Of Wonders and Wise Men

Of
Wonders
and
Wise Men

Religion and
Popular Cultures
in Southeast Mexico,
1800–1876

BY

TERRY RUGELEY

University of Texas Press
Austin

Requests for permission to reproduce material from this work should be sent to
Permissions, University of Texas Press, P.O. Box 7819, Austin, TX 78713–7819.

∞ The paper used in this book meets the minimum requirements of
ANSI/NISO Z39.48–1992 (R1997) (Permanence of Paper).

Library of Congress Cataloging-in-Publication Data

Rugeley, Terry, 1956–
Of wonders and wise men : religion and popular cultures in southeast Mexico,
1800–1876 / by Terry Rugeley. — 1st ed.
p.   cm.
Includes bibliographical references and index.
ISBN 0-292-77106-1 (alk. paper) — ISBN 0-292-77107-X (pbk. : alk. paper)
1. Mexico, Southeast—Religious life and customs.   2. Mexico, Southeast—
Religion—19th century.   3. Mexico, Southeast—Church history—19th century.
4. Mexico, Southeast—Civilization—19th century.   I. Title.
BL2560.M6 R84   2000
277.2′6081—dc21
00-029909

Contents

Acknowledgments

There are many people who deserve recognition for their role in bringing this work about. More than anyone else, Bill Beezley inspired and encouraged me to attempt a cultural history, and the text has profited from his critical reading. William Taylor and Grant Jones read and commented on earlier drafts of the work. John Hart, Gilbert Joseph, and Allan Burns provided support and encouragement. As always, Michel Antochiw shared his encyclopedic knowledge of southeast Mexican history. Hernán Menéndez Rodríguez has worked tirelessly to promote historical research in the pages of *Por Esto!*'s literary supplement, *Unicornio,* and consistently offered a forum that allowed me to present preliminary versions of parts of this book to a Mexican readership. Thanks to my colleagues at the University of Oklahoma Department of History for an environment conducive to research and writing. Stephanie Jo Smith checked references and offered suggestions while I was working in Mexico.

This work would never have come about without the efforts of the many archivists of Mérida and Campeche, professionals who made historical research a pleasure. In Mérida, I am deeply indebted to Dra. Piedad Peniche Rivero, director of the Archivo General del Estado; and to Jorge Victoria Ojeda, Jorge Canto Alcocer, Candy Flota García, Andrea Vergoda Medina, and all others at the AGEY, a mecca to historians in southeast Mexico. A second home away from home for me has been the Centro de Apoyo a la Investigación Histórica de Yucatán and its sister facility, the Hemeroteca José María Pino Suárez. For their hospitality and assistance, I thank directors Luis Alberto Solís Vázquez and Enrique Martín, as well as Yolanda López, Beatriz Heredia de Pau, Patricia Martínez Huchim, and many others. I will never forget the summer mornings in the Archivo Notarial of Yucatán in the company of Rinelda Cauich Ayora and Jorge Gaumer.

Needless to say, a project of this sort would not have been possible without consultation in the cathedral archives of the peninsula. For his generosity I warmly thank Padre Jose F. Camargo Sosa, director of Mérida's Archivo Histórico de la Arquidiócesis de Yucatán. Additional access to this same collection was possible through the microfilmed materials at the University of Texas at Arlington, for which I am indebted to the services of Maritza Arrigunaga y Coello. Thanks to Padre José Manuel Casanova Medina for his ongoing permission to research in the cathedral archives of Campeche. There I benefited from the work of Ney A. Canto Vega, who, in addition to carrying out a splendid reorganization of the cathedral archives, allowed me generous access to the collection.

Financial support for this book came from the Oklahoma Foundation for the Humanities, the University of Oklahoma Research Council, the dean of the University of Oklahoma College of Arts and Sciences, and the American Philosophical Society.

Thanks to the erudite Father Joe Meinhart for calling to my attention John Wesley's observation on Calvinism, one with which most nineteenth-century Mexicans would have readily agreed.

I extend my general appreciation to family and friends in Mérida who supported and encouraged this project.

Finally, special thanks above all to my wife, Margarita, who traveled with me to archives throughout Mexico and Belize, lived with me in Peto, and put up with endless revisions: "Láayli'e' táan in tuklikech."

A Note on Orthography

Maya words used in this text follow the modern orthography used in the *Diccionario básico español-maya, maya-español* by Ramón Bastarrachea, et al. (Mérida: Maldonado Editores, 1992). The only exceptions have been certain place names and last names that have retained certain traditional colonial spellings: for example, *h* instead of *j, u* for *w, th* instead of *t',* and *dz* instead of *ts.*

English translations for the titles of folktales published in Spanish are my own.

All monetary values are in Mexican *pesos* and *reales* (one *peso* = eight *reales*).

Sour godliness is the Devil's religion.
—*John Wesley on Calvinism*

The day will come when you see
everything you do
reflected in a pool of water.
—*Maya riddle*

Strange Lights, Mysterious Crosses, and the Word of God Denied

The year 1815 began much like any other in the Mexican port of Campeche. Fishermen hauled in their catches of bass and baby sharks, Maya peasants came from the countryside to sell corn and vegetables, soldiers trained in the plaza, the city's cannon factory churned out its wares, servants brewed cups of chocolate for their masters. Little did the citizens of this tranquil town suspect that a miracle was about to visit them.

It came, as scripture had prophesied, like a thief in the night. In January a servant was splitting wood in the Campeche home of a certain Arturo Alvarez when he discovered the image of "two perfect crosses" in a piece of kindling. This event sparked wonder throughout the town. Public excitement increased several nights later, when Alvarez and his wife awoke to discover the room filled with a strange, splendid glow "which did not cause them fear." Inevitably these miraculous occurrences brought an investigation by the church. From his cathedral in Mérida one hundred miles away, the Spanish-born Bishop Agustín Estévez y Ugarte appointed Padre Agusto de Solís, himself a native of Campeche, to investigate. But Solís was not impressed. Deciding that the images were a fraud, he confiscated the wood and sent it to the bishop, along with the following comments:

> I greatly distrust the miracles of these people; the rabble of this city are highly prone to feign miracles around whatever appears mysterious; every day they are

finding crosses to excite and interest the devotion of the vulgar. Many times they have brought me [the shapes of] palm leaves accidentally formed by the candles for the dead, and so forth . . . All things should be expected of the Almighty, but it is unlikely that He should make crosses appear in the house of a nobody.[1]

The crosses disappeared into the bowels of the great cathedral. Estévez and Solís spoke no more of the matter and turned their hands to more worldly affairs. But for the people of Campeche, the investigation was a *carpetazo,* an official cover-up with sinister overtones. The crosses were obviously some immense and divine message to the people, yet the church, which was supposed to be the earthly hand of God, had chosen to conceal them.

In the distance of 180 years the wonder of the kindling crosses continues to open a nest of questions. Why here, and why in kindling wood? Was it significant that a servant found the crosses? Did masters and servants equally share the status of witnessing a miracle? How could Alvarez and his wife have felt so calm in the presence of otherworldly light? Did it matter that priest and parishioners came from significantly different socioeconomic levels? Was it germane that the peninsula had just emerged from a political crisis that had questioned the legitimacy of the church?[2] Or that armed insurgents, as everyone knew, still roamed the interior of central Mexico, demanding independence and social change? Finally, why did the church insist on denying the people their moment with the Spiritual?

The paucity of documentation prevents concrete answers in this instance. But these questions capture all the dilemmas and contradictions of religion as a cultural field, a symbolic framework for life, in early nineteenth-century Mexico. While presiding over the great medieval spectrum of wondrous beliefs and entities and the many imperatives that this spiritual world created, the church also assumed the role of enlightened skeptic, reviewing and proscribing accounts of visitations that rose spontaneously among the people. While asserting the limitlessness of divine power, the church also had to confine that power to a realm of possibilities acceptable to Yucatán's social hierarchy. In this episode, part of a larger dialogue over the meaning and use of religion, Padre Solís found himself opposing the faithful. He knew them not as people (*gente*) or parishioners (*feligreses*), but rather as the rabble (*populacho*). He remembered the townsfolk by the endless series of apparitions they had witnessed, apparitions that threatened to overturn social convention by arousing "the devotion of the vulgar." Underscoring the tensions was the investigator's contradictory perception of a visitation's effects, the calm, glowing light that served to agitate (*alborotar*) the populace. As its conservative proponents always insisted, the Catholic religion did help unify a nation connected by little else, but the kindling crosses remind us that religion also served as an arena for contentions and differences among the faithful themselves, and it is precisely the tension generated by ambiguities of unity and difference that invite the curiosity of the late-twentieth-century observer.

This is a book about nineteenth-century Mexicans and their religion. What I have tried to uncover are the popular cultures behind wonders like the kindling crosses—the enormous and often hidden context of roles, beliefs, folkways, popular piety, and religious practices. My approach is a simple one, perhaps even obvious, but I think it opens doors to subtleties and historical scenes that we, in our rush to sketch out the political economy of rural society, have tended to ignore. Put simply, the popular cultures of these people mattered, and religion formed a major strand of those cultures.

This book grew out of material that I began to accumulate during an earlier study on the origins of the Caste War of Yucatán. While writing on the more concrete issues of taxes, land, social mobility, political alliance, and revolution, I realized that we knew little about the people who lived within these structures, the men and women who wore generic socioeconomic masks but seldom revealed their thoughts, their private triumphs and failures, or their dreams of how things should be. The question was how to get into the more intimate corners of a folk now dead for over a century. Things that interested them included their love lives, music, jokes and stories, political views, ambitions, their personal pride and petty vendettas. All of these appear in varying degrees in the archival documents. Ultimately, however, one cultural dimension stood out above the others: religion. Religious culture has the distinct advantage of being well documented, since the church was the best organized and most stable bureaucracy of its day, while its members composed the most educated and literate sector of the population. Religion was also broadly encompassing. Religious culture cut across class and ethnic lines; it held many meanings and many voices. At times it papered over conflicts but at others became the vehicle of their expression. It offered a path for exploring how human beings lived and thought beyond the familiar descriptions of land, taxes, haciendas, and peons.

The chapters of this book spin out of several related questions. The first concerns the social context behind rural Mexico's apparitions and oracles— the mysterious crosses of Campeche, Jalisco's Virgin of the Maguey plant, or any of a thousand others. Yucatán has what is arguably the most extraordinary and successful of all of Mexico's many apparitions: the Speaking Cross. In 1847, tensions involving taxes, growing political violence, land pressures, and the declining social position of the indigenous elite sparked a massive rural rebellion known as the Caste War. The rebel ranks consisted mostly of Maya peasants; they enjoyed initial success, but after the spring of 1848 the state regained the upper hand and began to beat rebels back into the forests of the southeast. Manipulated and probably created by the generals, the oracular cross preached war to the death. It rallied the rebels in their hour of need, and its cult survived to become a folk religion still prevalent in rural areas of Quintana Roo.[3]

Meanwhile, apparitions continue to punctuate the region's recent history. What nineteenth-century persons, places, and practices lie behind these? While Farriss's important 1984 study concentrates on the deep past of Maya peasant religion, I have chosen to reconstruct the period of 1800 to 1870, the seven decades of historical experience that surrounded the Speaking Cross, to see what tendencies and meanings were current at the time of the cult's formation.[4] I have also tried to explore diverse parts of the social spectrum because I am convinced that classes and ethnic groups were more interactive than we have tended to portray them. This is not to say that such separations did not exist, but as contemporary experience teaches, it is possible for different ethnicities to borrow and imitate without becoming a single people or even necessarily liking one another. What I have found is that although certainly eye-catching, apparitions that we might term wondrous or miraculous were merely a small part of a far greater canvas of popular religious culture.

A second and related point that impressed me was the dual orientation of the people. While revering an idealized past, a time of virtue and devotion, Yucatecans were busily working to bring that age to an end. Their project was not the invention of tradition (that is, a tendentious doctoring of the past) that Eric Hobsbawm and others have described for modern Britain, although at selected moments, such as with the organizations of urban piety described in Chapter 3, that analysis does apply.[5] Rather, it was a prolonged ambivalence toward the old and the familiar. With the exception of certain *comecuras*—literally "priest eaters," or rabid anticlerics—most people claimed to be devout Catholics. And yet Yucatecans, in their quest for economic growth and state formation, were busily curtailing the powers and privileges of that ancient institution. Consistent with William B. Taylor's analysis of eighteenth-century Mexico, priests here were losing their power to tax, their old privileged access to peasant labor, their near monopoly on education, and their supervision of life passages such as birth, marriage, and death.[6] Property owners launched a sustained attack against religious restraints on exploiting indigenous peasant labor. Urban intellectuals began to assert the right to think and speak for themselves. Peasants, too, changed their world, if only by growing in number; beyond that, many of them took advantage of larger changes in the society since 1750 in order to carve out a cultural and economic independence from the *padres*. Most Yucatecans participated inadvertently in these changes, just as most people today make hundreds of small, daily decisions that ultimately help to uproot their old ways. But participate they did. The situation was thus often the opposite of Hobsbawm's invented traditions. People acted one way, while a persistent past lived on in their thoughts, attitudes, and cultural decor.

As a corollary to the above, the tensions between innovation and older culture are worth studying for the ambiguity of their results. In some ways, at least, the new secular tendencies prevailed. Particularly since the 1910 Revolution, the nation-state wields final power; priests have lost both their privileged access to property and their ideological monopoly. Old-time Catholicism now faces stiff competition from the evangelical sects that have exploded throughout Latin America since the 1970s. Perhaps more debilitating from the believer's view is the creeping dry-rot of consumer materialism. In Mérida, the *centros comerciales,* or shopping malls, are now becoming the new cathedrals, while those searching for a modern-day Garden of Earthly Delights need look no further than Cancún.[7] At the same time, however, the old ways have proven remarkably durable; approximately 86 percent of peninsulars are still at least nominally Catholic.[8] Most of the features explored in the following pages—processions, fiestas, the cult of saints, the prestige of priests, and even the old antireligion of anticlericalism—have their modern counterparts, and throughout the book I have taken care to note those continuities when appropriate. Folkways enjoy special strength in the countryside. Indeed, Redfield's prediction of the rural community's modernist transformation has, along with Christ's return and the global revolution, suffered from repeated rescheduling.[9] There is nothing unusual about this, since peasantries and ethnicities have proven remarkably stubborn everywhere. But Yucatán's modernization has been particularly ambivalent, partly because of its isolation, partly for its ongoing underdevelopment. Hence this study of a persistent past and its nineteenth-century advocates and adversaries.

Questions regarding both the motive for miracle and the persistent past lead to a larger issue of how multiple beliefs, interests, and worldviews can function together with the same, ostensibly monolithic cultural system. When viewed from below, the Mexican Catholicism of the early nineteenth century emerges as something more than a hierarchy and a set of doctrines. Rather, its inclusivity allowed for an enormous amount of discussion and change, a polyvocal cultural field that internalized all voices of the society, even the dissident and diametrically opposed. In this mansion there were indeed many rooms, and in the course of the book I hope to enter as many as possible.

Finally, I hope that such an approach can help counterbalance what I think has been a stubborn bias in the historical literature on Mexico's southeast region. Here the publicity has been not only bad but superlatively bad: Mexico's most prolonged conquest, the cruelest *auto-de-fé,* the largest peasant uprising, the worst labor conditions, the most decadent planter class, the most radical socialists, the hardest of hard-shelled reactionaries, the most cynically exploited *ejidos.* These profoundly somber tones give little hint of the joy that people took in their world, or the at-times zany quality of life that prevailed in the rural villages. The darker version fails to explain what gave people such a sense of belonging to a place, much less of being the *elegidos de dios,* God's chosen. *Of Wonders and Wise Men* will, I hope, contribute toward a more finely developed picture of daily life in a moment of Mexican history, something that thus far I have been able to find only in Luis González's excellent recreation of rural Michoacán, or more recently in Paul Vanderwood's study of the Tomóchic conflict of the Chihuahua sierra.[10] To find this other Yucatán I have followed the suggestion of Murdo MacLeod, who, in an essay on Mexico's colonial violence, urged for "a return to the most obscure colonial documentation," with the hope that little-known documents of nineteenth-century Yucatán hold keys to understanding how things really were, and why.[11]

The Time and Place

This is not a book about the Great Events; rather, it concerns the lore and longings of a people who simply considered themselves normal and who did not see historical contours and changes as we see them now. To them, their life was the natural way of life; the great episodes that fascinate historians were interruptions, and usually unpleasant ones. But because so much of what happened to them did connect with larger episodes, a quick synopsis can help put us in the place and time.

Throughout most of its post-Conquest history, Mexico's southeast peninsula has been a separate if related part of a larger nation. Lack of commercial economy had perpetuated both a tribute economy and indigenous-village structure in the region during colonial times; after the worst of the demographic collapse, the countryside began a gradual population recovery coupled with increasing land commercialization. Tribute—and from the late Bourbon period onward, taxes—remained the state's and church's main way of wringing surpluses out of the Maya peasantry. At the dawn of the nineteenth century, southeast Mexico was a patchwork of villages, haciendas, and small ranchos, all influenced by the markets and political dictates of the three or four regional cities. Villages retained much of their political autonomy, and the Maya town councils, or *repúblicas de indígenas,* continued to generate paperwork concerning land, legacies, and sundry affairs. Independence came peacefully here, but the attendant political wranglings helped spark Maya consciousness of the possible, leading to the Caste War. This conflict erupted in 1847, subsided around 1852, but resurged toward the end of the decade and continued until the late 1860s. Thereafter, Yucatán followed a fragmented evolution. In rebel territory, rebel holdouts reorganized themselves into a military-theocratic maroon community built around one or more oracular crosses. In the deep south, refugees and former combatants, the so-called *pacíficos,* swore loyalty in exchange for almost complete autonomy. Finally, in the older colonial centers of the north and west, a hacienda-based culture became increasingly dedicated to the production and sale of henequen fiber. For peninsular elites, a strong influx of henequen profits helped isolate them from popular cultures and led to an imitation of the *beaux artes* culture of Porfirian Mexico.[12]

During all this, Spanish colonial Catholicism formed one of the society's fundamentals. As every student of Latin America knows, the conquistadors arrived with friars at their side and, with seven centuries of Catholicism, intimately identified with Spain's expansive warrior nationalism. Regular orders such as the Franciscans (who enjoyed a long monopoly in Yucatán) composed the only institution capable of winning over the indigenous peoples and tempering the darker aspects of colonialism. The friars set up missions, built churches, taught natives the basics of Christian doctrine, and endlessly worried over their converts' relapses and idolatries. Among the colonizers, Catholicism continued to provide an intellectual framework for life, a road map for things spiritual, a marker for life passages, a source of both prestige and economic security, and a provider of numerous services, including education, training, and legal expertise. In short, Maya and Spaniard alike had

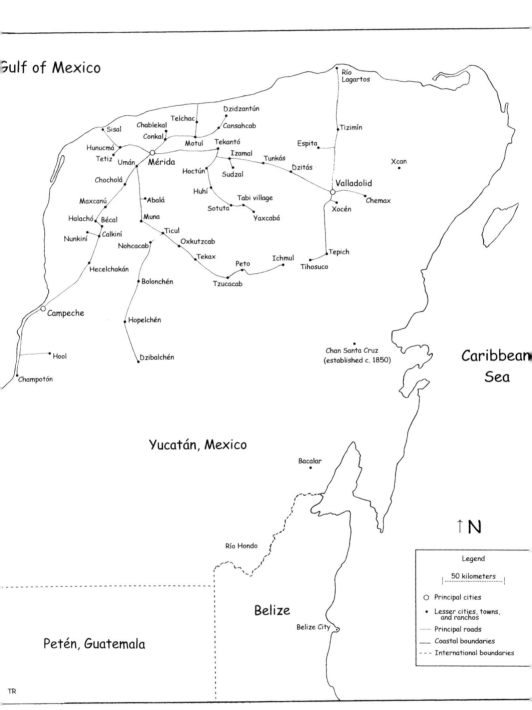

Gulf of Mexico

Río Lagartos

Dzidzantún
Telchac
Cansahcab
Chablekal
Tizimín
Sisal
Conkal
Hunucmá
Motul
Tekantó
Espita
Tetiz
Izamal
Tunkás
Xcan
Umán
Mérida
Hoctún
Sudzal
Dzitás
Chocholá
Huhí
Tabi village
Valladolid
Maxcanú
Abalá
Sotuta
Chemax
Halachó
Bécal
Muna
Yaxcabá
Xocén
Nunkiní
Calkiní
Ticul
Nohcacab
Oxkutzcab
Tepich
Hecelchakán
Tekax
Ichmul
Tihosuco
Peto
Bolonchén
Tzucacab
Campeche
Hopelchén
Chan Santa Cruz
(established c. 1850)
Hool
Dzibalchén
Champotón

Caribbean
Sea

Yucatán, Mexico

Bacalar

↑ N

Río Hondo

Legend

50 kilometers

○ Principal cities
• Lesser cities, towns,
   and ranchos
— Principal roads
— Coastal boundaries
- - - International boundaries

Belize

Belize City

Petén, Guatemala

TR

Map 1. The Yucatán peninsula, c. 1821.

to consider what the church had to say in matters great and small. During the eighteenth century the Spanish Crown began to phase out the regular orders in favor of the less talented, if more pliant, secular church hierarchy; it also began a gradual reduction of overall church power in favor of centralized state-building. Between 1821 and 1876 the church lost its power to tax, to impose tithes, to hold properties beyond the church and rectory, to dabble in politics, to celebrate masses outside the church, and to serve as lenders of money. Nevertheless, three centuries had engraved Catholic ways of thinking into the people, and the church's influence persisted at an unofficial level even after these reforms had taken effect.

The principal object of so much religious passion and quarrel, the colonized Mayas of Yucatán, never fit easily or perfectly into the vision the colonizers mapped out for them. Maya religiosity, which has generated its own huge corpus, focused on supernatural forces that influenced daily life: entities such as field gods, rain gods, the saints, dead relatives, and an assortment of local beings that helped or hurt according to their whimsy. Much depended on the generosity of the gods, so people kept them in a good humor through a combination of presents and promises. Among other things, the deities expected special dinners, complete with liquor and cigarettes, before, during, and after the planting. In hard times Maya peasants could work out a bargain with the saints by offering to perform some public act of devotion. Religious activities such as processions, ceremonial banquets, and special prayer sessions were communal. Whatever their effect on the gods, these activities at least gave their participants a sense of order and safety, and helped paper over the hive of intrigues and jealousies that plagued the rural village. At the same time, apparitions validated both individual hopes and popular beliefs; in difficult moments some saint or another was likely to appear with messages of hope and inspiration, maybe even cure a disabled leg or open the ears of the deaf. Mayas saw themselves as Catholic, a system taught to them from birth and through which they could lay claim to basic civil rights in colonial Mexico; but what the friars said was not always what the Mayas heard, and the peasants' brand of faith did not preclude features that had little to do with the doctrines of the Mother Church. Far from being mere objects of meditation, for the Maya religious items such as crosses and rosaries had magical powers in and of themselves. Village life pulsed with the dangers of ghosts, witchcraft, and mysterious evil winds. Folkloric prescriptions usually served as a shield, but the more difficult cases called for the intervention of a h-men, or shaman, steeped in the older beliefs, a man for whose services the customer could expect to pay dearly. Maya in its names, local flavors, and particular details, the system nevertheless followed larger contours similar to those found in other parts of Mexico, a syncretized folk Catholicism that transcended specific ethnicities but was usually strongest in rural areas and among people of indigenous descent.[13]

It is important to note, however, that other voices added to the off-key chorus that was popular religious culture. These included the village priest, the high clergy of the cathedral, the urban merchant, the rural patriarch, the foreign traveler, and political authorities—scrupulous and otherwise. Women from all ends of the social spectrum often enjoyed particularly close relationships with the church and its lay organizations. Cities and towns were the homes of such diverse folk as day laborers, artisans, soldiers, traveling merchants, displaced peasants, and even heretics and criminals. Rather than simply rehashing the now familiar aspects of Maya peasant rural religion, I hope that the chapters of this book capture more of the polyvocality that prevailed in the days between the departure of Spain (1821) and the rise of the dictator Porfirio Díaz (1876).

Writing Popular Cultural History

A history of popular culture may get us closer to the elusive horizon of things as they really were, but writing such a history is no simple task. Even after years of intense self-criticism, particularly among the European historians who pioneered the approach, popular cultural history still struggles with certain basic issues and questions.[14] On the following interpretive and methodological points it is impossible to strike an equation that will satisfy everyone, in large part because understandings of culture rise out of deeply ingrained worldviews and personal experiences that by definition are not universal. Nevertheless, the following pages lay out some of the problems and explain my own approach to them.

The first pitfall concerns a related cluster of conceptual and definitional problems. What is culture, and perhaps even more perplexing, what is not? The word has many meanings, ranging from arts and crafts to intellectual constructs to a common anthropological usage referring to the totality of a people's learned information and practice. Should cultural studies explore the intellectual and more overtly symbolic elements of culture, or should it include a broader reading that includes their "material" lives, reading these also as texts? Most cultural historians put aside the vision of a totality of learned behavior and information in favor of a somewhat more limited realm of shared meanings and values and symbolic ways of enacting them.[15] This approach tends to stress such things as beliefs, attitudes, public behavior, entertainment, and modes of expression, and it is the approach that I have followed throughout.

It is increasingly clear that cultures are not only multiple but interrelated as well. This question weighs heavily on nineteenth-century studies of regions like Mexico, since such areas remained strongly colonial and, at least in earlier renderings, split between peasants and Hispanic elites. Seldom has this been truer than in the historical and anthropological literature on Yucatán, land of Maya and Spaniard. There is a danger of thinking in terms of apartheid cultural systems for elites and masses, which virtually all recent cultural commentators have attacked. But this still leaves room for related questions. Where and how is culture made, and by whom? Do the folk, whoever they happen to be, produce their own cultural components? If so, is it in isolation or through dialogue? Does popular cultural production imply a completely different set of components, of names and stories and beliefs that were fundamentally "other" to the Great Tradition? Or is it simply a different way of looking at the artifacts of the Great Tradition, a tendency to invert meanings and stand the social world on its head? Even with shared cultural symbols, it is still possible to have radically different visions. Nor are these visions necessarily locked in total warfare—a notion that derives, I think, from a too-close adherence to resistance theory—but rather share certain points of agreement.[16] A related matter concerns the difficulty of creating an appropriately subtle taxonomy, one that would allow us to distinguish between subcultures and countercultures.[17] The latter are less evident here than in the modern industrial world, but as the subtitle of the book suggests, I have followed the approach of multiple though closely related popular cultures, with variations for Maya villagers, hacienda peons, urban rabble, aspiring bourgeoisie, and the women of cities and towns.

Naming the practitioners of these cultures can be difficult. At times rural people referred to themselves as "we of village such-and-such," at times through the old colonial status of *indio* (Indian), at other times as *macehuales,* an old Aztec term for a commoner that came to be generalized throughout much of Mexico. They used these terms irregularly, and I hope that I will be pardoned for not adopting them. My own writing fluctuates between the modern terms "Maya" and "peasant" (*campesino*); the former is an ethnic description, the latter a socioeconomic category (a politically disenfranchised people living primarily through subsistence and whose surpluses are drawn away by elites). Throughout this book I have tended to use the two interchangeably, in part to vary the diction, in part for the simple reason that most rural Mayas were peasants and most peasants were Mayas, with some wiggle room on both ends.

Another part of the problem here is that until recently we have known relatively little about elite culture in the region. Studies of southeastern Mexico have enjoyed several advances over the past few years, particularly regarding the organization, mind-set, and social vocabularies of the colonial Maya.[18] But there has been far less interest in the nineteenth century's pre-Porfirian elite religious culture.[19] Howard Cline's 1947 study of peninsular society was accurate in many regards, but Cline was certainly wrong when he asserted that the peninsular church was uninfluential.[20] It is clear that its weakness was relative; it was less influential than in the days of the Franciscans' millenarian kingdom but still integral to all levels of society. Moreover, the church played a leading role in peninsular economic development, its wealth being partly institutional, partly the private success of individual members. Finally, it was not monolithic but internally divided; it did not exercise an unrestricted power over the peasantry, but rather had to negotiate with them at all points. Lay believers were every bit as important as the men who served as their spiritual guides. The institution still enjoyed great vitality, and its doctrines and practices formed part of the core religious culture of all classes. In this study I hope to restore some missing pieces in the balance between the elite/peasant religious cultures.

A second problem concerns something we might call "internal resolution." How unified are cultural systems within themselves? Architectonic theorists tend to envision links between diverse phenomena. However, such theories often disintegrate under scrutiny or upon repeated application. The collapse of totalizing paradigms has led to the conclusion that cultural fields may not have the coherence and organization that we wish to ascribe to them. In the postparadigmatic wreckage, I think it is useful to see cultural mores as being like "language games," which Ludwig Wittgenstein used to characterize the totality of language: strands of practices or beliefs that bear family resemblances to one another but lack a single function or common denominator.[21] Cultural practices relate variously (and not always consistently) to ethnic conflict, to gender roles, to individual anxiety over the elations and miseries of life. To this must be added a large amount of artifact and unassimilated bodies that cultural fields tend to acquire over time, perhaps like a reef of many different plants and corals. This diversity of function helps explain why anthropologically based history tends toward such divergent readings, with authors like Clifford Geertz stressing the underlying unity of culture—the shared understanding of the Balinese cockfight—and Marshall Sahlins arguing for a difference of readings within the same general society.[22] This, perhaps, echoes an old historical debate, the split between conflict and consensus. Does culture unite people, mediate their differences, hold them together, or do societies (such as nineteenth-century Mexico's) have separate cultures that reflect class, ethnic, or gender struggles? Or do they somehow do both? An earlier, nation-centered literature tended to stress the former, with increasing emphasis on conflicting readings from the 1970s onward. Most recently, a popular and subtle synthesis has been to explore how seemingly unified cultures in reality contain different ways of thinking—that is, to see how those conflicts can continue beneath the ostensibly unified surface of shared culture and vocabulary.[23] This is the path my own study tries to follow. The people found a motive for miracle in the nooks and cobwebs of official doctrine, places where their social betters had intended no miracle.

In this book I have striven throughout for a high level of detail in an effort to bring cultural tendencies to their sharpest resolution. Without sacrificing interpretation, there must also be a descriptive imperative that moves people to write cultural history. Moreover, though it would have been satisfying to lay out a grand Mexican synthetic vision resembling Peter Burke's study of early modern Europe, the limitations of preexisting research in nineteenth-century Mexican culture impose boundaries of their own. We simply lack sufficient case studies for meaningful synthesis. Drilling deeply enough to hit popular cultures has therefore meant minute archival work in one province, but with hope that the same aquifer extends into other historical subsoils as well. I have also tried to diverge from the too-anthropological approach favored by those who have written more strictly ethnohistorical pieces. *Of Wonders and Wise Men* at times favors the story over the generalization because I wanted above all to put life back into the skeletons of these forgotten country people. The book therefore follows a combination of approaches. The chapters on folk knowledge (1), urban piety (3), icons (4), and anticlericalism (6) offer broad surveys of their subjects. But I have alternated these with individual case studies as another way of recovering nineteenth-century people, places, and practices. To represent the high end of religious culture, we find Raymundo Pérez, rural pastor, entrepreneur, and all-around wise man, the paragon priest of the nineteenth century (Chapter 2). The hacienda-based cult of San Antonio Xocneceh (Chapter 5) serves as a case study of how peasant piety weathered the liquidation of *cofradías,* or land-based lay brotherhoods, of the late Bourbon period. Finally, the scandals of the Petén, the Yucatecan church's jungle outpost, open a window to all the local meanings and local politics attached to national religion (Chapter 7).

A third problem, one more distinctly related to method, concerns the difficulty of penetrating through elite-filtered sources. U. S. and European scholars have had a hard enough time reconstructing the popular cultures of their relatively literate and documented world; the challenge increases when we move to Latin America's turbulent nineteenth century.[24] Here we have a colonized peasantry, few of whom even spoke the official language of Spanish. Peasant production of documents declined over the century—largely related to the abolition of the Indians' corporate legal identity and the elimination of institutions such as ejido lands and the repúblicas de indígenas, and to the state's increasing intolerance of and refusal to archive Maya-language letters and petitions. But other complications intruded. There was little nostalgia here for the disappearing folkways of the past. Many of the literate urban creoles wanted to throw the past out with both hands and get on with the business of imitating Europe. The political confusion of the century included four separations from Mexico (in 1836, 1840, 1845, and 1846), innumerable coups and political uprisings, and the Caste War of 1847 onward. Indeed, few creoles cared to romanticize a band of peasant guerrillas who had just stolen their worldly goods or burned down their haciendas, and so few bothered to collect folklore or preserve the antiquarian past. Nor did the Catholic friars, important sources of writings on Europe's medieval folk culture, produce much of benefit. The Franciscans were secularized in the region in 1821, and the secular church itself suffered a century of tumult as the Mexican state-builders stripped it of its wealth, its privileges, and its leisure for scholarly pursuits. For all these reasons, the task of reconstructing a history of popular culture here is daunting.

Yet it is by no means impossible, as I hope this work shows. Although the problem of sources persists, it is also true that elite culture produced a huge and not necessarily contrived documentation that covered many aspects of its society. Maya peasants and urban rabble constantly enter into that documentation. We find them, for example, in notarized transactions, wills, court cases, and petitions. Surviving paperwork does show how people acted, and with thoughtful reading can also provide some window into their thoughts and attitudes. In the twentieth century, when popular culture became a subject of more interest, collections of folklore began to proliferate, and I have used these throughout, particularly in my examination of folktales and folk beliefs.

Finally, and as a coda to these problems, there is the dilemma of historians ourselves: while we often disdain popular enthusiasms in our own day and age, our writings can celebrate these same sorts of beliefs among peoples of the past.[25] The observation is as germane as when Gerald Strauss posed it seven years ago. It is not so much a question seeking an answer but, rather, a caution that historians should bear in mind when resurrecting the resistance and dissonance of popular sectors past.

Wonders and wise men are not easy things to speak of. But for historians there is a great deal to say about how the beliefs and institutions we create to deal with our anxieties interact with a world where real human beings work real jobs, blister our hands, and drink liquor at nightfall. Politics and piety collide, or perhaps collude. Devout laymen subtly convert their faith into a business network. Mysterious apparitions undermine the cult of officialdom, and dissidents gather around doctrines that in their original surroundings seem bizarre, exotic, and above all dangerous. Such things happen daily, throughout all lands and among all peoples. The motive for miracle lies somewhere therein. It is for this reason that the trifling chicaneries and backyard marvels of the pious in a dusty Mexican province of the last century are of some interest to us, and that those long-dead Yucatecans, in their quarrels with God and each other, deserve still a few more pages.

Of Wonders and Wise Men

Geography, Misery, Agency, Remedy

*The Unwritten Almanac
of Folk Knowledge*

THE MAYA PEASANTS of the nineteenth century had a way of knowing the world that they handed down from parent to child in a kind of oral compendium, a hodgepodge of wisdoms, techniques, and tidbits that everyone should learn and repeat. Comparison to an encyclopedia would suggest greater order and structuring than really existed, and so perhaps a better metaphor would be the almanacs once popular among farmers, a book loosely built around the calendar but with all sorts of additional insertions, a book with no clear-cut beginning or end, no homogeneity of style, something best read at random. It was, in sum, an oral folk almanac.[1]

The almanac's calendrical basis is well known: slashing, burning, and planting fields in spring, tending in summer, harvesting in autumn. What concerns us here is another major part of that almanac, the folktale, and how it might open a window to popular beliefs and attitudes inaccessible through the documentational memory of church and state. European cultural historians have already shown how tales of giants, wolves, and magic trees can reveal something fundamental about peasant life. This same line of analysis, I think, can apply to southeast Mexico as well, "a land where good tellers of stories are highly esteemed."[2] Like their counterparts in other areas of the world, peninsular folktales, or *cuentos,* operate in many dimensions, but what places them at the heart of this study is their grounding in the wondrous, the miraculous, the incredible. Perhaps the term "miracle" overstates, since the people who told such stories saw them as part of the natural world; nevertheless, the stories told of things that happened only rarely and that made people look up and pay attention. In fact, of the entire corpus collected from 1900 onward, relatively few stories rest on what *we* would see as natural terms. When the peasants told their past, the animals talked, Jesus walked among the cornfields, rain gods and spirit protectors meddled in the affairs of mankind. Maya folklore collector Allan Burns wrote with great insight when, borrowing the phrase of his informants, he described their narrative genre as *secreto'ob,* or secrets; the name refers not to who may or may not hear the tales, but rather to their wondrous and astonishing content.[3] We do not need to insist that people believed these tales and sayings in a literal way (although to a certain extent they did, and do).[4] A closely related genre, the *creencias,* or popular beliefs, were really half-beliefs that coexisted with empirical knowledge, like bromeliads clinging to trees in the Yucatecan forest. What mattered was that the people chose these themes as the building blocks of their cultural world, and they did so on the basis of historical experience.

Mexican folklore has remained under-utilized as a historical source, perhaps because Mexican provincial elites lagged a century behind their European counterparts in discovering their peasantry, who were the main vessels of such knowledge.[5] Early Franciscan friars recorded some amount of religious/supernatural lore, while nineteenth-century authors made only minor and unsystematic attempts to record folk beliefs.[6] The major exception was Daniel G. Brinton's "The Folk-Lore of Yucatan," an 1883 piece from the *Folklore Journal* that drew on nineteenth-century manuscripts, some of which are no longer extant.[7] Manuel Rejón García's *Supersticiones y leyendas mayas* (1905) constituted another early attempt to capture rural folkloric beliefs.[8] The great change came in the 1920s and 1930s with revolutionary indigenism and the arrival of the multifaceted Carnegie Project. The first contribution from this endeavor was the legends recorded by Robert Redfield and Alfonso Villa Rojas in their studies during the 1920s.[9] Neither man saw folktale collection as his principal mission, but their ethnographies included appendices of unvarnished cuentos that reflected the oral literature of Chan Kom and Tixcacal Guardia. A far more important body comes from Redfield's wife, Margaret Park Redfield, who amassed a relatively neglected corpus of legends and riddles from the town of Dzitás at the time of her husband's fieldwork.[10] Manuel Andrade, a Cuban-born anthropologist from the University of Chicago, collected twenty-five folktales from Chichén Itzá in 1930.[11] The presidency of Lázaro Cárdenas (1934–1940) helped maintain interest in folk culture as part of its nationalist-populist political project; it was during this time, for example, that Mérida's Museo Arqueológico translated and reprinted the Brinton piece. Enthusiasm spread to Mérida's urban intellectuals, resulting in *Yikal Maya than* (*The Sound of Maya Words*), a bilingual literary magazine that between 1939 and 1955 served up folktales whose rough original contours are still recognizable beneath the pseudoelegant vocabulary that contributors lathered upon them.[12] Recently there have been systematic attempts to collect Maya peasant folklore in less prettified (and far more potent) form, including the Allan Burns study (1982) and the National Indigenous Institute's multivolume *Colección letras mayas contemporáneas* (1993).[13]

Despite the lateness of serious collecting, there is reason to link the lore we do have with historical changes in Mexico's pre-Porfirian nineteenth century. The basis for this approach lies in a modified version of arguments posed in the 1940s by anthropologist Ralph Beals. Intrigued by the preponderance of identifiably European motifs in Mesoamerican folklore, Beals argued that Hapsburg policies had tended to separate the Spanish and Indian peoples into their respective *repúblicas,* while the friars' initial contribution confined itself to the lore of Christian doctrine, stories such as Noah's ark or the persecution of Christ. (Garbled versions of biblical stories remain a standard of rural Mexico's oral literature.) A second wave of European folk knowledge began to inundate the rural villages with the Bourbon reforms and continued with Mexican independence and afterward. Yucatán itself followed this demographic trend. There the hacienda system grew steadily in the eighteenth century, while from 1821 to 1847 the sugar-based economy of the south and east boomed as people left the old colonial northwest for newer opportunities. The period may have brought increasing land pressures for the Mayas, but it also expanded their repertoire of folkloric information, with rapid additions to the available corpus of stories, songs, creencias, narrative motifs, fictional characters, proverbs, and home remedies. The folkloric exchange continued after 1847 as the army dragooned thousands of men, both Maya and Hispanic; once the initial fury of the Caste War had quieted, the state still rousted men out of their villages by the hundreds to serve in guard units known as *cantones* and, later, *colonias militares,* outposts of epic boredom where there was little to do except kill the time by talking and telling stories. Throughout these years, preexisting Maya elements did not disappear, as Beals suggested (an overstatement that caused critics such as Paul Radin to overlook the historical value of his theory), but rather merged with selected parts of this new and powerful wave of folk knowledge. For this reason, then, I think that the peninsular folklore that survives today tells us something about attitudes and social mores that were constituting themselves in the nineteenth century.[14]

Yucatecan folklore is in this sense no exception to the tendencies noted in other parts of Mexico. Many of the stories that circulated among peninsulars arrived with the Spanish, even though Spain itself may not necessarily have been the folktale's point of origin. Two particular examples illustrate this point. "La Pobreza," the story of an old woman with an enchanted tree, was in fact a version of "Bonhomme Misere," an old French folktale of approximately the same plot. (Unlike the European prototype, who was male, the Maya protagonist, La Pobreza, is a poor peasant woman: Bonhomme Misere underwent a gender change as well as a renaming in crossing the Atlantic, although the name retained its conceptual content.) La Pobreza wants to stop people from stealing the fruit from her tree, and through a magically obtained wish sees to it that nothing can be removed from its branches. When Death himself comes to call, La Pobreza tricks him into climbing the tree, from which he cannot escape. For years people stop dying as La Pobreza's tree imprisons the Grim Reaper.[15] Similarly, collectors have turned up at least one version of the Aladdin story, in which "Aladín" carries out many of the same tasks as his Middle Eastern prototype.[16] The peninsular Aladdin finds the same bottle, conjures the same genie, and travels the same path to riches and glory. Here, too, a malefactor robs him by promising new lamps for old, only to be undone in the end, with Aladdin marrying the princess. These selected examples were clearly Old World imports in both the plots they recounted and the lessons they taught. To them we can add scores of others, including stand-bys such as the boy assigned impossible tasks by a cruel king or the adventures of the old Spanish dunce Pedro de Urdemalas.[17] Items from the 1930 collections of Manuel Andrade from the area around Chichén Itzá bear the strong imprint of European influence. Similarly, the often-recorded riddles, or *adivinos*, of Maya peasants in fact have counterparts throughout the Hispanic world, including Spain and New Mexico.[18] Some of their building blocks derive from a pre-Columbian repertoire or dwell on more local and indigenous themes: the house, the *milpa* (cornfield), the village, the jealous in-laws, and the guardian spirits of the fields and forests. Others clearly are European overlays. Except in selected cases, I have not attempted to reconstruct the ethnic genesis of individual beliefs. Peasants adapted narrative materials to suit their own interests, and to my knowledge all existing collections of stories demonstrate heterogeneous roots. What rural Mexicans did choose to take, I would argue, reflected certain important social values, certain common historical experiences, as well as a shared vision of supernatural forces as undergirding human experience.

This chapter attempts to reconstruct folk beliefs from two principal sources: the narrative of folktales and the related but far less structured body of creencias. I have to admit beforehand that it is impossible to determine with finality how accurately all of this represents the forms of the stories that circulated in the nineteenth century. But evidence suggests considerable retention over the years, at least in the stories' skeletal forms. Many of the tales still bear the stamp of colonized peasants, and the fact of their widespread currency—different versions of the same tale occasionally crop up in different towns and among different informants—suggests a certain antiquity. I have therefore treated much of the available material as folklore, not "fakelore," even though a more systematic inquiry into the collection of oral traditions in the peninsula may amend the picture somewhat.[19] Rather than trace motif evolution, I have tried to follow a method used profitably in other folklore-rich areas by linking the motifs, themes, and overall perceptions contained in surviving folklore to historical processes of the time when these stories circulated.[20]

Geography

All Mexicans knew that they lived in part of a great expanse known as the world—but what was the world? The answer differed according to who was speaking, because in all cases people had popular constructs that helped situate them in their town, their society, and in the bigger picture of things, places, and powers that were ultimately unseeable. In almost all cases, however, religious constructs—whether of high orthodoxy or folk Catholicism—helped shape this picture.

Perceptions of the wider world differed radically. Educated Yucatecan elites, such as writer Justo Sierra O'Reilly, had an impeccable understanding of geography and world affairs. But most were not so favored. Members of this class likely had traveled at least once in their lives: to Spain, Cuba, France, New Orleans, or even New York City. But the intelligentsia was microscopic, easily less than 5 percent of the population. Even most creoles had limited exposure to science, learning, and the wider world; the Catholic Church exerted a strong control over education, and the creoles' own worldview was conditioned by the belief in the hand of God, the agency of saints, and the efficacy of ritual and prayer. Beyond these few elites stood the great mass of Maya peasants, who operated through a worldview that was at once highly practical and intensely wondrous.

The world was many things, but it was first and foremost a geographical world, a panorama of physical and social—and supernatural—spaces. The learned had made their own conquests of this dimension a long time ago. The history of Caribbean navigation and the problems of colonization had generated a series of peninsular maps that progressed from guesswork to accuracy. After several inferior colonial attempts, a fairly detailed peninsular map appeared in 1734, followed by an improved version in 1798.[21] Cartography owed its advances in no small part to the patronage of military corps, which, on behalf of the states that generated them, tried to delimit their territories for purposes of defense and development.[22] But in reality few people had ever seen such maps. It was not that people never left their towns or villages; on the contrary, the *campesinos* traveled a great deal in search of land, trade, fiestas, and sweethearts. It was a rare village indeed that did not send someone to Mérida, at least once every few years, on matters of law or commerce. People simply learned the world's shape by passing through it. This in turn affected how people represented the world among themselves. City maps, for example, did not exist; Mérida had no street names, only corners with picturesque markers like "The Elephant" or "The Camel." Prior to the late 1800s, even the real-estate sales of the urban elite lack specificity; title transfers normally identified houses and lots by some well-known reference ("near the house of Dr. Raymundo Pérez") and today are virtually useless in pinpointing exact locations. The countryside, meanwhile, was even more idiosyncratic in its reference points. The immediate world consisted of villages, house sites, trees, foot-worn trails, and human-created field markers known as *mojoneros,* usually a pile of stones. Thus, few survey maps of rural property exist for the early nineteenth century. Specific lands often have poetic names that suggest folk labeling: "over the cenote," "place of the five points," "the ceiba tree." These names have enjoyed a surprising permanence among Mayas and Hispanics alike. To rural peasants these lands had a unique identity, a recognizability, that made them emerge out of the vast backdrop of wilderness. This tendency to reveal itself was, in turn, consonant with a larger worldview; information regarding strange peoples and faraway lands formed a primordial chaos that was unimportant and perhaps unknowable—a great indeterminacy. What mattered was learning the key points that emerged from the chaos, the points affecting daily life.

Maya peasant accounts of supernatural geographies—heaven, hell, the land beyond the seas—varied widely, a reflection of the great indeterminacy. The nature of the soul, its relation to personal identity, its destination after death, and the duration of its stay in the afterworld were all matters of uncertainty, and surviving accounts vary from one anthropological source to the next. Most accepted that beyond their land lay the four cardinal points, each with its rain god, or *cháak*. But by the early twentieth century few could still recite ancient notions of a fifteen-layered universe: seven layers of heaven above, seven of hell below, and the plane of human existence in the middle. Others speculated on an afterlife similar to Buddhism's, where souls were periodically recycled according to the virtue of their previous lives. However, the majority simply had no knowledge of or particular concern about these more abstruse points.[23] This sort of indeterminacy is not unusual for a peasant society; studies of contemporary Andean peasants, for example, find similar uncertainty and even skepticism about afterlives and Otherworlds.[24] These beliefs survive as dogmas only when politically reinforced by a religious hierarchy, something the folk world lacked.

One of the more playful narrative explorations of the cosmological Otherworld comes from "The Man of the Earth," the story of a farmer who accidentally wanders into the home of one of the four cháaks. The cháak takes him in as a helper, but the man finds himself unable to manage the superpowered objects of this outsized universe. Ordinary things like watermelons and chickens cause fatal accidents, and the god must repeatedly reanimate his hapless servant. The cháak's bullets do not merely kill but also incinerate intended quarry. Attempts to manage a sacred rain gourd and spoon result in floods. Eventually the exasperated cháak gives up and sends the man home; after what seemed only a few nights away, the farmer discovers that fifteen years have passed on earth![25] A similar chain of events appears in a story that Brinton picked up from the now-lost manuscript of a nineteenth-century Tihosuco author. Here, a peasant discovers a tall, mysterious stranger in his milpa, gathering ears of corn in a basket. The stranger (in reality a *balam* or *yumtsil,* a field god) explains that he has simply come to reclaim a bit of what he himself had given; he sits down to smoke a giant cigar, but the flint piece he uses to light it gives off sparks of lightning and thunder. The terrified peasant faints, awakening to find that his entire milpa has been leveled by a hailstorm.[26] More explicitly Christian versions of this same story turn up in Zacatecas, or in Oaxaca, where San Isidro, patron saint of agriculture, plays the same role as the Yucatecan balam; these variations presumably reflect a shared tradition of missionary evangelization as well as a shared belief that the Otherworld was in every way bigger and better than the cornfields of home.[27]

Within the circumscribed geography of the known world, the most important division was between the village and the bush. To judge from the early ethnographers and surviving Maya folktales, few distinctions mattered more than this. The village was a knowable, predictable realm that humans had carved out of the great indeterminacy. Redfield underscored this point in his much criticized but often incisive synthesis of 1940.[28] Matthew Restall's recent (1997) analysis of the *kaaj*, or village unit, elaborates a similar point: in popular rural consciousness, the village stood forth as that which was known and (unlike the *kool*, or milpa) relatively permanent.[29] The indeterminacy of its necessary foil, however, the *k'aax* (*monte* in Spanish, "wilderness" or "forest" in English), partook heavily of the supernatural. Indeed, few motifs recur as frequently in Maya folklore. The story that Yucatecan peasants have retold countless times runs like this: A man must perform an errand, or return home; against all warnings and common sense, he insists on walking at night through the monte. Here he encounters a devil or supernatural beast. In most accounts the creature does nothing but by its mere presence, or supernatural "winds," poses a threat. The man chases it away by throwing stones, shooting it, or attacking it with a knife, or eludes it perhaps by the more prudent measure of simply running away. His hairbreadth escape serves as a warning to young daredevils of the village. In other variations, balams were known to abduct young boys who lagged behind their fathers when walking through the monte; the message in these tales was that children should learn to keep up with the demands of the adult world.[30]

Within the mundane realm, the popular mind also endowed certain selected spaces with special, even magical, significance. Prior to the eighteenth century, the church had designated the earth's sacred places. Many of these had been under sustained assault but were still held in certain instances. One such practice was sanctuary, or the right of pursued criminals to seek refuge in the church. In November 1839 Eligio Poot had his conviction for (undeclared) crimes reversed because he had been dragged from his hiding place in the Conkal church "without the proper formalities."[31] Another reserved space was the cemetery. This had traditionally stood beside the church; people were buried in the atrium or, if socially privileged, within the walls or beneath the floor of the church itself. However, the old days of churchyard burial were passing as state builders began to move cemeteries away from populated areas and outside of church control. The *ayuntamiento* (municipal government) of Mérida took the lead by purchasing the hacienda Xcoholté, formerly the property of Joaquín Lara, and using it as a place for burying the city's dead. In the long run this simple health measure played a critical role in controlling plagues and water contamination, but its effects would not make themselves known for some time. Meanwhile, folk reverence persisted. During the Caste War, rebels still buried revered leaders in the church atrium, as happened with Cecilio Chi in Tepich.[32]

The Yucatecan folkloric geography *par excellence* was and is the tunnel. Legend holds that mysterious tunnels connect to key points of the peninsula, such as the cathedral in Mérida, the church in Valladolid, or the ruins of Chichén Itzá. Rejón García records this belief as early as 1905 in regard to the caves of Kaua, and certainly it is much older than that.[33] However, the belief still flourishes today in the countryside, where locals like to recount how thousands of people hid in a nearby cave for ten years during the Caste War. Even many meridanos are convinced that their old colonial structures, particularly the cathedral and the nunnery, were originally linked by a tunnel network "in case the Indians attacked." Victoria Ojeda noted that such legends are actually common to colonial Mexican cities.[34] Here, at least, tunnel belief rests partly on the evidence of the senses: Yucatán is a huge limestone rock shot through with water-carved grottos, caves, and passageways, some of them quite spectacular and all populated with wondrous beings. Such was the case in 1890, when the Gascón traveler Ludovic Chambon was warned not to spend the night in the caves of Loltún, owing to "the spirits which guard its treasure, the enormous bulls that attack its profaners, and the avalanche of stones thrown by invisible beings."[35] However, the greater force of the belief appears to lie in a longing for ancient hidden knowledge, for a space unknown to colonial overlords. Unconditioned freedom survived the conquest by retreating to subterranean levels. The connection to seats of power suggest that the tunnel traveler will find a shortcut to justice and protection. The great limestone sinkholes, or *cenotes,* are also magical and connect, somehow, to an Otherworld. In Sudzal, for example, angry souls of people thrown in the cenote by "red soldiers" of the Revolution will drag bathers to their doom.[36]

In some cases the events of folk history left visual markers that explained the world to its rural inhabitants. Take, for instance, the story of the *burro tuunich,* or stone donkey, a syncretic word in a syncretic world. Many years ago, in this same town of Sudzal, a sorcerer sent a magical donkey to walk through the center of town; children foolish enough to ride on the donkey's back found themselves carried away to the bottom of a cenote. Eventually the townsfolk caught on and killed the sorcerer, at which point the donkey turned into the irregularly shaped stone that today sits in a field on the outskirts of town.[37] With a little imagination, the modern-day visitor can still see the burro's head, neck, and shoulders. For the people of central Yucatán this stone curiosity performed the same functions as the pillar of salt that was once Lot's wife: a signpost of history, a monument to the struggle against evil, and a comment on human affairs that stood out from the natural landscape.

As the tale of the burro tuunich suggests, strange geographies included strange beasts as well. Urbanites of the early nineteenth century, it appears, manifested little interest in natural history outside of tabulating livestock in their appraisals of haciendas. But rural folk knew of many additional creatures, mostly supernatural and better avoided. Huge winged serpents guarded cenotes. Tiny men known as *alux* roamed the woods and milpas, causing trouble when vexed but helpful if treated with respect. Under moonlight the *x-tabay* took the form of a beautiful woman to lure men to their doom. Tales of the seven-headed, hundred-footed *ek chapat* (literally, "lord centipede") apparently drew on Greek myths of the Sphinx, for this man-monster devoured any traveler who was unable to answer his riddles.[38] The *wáay chivo,* or "phantom goat," usually held to be a self-transformed sorcerer, had a habit of abducting the children and seducing the wives of men away from home and of digging up dead bodies for ghoulish intents. In some versions of its story, the villagers unite to hunt down the creature. After wounding it with a rifle shot, they follow its bloody tracks only to discover the village sorcerer lying dead or wounded in the hammock of his house.[39] Even as recently as 1937, a wáay chivo scare swept the town of Tekax when a barber, disappointed in his many attempts to seduce local women, disguised himself as the demon animal and menaced them in their homes at night.[40] Wáayes could appear in other forms as well: as cats, dogs, bats, and so forth. Beyond this, each animal species had its own supernatural king and protector. Devils took innumerable forms; for example, where a man had hanged himself, the devil appeared in the form of black dog. Whirlwinds, too, might be devils. Devils could even enter villages disguised as lowly creatures like mice.[41]

The world had its temporal geography as well. As various Maya ethnographers have pointed out, Maya peasant conceptions of temporal events are for the most part limited to events of the past two or three generations. The phrase "in the time of my grandfather" marks a story as extremely old. Beyond even that horizon, however, one body of oral tradition throughout Mexico concerns an unimaginably distant past, the Origin Time, in which the world assumed its current shape. Burns's "epoch of miracles" refers to precisely such an age: an epoch whose chronicles explain "how men got firewood long ago, how the corn grew long ago, how the corn was harvested long ago." [42] The period eludes quantification, but just as key activities and constructions set human life apart from the wilderness, so too certain narrative motifs staked out the coordinates of Origin Time. The first was an age when the ancient Mayas (*úuchben máako'ob* or *itza'ob*) ruled the earth, moving great stones merely by whistling. These accounts reminded the listener of former Maya greatness, usually with the suggestion that said greatness, like just about everything else associated with Origin Time, would someday come again. In other versions the world was once inhabited by a race of foolish dwarfs, or *p'uuso'ob,* who perished by flood.[43] Their rise and demise resemble other tales in which inferior or imperfect beings precede humanity, such as the antediluvian sinners of Genesis or the stick men of the Quiché *Popol Vuh.* Recent accounts, however, are far more charitable. The peninsula's modern-day informants see the little people as a race of wise progenitors that pioneered the basics of culture; according to these same informants, the p'uuso'ob are alive and well and living in (where else?) tunnels. These unusual beings come back from time to time to check on things.[44] The process of folkloric compression has merged the p'uuso'ob with the itza'ob, wise ancestors being more critical than foolish ones.

Another actor in this same mythical past was Jesucristo, here incarnated in a form hardly recognizable to Christian orthodoxy. A key event of Origin Time was the Jews' pursuit of Jesucristo across the peninsula; the Son of God was destined to lose this contest, but in the process he created the names of the birds and altered the natural landscape to its modern-day form. Jesucristo stories are particularly common in the Park Redfield collection, although collections from other parts of Mexico, such as Jalisco and Veracruz, contain virtually identical versions of the same. The story and its variations appear to be pan-Mexican.[45]

Finally, the urban masses had their own version of Origin Time. It lay not in some folk-biblical history, but rather in an unspecified early moment in their cities' histories, when the urban landscape took on its names and symbolic contours. Periods in question were broad: the halcyon days of the Spanish empire, the tumultuous nineteenth century, or the by now thoroughly mythologized Revolution. A Campeche street corner named "The Comet," for instance, was the place where citizens gathered to watch Halley's Comet in 1910, while the corner named "The Dog" commemorated the legend of a Spanish heretic who converted when he found his dog struggling with the devil in his daughter's bedroom (lack of faith leading to licentious behavior leading to dangers for home and family).[46] Similarly, Izamal's "Corner of the Deer" (the intersection of streets 27 and 24A) was where a cruel Spaniard had taken in a deer; in reality the soul of a deceased beggar, the animal worked a Dickensian transformation over old Don Rodrigo, mellowing him into the most generous man of the town.[47] Urban tales of Origin Time tilted far more toward the Hispanic end of the cultural spectrum, but nonetheless they performed functions similar to those of their rural and more predominantly Maya counterparts: explanation, orientation, the linking of human chronology with moral realization.

The world of early nineteenth-century Yucatán was thus much larger and more bewildering than a glance at maps, censuses, and property titles reveals. Peasant knowledge of geography rose through cumulative life experience, not through the necessities of state defense and administration. Primal distinctions existed within the realm of daily life: house, village, milpa, monte, and so forth. Popular knowledge, whether urban or rural, emphasized the here and now. Sacred spaces persisted in both narrative and practice. The deep background of this knowledge, however, had far less resolution than the immediate present. Larger questions of time and geography faded into indeterminacy. Above all, however, the conceptual background was shot through by an inchoate popular religiosity that relied upon a hodgepodge of the known, the unknown, and the invented.

Misery

Part of the world that everyone came to know sooner or later was misery: poverty, illness, hard labor, hunger, isolation, loss, humiliation, death. For the poor masses—and for everyone else—the impulse to wondrous belief sprang partly from the world's inescapable blows. Peninsular life had beauty, but it also suffered through stretches of hardship that humans were powerless to control. Impotence before these forces gave folk religion much of its appeal.

Perhaps the most terrible and least explicable of human suffering was illness, singularly acute in the pre-Porfirian nineteenth century. This was no stranger to the peninsula, since waves of illness relating to malnutrition had accompanied the Classic Maya collapse.[48] The situation worsened with the European-brought microorganisms. The population began to rebound around the middle of the seventeenth century, but Yucatán suffered epidemics of smallpox in 1824–1825, cholera in 1834–1835, cholera again in 1850–1854, and occasional outbreaks of both of these, plus measles, between 1854 and 1876. No history has yet documented the suffering these diseases inflicted, but it was clearly terrible. A physician who observed the 1825 typhus outbreak in Tunkás observed, "This is a vile, malignant, putrid illness recognized by its signs and symptoms, and with the bloodletting and infinite other barbarities to which [the Indians] are accustomed, some hardly last three days and others until the fifth day, throwing forth a vile corruption an hour before they die."[49] These epidemics remained etched in human memory, and references to them turn up in documents as late as a half century after the fact.[50]

Medicine offered only faint hope. In those days germs and viruses were unknown, and high medical officialdom understood most disease as the result of miasmas, or fetid and contaminated air. In addition to its conceptual limitations, medical practice had made only limited headway in the region and was primarily restricted to urban elites. Spanish colonial administrators introduced smallpox vaccinations to the peninsula in 1801, when royal surgeon Francisco Xavier Balmís made his trip through the Americas.[51] After 1821, Yucatecans tried to maintain the initiative; innumerable records remain of smallpox serum being sent to remote parts of the peninsula, usually to children. But vaccination serum, kept in impregnated cloth or sealed between two glass plates, suffered from uneven quality and was insufficient for the total population, even though many Maya peasant children were vaccinated from 1801 onward.[52] Sanitary and medical practices were indeed making inroads here, but it would be decades before they held out much real hope to anyone. In the countryside, cures took a more homegrown twist, as, for example, with Padre Baeza of Yaxcabá, who advocated powdered boar's tooth as a remedy for internal ailments.[53] Meanwhile, plague and illness had a second cousin in famine. Crises of harvest had flogged Yucatán repeatedly since recorded memory, drought and locusts being the main causes, followed in later years by political conflict. In the central region, improved health care and urban sanitation had begun to temper the severity of plagues by the mid–nineteenth century; but rural Yucatán was slow to change, and epidemics contributed to at least seven food shortages between 1807 and 1843.

Not surprisingly, then, illnesses turn up as a recurrent motif in folk knowledge. Although beyond the scope of this book, the unwritten encyclopedia of herbal remedies formed a central component of the repertoire of the *h-men*, or Maya shaman, then as now.[54] Rural folk had other recourses as well, including quarantining afflicted parties or providing them with greater allocations of food. Perhaps the most common response was flight, since peasants had learned through experience that once set in motion, political and biological misery traveled through human agents, and that it was best to avoid these by hiding in the forest. They believed that physical ailments came from witchcraft, or failure to keep peace with the gods through sacrifices and prayers, or else from the violation of the innumerable supernatural tripwires that might bring on evil winds.[55] Such winds had European origins but found counterparts among beliefs of the colonized Mayas. They appear to have followed no prescribed form; like geography and witchcraft, the winds were amorphous and had as many descriptions and analyses as there were informants. In recorded folktales, evil winds entered as a result of contact with supernatural beings, such as guardian serpents.[56] In other cases, winds spun out of bad places, as they can do today in the corrals of abandoned haciendas.[57] An obsession with miraculous cures also underlay much of Catholic attitude and ritual in the nineteenth century; it reflected more the popular than the learned end of Catholic culture, but whatever its social base, it was a strong obsession based on pressing historical problems.

Certain monster stories, in fact, reflect concerns about sickness. The x-tabay, probably the best known of Yucatán's mythical beasts, offers a case in point. This supernatural denizen appeared in out-of-the-way areas, usually at night; it took the form of a beautiful woman with long, flowing hair, with the aim of leading men to their doom. When not thus engaged, the x-tabay lived in the trunk of a ceiba tree. Accounts of the x-tabay are common, and even today it is one of the few tidbits of rural folklore universally known to urbanites.[58] Probably, as some have suggested, the x-tabay derives from a pre-Columbian Maya deity. But it is difficult not to see its stories as metaphors for venereal disease, a punishment for sexual indiscretions and marital infidelities. In most versions, a man going through the monte at night is accosted by a beautiful woman, with whom he has relations. Thereafter, his penis becomes weak (diseased or impotent), and a h-men must intervene. Even in narratives where the man resists temptation, an implied hint of marital infidelity remains present. The x-tabay appears to have been rural storytellers' way of giving their lesson a supernatural reinforcement. A nightclub in contemporary Mérida carries the name, as well as the moral danger, of this mythical creature.

If sickness absorbed the peasants, it is equally difficult to overlook the ubiquitous violence of Maya folktales. As with twentieth-century urbanites and their movies, the taletellers of rural Yucatán made death and mayhem regular scenery in their craft. In fact, the cruelties the peasants inflicted upon one another in their folktales are often astonishing: a wife kills her husband by sticking a sharpened pig bone in his head.[59] An unfaithful woman poisons her spouse with an enchanted fat that goes up his nose and suffocates him.[60] A jealous man seals his wife in a coffin and throws it into the ocean.[61] An angry husband forces an old lecher to eat baby excrement.[62] And when humans are not the culprit, there is no shortage of gods, demons, and monsters to do the same. A woman who dares to walk through the monte alone is torn apart by a demon with long fingernails.[63] A devil keeps herds of human children like goats, to be eaten at his leisure.[64] These motifs functioned in part as the peasant equivalent of modern-day cartoon violence: a plastic medium in which the imagination could run riot without causing real pain. But in part it was the harshness of rural life that lent them believability. The audience to such tales knew beforehand that life was hard and people made each other suffer.

Beyond the obvious problems of sickness and violence, the peninsular world also abounded in magical dangers of both Maya and European origin.[65] To counteract these the people used divination to see the future, ward off illnesses, and better coordinate their lives with the supernatural forces that surrounded them. Not surprisingly, many popular methods for divining the future related to death. Unlucky omens (in Maya, *tamax chi'*, or "deep speech") included snakes with red eyes, but there were many others. To see a tarantula or a scorpion carrying her young on her back meant a death in the family, as did a blackbird flying through the house. Removing a butterfly at night from your house would kill a relative. However, of the many unlucky omens in this unlucky land, the worst was to be caught lying face-up in a hammock when the owl hooted. This fear became proverbial throughout greater Mexico: "When the owl cries, the Indian dies," ran the expression. The only recourse was to sit upright and pray. Mothers turned the children on their side and placed an overturned shoe beneath the hammock in order to protect the children's souls.[66]

The folklore of dream interpretation crackled with dangers of all description. Dreams normally foretold the future, but the vast majority of known interpretations referred to futures that were explicitly unhappy or dangerous. For example, dreams of floating in the air or having a tooth pulled spelled doom. Dreams of red tomatoes meant a dead child. A man who dreamed of going to a strange city or having a bull enter his house would soon attend a funeral. Other death dreams included ticks and broken pitchers. At the same time, even those that were not necessarily death-related might still be portentous. A dream of a naked woman meant that the dreamer would encounter a rattlesnake the next day. In dream language, a house on fire meant a family member with fever. Snakes meant a quarrel with the spouse, while white horses gave a clear prediction of rain.[67] Burns found that Maya informants regarded dreams as a kind of telephone call from the Otherworld, but judging from other collections it appears that many of the messages were unhappy ones.[68]

Many popular beliefs and dangers surrounded the household, an area that more than any other was the special purview of women. Here, intrusions of the natural world (birds, insects, snakes) into the household usually boded ill. Fireflies in the house meant a coming fever.[69] Some of the more innocuous house beliefs involved the lowly broom; sweeping at night, for example, could lead to a life of poverty.[70] Sweeping over the feet of a girl meant that she would marry an old man—perhaps the message was that keeping children in the house would keep them from meeting potential spouses.[71] Putting a broom behind the door would bring a long-winded guest, together with a powerful urge to use the bathroom.[72] This last belief seems little more than a recognition of unhappy coincidence. However, the creencias did hold out the hope that people had some control over their fates and that with caution they could avoid unpleasant situations.

A huge number of folkloric beliefs also pertain to the perils of pregnant or menstruating women. Most of these bewildering prescriptions involved evils finding their way into the womb, endangering the health of the child and hence of the community itself. Several involved sympathetic magic between the umbilical cord and other ropes and strings. When sewing, for example, a pregnant woman should never lay the thread over her shoulder, or the umbilical cord would strangle the fetus; stepping on a rope or leaping over a horse's rein had identical results.[73] An expecting mother who saw a snake should not run immediately, because the "force" of the serpent could enter her body. Blowing into a bottle would cause her to have insufficient air when the time for delivery came.[74] A pregnant woman who scratched herself during a full moon or an eclipse necessarily transferred the mark to her baby; the only remedy was to drink the water used to wash a millstone.[75] Bathing with too much water would result in excess liquid in the womb. To avoid miscarriages, the mother-to-be should eat roasted iguana seasoned with *k'uyub* (*achiote,* or annatto seed). If still nursing her baby, the mother should not go into the monte, because a snake known as *x-chayil kaan* would smell the milk and pursue her.[76] If there is a consistent theme in these accounts, it is that women, and particularly pregnant women, were filters capable of catching all sorts of evils and transmitting them to their children. Pregnant females had received the fertilizing influence of the male, and their ability to absorb other influences remained acutely heightened during pregnancy. Expectant mothers could also absorb their own sins and transmit them to their children: a woman who ridicules a hunchback will bear a hunchbacked child, while a woman who boasts that childbearing is easy is likely to die in the process, possibly the result of twins or triplets.[77] This last creencia touched at one of the core lessons of peasant folklore: the importance of humility and stoicism, here articulated for the benefit of too-arrogant women.

If pregnant women risked absorbing dangers, menstruating women were capable of releasing them. As in many societies, menstruating daughters could make their brothers ill and hence needed to be separated (presumably a reflection of the fact that the daughters themselves were now sexually vulnerable). However, the situation had advantages: eating limes during menstruation helped remove stains from clothes. In other versions, it was prohibited to eat oranges or limes, wash one's hair, or take a bath. In fact, the whole process was shrouded in mystery, and it was widely believed to be a sin to inform a girl of the menstrual process before she had experienced it.[78] Finally, if all this became too complicated, a woman could immediately terminate the menstrual period by eating coconut meat. Virginity also mattered, even though among rural Mayas it was not as de rigueur as for the status-conscious urban Spaniard.[79] Rural folk believed that they could detect virginity if the woman could walk without swaying or if she had narrow hips; conversely, a girl who was not a virgin and who took in her hands the flower *naj* plucked from a cenote would cause it to stain. A *limón* fruit thrown in her path could also predict the same thing; if when opened the seeds separated, the girl was no longer a maiden.[80]

Animals proved critical in feeling out supernatural dangers. Dogs could see ghosts and frightened them away with their bark. Chickens cackled at night for the same reason.[81] Dogs, nevertheless, were the superior animal for their intelligence and loyalty, and offered such additional advantages as absorbing spells intended for their masters. In one recurring motif of Maya folktales, two loyal dogs revive their master after he has already died and been buried in the walls of the local church.[82] In at least one version it was Jesus' faithful dogs, Chainbreaker and Batichuyu, who revived him after crucifixion.[83] "The Dog and the Devil," a cuento that Martínez Huchim collected in the

Tizimín area, relates how a dog saves his master from being eaten by a devil; the devil agrees to the dog's challenge that he must first count all the dog's hairs, but each time he reaches the end the dog begins to wag his tail, and the devil loses count.[84] However, woe to the man whose dog dragged its rear end in the dirt, for it was marking the place where its master would soon be buried.[85] The praying mantis (*ts'awayak'*) brought nightmares, especially if it perched on a sleeping body.[86] White butterflies, to the contrary, were favorable, because when clustered at the entrance to a milpa a fine harvest was certain.[87] Swallows flying low meant rain, as did ants carrying their young.[88] The song of a cicada known as *choch* did so as well, while another cicada, *chipitín*, foretold drought.[89] A dying iguana was capable of slinging off its tails, "inflicting a poisonous wound." Moreover, iguanas could bite a person's shadow in order to cause severe headaches.[90] Speaking the name of the animal you were hunting ensured that he would elude you.[91] In modern-day Yucatán, and even in urban Mérida, few creencias are more prevalent than the notion that a dragonfly (*tulix*, often the corruption *turix*) in the house means a visitor is coming.[92] Its counterpart, the huge but benign black moth known as *x-majannaj* ("renter"), means a visit of longer duration. Plants, too, spoke of the future. Thin corn husks predicted a mild winter; thick ones were a sign of prolonged chills.[93] In some cases, even inanimate objects were believed to have life; one should never speak ill of tobacco and liquor, ran the saying, because they had "ears" and could take revenge.[94]

Misery, then, was all around. The repeated contagions, the hungers that resulted from drought, plagues, and the Caste War, the uncertainties of pregnancy and childbirth—all these were key features of nineteenth-century life. Most were not unique to that period, but they all struck in heightened form as a result of population growth, political instability, and widespread violence, and all found their way into the body of the folklore then forming.

Agency

Misery entailed agency. In this world, bad things did not simply happen but, rather, happened as a result of malice and personal intent. When peasants told stories, they tended to place personal machinations and evil behind much of the suffering.

Narrative agency was a delicate matter, since it involved naming names—even if those names referred merely to generic socioeconomic roles. Perhaps this was one reason for a large number of tales in which animals serve as protagonists. These stories were often allegories; their narrators used them to convey some truth about life in a form that was comprehensible but also non-confrontational. Animals seemed more stereotypical and did not lend themselves to lengthy exploits. Their stories tend toward brief vignettes that impart a simple, clear message. Animal allegories were usually shorter than human narratives. Levi-Strauss cautions against assuming that animals are chosen for myths because of inherent characteristics; nature, he insists, is culturally constructed rather than empirically deduced.[95] In some cases the roles assigned to specific animals do indeed seem to hint at some uncharted mythic structure. Why, for example, is the *tsutsuy* good but the *sak pakal* bad? Both were species of wild doves. When Jesucristo fled from the Jews so long ago, the former sang *tsu tsu bey* ("the road is closed"), while the latter sang *petek tsuk che'* (roughly, "he's in the briar patch"), thus betraying his location.[96] These fanciful readings of birdsongs were constructions based first on cultural values and only secondarily attributed to nature. Or: why did the squirrel cruelly deceive the wild dove into killing her children? She believed his story that a great flood was coming, and afterward would always cry, "*Ku'uk tu tuus,*" "the squirrel lied." We know that this story circulated at the beginning of the century; perhaps, as the agrarian schoolteacher Santiago Pacheco Cruz suggested, it reflected a distrust that was the legacy of colonialism.[97] Viciousness and gullibility were recognizable human traits, but why these animals as vehicles?

At the same time, certain other tales and folksongs seem to use animals because something about them called to mind a facet of human behavior.[98] The bat, for example, was an animal that defied taxonomy: was it closer to birds or rats? It is not surprising, then, to find the bat as a neutral protagonist in a fable about war. The story goes that once all the animals went to war, but the bat could not decide which side to join and so fought with whatever group happened to be winning at the time. Infuriated by his opportunism, the others informed him that switching sides was unacceptable. The bat then elected to remain between the two groups, and when the next battle came, he was crushed between them. The moral: You have to choose.[99]

A similar device operates in the story of "Siete Colores" (Seven Colors), a bird of singularly exquisite plumage. Originally he was the ugliest of all birds, but the others took pity and contributed a few of their own feathers, transforming him into a multicolored marvel. But Siete Colores now spent all his time admiring himself in the mirror and was unable to warn the others when a hunter was coming. For his vanity God condemned Siete Colores to live in a cage.[100] The story distills peasant attitudes toward people and things that are beautiful but essentially useless. Dogs, to the reverse, were homely, mangy, and potentially vicious, but they also served humans with loyalty and are treated in the stories as privileged beings. Even in real-life villages, where their conditions were decidedly unregal, dogs still ran free in the streets, houses, and even churches.[101]

Unquestionably, however, the more compelling products of folktales involve the deeds and misdeeds of human beings. In Maya cuentos, the hero of the action is young. He lacks significant prospects beyond his milpa. Moreover, his struggle is often generational. Older members of the village—parents, in-laws, petty merchants—control the wealth of his world. They disdain the young man; in fact, it is hard to ignore how often the heroes begin their careers described as foolish, lazy, shiftless, deceitful, and so forth. Either these epithets prove to be false, or else they work to the young man's advantage as he systematically defeats his enemies and takes possession of his world.

Among heroes, few traits mattered as much as cunning. Underdog culture tends to prefer cleverness, since success by strength and power is out of the question. This holds true for Grimm's European folktales as well as for the slave narratives that Joel Chandler Harris distilled into the Uncle Remus stories. Mexican peasant tales often utilize the rabbit as a symbol of the little guy who uses his head; in fact, the most common and widespread of all narrative structures in Mexican folklore are the *conejo/coyote* stories, in which one or both of the characters function as tricksters.[102] In Yucatán Juan T'u'ul (John the Rabbit) recurs as a stock character.[103] (This character is not to be confused with Juan Tul, who was a protector spirit of cattle and had a specialty of retrieving lost animals.[104]) We also find stories of rabbits outwitting foxes, rabbits defeating giants, and ticks outhunting pumas.[105] The lesson in all of these was that weakness was really strength, and that the peasant, however much an underdog, would triumph in the end.

While male heroes predominate, there are occasionally heroines, such as that in the story of "The Girl Who Became a King."[106] Thrown out by her tailor husband on false accusations of sexual misconduct, the girl eventually enters the king's court disguised as a man, and in fact uses an artificial penis made of tin so that other men of the court can see her urinating. The woman eventually reunites with her husband; they become king and queen and see to it that her false accusers are burned alive. In this somewhat bawdy story of gender transformation, the woman has to assume male identity to become a protagonist.

Since heroes grow insipid without foils, the narrators peppered their stories with the misdeeds of certain fairly predictable stereotypes. In Origin Time narratives collected by Redfield and Park Redfield, Jews often served as the evil agents who motivated the narrative action, usually through their wicked pursuit of Jesus. Any peasant who listened casually to the main readings of the liturgical year heard tale after tale of Christ's passion and betrayal. Few had any concrete idea of what a Jew was, where Jews lived, or what they believed, but it proved temptingly convenient to paint them into stories as all-purpose traitors and malefactors. This folk anti-Semitism, common throughout Latin America, is evident in quite a few of the stories collected by Margaret Park Redfield.[107]

Devils put in regular appearances as well. On almost all occasions they are highly dangerous. One archetypal Maya devil story concerns the demon imprisoned in a grotto. Through sweet talking and insincere promises, the devil cajoles a naive peasant lad to release him, then announces his intention to eat the boy. But the story ends happily when a fox cleverly tricks the devil into reentering the grotto and seals him up once again.[108] Similarly, in "The Poor Charcoal Maker," the devil gives his hapless victim twenty thousand dollars and twenty years in exchange for his soul; the *carbonero* is saved only by the intervention of an old woman who frightens the devil away by exposing herself.[109] There are at least a few cases in which the devil is a useful associate; when properly approached through the correct rituals, for example, the devil could inform men of their wives' infidelity.[110] The ambiguity features in folklore from other parts of Mexico as well.[111] Despite the exceptions, however, devils are usually bad and are best avoided.

Curiously, however, the bulk of surviving folklore makes little use of villains such as *hacendados,* priests, predatory officials, marauding soldiers, and so forth. In fact, there are only rare instances in these tales when *ts'uulo'ob,* or white non-Mayas, enter at all. Peasants more commonly reserved narrative roles for forces closer at hand. Perhaps the only exception to this rule is a cuento that Andrade picked up in Chichén Itzá, "The Batab Cazuela," who suffers having his daughter as well as his kingdom taken over by unspecified but clearly rapacious foreigners.[112] The story strongly suggests a consciousness of archaeological expropriation by non-Mayas. Another recognizable intrusion by non-Mayas takes place in the story of "The Lazy Man." The man finds himself pursued by a monster, but the local magistrate—a fox, significantly—saves him. In return, the fox-magistrate demands all the man's chickens, a symbolic way of saying "everything he had." Peasants apparently recognized this sort of exploitation as the price of doing business with officialdom. But the broader (if violent) humor of the story spins out of the magistrate's unsuccessful attempts to collect on the debt: the peasant's wife knows nothing of the deal, and sics her dogs on Señor Fox, who is torn to pieces.[113]

However revealing, the two cases shown above were also exceptional. Far more common as evil-doers were local rivals, jealous neighbors, and wicked in-laws and stepparents—troublesome, but essentially of the community. If these characters seem to come directly from the central casting of the closed corporate village, it is because their jealousy and intrigues were familiar to most peasants. "Joselita and Petrona" recycles the well-known wicked stepmother who conspires to have her two innocent stepchildren abandoned in the woods (they return and kill her instead); this particular motif is known to have circulated in Tabasco in the 1880s.[114] In "The King and the Three Sisters," a young woman marries a king; her two sisters are livid with envy and, acting as midwives, take away the girl's newborn infants and replace them with dead animals.[115] Or, in Burns's "Story about an Unusual Marriage"—one between a man and a vulture—the humor depends on a discomfort that everyone understood: having to live with in-laws, in this case carrion-eating birds with a taste for human waste.[116] Relatives constituted the necessary problem—the connections without whom life could not continue but also one source of the latent tensions at the village's subatomic level.

Another manifestation of family tension was the fear of adultery, unpopular anywhere but particularly threatening in peasant villages, where the bond between husband and wife formed the basis of material existence. Men built houses, hunted, and farmed the milpa, while women were expected to do everything else. Available census information for the years before 1847 together with more recent anthropological work demonstrate the rarity of single households and, conversely, the importance of the dyadic bond.[117] In virtually any narrative structure things have to go wrong before they can go right again, and for this reason the home often serves as the setting for sexual jealousy and betrayal. In one archetypal tale of adultery, the guilty woman (apparently men were telling the story) uses witchcraft to change herself into an animal in order to meet her paramour. To quell suspicions, the *x-wáay* or *x-pul ya'aj* (female witch) leaves behind her head in the hammock, making it appear that she is there sleeping.[118] The wronged husband takes revenge by destroying the head, thus making it impossible for the wife to return to her old life. In a version from Xoccén, the x-wáay eats the baby when her husband goes hunting.[119] This story of the wife who turns out to be a witch has circulated extensively throughout Mexico; numerous variations have been recorded in Chiapas and central Mexico.[120] On one level, the narrative denotes a disdain for women who fail to carry out domestic obligations. On another, however, the fear of marrying a witch also reflects anxieties over the unforeseen hazards of matrimony in a culture where couples joined at a very early age and without clear knowledge of one another's character. Finally, stories of witchcraft target the wife, since a well-known sexual double standard applied between men and women; wronged wives usually had to suffer betrayals in silence, and stories of husbands who turn out to be wizards are relatively unknown.

With or without benefit of marriage, there was plenty of witchcraft, or *hechicería,* to fuel nineteenth-century taletelling. Witchcraft usually functions as an objectified version of the jealousies and suspicions that undergird village society; it is the scourge of rural life everywhere. In some cases it functioned on a one-to-one basis: someone wanting to spoil the luck of a hunter, for instance, could buy deer meat from him and throw the bones in a cenote.[121] But the special knowledge involved made witchcraft by third parties more the norm. Rural Mayas considered death a satisfactory plot resolution to tales of sorcery, since, as with the x-wáay, such tales typically end with the enchanter being burned to death.[122] In "The Mare's Son" the wicked stepmother and her accomplice daughter are tied to a tree and forced to breathe chile smoke until they vomit to death.[123] These plot-twists, gruesome and seemingly fictional, in fact reflected real-life experience. Preoccupation with spells and sorcery thrived in the nineteenth century. Most hechicería was (and is) the work of professionals, or at least was attributed to them. It is also a fact that Yucatecan villagers commonly used spells to find happiness, take down a rival, or bring back lost love.[124] As in the stories, communities could deal harshly with people who cast spells. In Kantunil-kin, a *pacífico* community that formed in the late 1850s to the northeast of Xcan, Maya peasants were willing to burn x-wáayes publicly as late as 1866, their intended victims saved only by the authorities' quick intervention.[125] Nevertheless, the villagers must have been drawing upon a fund of practical experience accumulated from episodes when the authorities were not timely enough. Even in Chan Santa Cruz, the generals were known to deal harshly with those who practiced witchcraft.[126] For sharper resolution, we might consider the remarks of archaeologist Thomas Gann, who traveled extensively in the areas of Belize and Quintana Roo in the early decades of this century: "The heaviest punishment is inflicted for witchcraft or sorcery, as the *puyla,* or sorceress, is greatly dreaded by the Indians. She is literally chopped limb from limb; but whereas the bodies of other victims executed in this way are always buried, that of the puyla is left for the dogs and vultures to dispose of."[127] The village's varying reactions—the simultaneous admiration and fear of hechicería—reflected a contradictory attitude of fear and fascination regarding otherworldly forces, in turn a reflection of forces latent in the village itself.

Mexican folktales raise an interpretive problem in their reluctance to pin blame on extracommunal forces: landowners, officials, priests, and so forth—the actors that most historians point to as sources of pressure for the average peasant. This is, in fact, a reticence or discretion that they share with other folklores of the world. At least three explanations come to mind, none of them entirely satisfactory in and of itself. The first could simply be faulty collection. After years of retelling the fakelore of Paul Bunyan, for example, we now have evidence that northern loggers preferred to spend their free time playing cribbage or talking Wobblie politics.[128] Methodological distortions or peasant evasiveness may have played a hand in Yucatán as well. Nevertheless, it is difficult to believe that peasant informants consistently altered their tales to spare the feelings of anthropological collectors in a way that falsified virtually the entire corpus of known folk narrative. Moreover, when speaking to anthropologists of history, peasant informants demonstrate no such reticence in their stories of the oppressive prerevolutionary labor conditions, often referred to as "the time of slavery."[129]

A second possible explanation is that these tales work better in a hermetically contained world where the folk exist on their own. That is, in their oral literature the Maya peasants liked to conjure up a world in which they alone operated, perhaps since the doings and motivations of elites seemed incomprehensible to them, perhaps because stories that touched too close to reality ceased to be entertaining. This uncomfortable intensity may help explain why art movements of social realism are often brief.

Still a third possibility is that the selection of in-laws, Jews, Negroes, and devils reflected a tendency toward lowest common denominators in narrative symbolic structures. Peasant relationships with non-Mayas were in fact complex, and villagers relied on these powerful outsiders as often as they quarreled with them. Within each audience of a folktale there was a potential range of opinions regarding specific ts'uulo'ob, all of which tended to be controversial. Peasant dealings with their largely Hispanic higher-ups generated far greater ambivalence. Such relationships had their root in colonial administration and tributary practices. Priests, officials, property owners, and even *santos* could do things for the average Maya, but patronage demanded continued gifts in a process of unequal reciprocity. Patronage ties continued to flourish throughout the golden age of haciendas.[130] The point is that peasants looked uneasily toward patrons but had a hard time casting them as unvarnished malefactors.

Some inkling of this point glimmers beneath the surface of "The Fire God and the Rain God."[131] When the Creator was dividing up work for his helper gods many epochs ago, the two aforementioned were so lazy that they did not show up to receive their assignments. Fire and Rain, the two deities most important to peasants, had to be bought by promises of continual offerings, or else the peasants would suffer. The same was true for other potential bene-factors, whose real-life ambiguity disqualified them as the appropriate stuff of cuentos. As with Hollywood and its villain preferences (Nazis, Middle Eastern terrorists, Colombian drug lords, greedy corporations), there was an inclina-tion to seek stock figures whom all could comfortably despise.

Remedy

Crops died, babies cried, plans failed, the husband was a drunk, and the au-thorities took everything. What recourse for such miseries? While much of peasant lore focused on the hardships of life, it also pointed to solutions and salvations. Virtually all socioeconomic studies of peasant society stress risk avoidance as an important trait; similarly, one subtext of Yucatecan folktales emphasizes that caution and prudence are necessary for a long, happy life — and afterlife.[132]

One solution the cuentos never mention is technology, a fact that directly links the formation and general ethos of Yucatecan folklore to pre-Porfirian history. The reason for this is simply that key transforming technologies had yet to appear. Neither gas nor electricity illuminated the darkness of rural nights, while rapid travel meant horseback or horse-drawn carriages on the few suitable roads, or else Indian portage in the *koché* (hand-held carriage). Soldiers fought the Caste War with single-shot rifles. Even the midcentury hacienda, while larger in scale than traditional land-tenure systems, would still have been technologically recognizable to a Maya of 1600. The mechanized henequen rasper was the lynchpin of later economic growth and transforma-tion, but it was not invented until 1855. The telegraph came a decade later, during the French Empire (1863–1867). Yucatecans opened their first railroad, the Progreso-Mérida line, at the comparatively late date of 1881. Moreover, it would take years for these inventions to have a beneficial effect on the lives of most rural people. The age of mechanical marvels, as well as our own quasi-religious belief in the power of technology, lay far in the future, and the age's folkloric solutions crystallized a worldview that saw remedy as either human or superhuman, with little in between.[133]

The best way to escape trouble was not to get into it in the first place; accordingly, a large number of folk tales caution against such destabilizing faults as pride, excess, jealousy, and cruelty. One example of this comes from the various examples of the *kuxa'an suum,* or Living Rope, in a parable against human avarice that can be documented at least as early as 1865.[134] The story concerns the discovery of a chest, usually hidden in or near a cenote or archaeological ruin, within which lies a miraculous rope that has no end. When the discoverers try to cut the rope, it bleeds. The narratives go on to recount that the rope reaches all the way to Mérida, and in at least one version, on the Last Day it will stretch to the top of Mérida's cathedral. The powerful of the earth will have to walk the rope; those who have used their power wisely will pass unharmed, while the unjust, including *caciques* who exploited their people, will fall to a horrible death. In other versions, there is a race to carry tortillas to Mérida via the rope; the Spanish king sends his contestant on a horse, who cannot mount this too-narrow highway, while the Maya king sends his on a squirrel, who travels it effortlessly. The Living Rope story speaks of an apocalypse to come but softens the message with hope for a moral order. More than anything else, it appears to be some sort of world umbilical cord, a vital tissue that, like the tunnels, leads from the deep past (from the *úuchben máako'ob,* who placed it there in Origin Time) to a powerful but just future (in this case, the cathedral of the so-distant capital). There is a frank aggression in the human attempts to unearth the Living Rope, and those who do so usually appear in the story as plunderers. But while they can cut and wound, final justice lies with the rope itself, which will provide the means of sorting out human beings in the hereafter. The story of the kuxa'an suum draws directly from the pre-Conquest symbolism of an umbilical cord that connected the lords of Chichén Itzá to the heavens;[135] through the course of centuries it underwent a democratization, eventually serving less as a marker of nobility and more as the dormant protector of Yucatán's ethnic underclass.

Another widespread cautionary tale chronicles the adventure of the dog who learned to speak. A poor woman who carries well-water every day curses the family dog for his uselessness; "You can't even sing!" she says in disgust. One day she returns home to find the dog rocking the baby in a hammock and singing to it. In her amazement the woman drops the water buckets she is carrying, and the puddles grow to become certain ponds, or *lagunas,* known to the real-life listeners. When viewed through the structural analysis of Levi-

Strauss, this origin myth seems to spin out of the tension of several opposites: human versus animal, scarcity versus excess, home versus natural landscape. Here, the resolution to one opposite (the dog's adopting human nature) leads to the resolution of others, as overabundance of water now replaces water scarcity, so much so that the house is engulfed. On one hand the audience learned not to abuse animals; on the other, "The Dog and the Creation of the Lagoon" reinforced a peasant stoicism about matters that defied technological solution. Listeners came to understand that certain situations, such as the separation of home and well and the limitations of dog labor, had to be accepted, no matter how much hardship they brought; they came from necessary divisions of the world, and to undo those divisions was to risk everything. If dogs really *could* work for us, who knows what other unthinkable changes might follow?[136]

Excessive expectations, then, were a form of hubris that brought unfortunate consequences. A similar warning appears in the story of the man who wanted to see the dead. His motives vary: in some versions the protagonist is investigating spirits who haunt his patio, while in others he is merely curious. The method, however, invariably consists of putting a dog's tears in his own eyes; dogs could see ghosts and, through a process of contagious magic, imparted that same power. But mankind was not meant to see the dead. As a consequence of this rash experiment the man is struck mute by terrifying visions and soon dies.[137] Similarly, during the night of October 31, which initiated observations of Day of the Dead (*el día de los muertos,* or *janal pixan*), people should avoid looking out into the streets, lest they see the procession of dead spirits and consequently suffer some terrible punishment; the secretive dead were likely to carry off the family's baby, leaving only its bones in the cradle. Like the adventure of the talking dog, these stories stress the optical and spiritual limitations of the human being.[138]

Pride was bad, beauty was false, good luck brought the inevitable reversal of fortune. We find these same lessons in "The Story of the Two Women," who lived many years ago in the village of Cansahcab. Born on the same day, they were nonetheless different in every way. One woman was beautiful, charming, and popular, yet at the same time vain, self-centered, and deceitful. The other lived a saintly life but was so ugly that everyone avoided her; she lived in seclusion at the edge of the village, her only company being the animals and poor travelers for whom she cared. One day the two women died. To everyone's amazement, the body of the beautiful woman decomposed rapidly, and it filled the town with a noxious stench. But the remains of the ugly woman released a heavenly scent—some say it was the smell of roses—which overcame the stench of the vain woman.[139]

The message in all these stories was clear: Rather than beauty or brilliance, it is patience that overcomes many of the obstacles of life. As Redfield noted, Maya peasants see themselves as separated from ts'uul by their ability to endure hardships, to wait out difficulties, to survive in the bush.[140] Another cuento plying this same lesson is the story of María Muuch.[141] Born to average parents, María grows up to be a huge frog (*muuch*), although in other regards a cheerful and dutiful daughter. A local boy (the son of a king) discovers one day that when coy María bathes in the cenote, she takes off her frog skin and becomes a beautiful girl. Despite opposition from all quarters, especially from his royal family, the boy marries María and goes to live with her in a hut. But patience pays off. One night, when the young husband appears to be asleep, his warty wife finally doffs her skin; he seizes it and forces her to accept her human form, and in the end he and María return with enhanced prestige to the royal family. This tale's European motif (lovely girl in animal skin or beggar's clothes) has turned up in Jalisco folklore collections as early as 1912; here, its surrounding story links patience and persistence to the sexual transition from awkward girl to mature spouse, in this case set against generational opposition from in-laws.[142]

But narrators and audiences knew the limitations of their own kind. Experience had taught them that peasants, however stoic and cautious, still suffered.[143] This was particularly true in the nineteenth century, when despite adherence to all the old traditions the world around the Yucatec Mayas continued to change, and change rapidly. Awareness of suffering was a recognition of who had power and who did not; but it also acknowledged a hard truth about human truculence and discontent. In the end, and despite all possible warnings, people would still persist in getting into trouble. One symbol of this stubborn willfulness came from the story of the boy who wanted to learn the ways of the h-men. Despite his master's warning to keep his eyes shut during a spiritual exercise, the sorcerer's apprentice opens them anyway; his disobedience unleashes a serpent demon that the master has been struggling to dominate. The h-men regains control only after superhuman effort.[144] Of course, a two-edged sword operated here. As in most myths, the act of primal disobedience (or sometimes mere forgetfulness) launches the hero into terrible suffering but also sets the stage for narrative action. The apprentice's error or subconscious flouting of instructions, what mythographer Joseph Campbell refers to as "the blunder," like Adam's sin or the Greek sacrilege at Troy sends the hero on his journey and allows him to show his mettle.[145] Sin we should not, but sin we do. For that reason, folk wisdom entailed a huge number of cures, remedies, and magical ways out.

In some regards divination itself offered the cure—forewarned was forearmed. But beyond that, the popular culture of both ethnic groups prescribed a fragmentary series of remedies that in one way or another had their basis in the supernatural. To heal scars, apply the dust found on the crossbar of doors and windows.[146] To cure syphilis, eat snake, bones and all, cooked in an earthen oven.[147] Men and women alike learned to remove their hat when crossing the front of churches (today the sign of the cross substitutes). The more orthodox stood and prayed quickly when hearing the church bells toll at hours of *oración*.[148] It was imperative to say "Jesús" when someone sneezed because the devil was capable of entering through the open mouth.[149] If a turkey died on your patio, it was important to bury him on the east side of the *k'an xul* tree to keep the other turkeys from dying as well. All new enterprises should begin on Monday or Saturday, never on Tuesday or Friday (an obvious European import, since there was no pre-Hispanic week per se).[150] To protect against the devil, put a new piece of paper over the soles of your shoes every day.[151]

The number nine had rich significance, a fact perhaps derived from the Christian *novena,* or nine-day prayer, which enjoyed profound popularity in all quarters. At the same time, the number's importance may well have carried over from pre-Christian beliefs, since one of the incarnations of the sky god *Itzamná* was *Aj Bolon Ts'akab* ("Nine Fertilizer" or "Nine Inseminator").[152] Whatever the origin of its associations, the number clearly carried a mystic power well into the twentieth century. To avoid respiratory illness, hang up a gourd of *pozole* for every member of the family for nine days, then drink it. The man who came across a centipede should divide it into nine parts for good luck; a green snake with red eyes got the same treatment, or else whoever saw it would die within a year.[153] If a woman had trouble giving birth, her husband should pass under her hammock nine times.[154] Nine leaves of the sour orange in hot water cured stomach ailments (it works, although the actual number of leaves may vary). To cure headaches, rub a rattlesnake's rattle nine times over your temple.[155] In fact, the number nine's importance seems to have made the word *bolon,* or "nine," virtually synonymous with "sacred" or "blessed." Hence its usage in place names, such as Bolon-Tabi (a town whose Virgin cult is described in Chapter 4), or in the term *aj bolon pixan,* Maya for the patron saint of a village. Again borrowing from European traditions, the number thirteen was profoundly unlucky.[156]

Drink offered another palliative for humanity's woes, especially if it was magical, ceremonial drink. Before the coming of the Spanish, the Maya drank *balche',* an anise-flavored liquor made from the bark of certain trees, or else the fermented corn beer *chicha.* At least originally the practice had strong religious overtones, since pre-Columbian Mayas saw intoxication as a way of getting in touch with the divine; heavy drinking bouts, which the Spanish normally referred to as *embriageces,* formed crucial punctuations in the ritual year. But by the late eighteenth century, *aguardiente,* a crude sugar rum, was flooding the countryside. Valladolid produced a specially flavored variety known as *anís.* Both packed more of a wallop than the indigenous brews and quickly became the cure-alls of choice. One priest summed up the experience of his whole class when he wrote, "I like my predecessors have recognized and punished the repeated excesses which the Indians, whether of the república or not, commit with their continual drunken sprees." [157] Rural ills included fear and emotional stress: soldiers on both sides fought the Caste War heavily intoxicated, with drinks of aguardiente as part of the standard breakfast ration. [158] In sum, an activity that had strong religious overtones remained one of the people's standard ways of dealing with problems.

There was also a penitential tradition here. Maya peasant religion involved mortifying the flesh, again a pre-Columbian/colonial convergence. Ritual bloodletting was the passion of the Maya elite; this sport of kings presumably had a correlate among the common people. The colonial Catholic Church also encouraged penitential flagellation, and although the practice began to decline in the late 1700s, it clearly survived in many nooks and crannies of independent Mexico. [159] Church-sanctioned self-flagellation still had its moments, as witnessed by the traveler B. A. Norman in 1843:

> After the usual ceremonies were concluded, a large Indian prostrated himself upon the floor before the altar, carefully adjusted his limbs, and laid himself out as if he were preparing for burial. Men, with coils of rope about their hands, representing crowns of thorns, dressed in loose garments, and bending under the weight of a heavy cross, then entered and tottered up the aisles. A cross and skull were then passed around; the bearer repeating in Latin, as they were handed to be kissed, "This is the death, and this is the judgment!" When this form had been concluded, we were all supplied with whips, (I declined to avail myself of their politeness,) the lights were extinguished, and all was darkness . . . While I was speculating upon what would probably occur next in the order of exercises, my meditations were suddenly interrupted by the sound of stripes rising and echoing through every part of the vast edifice . . . This penitential ceremony continued for the space of fifteen minutes, at least, without intermission. [160]

Even beyond these more overt forms, there remained a kind of penitent or flagellant religion practiced by priests in the countryside who found that whippings "administered with tenderness" were the shortest way to the Indians' souls.[161] The Catholic ritual of confession also built on both European and Maya proclivities.

The people appropriated other church-sanctioned remedies as well. *Santos* figured prominently in superstitious remedies, usually in regard to actions performed on their day. If a man had a fruit tree that would not bear, he should whip it twelve times, preferably on June 24, the day of San Juan.[162] Cutting hair on that same day made it grow back thicker than ever.[163] Prayers to San Antonio could bring sweethearts. (See Chapters 4 and 5 for further discussion of the role of santos.) In addition to these folkloric prescriptions, popular religious culture had at least two other officially sanctioned remedies for everyday woes: *promesas* and *misas*. Both are common today but, unlike in earlier times, are likely to be taken in conjunction with medicine, if affordable. The former consists in a promise made privately to a saint; if the santo delivers, then it becomes a grave moral obligation to carry out the promise, usually some public display of veneration.[164] Promesas carry strong folk appeal because they are personal contracts between the person and the saint, without the help of the priest, and because they require no payment in advance and often a final payment that is nothing more than symbolic action. For those with a little money, though, the practice of hiring priests to say misas (masses) for the soul of dead relatives was an important way of dealing with life's problems. The practice had parallels with the ancestor worship of pre-Columbian Mayas. Benefits accrued indirectly, since the soul of a dead ancestor in heaven meant probable spiritual intercession for the living descendent. Padre Bernardo Valdez requested in 1819: "It is my wish that my death being verified, two sets of Gregorian masses be said for my soul, one after the other, so that Our Holy God pardon my faults and sins";[165] Padre José María Marin stipulated in 1835: "It is my wish that after my death a novena of masses be made in suffrage of my soul, and more if they be Gregorian."[166] The cost of the procedure tended to limit it to Spanish creoles. Of course, these religious deeds served practical ends as well. By paying other priests to say masses for his soul, the dying father kept his capital within families and within the institution. Special misas provided an important contribution to maintaining the Mexican priesthood and, unlike property, education, and the control of life passages, was something that the state could not take away.

Finally, and returning to an earlier point, there was the whole world of spells and counterspells. These differed from the humbler practices in that they required a religious specialist (the h-men) and were often public rituals. A recurrent motif in folktales, for example, involves the bewildered victim (of spells, evil winds, and so forth) who at last consults with a h-men to solve the problem. In the story "Cured by Nine Priests," a man who foolishly shoots a guardian serpent needs the help of a lucky number of h-men to undo the karmic damage.[167] This and similar beneficial interventions pointed back to magic's old duality and in turn to larger features of the social world. Weather, patrons, priests, and family all aided the peasant, but they were equally capable of destroying him. As with the dilemma of modern technology, dimensions of peasant knowledge necessarily entailed both good and evil use.

Beneath the many tales of magical solutions runs an extremely potent theme: social mobility. The pairing of magic and mobility was hardly coincidental. As is the case with virtually all popular stories, the appeal of folktales in the Andrade collection rested heavily on wish fulfillment.[168] These stories circulated among a people who lived close to the bone and who had little chance of getting ahead. In "The Good and Bad Brothers" ("El bueno y el malo"), the long-suffering good brother eventually rises to become king by carrying out the impossible tasks of hanging fruit on a tree, returning spilt gunpowder to its sack, and making the king's daughter conceive and give birth overnight.[169] That, the narrator implied to his audience, was the probability of striking it rich. Along these same lines, stories of buried treasure constituted the greatest of all miraculous opportunities, the perfect symbol of wealth materializing out of nowhere in a land without opportunity. In these stories ghosts or wondrous signs lead someone to a crock (*botijuela*) of old coins buried under the floor of an abandoned house. But hidden treasure, like dreams of mobility, often goes bad; contact with the ghost's evil winds proves fatal, or else the man is foolish enough to mention his treasure, thus causing it to disappear instantly.[170] Part of the appeal of these stories of good fortune was that there was just enough reality behind them to make them the repository of hopes and dreams. Well into the 1850s and 1860s there were still relatively affluent Mayas in Yucatán who could hold their own against growing land concentrations and export economies; like the myth of the self-made man in the United States, favored exceptions kept the aspiration alive, if only in a narrative context. (On a more literal note, and contrary to biblical injunctions, rural people really did bury money. Some Mayas believed that they could return to claim it after they died. But the greater motive was the quest for security in a war-torn world. If we are to believe the generals of Chan Santa Cruz, they had buried some 200,000 pesos, in those days an immense fortune, throughout various points in the forests of Quintana Roo.[171] I have never run across a documented case of someone actually finding it, but maybe they learned from the stories and kept quiet.)

The persistence of buried-treasure lore was recently brought home to this author during a residence in Peto in February and March of 1999. I was assured that people there often found buried pots of money that dated from the pre–Caste War years, although I was never able to locate anyone who had actually done so. Informants explained to me that upon finding such money it was necessary to use part of it to pay for a special mass, or else share it with friends; failure to do so would result in some horrible fate. For example, rumor had it that the foreman of a low-income housing project in Peto had absconded after his bulldozer turned up a crock of old coins. But since he had failed to carry out the necessary protocol, the locals had the satisfaction of knowing that he would die within a year. The common theme of these tales is that the stingy will suffer in the end.

Mobility may have been social, but in cuentos it often took the symbolic form of sexual attainment. A significant number of these stories concerns the search for a bride, a husband, or a lover; a prettier face or a larger penis. Only a scant distance separates sexual attainment and social mobility. The adventurous young man's final prize is usually joint: the king's daughter as well as the kingdom. Quite a few stories in the Andrade collections follow this plot. "Chipitín the Hunter," a lad who can magically transform himself into various animals, enters a kingdom disguised as a tiger. He can defeat a local *javelina* monster only if one of the king's daughters will allow him to suck her breasts. The javelina monster, it turns out, is actually a wizard in animal form, and Chipitín eventually finishes him off by sleeping with *his* daughter as well.[172] In "The Three Girls," the adventuresome hero makes off with the king's daughter, who had been hidden inside an orange dangling on a tree and protected by a giant.[173] Similar motifs recur in "The Seven Rays of the Sun," "The King and the Bandits," and "The Lying Son-in-law."[174] These stories are as notable for their ribald quality as for their structure; even to the present, Maya peasants speak about sexual matters and bodily functions with a casualness that shocks urbanites.

In all cases, social advancement involves marriage or at least sexual conquest. The close link between sexual attainment and social mobility points to generational tensions inherent in the peasant village. The Maya peasant matured in a community in which the resources of the world were limited.

Often it was his own parents, or the people of his parents' age, that monopolized the good things of life. Surviving documents of pre-Porfirian Yucatán make it clear, for example, that upper offices in the Indian república, as well as land-holdings among Mayas, were concentrated in the hands of mature individuals, usually fathers and grandfathers. As Redfield and Villa Rojas put it, "Parents and older brothers and sisters begin very early to ask the child to perform small services; a habit of obedience is generally acquired, and departures from it are very exceptional. The duty of obedience to and respect for one's elders is implicit in conduct and conversation." [175] A young man entered this world only slowly. He began his productive life early as his father's field hand. Later he moved up in the world by marrying the daughter of an established family and by succeeding in spite of the in-laws' skepticism. In fact, the first year of marriage involved a labor debt known as *jaankab,* in which the groom went to live with and work for his bride's parents, who would continue to keep an eye on their new son-in-law even after he had carved out a separate household.[176] To compound matters, the Maya testators of the nineteenth century typically divided their lands among their various children, so that the ambitious son and heir had to begin the process of land accumulation all over again. So too in public service, men came to the title of *batab* or *cacique* only after lengthy stints in lower office.[177] Age bestowed wealth and authority in this world; moreover, the pattern extended throughout much of rural Mexico and Guatemala, land-based societies where resources trickled from father to son and where the key internal conflict was often generational.[178] But in folklore narratives, the protagonist leaps over the Oedipal divide, supplants the parental figure by possessing his daughter, and assumes the rights of elderdom.

In pursuit of the elusive objects of power and desire, human protagonists typically fall back on supernatural means. The first of these, the magical fetish, constitutes a standard prop of rural Maya narratives. Returning to "Chipitín the Hunter," we find the hero befriending a puma, a tiger, an ant, and a seagull; in return, each of the animals gives him a piece of its body that enables Chipitín to transform himself into the animal in question.[179] With the help of these objects, Chipitín manages to overcome his difficulties and marry the daughter of the king. Magical aids appear in other contexts as well. A peninsular folk belief still common in rural parts holds that the stone found in one of the deer's stomachs, a smooth white object known as *tuunich keej,* brings infallible success to the hunter. Overuse can backfire, however, and the overambitious hunter is likely to find himself roughed up by a gang of tough-talking, angry deer demanding their stone back. (Moral: Don't ask too much from your patrons.) [180]

Beyond magical devices, protector spirits provide a second line of assistance for the human hero. In fact, it is usually a protector spirit who gives the hero his or her magic object in the first place. In another version of "Siete Colores," for example, Seven Colors is a magical beast; when a young hunter frees him from a trap, he becomes the boy's patron and launches him on a career to kingship, despite the jealousies and evil plots of his brothers.[181] At least two factors lay behind these supernatural aids. The first was that mobility was essentially improbable, at least in the large scope envisioned by the cuentos. The second is that intercession and patronage were normal peasant means of dealing with problems. In the case of virtually any difficulty, peasants began casting about for help from outside forces: from priests, from government officials, from rival landowners. In this sense, supernatural narrative components of the cuentos encoded the values and strategies of daily life.

The Present Day

Between the Yucatec Mayas' demographic nadir and the technological leaps of the Porfiriato stood an age of folklore formation. The pages of the people's folk almanac grew slowly throughout the eighteenth century as Spaniard and Maya made contact on estancias and haciendas, and accelerated dramatically after 1800 as peoples of varied ethnic descriptions and cultural orientations flooded into the south and east of the peninsula. This period of folkloric formation both preserved and transformed important antecedents in Hispanic and Maya cultures; it prospered in an age of increasing communication as yet free from the molding influence of a national media. The formation itself constitutes one of the most positive of all the legacies of prerevolutionary Mexico, and largely for that reason it has endured to the present day—both for the historian who wants to understand what in life mattered to a peasant in 1847 and for the casual connoisseur who can still appreciate this folk literature's vibrancy, its sheer inventiveness.

Keith Thomas's *Religion and the Decline of Magic* argues that the age of scientific paradigm in England was preceded by the exhaustion of an enormous corpus of folk beliefs, beliefs that a growing sense of individualism rendered insufficient.[182] However, the persistence of such beliefs in the Yucatán peninsula suggests that the change Thomas described does not happen in and of itself, as if through some process of internal contradictions gradually sorting themselves out, but rather depends on specific material conditions that render beliefs less functional, less serviceable. The decline in question was never so complete in the Yucatán peninsula, and certainly had not happened in the nineteenth century, when a sense of community was still strong. Both early and recent twentieth-century folktale collections still stress many of the features of an earlier mentality, a popular culture deeply rooted in the wondrous. In the plazas of rural towns, people still see ghosts, such as the bleeding leg known to prowl the plaza of Ekmul.[183] Milpa farmers near Motul still encounter the mischievous dwarf race while in the monte. We do not need to go the entire distance in asserting literal belief in all cases. Rather, there was a combination of belief and artistic decoration, but the selection of these themes nonetheless tells us a great deal about what was in the minds of the people, what they found acceptable, and what they found compelling.

The themes and motifs of peasant folktales fall into some distinct patterns. Peasants lived in a world of folk geographical divisions beset with potential dangers that they chose to endow with a personal animus. However, there were also means of escaping or resolving these problems. Many of the lessons encoded in the cuentos, be they moral or supernatural, still survive. Cultural change in this region, as in other parts of Mexico, has always been a deeply layered process. New levels of technology, communications, worldview, and expectations take their place atop long-established folk beliefs.[184] There are numerous explanations for this in a place like Yucatán. The society's economic character—its dependent development as a supplier of basic agricultural products—has helped preserve rural life, thus conserving many of the folkways that Robert Redfield thought were passing from existence a half century ago.[185] Experience has taught peasants to hang on to the little they have, including their beliefs. Relative isolation from larger Mexico has also helped; although roads have linked the two since 1970, even bus travel remains expensive for Yucatán's rural poor, and airfare is out of the question. Finally, many of the pueblos' success stories fail to return home, at least permanently, from the heights of Mérida and Cancún, while high rural birthrates have helped maintain a base population for folk beliefs.

The question inevitably arises as to how these folkloric outlooks fit, or might fit, into the larger national picture. Recent studies of broad Mexican movements, particularly liberalism, have argued for peasant versions of the same. To a degree this seems plausible; certainly Maya peasants and Yucatecan liberals shared a vision of greater local autonomy. (But how local, and from whom?) Moreover, as I have indicated throughout, many of the folk motifs found in Yucatán appear in other parts of the republic. However, I think that we need to be cautious in calculating the benefit of shared folklore. The cultural frameworks in which Mexican peasants operated make it difficult to see how there could have been much meeting of the minds on any specific point or how applicable peasant political consciousness would have been on a broader scale. Folkloric beliefs have the power to endure; in some ways they impart that power to their subscribers. But the intense localism, the particularism, the sheer magic of these belief structures, probably disqualified them from serving as the basis of anything other than the underdeveloped, paternalistic political structures from which they emerged.

Power is usually reciprocal, and the power of belief is no different. Mérida may dominate the villages, but the villages have also colonized Mérida. With the accelerating collapse of the countryside, an avalanche of newcomers find themselves like the characters of Mexico's cinematic classic *Nosotros los pobres:* unconnected, unskilled, in a hostile and unfamiliar city with no savings and no social safety net, and with more motive to look for miracles than ever before. Here culture has to be retooled, and in so doing the retoolers often draw on the folk beliefs of older rural community life. Even among the upper–middle class it is a rare household indeed that does not know something of the creencias. Perhaps in the final analysis people value them for the simple fact that they have endured. Pesos devalue, programs falter, missionaries come and go. But a dragonfly in your house . . . that is something else entirely.

CHAPTER
2

Rural *Curas* and the Erosion
of Mexican Conservatism

The Life of Raymundo Pérez

T HIRTY MILES southeast of Mérida, in the sleepy hamlet of Hoctún, stands a church that was once the domain of a certain R. Pérez: Padre Doctor Don Raymundo Pérez y González. In a province that commemorates such favorite sons as Andrés Quintana Roo and Felipe Carrillo Puerto, the name of Raymundo Pérez is now utterly forgotten. Perhaps he wanted it that way. While alive, Pérez always scorned public scrutiny and popular opinion. In his only portrait the doctor eludes us with a sly and inscrutable smile, as though taunting the inquiries of posterity.[1] But the portrait's mere existence is revealing. Outside of the likenesses of certain bishops and governors, portraiture was rare in Yucatán before 1850. It is not entirely surprising, then, to learn that Pérez ranked as one of the wealthiest and most influential men of the peninsula. He represented the high-end of religious culture in the heady half century that preceded the Caste War, the learned mentality that was far removed from Yucatán's popular mélange of wonders, witchcraft, and magical beasts.

Why bother to resurrect this intensely private man? Pérez's life merits reconstruction because it captures the attitude and culture of the patrician class during Mexico's early national period, an unusual combination of colonial and republican values. The patrician liked to think of himself as a kind of Mesoamerican de Medici who combined wealth, power, virtue, and religious piety. Unlike the Spanish colonials of earlier centuries, men like Pérez had learned to get along without the idea of a king but still adhered to many of the features of Spain's monarchical, authoritarian society. Most favored an established church as a source of order and cultural unity. In economic thought they tended toward protectionism and monopolies. While willing to work through constitutions and electoral processes, they also believed in maintaining many of the paternalistic protections for the indigenous peasantry while restricting political power and social leadership to a limited circle of elites. In political terms, this view was identified with members of the Conservative Party who dominated Mexican state affairs until 1854.[2] The way of thinking served a particular set of interests, but it was no less real, and it constituted one of the driving visions of postcolonial Mexico.

It would be easy to dismiss Pérez as another case of elite arrogance. But in so doing we risk closing our eyes to unexplored dimensions of his day and age. What did such men see in themselves that defined their own uniqueness? How and when did their vision intersect with the lives of the less fortunate? Pérez may have been an arrogant man, but what makes him compelling as a historical subject was the extent to which he lived the vision. While many conservatives were metropolitan *hombres de bien* content to amuse themselves with the fine wines and theater venue of Mexico City, Pérez's understanding of conservatism came from his work in provincial business, law, and agriculture, together with some hard-earned lessons in dealing with the peasantry. He represented the organic conservative, a man from the high-end of Yucatán's religious culture who yet at the same time remained engaged, if perhaps disdainfully, with his lower-class countrymen and their expectations regarding what religion meant and what its practitioners owed to their people. His life also explains something about Mexican conservatism's decline as a social and political philosophy, since many of Pérez's various endeavors, by almost any definition successful, had the effect of undermining the way of life in which he believed and to which he dedicated his eighty-eight years on earth.

Pérez mattered from an institutional perspective as well. His life opens a window to virtually every aspect of the nineteenth-century clergy, that pivotal sector of Mexican society. Explorations of the Mexican church almost invariably deal with their subject through the lens of corporate power.[3] But church power was often more aggregate than corporate. It derived its identity from the power and wealth accumulated by its individual members *as* individual members. Studies of *capellanías, obras pías,* and high-church politics therefore tell only a part of the story. The search for the full character and meaning of this institution—and, by extension, of the age itself—turns us to men like Pérez.

Where Alligators Eat Christians

The first stage of this history reads as though torn from some novel about a young man from the provinces. Raymundo Pérez y González was born in the remote tropical outpost of San Felipe de Bacalar on August 31, 1768, the son of Juan de la Rosa Pérez and Luciana González.[4] The town itself was hardly a cradle of piety. Built as an outpost of Spanish progress, a check on the influence of both the British pirates and the Petén Mayas, Bacalar became a haven for smugglers and drifters. Its original Spanish population came to get rich on tribute from the local cacao trade, but Indian resistance and the competition from Venezuelan cacao soon ended these aspirations. Indigenous resistance and pirate raids caused Spaniards to abandon the place altogether in 1648.[5] By the time of Pérez's birth, Bacalar had recovered its Spanish population. Belizeans slowly developed logging and contraband in its northern district, and Bacalar became a entrepôt through which southeastern Yucatecans sold their agricultural goods to the hungry British woodcutters.[6]

The experience of adolescence here was formative. In later life Pérez exuded ambition, an almost haughty erudition, and an instinct for power— all a rejection of his backwater origins. Peasants and their simple rusticities bored him, even though in later years he grew comfortable with the elaborate pantomime of deference that the *indios,* almost from birth, learned to perform when in the presence of great men. He reserved special contempt for the many would-be *caudillos* and rabble-rousers found among Yucatán's rural creole population. These distastes and ambitions, formed in the remoteness of Bacalar, remained with him to his death.

Pérez was fortunate enough to seize on one of the few avenues of social mobility. His talent and intelligence eventually caught the attention of the village priest, who saw to it that young Pérez entered the seminary of San Ildefonso at Mérida, an institution that in those days served as one of the conduits of elite cultural transmission in early southeast Mexico. Training at San Ildefonso, which made the difference between an accomplished and a lackluster clerical career, was normally reserved for the favored sons of the capital and, to a lesser extent, of Campeche and Valladolid.[7] Here Pérez distinguished himself as a brilliant and precocious scholar. Among other pursuits he studied

Cicero, whose complex clauses and exotic flourishes informed his later public writings; many years later, during his occasional public wrangles, the doctor still had a tendency to bludgeon his enemies with Latin phrases, even though in private correspondence Pérez remained simple and direct. After completing doctoral studies in logic, metaphysics, and philosophy, he graduated with highest honors; holy orders came on April 11, 1792. He was now twenty-four.[8]

Upon graduation Raymundo Pérez entered into a system that lay at the heart of the conservative vision and of the rural Mexican experience. The parish organization that the Catholic Church maintained for villages offered an organic and all-encompassing method for integrating spiritual welfare and sacred precepts with the parishioners' social and economic needs. This holistic vision came directly from Europe's Middle Ages, and it called for the *cura*, or pastor, the most educated and talented individual available, to lead. Physician, confessor, records keeper, moneylender, political advisor, and paternal father: the cura was to be all things to all men. Imposed by the friars of the regular orders during the sixteenth century, the parish system had always operated in tandem with other forms of organization, including indigenous village/family structures and secular Spanish authority. It had functioned remarkably well during the two centuries of Hapsburg rule, and many of the features found in this book—cofradías, processions, the village saint, and even many of the motifs of popular folklore—were its legacy to modern Mexico. From the eighteenth century onward, however, church authority had been under attack from such forces as demographic growth, increasing commercialization, a decline in the church's missionary fervor, and the Spanish Bourbon administrators' campaign to replace the Hapsburg hodgepodge with a rational state built around a centralized, secular monarchy. These stresses notwithstanding, however, the parish system tenaciously persisted into the nineteenth century and still enjoyed enough spiritual and intellectual vitality to attract men of talent.

Pérez began his career as an assistant in the parish of Tepetitán, Tabasco, then little more than a swampy hinterland of the Yucatecan bishopric. In 1796 his cura took a better position, and Pérez himself assumed the office on an interim basis. This rise was precocious, since most priests did not assume curacies until their midthirties.[9] Macuspana, a small pueblo midway between Palenque and Villahermosa, yielded a generous annual rent of twenty-five hundred pesos. Pérez worked the parish with only one assistant, a coadjutor named Bernardo Mariano de Castro.[10] Given the low overhead and above-average rent, Macuspana provided a strong income for its cura, and it was here that Pérez began to accumulate his considerable personal fortune. It is doubtful, however, that he conceived of this as much more than a stepping stone to better things, since willingness to take on remote parishes was a common way for ambitious young priests to launch their careers.

In Macuspana the doctor learned some hard truths not covered in his studies of metaphysics. The first concerned the limitations of frontier life. On one hand, the rural parish was invaluable for its privileged access to peasant taxes and labor, as well as for the autonomy and prestige it offered to its cura. In Mérida the clergy worked in the shadow of the cathedral, that great institutional authority that always stood just around the corner; in the recesses of the countryside, the cura was a ruler unto himself, with powers and advantages that placed him on equal footing with local secular powers. But, on the other hand, the rural parish could prove an intellectual and cultural dungeon. The priest who had spent years in the seminary becoming the most highly trained and educated member of his society suddenly found himself shut off from that society, alone among illiterate peasants and the often crude Spanish settlers. This town/country dilemma was one that each cura resolved for himself. Some opted for city life and less autonomy. Others, like José Bartolomé del Granado Baeza of Yaxcabá, threw themselves into their rural responsibilities, only coming to Mérida "for matters of the community."[11] Still others, like the powerful Eusebio Villamil (Baeza's successor at Yaxcabá), became absentee curas, farming out their responsibilities to a string of assistants while indulging themselves in the political and intellectual stimulation of Mérida.[12] But Pérez had yet to resolve this conflict. The rusticity and the wet tropical ground reminded him of Bacalar, the hinterland he had struggled to escape. Rural Yucatán had intrigued the austere, mystic Franciscans who first colonized the peninsula, but Pérez was a robust man, physically imposing and worldly in appetites and still too young, too immature, to live up to the burdens of pastorship. He diverted himself with various tribute-related business ventures and by traveling through the villages of his parish with an entourage of friends, wining and dining at local expense.

These practices led to a second lesson, one that concerned peasants. Though in theory Pérez held immense power over them, he soon discovered that the lowly had a way of evening scores. Despite their image as hand-kissing subordinates, peasants were quarrelsome and litigious and could nurse grudges for years. Priests and property owners who violated long-standing rural arrangements did so at their own peril. In Tabasco, peasants smoldered over Pérez's tribute demands and impromptu banquets. It was for this reason that San Fernando and San Carlos, two Chontal-speaking auxiliary villages of Macuspana Parish, unexpectedly turned on their cura when church officials made a *visita,* or periodic inspection, in 1804.[13] Angry peasants produced testimony after testimony of high-handed abuses. Most centered around unpaid labor, corporal punishment (which Pérez acknowledged), exorbitant fees, and irregular visits to the pueblos during which Pérez forced the peasants to provide for him and his entourage. The most picturesque complaint charged that the doctor forced local fishermen to hunt alligators, used then as now for their meat and valuable hides; peasants objected because "they are ferocious and will eat a Christian."[14] It is difficult to accept such indignation at face value; nearly a century later, travelers found the people of San Carlos still hunting alligators, happily and without compulsion.[15] However, these rhetorical tropes did have the effect of turning Raymundo Pérez into a Roman who threw the faithful to wild beasts. Seemingly hegemonic doctrines such as colonial Catholicism's almost always function as a field of negotiation where everyone plies his interests. The church's investigation exonerated Pérez. But if peasants lacked the ability to directly control their cura, they were at least capable of annoying him to exasperation. The episode soured Pérez on Tabasco, heightening a discontent that had probably been building from the start. In 1800 he had applied for the Campeche curacy, but for reasons unknown withdrew the application.[16] Macuspana gripped the doctor's ankles like tropical mud.

The Pérez Promotion

Two years after the disastrous visita, fortune offered Raymundo Pérez a second chance. The key to further mobility was the opening of the *curato* of Hoctún in 1806. By now Pérez better understood the workings of power and law in his society. Rather than preparing his own application, he obtained the help of José Matías Quintana, a prominent Yucatecan attorney who was later to play a leading role in Yucatecan independence and whose sons, Tomás and, more particularly, Andrés, would earn a fame of their own. Quintana himself was another case of a prominent liberal creole with close ties to church polity and economy.[17] With a simultaneous endorsement from the governor of Tabasco, Pérez handily won Hoctún's curato.[18]

The change carried many implications. It resolved the long-standing conflict between social and cultural involvement and the need for a rural power base. For the next forty-nine years Pérez remained fixed at Hoctún; by the time of his arrival it was already a populous region with three auxiliary communities (Tahmek, Xocchel, and Seyé), high church rents, and twenty-five haciendas.[19] The majority (forty-five hundred) of the some fifty-four hundred inhabitants resided in the towns, but many of these ended up doing occasional labor on the estates.[20] As an investment target, Hoctún was a sound decision characteristic of Pérez: though not as dynamic as the southern sugar frontier, it was more solid and dependable, and it offered lucrative profits to the few wealthy individuals who could dominate through their control of finance capital.

Hoctún also had an important cultural advantage: its proximity to the capital. Pérez maintained a dual residence in Mérida, where his home became a common landmark in deeds of property. In essence, he became a commuter cura. But while Pérez sought cultured society, other motives informed his reassignment. There had been the unpleasant business of the investigation in 1804; in typical colonial fashion, the authorities suppressed this small-scale uprising only to respond to its grievances after an appropriate period of time had passed.[21] Moreover, tax collections in the area of Homún-Hoctún-Hocabá suffered chronic difficulties in the first decades of the century, and Pérez presented himself as a forceful hand.[22] In the following decade, Hoctún showed none of the rent-collection problems that had plagued surrounding parishes.

Pérez began his residence in high style. After an initial five-year residence he launched a general refurbishing of the church building and the decorations surrounding the santos housed within. Pérez invested the equivalent value of a small hacienda in these changes, hiring a team of Maya masons and completely restocking the supply of cassocks, shirts, and altar canopies.[23] On a more practical note, he ordered the construction of a public granary that was still in use sixty years later.[24] Although the great age of Mexican church construction had ended, ambitious curas like Pérez could still make their mark by organizing and financing such projects for the community. Sumptuous church decoration generated jobs, provided an outlet for local creativity, appealed to village self-esteem, and bridged popular and official notions of religious piety.

But new controversies followed. In 1812–1814 the ill-fated Spanish constitution provoked a ferment in the Yucatecan countryside, as an urban political group known as the *sanjuanistas* saw to it that peasant church taxes were abolished. The period made little real change in the peasants' social condition, but its impact on peasant psychology and expectation was profound. Peasants repeatedly gave themselves over to beliefs that all taxes were nullified and that

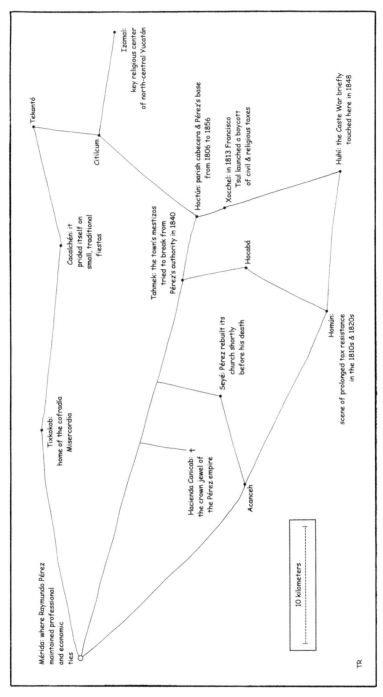

Mérida: where Raymundo Pérez
maintained professional
and economic
ties

Tixkokob:
home of the cofradía
Misercordia

Cacalchén: it
prided itself on
small, traditional
fiestas

Tekantó

Citilcum

Izamal:
key religious center
of north-central Yucatán

Hoctún: parish cabecera & Pérez's base
from 1806 to 1856

Xocchel: in 1813 Francisco
Tsul launched a boycott
of civil & religious taxes

Huhí: the Caste War briefly
touched here in 1848

Tahmek: the town's mestizos
tried to break from
Pérez's authority in 1840

Hocabá

Seyé: Pérez rebuilt its
church shortly
before his death

Homún:
scene of prolonged tax resistance
in the 1810s & 1820s

Hacienda Canicab: †
the crown jewel of
the Pérez empire

Acanceh

10 kilometers

TR

Map 2. Raymundo Pérez country: the Hoctún region.

all social obligation to the upper classes was at an end.[25] The parish of Hoctún was no exception. The spirit of rebellion against Pérez's control took place
in Xocchel, four kilometers southeast of the *cabecera* (administrative head
town). The governor had outlawed most of the abundant Maya contributions,
including the eggs and castor beans that the Indian children had traditionally given at doctrina classes. Pérez, like many curas, continued the practice
anyway, justifying his actions on legal fictions.[26] At this point the peasants
took matters into their own hands. The forgotten hero of this rebellion was
a certain Francisco Tsul, a leader who had roused "almost all the Indians of
Xocchel into rebellion." Tsul publicly dared to question the authority of both
the *alcalde* and the *ayuntamiento,* "saying that he would not even allow his
children to give eggs and castor oil, that the king had freed him," and that
corrupt local elites, including Pérez himself, were obstructing royal justice.
The episode was distinctly millenarian: Maya peasants believed that a distant
but all-good and all-powerful king had delivered them from bondage. They
acted upon common themes in the peasant conception of justice. But these
visions shattered when the peasants tried to realize them. When Tsul led a
group from Xocchel to complain to the bishop, Pérez decided that matters
had gone far enough and arranged for the local alcalde to throw them all in
jail. The sanjuanista propagandists seized on Tsul's aborted protest as a way to
discredit Pérez himself, lambasting him in one of their typically uninhibited
publications.[27]

Pérez's self-defense, published in an 1813 edition of *El aristarco,* is highly
rhetorical but still worth reading for its intellectual content, for it provides
considerable insight into the mentality and political ideals of creole conservatism.[28] The arguments regarding popular consensus now appear shaky as
applied to a colonial society where the few governed the many. But in overall structure they offer an intriguing glimpse of how churchmen saw themselves and their institution. Probably the least compelling feature is the essay's
predictable reassertion of clerical privileges. Corporal punishment, Pérez reminded his readers, was an accepted power of the cura. The doctor's high-
handed tone on these matters makes his unpopularity understandable. It is
doubtful, for example, that he won many friends by firing broadsides against
"these libertines given to the delights of Venus, these sodomites, these thieves,
tyrants, and oppressors of good men." More substantive is Pérez's exploration
of many points still at the core of modern church-state issues. He argued
that society accepted the church as countervailing authority to a totalitarian
state. Everyone, or virtually everyone, acknowledged its services. Moreover, if
such an institution existed, a class of religious specialists necessarily followed.

Society could eliminate the priesthood only if "all religious instruction is an invention of princes to keep people under their obedience."

While writing articulately of the church as a countervailing power, Pérez also urged state enforcement of church prerogatives. One might reasonably ask whether state enforcement of an established religion did not necessarily acknowledge state authority over religious matters. What was to keep Pérez's imaginary prince from manipulating church institutions to his own advantage? Pérez did not explicitly address this problem, but his essay implies that institutional autonomy resulted from a tenured priesthood that did not live in fear of dismissal or poverty. Implied also was a broad level of public mandate that made clerical autonomy possible. If a society accepts elite institutions as part of its identity, then it becomes the responsibility of its members to subsidize those institutions. The argument had broad application in justifying the various privileged classes of early national Mexico.

At what point, however, do institutions pass from autonomy to unaccountability? It was no accident to find Pérez exploring these issues during the first great surge of popular political movements in the peninsula. The doctor was living through one of those moments when the apparent consensus regarding familiar customs abruptly vanishes. On the whole, he seemed better prepared than most clerics for a reassessment of privileges handed down since the Conquest. While many of his colleagues reacted with nothing more than indignation, Pérez thought the matter through and presented his arguments in a public forum. Though speaking in defense of his own particular interests, he cut to the heart of many issues regarding the state, autonomous institutions, and their relationship to the people.

In argumentation as in life, Pérez's religious vision operated more on social than on spiritual terms. Doubtless there is a temptation to dismiss the early-nineteenth-century theological perspective as yet another version of some long-evolving Spanish absolutism, the product, as the doctor's sanjuanista critics charged, of "a certain theologian, educated in the darkness of the past century." [29] But the vision of interlocking moral and social orders is a long-lived one; most societies have their own version of theological or ideological bases for the current state of affairs. What matters is how thoroughly Pérez grounded his arguments on purely social terms. The doctor evinced little interest in the afterlife, spiritual beings, yearnings for redemption, states of grace, or the transcendental mysticism that had characterized so much of golden-age Spain.[30] Rather, religion existed to regulate earthly human affairs, and it did so by reinforcing the hierarchical relations of its participants. Like his portrait, the doctor's writings contained nothing that was otherworldly.

The essay's defensive tone foreshadowed Pérez's own political reorientation, for within seven years he joined the ranks of former conservatives and clergy who had gone over to the liberal Independence Party. Why? Certainly the events of the constitutional years undermined Spain's credibility as an upholder of order. At the same time, Pérez, like other prominent creoles, was coming to identify Spanish bureaucratic incompetence as an obstruction to his own ambitions. But in 1816, two years after the restoration of King Ferdinand to the Spanish throne, Pérez found himself involved in a land dispute with his *"enemigo capital,"* a Hoctún *vecino* named Pedro Manuel Escudero. Pérez linked Yucatán's interim governor, Miguel de Castro, with his problems, for he sent Castro an intemperate and almost threatening letter. In it he complained of the indignities he had suffered in Tabasco and elsewhere, and he concluded, "Your Excellency will be responsible to God, to the King, and to the Nation for whatever sad results." This was strong language. Shortly thereafter, Pérez learned of the official displeasure his letter had incurred and tried to reingratiate himself into Castro's favor. But this fence-mending failed to conceal that talented, upwardly mobile creoles no longer looked to Spanish officials with the reverence of old.[31]

Sensing that a break was probable, former enemies of the sanjuanistas signed aboard the party most likely to control Yucatecan affairs once the peninsula found itself independent. Wars with radical participants such as Miguel Hidalgo and José María Morelos were largely over. Consequently, the mass defection of individuals such as Pérez guaranteed that the more extreme demands of the sanjuanistas—such as peasant autonomy—would perish and that Yucatán's postcolonial political configuration would resemble more than anything the late colonial status quo, with prosperous creoles occupying all the highest offices. This strategy of co-opting secular political movements from within was already evident by 1813, when Pérez himself gained appointment as a deputy to the Spanish Cortes, or parliament; only the sudden collapse of that republican system rendered his appointment a dead letter.[32] By 1821 Pérez's reorientation was complete. This about-face did not escape the notice of his enemies, who still ridiculed him for it twenty years later.[33] But the strategy succeeded, for independence brought few substantive changes.

The Prosperous Pérez

Like many of the more affluent clergy, Raymundo Pérez adapted brilliantly to life in the new republic. He had already mastered the three bases of the new elites: law, property, and the requisite cultural orientation. Spain was no longer a factor. With a closely knit creole oligarchy holding power, and with an apparent initial consensus on established religion, there was little to stand in the way of his success. Wealth of individual clergymen varied widely, reflecting the contours of the larger peninsular society, but by any conceivable measure Pérez stood at the very top of the clerical economic ladder.[34]

Throughout his long tenure in Hoctún, Pérez enjoyed three financial mainstays. First, there were his parish rents, which returned to normal after 1814. Throughout the pre–Caste War period, Pérez, like other curas, spent a good deal of time defending his control over tax revenues, or obventions, for peasant settlements that tended to form on the outskirts of his parish. Some idea of the importance of obventions in the peninsula's overall economy comes from Pérez's repeated quarrels with curas of adjacent parishes who presumed to collect taxes from *ranchería* settlements that formed in the backlands between towns. These acrimonious disputes could go on for years. Pérez's quarrel over Ch'iich' ("bird"), a mushroom hamlet near Cacalchén composed of peasants originally from Hoctún, provoked an enormous dispute that, after six years, eventually ended in Pérez's favor.[35] In this and similar cases, the church tended to uphold the obvention privileges of the curas from whose parish Maya peasants had migrated against those of curacies to which they had come.

Agriculture was a second source of wealth. Most important was his main hacienda, Canicab. This was one of the larger of rural estates, valued in his lifetime at ten thousand pesos (an average corn/cattle estate sold at two thousand).[36] As his capital and connections expanded, Pérez also went into the agricultural purchasing business; he bought up grain and livestock from the estates in Hoctún and wholesaled them in the Mérida urban market.[37] In 1843, when the Mexican army invaded Yucatán and the treasury quickly evaporated, Pérez and fellow priest-entrepreneur José María Meneses covered the shortfall in exchange for exclusive rights to import beef into Mérida; for every head of cattle slaughtered, one peso accrued to the state.[38] The laborers for these activities were Maya peasants; like most curas, Pérez used his position as leverage to bring as many locals as possible into the hacienda workforce. Everyone in Hoctún was expected either to cultivate his own fields, to serve as an agricultural wage worker, or to perform made-up chores around the village.[39] This, merely one of many such plans operating at the time, epitomized Pérez's shrewd business management: it proletarianized the parish while still reserving ultimate control of the system for the cura himself.[40]

Third, the revenues from church rents and commercial agriculture allowed him to expand into loans and real estate. These latter two were reciprocal, since property development was the cause for lending while property itself was the standard collateral for loans. Pérez became one of the most active sources of credit on the peninsula: three hundred pesos to Antonio Solís, one thousand pesos to Simón Palomeque, two thousand to Pedro José Escovedo, one thousand to José de la Cruz Villamil, and one thousand to Pedro José Peniche.[41] He was, in effect, a personal banker to many of the most prominent creoles on the peninsula. At any given moment Pérez held multiple outstanding loans, always at the standard rate of 5 percent over four years. Moreover, in the course of his lending activities Pérez also became a significant developer of urban properties, particularly in the area of Mejorada, then the western edge of Mérida. His own house in Mérida, located near the Santa Lucía Church, appears from time to time in the notary documents as a landmark from which to orient other property.[42] Finally, Pérez dealt in haciendas as well, as, for example, with his purchase and resale of the hacienda Yaxcil, located in Hoctún.[43]

Collectively, these enterprises cast the doctor in a light considerably different from that which an older body of writings created for the clergy. It is undeniable that Pérez, along with Meneses (San Cristóbal), Eusebio Villamil (Yaxcabá), and Silvestre Antonio Dondé (Tekax), constituted a rich upper crust of the pre–Caste War peninsular church.[44] But *capellanías,* chantries, and pious works—instruments of clerical income that in fact had been declining generally since 1800—had become irrelevant to this distinctly modern entrepreneur, even though he would have defended them out of institutional allegiance.[45] In terms of economic practices, the principal feature separating Pérez from his secular counterparts was his right to peasant obventions. Liberalism, the defining movement of nineteenth-century Mexico, was a more diverse and heterogeneous movement than is commonly recognized and overlapped with people like Pérez at various points, including private enterprise, provincial and local autonomy, and faith in an ill-defined vision of prosperity and progress. Pérez represented a strain of economic liberalism within a socially and politically conservative church.

Economic power and experience also translated into institutional power, giving Pérez a considerable hand in determining the methods and ideological contours of the Yucatecan church. Indeed, wealthy and entrenched curas such as Pérez and Villamil probably had more influence on church policy than did Bishop Guerra, whose actions and decisions typically came in response to demands issuing up from the rural parishes, the true backbone of the institution. There was, for example, the case of the famous sermons of Joaquín Ruz. An enthusiastic Franciscan living in Mérida, Ruz had taken it upon himself to codify church training for contact with the rural peasants by preparing a collection of sermons translated into Maya.[46] But his knowledge of the language was almost entirely academic, and questions immediately arose as to his translations' validity. In 1835 the church set up a commission headed by Pérez and José Gregorio del Canto of Conkal. The commission condemned Ruz's work in harsh terms: "By the knowledge of [the Maya language] that I have acquired and practiced in the thirty-five years that I have administered the holy sacraments, to Indians as well as vecinos, . . . I must say that the entire corpus of the Manual of Exhortations, and the four books of sermons, is confused." [47]

Linguistic veracity was one thing, but there was also an unspoken political dimension to the Ruz corpus. A centrally designated body of sermons struck at the rural cura's ancient right to compose his own words to his own people. Again, there were liberal-Federalist overtones to Pérez's actions. Ruz's sermons subsequently fell into oblivion. Daily communication would continue to take place as the priests translated their messages into Maya, their second—and in some cases, first—language. Ruz did go on to publish four volumes of his project; however, although scholars occasionally toy with the Ruz corpus, there is thus far no concrete evidence that even one of its prefabricated sermons was ever preached to assembled Mayas or that its words had any demonstrable effect on the society and culture of the times.[48]

Despite these commissions, Pérez appears to have avoided high church office. After the death of Bishop Agustín Estévez y Ugarte in 1827, fellow entrepreneur-priest José María Meneses served as interim leader, but his Federalist and quasiliberal inclinations made Meneses vulnerable to the changing political winds; after the national conservative takeover of 1834, he lost the post to the more pliant José María Guerra.[49] Meneses had to content himself with the lucrative curacy of barrio San Cristóbal; he continued on as one of the peninsula's richest men for several more decades, while to the end of his life Guerra was known as the man who had "stolen" the bishopric, a fact that helped weaken his authority and left him open to rivals.[50] Pérez astutely avoided this factional war. Like a number of his clerical contemporaries, however, he did dabble in the secular politics of the early national period. With the Mexican state now assuming the old right of approving ecclesiastical appointments (*patronato real*), and without a clear-cut church-military alliance, younger priests in particular turned to politics as a way of defending church interests against the liberal agenda.[51] Raymundo Pérez was active in these affairs at least as late as 1834. However, brief service in both the executive and congressional branches convinced him that Yucatecan public affairs were not the ordered, rational world he had come to prefer. Democratic politics, even of the highly restricted sort practiced in prereform Mexico, involved a class of men far less talented and educated than the dedicated doctor. Pérez resigned prior to the Imán revolt of 1839–1840.[52]

Public life disappointed him, but there were still the pursuits of learning and culture. In 1834 he was appointed rector of the Academy of Science and Literature in Mérida, although we know nothing more on this point.[53] While he lacked access to the cultural amenities offered by a European university, Pérez himself enjoyed one of the best personal libraries on the peninsula. At the time of his death he had amassed a collection of nearly two hundred volumes, an extraordinary achievement in a time and place where 95 percent of the population was illiterate. The bulk of those works dealt with legal and theological issues; aside from Homer, Voltaire, and a handful of minor literary figures, the ever-practical Pérez had little interest in *bellas artes*. Purportedly the doctor donated many volumes to the academy long before his death.[54] Finally, like many Yucatecan intelligentsia, he subscribed to Justo Sierra O'Reilly's homegrown literary journals (see Chapter 3 for a partial analysis of these).[55]

Somewhat more elusive is Raymundo Pérez's sense of religiosity or spiritual vocation. In part this owes to the fact that the religious culture of the era's priesthood cast the vocational role in largely social terms; during the first half of the nineteenth century, pastors worried about such key issues as administering their parishes, adapting to the economic life of the new republic, and defending church interests through participation in the mudslinging atmosphere of national-era politics. In part, the apparent absence of spirituality is a mirage, since this dimension of human life left a smaller imprint on surviving documents. Clearly, however, the prevailing norms of popular religious culture defined in advance what Pérez and other parish priests had to do. We know, for example, that each year the doctor oversaw "the procession of the miraculous image of our Lord Jesus Christ in the atrium outside the church," a manifestation of spirituality that in the case of Hoctún attracted people of all classes from the surrounding towns and estates. Following the procession Pérez exposed the sacrament on the church altar for public veneration.[56] Beyond this, Pérez managed or coordinated seven different *cofradías* (investment funds, in this case) whose revenues helped subsidize the care and celebration of saints of the parish. Sacred images formed one of the corner-stones of popular devotion (see Chapters 4 and 5), and their care remained one of the cura's principal responsibilities. As always with Raymundo Pérez, however, the spiritual overlapped the practical, and the seven cofradía funds provided loan money for a variety of houses and haciendas, mostly located in Hoctún parish itself, including Pérez's own hacienda Chacsam, which at the time of his death carried an outstanding mortgage of five hundred pesos drawn from these sources.[57] Finally, from his few recorded views on spiritual matters, Pérez was known to opine that all priests should be allowed to preach, since even the worst were bound to say something useful, but only seasoned veterans should hear confessions, because the personal involvement of this sacrament required greater sagacity. This too seems in keeping with an overall belief structure that linked formal exteriors with an unobtrusive if paternal authority.[58]

Pérez also expanded his personal life in Hoctún. After settling in the parish he formed a common-law union with a certain Juana Medina. In 1821 she gave birth to Pérez's son Manuel, who, in the custom of the age for illegitimate children, took the surname of his mother.[59] Common-law unions for priests were not unusual in those days; parishioners only objected if the relationship became scandalous or irresponsible, problems that were not the case here (see Chapter 6 for further discussion). On the contrary, Pérez treated Manuel with the utmost consideration: in 1835–1836 he sent the boy to the United States for two years of study at St. Louis University, a Jesuit school patronized by many wealthy Mexican families in the nineteenth century.[60] A second son, José María Medina, went on to become a prominent citizen of Motul.[61] Manual Medina eventually inherited the bulk of Pérez's estate. By that time he had come to occupy a seat on Mérida's prestigious ayuntamiento.[62] When as a young man he made his 1849 address to the city's Academy of Science and Literature, he chose as his theme the importance of education, with twin emphasis on commerce and religious orthodoxy.[63] Manuel was truly his father's son.

Despite his frustrations with politics, in 1840 the doctor could look back with pride. In his three decades at Hoctún he had become the most important individual in the region, a wise man in church affairs, a figure of diversified wealth as important in Mérida as in his own quiet parish. "Seest thou a man diligent in his business? He shall stand before kings." With the prochurch conservatives back in power in Mexico City, there was little motive indeed to seek miracles here, only stability.

The Imperiled Pérez

Despite all of its accomplishment, however, this well-ordered life was about to feel the cuts and traumas of revolution. The Caste War, which erupted in July 1847 and raged for some three decades, remains one of the central events of southeast Mexican history, and it conditioned much of the last sixteen years of the life of Raymundo Pérez. To begin with, Pérez witnessed the rapid transformation of demography and land tenure. Peninsular population began to shift from old traditional colonial centers like Hoctún as people moved into the south and east. He himself took no part in the scramble for public lands (*denuncias de terrenos baldíos*) that raged between 1841 and 1847.[64] Perhaps, as his hagiographers later claimed, he understood the danger of tampering with rural customs. But in fact he had little incentive. By 1841 land tenure around Hoctún was thoroughly codified; the denuncias were economically irrelevant to a man as established as Pérez, and the politicians who promoted the land rush, men such as Miguel Barbachano, instead catered to a crass frontier *nuevo riche* that would have turned the stomach of the dignified doctor.

Nevertheless, prewar tensions asserted themselves in other forms. The Caste War was as much about local autonomy as it was about land, and in this regard Hoctún was no exception. An older generation of creole patriarchs such as Pérez monopolized municipal politics in the cabecera. Their stranglehold provoked poorer and less educated mestizos to relocate to Tahmek and Xocchel, where they formed municipal juntas of dubious legality. The act had provocative implications, since towns with their own juntas theoretically enjoyed control over their own tax and labor arrangements. In their efforts they were able to enlist the support of local Maya peasants. Many of them made a living by making charcoal and selling it to the wealthy bourgeoisie of Hoctún, but as in other small towns they resented the extractions resulting from cabecera dominance. Pérez quickly acted on behalf of the cabecera's elite: he filed suit, making a great deal out of the fact that the defectors were illiterate, poor (one was a mere tailor), and had not fulfilled their requisite military service. The tendency of less privileged non-Mayas to build alliances with Maya peasants would return seven years later when the Caste War evolved out of the patron-client relationships in the eastern towns of the peninsula. For the moment, however, Pérez managed to win his suit and resolve the matter entirely to the satisfaction of himself and of his fellow traditionalists.[65]

Pérez's last great act before the war was an ecclesiastical division committee. By the summer of 1843 Yucatán's civil wars had virtually abolished church taxes, placing the church on an annual stipend from the state government. These funds were far below the obvention revenues of fifteen years earlier; Bishop Guerra had to convene a panel to divide the revenues among existing parishes. He chose Tomás Domingo Quintana (brother of Andrés Quintana Roo), Eusebio Villamil, and, of course, Pérez. The committee proceeded along the basis of size, and thus directed more money to the more populous parishes—including Hoctún. The church remained a multitiered institution with personal and institutional power dependent on personal connections and favorable political appointment.[66] Eventually the crisis blew over, and many curas returned to the collection of obventions, legally or otherwise.

Meanwhile, however, larger crises were brewing. In November 1846 a group of Campeche-based elites led by merchant and former militia officer Domingo Barret pronounced against Barbachano and Mexico and threw Yucatán into its last great factional revolt.[67] Pérez, like other wealthy men, involuntarily subsidized the new regime in its struggle against counterrevolts. In April 1847 the revolutionaries drew up a list "of property owners and capitalists" who were to support the pro-Barret troops of General Agustín León; the loans were forced, the lenders in question being assigned to a certain category of loans based on a reckoning of their total worth. The list was a *Fortune*'s Five Hundred of the peninsula. Raymundo Pérez appears as number nine. His "loan" of 210 pesos placed him ahead of such better known hacendados as Simón Peón, at a mere 15.[68] But in the long run forced loans failed to contain the peninsula's factional instabilities. Weak revenues generated quarrels and revolts, while increasing privatization of land hurt peasant subsistence. Finally, the rural political struggles of the 1840s demonstrated the effectiveness of political violence in accomplishing one's goals (although the long-term consequence of the mobilizations, rural destabilization, was largely ignored).[69]

We know comparatively little about the events of the Caste War in the parish of Hoctún. By the time the rebellion had reached the communities around Ticul, it had already lost much of its original momentum.[70] Hoctún became a haven for many families fleeing from the deep interior; much to their relief, the parish itself did not fall to rebel forces, since federal troops managed to repel them at the battle of Huhí, eleven kilometers to the southeast. (Ironically, there was another Raymundo Pérez operating during the Caste War, a rebel caudillo who accepted peace terms in 1859, near Tizimín; there is no known connection between the two men.[71]) Although catastrophe was averted, the Caste War had searing psychological effects, not only for Pérez, but for the Yucatecan clergy and for the creole community in general. Fabian

Carrillo, the lawyer and noted political conservative who delivered Pérez's funeral oration, reported a moment when Pérez "saw reflected in the towers of his church the splendor of the flames."[72] This story was largely fiction, since as far as we know nothing whatsoever happened in Hoctún during the war. Nevertheless, like other and similar anecdotes of the Caste War, it revealed the sense of frustration, disillusionment, and betrayal that many creoles nursed toward those whom they considered their social and ethnic inferiors in the postcolonial era. Carrillo softened the implications by assuring that for Pérez the revolt was no surprise, that in fact he had long predicted it. This, too, was indicative. Within decades of the war's opening, it had become fashionable, particularly in conservative quarters like the church, to claim to have foreseen the conflict; sudden breaks with the old colonial structures, the implication ran, were the underlying cause. This argument was in many ways correct. But those who advanced it, sectors such as the clergy, had usually benefited from the old system. Moreover, it ignored the fact that many of those same conservatives, Pérez chief among them, had adroitly straddled the two worlds, availing themselves of the opportunities of economic liberalism while simultaneously holding on to the benefits accorded them by the old colonial order.

On the whole, Pérez and Hoctún survived the Caste War in good shape.[73] When the conflict receded from the northwest, Pérez launched a general refurbishing of the parish. He financed not only construction of a church at Seyé but also the restoration of the church at Tahmek, "over its old foundations."[74] (For the latter project he provided in advance 750 pesos in silver, relying on pledges of local families to cover the remaining 250 pesos.[75]) There is no evidence that building damage was war-related, and in fact these structures were liable to a wide variety of accidents and to natural deterioration. Even many of Yucatán's picturesque destroyed churches suffered their damages at a comparatively late stage of the war, or many years later through unrelated wear and tear (see Chapter 4). Canicab and Pérez's other haciendas remained in operation. Like many property owners, Pérez managed to exempt his Maya peons from military service; eager for military initiatives, Yucatán's landholding classes were even more desperate to hang on to their own labor force.[76] Finally, Raymundo Pérez also continued numerous loan and real-estate activities in Mérida.[77] In 1855 he made his last significant purchase, a five-thousand-peso house in the Mejorada region.[78] Here, too, Pérez's career managed to capture an important dynamic of the day and time. The survival of his own personal wealth provided a reservoir of capital that helped certain sectors of the Yucatecan economy, particularly urban real estate and northwestern haciendas, to recover from the war with relative speed. His 1848 loan of two thousand pesos to Manuel José Peón on hacienda Mukuychén, in Abalá, is only one example of internally financed survival and reconstruction.[79]

The Pérez Passing

Hoctún survived, but calamity and old age eventually took their toll on the doctor. By the time of the Caste War he was already the oldest cura (seventy-nine) on the peninsula.[80] He lived on in the parish of Hoctún, remaining spry and sharp into his eighties, "although stooped in posture."[81] But he now passed along much of the administrative affairs in Hoctún to his coadjutor, Luis Francisco Ricalde. To the end of his years Pérez remained embroiled in disputes with neighboring curas over the rights to religious fees from outlying peasants. He charged ten reales for a first marriage, four for the candles in religious ceremonies, and six for masses: prices the Caste War rebels had laid out as the preconditions of peace.[82] Like the church as a whole, Pérez survived by learning to demand less.

Power and wealth did not mean immortality, and so it was inevitable that one day sad tidings came from Hoctún. On November 17, 1856, Ricalde wrote to Bishop Guerra: "I scarcely have the spirit to give Your Illustriousness the unhappy and ill-fated news that at five in the afternoon, Sr. Dr. Don Raymundo Pérez passed away."[83] The timing of his death dripped with historical symbolism. In one sense the old cura died with his home village of Bacalar; in a little over a year it fell to the hands of Caste War rebels, who retained possession for nearly fifty years.[84] He also died at precisely the time when the national Liberal Party determined to break up the wealth of the church once and for all. In 1855 the Ley Juárez abolished many of the social perquisites Pérez had so defended, and in the following year the Ley Lerdo stripped the church of its corporately held property.[85]

With the demise of Pérez, Yucatán lost an important link with the past, since he constituted one of the old guard who had started their careers under the Spanish Empire. Another elderly entrepreneur-priest, Eusebio Villamil, died two years later; Bishop José María Guerra died in 1863. By 1867, only the ancient Pedro José Hurtado of Bécal remained. Hurtado himself had been part of the Spanish entourage of Bishop Agustín Estévez y Ugarte that had arrived in 1797. He had survived the constitutional crisis, independence, the Caste War, the reform, and the French occupation.[86] But Hurtado alone could not prevent the inevitable: the Yucatecan church was losing its institutional memory of colonial times.

The old adage warns us to speak no ill of the dead. But in his funeral oration, Fabian Carrillo outdid this by suggesting that the Caste War had bankrupted Pérez.[87] The claim must have provoked silent smirks from its audience, who knew perfectly well that Pérez had died one of the richest men in southeast Mexico. His estates continued in working order, and the war in no way touched his lucrative trade in Mérida real estate. The episode was an example of the kind of shabby deceptions to which Yucatán's propertied classes were prone. Indeed, even as the grave diggers were laying his body to rest, his heirs were counting up the pesos of the Pérez empire. The doctor's will, originally filed among the notarial papers of Izamal, is now lost.[88] But references turn up in other documents, much like the wreckage of some great lost ship floating to the surface.[89] These papers suggest a complex document disposing of enormous wealth. Even after the many donations of his last years, the Pérez estate still included over forty thousand pesos in either cash or debts owed to the doctor. Pérez had provided for numerous gifts of houses, as well as individual cash gifts of one to two thousand pesos. His heirs had to send one gold chalice to Havana in order to get top price.[90] And, of course, there was property. By this point Canicab was the sixteenth-largest hacienda on the peninsula.[91] In addition, Pérez owned four other haciendas, all economically active at the time of his death.[92]

The funeral oration also reports many charitable gifts for the rural peasants of Hoctún. This would not be surprising, for it had been a custom among the wealthier curas of the late colonial period to provide legacies—a custom the curas saw as a privilege and the peasants interpreted as a right. It was indicative of the deterioration of the rural social fabric that the custom had begun to fall off after independence, when the cash nexus increasingly became the basis for human relationships. Pérez, steeped in the older tradition, tried to maintain these more genteel gestures of the moral economy in the face of the commercialism he had also embraced.

The past 150 years have buried the memory of Raymundo Pérez far deeper than six feet under the earth. A talented but haughty man who held himself aloof from the public, Pérez made little effort to perpetuate his own memory. Later Yucatecans wrote two biographical sketches of him, both reworkings of Fabian Carrillo's 1856 funeral oration. Indeed, by the 1880s details regarding the previous generation were growing hazy; Pérez himself was absorbed into the world of Yucatecan folk knowledge. When Serapio Baqueiro passed through Hoctún in 1881, he found that among Maya porters, the doctor was legendary as a big tipper, while hacienda owners canonized him as an early apostle of henequen cultivation.[93] But in his day Pérez's social and political career epitomized many of the dilemmas that confronted rural Yucatecan society in the first half of the nineteenth century. Spanish colonial society had always maintained its legitimacy by brokering the intentionally fragmented peoples of the Americas, most particularly the conflicting interests of Spaniards and Indians. After 1821 the creole heirs to the Americas sought to play both roles at once: the detached administrator and the ambitious entrepreneur. The tensions generated by these dual and often contradictory identities eventually tore Mexico apart.

Few sectors of the society better epitomized the problem than did the clergy. Mexico's rural church was largely tied to the older economy of tribute, the legacy of the missionaries' spiritual kingdom. This held true despite the near total disappearance of millenarian fervor. Rights to tribute demanded a certain moral claim. However, the padres of the countryside were not necessarily hidebound reactionaries. They welcomed economic developments such as commercial agriculture, urban real estate, infrastructure development, and the business of retailing and wholesaling in the domestic markets. However, they wanted to assimilate these new opportunities with the security of the persistent past and its lingering virtues, the parish system that defined them socially and spiritually and that they had been trained to defend. In this dual orientation they differed little from many nonclergy, including the Mayas, who were far more receptive to new possibilities than previously supposed.

The justification for having the best of both worlds rested in an almost classical ideal that combined piety and power, an intersection of colonial and republican values. Material wealth and worldly political power cloaked themselves in moral righteousness. In the years before the Caste War the ascendancy of such men was still possible; they thought it natural to associate education, religious vocation, and the adroit domination of economic and political matters: "The rich ruleth over the poor, and the borrower is servant to the lender." But the war robbed them of much of their material well-being and, beyond that, momentarily punctured the smug sensibilities that had surrounded these rural overlords. What makes Pérez interesting is the degree to which he fulfilled this hybrid ideal. Pérez mastered the theological framework of his time as well as its economic opportunities.

In the final tally, though, his life may be less noteworthy for its continuities than for changes that help explain the decline of Mexican conservatism as a coherent social and political movement. Nineteenth-century conservatism is normally seen as the Spanish Empire without the Spanish, an attempt to perpetuate the political and social institutions of colonialism, but under creole supremacy. These institutions included an established church, economic protectionism, trade monopolies, authoritarian politics, and paternalism toward the indigenous communities. Engaged in a life-and-death struggle with liberalism and its project of laissez-faire capitalism, the conservatives self-destructed through a disastrous alliance with French imperialists. What finally emerged from this conflict was the Porfirian synthesis, an arrangement that combined the economic strategies of liberalism with the authoritarian political mechanisms of the conservatives. There is much truth to this account. However, the evidence suggests that conservatism also declined through a process of internal erosion. Entrepreneur-priests such as Raymundo Pérez, José María Meneses, and Eusebio Villamil gradually adopted so many of the liberal capitalist practices that conservatism as a distinct and holistic political ideology no longer made sense. True, Yucatecan partisans were still arguing in conservative terminology in the 1850s and 1860s, but the material basis of society and the daily experience of human participants normally do change before rhetoric and public postures have time to catch up. Thus, while historians have focused on deconstructing Mexican liberalism, we would do well to consider the internal metamorphosis of conservatism and of conservatives as strands of both provincial and national change.

The Posthumous Pérez

Classic Mexican conservatism crumbled with the deaths and conversions of its individual members. But men such as Raymundo Pérez left a patrimony — their wealth, their estates, and their ideological structures — for a future generation to adapt and to reinvest according to the changing times. The transfer was often a messy process, particularly in eras as chaotic as the two decades that followed Mexico's reform laws. For this reason the public controversy that had occasionally ruffled Pérez during his lifetime refused to disappear; indeed, the last and certainly the most sordid episode in the doctor's long history took place after his death in 1856.

As executor of his will Pérez had chosen his son Manuel Medina. By now Medina himself was a family man with two daughters, María Francisca del Francito and María de los Angeles (Pérez had died a grandfather).[94] He may have retained his father's business acumen, but in the long run he turned out to lack the latter's moral sense: Manuel Medina went on to become one of the more outspoken champions of selling captured Maya prisoners as slaves to

Cuba.[95] This sort of opportunism also informed his management of the Pérez estate. Rather than execute the many articles according to the letter, Medina undersold numerous properties, failed to inventory all the fixtures and assets of the estates, and kept double books that allowed him to pocket the difference. His partner in this scheme was none other than Fabian Carrillo, the conservative lawyer who had delivered Pérez's funeral oration and who had authored a moral treatise on the dangers of avarice two years earlier.[96] On top of all this, Medina loaned himself money from a trust fund his father had set up to aid a young Maya boy of the parish, Refugio Ek.[97] Angry heirs pursued Medina through a legal process known as *ocultación de bienes,* or an inquest into concealed property inheritance. Even Medina's own mother filed suit against him. The case dragged on for nine inconclusive years, by which time the statute of limitations for many of these accusations had expired. In 1865, the courts, now under the ill-fated French Empire, ordered a complete inventory of Pérez's property and debts, but no record of its findings survives.[98] Indeed, the lawsuit seems to have made little impact on Medina; judging from his elaborate and well-maintained crypt in Mérida's general cemetery, he died in comfortable circumstances. Wealth had a peculiar way of staying put.

Hoctún itself went on without Raymundo Pérez. His longtime assistant Luis Fernando Ricalde stepped up to assume the role of cura; Ricalde stayed in office almost as long as his mentor, serving until his death in the late 1880s.[99] Located in the heart of the henequen zone, the town flourished during the boom years of cultivation and then declined as plastic fibers and foreign competition gradually put Yucatán's henequen industry out of business. Today Hoctún is memorable chiefly for the gravestones of its public cemetery, featuring colorful folk-art recreations of Maya huts, Mexico City's Latin American Tower, and the Castillo of Chichén Itzá.[100]

Canicab, the crown jewel of the Pérez empire, had its own checkered sequel. After the cura's death the estate eventually passed into the hands of the Liborio Cervera family. These new owners took advantage of the henequen boom, replacing corn and cattle with hundreds of acres of green gold and supplementing human labor with steam engines and defibrating machines. On the great chimney of the processing plant visitors can still make out the numbers 1888, a landmark year in its economic life. Eventually, however, Canicab went the way of the other great henequen haciendas. The victim of revolutionary land redistributions and shifting world markets, it fell into permanent decline after 1930. Some of Canicab's deteriorated remains are ejido property; other small fragments have become private housing, while the village that has grown up within and around it suffers from profound stagnation and unemployment. Whatever his views on change, it is safe to say that Canicab's former owner would not be pleased.[101]

The trajectory of Padre Doctor Don Raymundo Pérez y González carries a moral tenor similar to that of a cautionary tale from the Middle Ages. *Ubi sunt:* "Where now are the rich and powerful?" For five decades Pérez dominated the religious and economic affairs of his world. But when his survivors buried him somewhere in the ancient parish of Hoctún, his fortune sank from view and his name passed from the memory of the living. The exact location of his remains is unknown.[102]

The Bourgeois Spiritual Path

A History of Urban Piety

AFFLUENT AND ERUDITE priests like Raymundo Pérez had no monopoly on piety. Urbanites, residents of the grand cities of Mérida and Campeche, and even the townsfolk of the smaller, interior communities such as Dzitás and Pustunich, had their own ways of staying in touch with the sacred, and it is to their story that we now turn.

Yucatán's tales of urban piety drew from a tradition of a public, ceremonial culture built on the medium of religion. The search for social self-definition through links with the church has a long history in Europe and elsewhere. From the Middle Ages onward the growing bourgeoisie had carved out its own way of simultaneously celebrating itself and the Almighty. Parades, guilds, carnivals, and ostentatious public prayer provided the routine protocols of city life.[1] In more recent times, nationalism and high-tech consumption have picked up where religion left off. These various strains of urban piety serve diverse purposes. Organized activities provide outlets for belief and hope. They bring individuals out of their isolation. Particularly in earlier times, before the rise of the welfare state, lay brotherhoods provided a modicum of security and support in a notoriously insecure world. Perhaps the most significant aspect of urban piety has been its inextricable relationship with social prestige and class ascendancy. It is almost in the nature of these affairs that pious behavior takes place in public. That secret individual piety existed cannot be doubted, but much of urban piety was designed for social display and public consumption, and this is what caused it to leave such an imprint on the historical record.

As one final remark by way of introduction, it is important to acknowledge, and hopefully compensate for, some of the vagaries of the term "bourgeoisie." I use this term not in the Marxist sense of their relation to means of economic production but, rather, to characterize urbanites who saw themselves as being quite different from the people of the countryside. At times that difference could be more imagined than real; rural and urban values shared connections, just as Mayas and Hispanics shared some values and cultural beliefs, but city life does have a way of causing people to turn their back on the ways of the milpa. Moreover, though at the core of many of the following episodes stood a well-educated, high bourgeoisie that wrote, read, planned, financed, and organized, this elite core still managed to bring along with it a large number of less affluent urbanites who watched, imitated, participated in, and even initiated and modified the ceremonies of public piety. In this chapter I have tried to pick apart the various layers of urban culture when possible, but with an understanding that the groups did indeed interact.

Pious Literature

For some urbanites it was not sufficient to act piously. The desire to understand the sacred, to bring one's thoughts into line with church rituals and teachings, led many to begin by *reading* piously. Members of the intelligentsia are probably a minority in any culture; for the majority, it was enough to attend the ceremonies, march in the processions, and speak, inwardly or outwardly, with the divine power. But those who drew their sense of the religious from intellectual engagement enjoyed a significant body of devotional literature that framed religious experience in written language and, by extension, in thought itself.

The first question of this literature concerns its origins. Were Mexican provincials net importers of religious culture, or did they generate their own spiritual writings? The answer is mixed. To begin with, the intellectual culture of Yucatán's early national period drew in part from a rebirth of church piety that owed its life to the social and political developments of Europe. European Catholicism and the ultramontane spirit enjoyed a renaissance between the decline of French revolutionary fervor and the eruption of anti-Vatican attacks from the Italian state builders in the 1860s. The remains of the deists Voltaire and Diderot were temporarily removed from the Panthéon; the Jesuit order returned to life; and European intellectuals such as Lamennais, Lacordaire, and Montalembert wrote new justifications for the Catholic institution and its social power.[2] One direct manifestation of this new spirit of piety was the doctrine of the Immaculate Conception in 1854, dutifully promulgated by Bishop Guerra even as the Caste War simmered in the hinterlands.[3] In sum, international political events helped to relegitimize the Catholic faith and to revive its cultural production.

Judging from surviving collections, however, most of the peninsula's pietistic works, whether in newspapers or printed separately, came from Yucatecans themselves. This was all the more noteworthy for the fact that the first peninsular printing press did not crank into action until 1813, when the early newspaper *El aristarco* appeared under the direction of liberal thinker and later statesman Lorenzo de Zavala.[4] Little suggests a strong Mexico City presence; rather, pious writings evolved out of a tightly knit group of privileged, fairly conservative meridanos who enjoyed close relations with the clergy. The "Generation of 1840" was led by Justo Sierra O'Reilly (at times writing under the penname/anagram José Turrisa) and included writings by Gerónimo Castillo, Juan José Hernández, and Vicente Calero.[5] O'Reilly was in some regards a liberal, but was also the son of a Yucatecan priest and at least prior to the Caste War had a deep regard for the institution.[6] In addition, there were polemical writings produced by the clergy, items similar in tone and argument to Pérez's 1814 self-defense. These writings were not monolithic, but they shared enough common themes to permit a discussion of their overall ideas and orientations.

What exactly did the Yucatecans contemplate when engrossed in devotional literature? Piety is not self-defining, and people can be looking for many different things when they aspire to read religiously. The old Massachusetts Puritans read jeremiads.[7] Liberation theology stresses religion as both an end and a mean in community self-realization.[8] Existentialist Christianity emphasizes moral agency in an amoral abyss—Kierkegaard's metaphor of "life as treading water with ten thousand fathoms beneath us."[9] In fact, however, none of these models seem to have operated in Yucatán's early national period. While plying diverse themes and functions, the bulk of its production related to a postcolonial project through which the peninsula's creole elite justified their own political domination while underscoring selected links with the Spanish colonial past.

One task of pious literature was to perpetuate the old dogmas of cosmology. As with peasant mythologies, religion performed the critical duty of orienting urban peoples to their place in history and the universe. The readers of Mariano Rodríguez y Cantón's 1826 almanac, for example, could find a universal chronology that placed intensely local events within the context of a biblical-cosmological time. The burghers of this small, isolated province took a certain consolation in knowing that "the terrible storm which struck Campeche" happened exactly 7,005 years after the creation of the world, or that a fire in Ichmul ranked alongside the conquest of Mexico as a topic of mention.[10] Oddly enough, however, the church itself was losing interest in the afterlife, the realm that had so entranced the artists and theologians of the Middle Ages. The subject is absent from Yucatecan pious literature, with the possible exception of the prayer booklets known as *novenarios,* themselves a remnant of earlier traditions. In fact, fire and brimstone were waning in worldwide Catholicism by the late eighteenth century.[11] These concerns became the almost exclusive property of evangelicals, who needed strong tonics for the strong sins of the backlands, and to justify popular revolt against the patrician authorities of the early-nineteenth-century United States.[12] Church doctrine regarding cosmology still sat on the books, but it had begun to take on a quaint and slightly anachronistic tone, partly for its harshness, partly for its odd specificity. For example, the 1838 *Sumaria de las gracias* provided a roster of fees for religious services both in Mérida and the rural towns, complete with a long list of holy deeds and their corresponding time off in purgatory. Mere church attendance on average Sundays removed ten thousand years of torment; special occasions included the day of San Esteban, the feast of San Juan, and the day of the circumcision of Jesus (each worth twenty-eight thousand years); and for visiting the church on the Friday after Palm Sunday, the sinner received plenary indulgence "and many other pardons beyond count."[13] In no small degree, the growth of Mexican liberalism reflected an urban bourgeoisie that was losing interest in the *Sumaria*'s brand of everlasting discomfort.

By the 1820s the Catholic intelligentsia were increasingly absorbed in social issues and promoted the church as the bulwark of order and stability in an age gone mad with revolution. Peninsular pious literature consequently stressed social stability, the underlying concern of postindependence creoles who had witnessed the upheavals of Haiti and Hidalgo. Of the diverse beliefs of Mérida's conservative elite, few were more pervasive than the idea that religion was necessary to form an organic, hierarchical society. Juan José Hernández put the matter succinctly in a poetic epigram: "All society is arranged/ with every station according to its station/ To that end the people keep plowing/ and the priests of the altar keep praying." [14] This social-ethical voice often had to compete with a popular spirituality that preferred wonders, visitations, and miracle cures, features common to episodes such as the kindling crosses, but it was nonetheless a strong voice that defined a major part of nineteenth-century Mexican thought and attitude.

In no small part, then, pious literature of the day stressed the beneficial nature of conservative, elite rule. This was a bourgeois culture looking for sweetness and light, a spiritual equivalent of Howard Cline's "age of progress." Satan put in only rare appearances; the allusions to the devil in the prayer book *Devoción a la escala santa* are atypical, and, significantly, derive from an eighteenth-century leftover. [15] Much more to urban tastes was something like the saccharine "Historical-Religious Song in Praise of the Virgin Mary" retailed in Mérida in 1864. [16] Similarly, J. A. Cisneros's long rhapsodic poem "To Religion" begins with the conceit of everyone—Jews, heretics, heads of state, even corrupt priests—conspiring against the Virgin Mary, but concludes with the Virgin's inevitable triumph and a world restored: "In all the world there is nothing/ without you, Oh holy religion!" [17] To modern tastes the works of authors like Cisneros, Sierra O'Reilly, or the later bishop and church ideologist Crescencio Carrillo y Ancona are likely to appear syrupy and apologetic. They tended to gloss over social conflicts and to ignore large sectors of the population and peninsular culture. Urban readers of the nineteenth century, however, seemed to have preferred them.

The genre of church history neatly captured this tendency. Unlike the anticlerical liberals discussed in Chapter 6, conservative elites still took the church as their partner in rule and did everything possible to present the institution in a progressive and highly flattering light. Justo Sierra O'Reilly in particular liked to recount historical tidbits on priests and bishops, even though in his later years he became somewhat embittered toward the church. On the late Padre José María Loría, "the sweetest of characters," he wrote, "His soul, which was a treasure of noble and philanthropic sentiments, suffered grievously with the misfortunes of mankind." [18] Fabian Carrillo's prevarications about the late Raymundo Pérez were no accident, but rather designed to pose conservative-clerical rule as the proper alternative to Caste War–related violence.

Admittedly, not all the conservative authors were so enamored of progress. The most extreme of reactionaries, Vicente Calero, celebrated the Conquest as the triumph of religion and used his pen to blast every facet of the modern age. As he articulated in essays such as "Lent" and "The Bible and Contemporary Literature," western society had been on a long downhill slide since the Renaissance and, more particularly, since the French Revolution. The dyspeptic Calero loathed the frivolity that had grown up around events like Lent; processions and carnivals, he believed, had to be replaced by thoughtful, even grave meditations in parks beside the church. This change would come about by education and above all by "effective preaching." He took some comfort in the belief that poets everywhere had lost interest in Greek and Roman mythology, and were instead turning to the Bible as the true source of inspiration.[19]

Calero's brand of killjoy Christianity had little chance of gaining popular acceptance. Few other authors took so dour a view, and even priests themselves do not seem to have been much inclined to this sort of asceticism. However, they did share with Calero a vocabulary that threw power and sanctity to the religion that linked them to their sacred past—*precioso* (precious), *sublime* (sublime), *sublimidad* (sublimity), *belleza* (beauty), *las eternas máximas* (the eternal maxims),and *los himnos consagrados* (the sacred hymns). These motifs ripple through the genre of church elegy, for example, in which the author enters one of the peninsular churches and finds himself in a state of spiritual transport. "What a deep impression," wrote Sierra O'Reilly of the Mérida cathedral, "that I still feel the indelible stamp which it impressed with such vehemence on my brain!"[20] The same conceit appears in Sierra O'Reilly's essay on the Havana cathedral and in "El camposanto," a stock piece of romantic rhapsody set in Mérida's cemetery, where the author goes "to learn the holy fear of God."[21] These Hispanic equivalents of Thomas Gray's country churchyard employed Yucatán's religious edifices, with all their colonial associations, to connote immortality and the sacred.

Whether in the physical or the abstract, then, the church radiated power. In keeping with this authoritarian ideological project, stable social mores demanded the construction of antiquity. It hardly mattered whether this was an expropriated Maya antiquity or one brought over from Spain. Formulaic pieces of local antiquarianism concerning the ruins of Uxmal and Chichén Itzá, or reprints of foreign observations on peninsular archaeology, served more to paint a sepia-toned past than to build archaeological knowledge.[22] The many histories of bishops and convents also celebrated the hierarchy of colonialism.[23] In all cases the writings posit an ancient and deeply devout culture that could selectively pluck out baubles of modernity for itself without risking larger and more radical social change. The pursuit of an ancient identity was inconsistent: Sierra O'Reilly and others had only limited interest in the scientific retrieval of the past. Rather, their literary project fed vicariously on the work of John Lloyd Stephens (who had his own tendency to orientalize foreign cultures) as grist in their effort to construct a postcolonial ideology.

At the same time, celebrations of Maya antiquities usually had a subtext of underscoring what the elite saw as the stupidity and barbarism of contemporary Maya peasants. These same themes crept into unexpected corners. For example, Juan José Hernández's bogus ethnography, "El indio," although in some ways a rehash of all the old stereotypes of Maya peasants, was in reality an attack on Hernández's less-than-religious enemies. A close personal friend of Vicente Calero, Hernández set up the *indio* as a metaphor for liberals: stubborn, brutish, willful against the church, and living in a state of nature like wild beasts. "Why is it not preached to the Indians that isolation is contrary to society, and that religion cannot exist without the latter, and equally, as some politicians want, that society cannot exist without religion?"[24] In both its expropriation of an indigenous past and its denigration of contemporary peasants, the local antiquarianism of the early nineteenth century served as an intellectual precursor of later revolutionary-era indigenism.

Another genre of pietistic literature, the printed *novenario,* enjoyed far more popularity and, with its emphasis on cures and wondrous intercessions, had pronounced links with a prebourgeois past. (The components of a cultural field seldom evolve uniformly.) The *novena,* or nine-day Catholic prayer ritual, characterized Spanish piety but also came to constitute a major element of Maya folk religion as well; in the 1930s Redfield and Villa Rojas described Chan Kom's novenas as single-session prayers similar to rosaries, while the term *novenarios* referred to ritual prayer over nine successive nights. These relatively common events occurred either on name days or in fulfillment of a promise made to a santo in return for some favor.[25] Much of their popularity lay in the fact that the reader did not have to be among the high intelligentsia to comprehend them; like the santo cults described in Chapter 4, they allowed common people to get in touch with the sacred without elite guidance, a trend that continues today with the unofficial novenarios to unofficial saints sold in Mérida religious bookstores catering to the lower classes—much like the artifacts of Mexico City's massive Mercado Sonora.

Originally made to serve as a guide for people carrying out the novena ritual, the novenario became a meditative work in and of itself. These small volumes were extremely prevalent in the peninsula: between 1810 and 1870 we find at least thirty-one, with an assortment of other small devotional items of similar character.[26] The novenarios' average size was 10.5 centimeters wide by

15 centimeters tall. Running anywhere from eight to thirty pages and bound in a thin paper cover, the booklet normally consisted of a small opening prayer to be said each day, followed by the nine specialty prayers. Smaller and far simpler prayer books known variously as *votos, donaciones,* or *devocionarios* performed similar functions for those without the time or patience to go through an entire novena.[27] Typically they included a statement of the Vatican's official approval. The works were anonymous, or else purported to have been written long ago and far away—by an Italian monk, by a talented novice, "by a priest who once served under the threshold of that holy temple."[28]

Novena prayers spoke to several needs. Some were for routine reverence of the santo, to be spoken during his feast day. Others, such as the novena to Santa Apolinara, patron saint of toothaches, or to Santa Lucía of the eyes, were performed on an as-needed basis.[29] Whatever the occasion and motive, the stock device of the novenario was fulsome praise. Often this operated through an appositive construction in which the authors enumerated the santo's many identities in order to more fully comprehend his majesty. Such was the strategy featured in the "Novena to the Sacred Heart of the Most Holy Mary," whose long list of her epithets included "most holy Mother, most pure Mother, Mother who is intact . . . mirror of justice, seat of wisdom, cause of our joy."[30] The 1851 *Manual of Virtue* encouraged people to focus on the meanings of the Lord's Prayer through a fifty-five-page textual analysis of each individual line.[31] These sorts of intellectual embroideries on dogma came straight from the baroque times of old Mexico, but they still enjoyed a popular audience in the mid–nineteenth century. They were the remnant of a traditionalist society in which speech reproduced formulas and motifs in endless combinations; they retained a high degree of what Walter Ong referred to as "orality," whereas the pious compositions of the urban bourgeoisie showed strong authorship, with the balanced preparation and the finish available only to written, edited works.[32]

Despite generous portions of sweetness and uplift, however, novenarios sometimes borrowed from the old penitential tradition. The style and phraseology at times consisted of verbal self-flagellation, as sinners castigated themselves in hopes of drawing the santo's sympathy. The novenario of Abraham, for example, implored that God's call "may impress on our hearts with strong desires to do penance for our sins, to mortify our senses, to torment our bodies, and to subject to reason the rebellion of our passions."[33] Similarly, the *Devocionario* of 1839 could address Mary as "you who washed away the leprosy of my sins with the fountains of your blood."[34] The 1849 *Oraciones* also harkened back to an older Spanish tradition of mysticism and personal communication with divine forces.[35]

In sum, urban devotional literature filled a variety of roles in provincial society. It mediated between a lingering past and a desire for the benefits that accompanied economic change. It constructed what a conservative bourgeoisie took as the national heritage. And it carried on diminished versions of earlier pietistic traditions. The bulk of peninsular literary production was informed by the values it posed. And there was one other important consequence of this literature. As scholars of nationalism have observed, the act of reading can build a shared consciousness.[36] Unlike fiestas and processions, pouring over devotional literature took place in private, but at the same time, people could read alone together in different rooms, in individual houses, in cities separated by many miles. The limitations of colonial society, which included an illiterate, marginalized majority, meant that works like the *Museo yucateco* enjoyed only limited circulation. Yet within a small cohort the constant mental rehearsing of pious themes became a marker of identity, one that would serve a political function even when its original tenets of devotion had lost much of their immediacy.

Pious Organizations

Words without deeds were arid. The bulk of the urban bourgeoisie chose pageantry over pamphlets, and for nineteenth-century Mexicans the institution for enacting their own special brand of urban piety was the *cofradía,* a form of lay brotherhood or sodality that had emerged in Europe in the 1200s and that loosely based itself on the mendicant orders.[37] Cofradías became a mainstay of colonial Mexico City, Lima, Bogotá, Salvador, and elsewhere; even Brazilian slaves had their own version, based on the practice of mutual aid.[38] The conquistador Francisco de Montejo the Elder first brought the cofradía to Yucatán in the mid–sixteenth century. Within fifty years all barrios of Mérida enjoyed such organizations. In practice, urban cofradías amounted to colonial rotary clubs, in which prominent citizens celebrated their place in the social hierarchy by conspicuously attending mass and other religious events. Revenues almost always took the form of dues, although there were exceptional cases of cofradías built on endowments, as illustrated below.[39] Whether large or small, they provided important sources of loan capital in a society without banks.

The urban cofradías did many things, but first and foremost they supported the clergy. Prior to the 1840s curas had plump revenues from the peasant church taxes known as obventions.[40] But Santiago Imán's revolt of 1839–1840 and the subsequent Caste War gutted church funding; at least some of the church's goods were sold to finance the war effort, while obventions, now referred to as the *contribución religiosa,* fell from nineteen reales per married couple to a mere seven, a decline of over 60 percent from their pre-1840 value.[41] Moreover, payment during the turbulent 1850s and 1860s was irregular at best. It was therefore imperative that the church make up the deficit. This took place through organizations of voluntary contribution, much in the way that professional fundraising and charitable giving have risen in the United States with the decline of government funding. The great transition of the nineteenth-century Mexican church was the transition from a compulsory to a voluntary organization, and urban sodalities formed a critical thread in that history.

The survival of these operations was not a given. On the national scale, they appear to have suffered high mortality rates, making instability one of their most prominent features. States in other parts of Mexico began the nineteenth century with thriving cofradía systems. The densely populated bishopric of Puebla had some 955 organizations, including both rural and urban. That of Guadalajara had 338, Guanajuato 47; about a third of these operated on dues, while the remaining majority survived on the returns of money invested in land, houses, livestock, and sundry business transactions. However, by 1822 many of these had fallen on hard times, mostly the result of destruction and economic decline associated with the wars of independence; phrases such as "destroyed by the wars" form a leitmotif in their lists of property holdings.[42] The bishop of Chiapas reported an even gloomier situation in 1856: "There are almost no [cofradías] in all the diocese which appropriately deserve the name."[43] Sonoran-Sinaloan brotherhoods consisted of either Indian organizations possessing a few cows or urban chapters of the cofradía of Nuestro Amo, based exclusively on monthly dues.[44] As for Guadalajara, an 1856 ecclesiastical report summed up the situation as follows:

> Before the year 1810 there were few villages that did not have one, two, or even more. As a result of political upheavals, nearly continuous and for so many years, they have suffered ruinous thefts of their holdings; and as many consist in little more than furniture or a bit of invested capital, more than a few have disappeared altogether. Those which remain, never grand affairs to begin with, find themselves in such a state that few are able to cover their operating costs.[45]

There were, of course, the favored exceptions. Oaxaca's Precious Blood of Christ enjoyed a portfolio of 10,593 pesos, all invested in productive real estate.[46] But the larger point here is that whether Indian or Spanish, urban or rural, the Mexican sodalities underwent ongoing evolutions. Most reached the middle of the nineteenth century in the poor condition described above, only to face the challenge of the Liberal reforms, which stripped both prosperous organizations and penny-ante banks of their right to hold and loan capital.

Southeast Mexico mirrored the national experience. Institutions such as the cofradía of the Virgin of Merced (1809) wrote elaborate guidelines, only to vanish altogether from the historical record.[47] In 1851 a series of dramatic religious awakenings, poorly documented but probably associated with Caste War tensions and the liberal menace, swept the city of Campeche, giving birth to the organization Sacred Heart of Mary—but who could count on such fervor to last indefinitely?[48] Moreover, in some cases the church appears to have been reluctant or, at least, slow to grant approval for their formation. For example, Bishop Guerra gave a tentative verbal approval for the creation of a cofradía in Santiago, Mérida, in 1860; but this was not officially ratified until his successor, Leandro de Gala, signed the papers three years later; the organization itself did not get around to writing its regulations until 1868.[49] Doubtless in this case the delays owed something to the political upheavals of the Second Empire. But the fact remains that urban cofradías were large public undertakings that required a great deal of planning and organization, and that without careful administration these same undertakings could easily disintegrate. Since repeated failures would only serve to discourage later efforts, the church had to exercise prudence in granting approval to would-be cofrades.

Beyond the problems of internal dynamics, peninsular sodalities also felt the changes of their day and time. Prosperous during the decade of political conservatism (the 1830s), they also suffered under the wave of anticlericalism and the antitax groundswell that followed the Imán revolt. When Alejandro Marín y Escalera accepted the position of *mayordomo,* or chief administrator, for the cult of Señor de Amor of barrio Santa Ana, Campeche, in 1846, he did so on the condition that someone else be appointed to collect the dues; he did not want to deal with "the ugly mood against mayordomos which enemies of bad character have stirred up in this city."[50] Similarly, Valladolid's cofradía of Santísimo Sacramento (the Blessed Sacrament) fell into inactivity after a decade of Caste War–related violence reduced the power of the town's land-based elite.[51] The Campeche-based Sacred Heart of Mary got off to a roaring start in 1850, then faltered before certain "sad events" (probably the Liberal reform) and had to be reawakened in 1886.[52] To take one final case, few organizations outdid Campeche's own chapter of Santísimo Sacramento as a barometer of national politics. The brotherhood began in 1753, fell apart during the upheavals of the early national period, rose again in 1878 under the peace of Porfirio Díaz, disintegrated once more when the Revolution came in the mid-1910s, then made its final return in 1932 as revolutionary anticlericalism began to subside.[53]

Another problem was that ostentatious public piety carried considerable overhead. For example, the cofradía of Nuestra Señora del Rosario tried to stage annual fiestas by using proceeds from an endowment of the late doña Josefa Roo. But its financial records for the years 1810–1828 show it running a deficit of 3,456 pesos. Annual fiestas for Rosario ranged from 196 to 308 pesos, with an average cost of 222 pesos. How exactly was this money spent? Taking 1816 as a nearly average year, we find that 59 percent went to pay priests for singing masses or preaching a special sermon; the second major cost was candles (27 percent) and fireworks (10 percent), with assorted small payments to musicians and carriers of statues. The revenues on small loans to Yucatán's relatively stagnant private sector simply failed to cover these cumulative expenses, and the church had no choice but to stipulate that the back debt be paid gradually out of the remaining principal, itself a mere 3,700 pesos.[54] After 1828 there are no further references to the group. Still, there is no reason to consider the case of Nuestra Señora as exceptional, for latter-day urban brotherhoods continued to rise and fall. Valladolid's cofradía of the Virgin of Guadalupe went through similar ebbs and flows and was once more reorganizing itself as late as September 1910, three months after the city witnessed a minor uprising commonly tagged as "the first spark of the Mexican Revolution."[55] In Chocholá, during the constitutional crisis of 1812 and its attendant economic hardships for the church, the pious of the town drew up a contract for a cofradía to provide burials for members and their families; the original signatories pledged themselves to a one-peso annual contribution. But was this contract binding for future generations? The founding cura, José María Badillos, certainly thought so, but by the early 1830s some disgruntled townsfolk, led by a certain Luis Polanco, were trying to do away with the organization and with Badillos' insistent collection attempts, arguing (correctly enough) that contracts signed by their parents carried no legal onus for themselves.[56] Changes of enthusiasm and economic conditions therefore made urban cofradías more of a process than a permanent fixture.

Finally, individual leadership made its mark on the fortunes of the cofradía. More often than not this meant a charismatic young cura; the well-documented sodality of Santísimo Sacramento rose and fell on the vitality of Padre Gregorio Ximénez, a key figure in the religious, urban, and educational history of prereform Campeche.[57] Similarly, Padre Valerio Canto y Sosa was instrumental in reviving Campeche brotherhoods in the 1880s.[58] The padres found collaborators among a small group of prominent, religiously devout men who saw such organizations as a civic and spiritual duty, who helped draw up the charters and constitutions, and who bore the lion's share of time-consuming ceremonial office. Such organizational structure varied, but the critical role was usually that of mayordomo, or general overseer and manager. At least in some cases, and less by rule than through general consensus, the role of mayordomo was hereditary. In Campeche's cofradía of San Román, for instance, the Marcía family had traditionally held the privilege.[59] *Mayordomía* could also run the risk of dictatorship, another factor in cofradía decline; something like this appears to have operated in Santísimo Sacramento, for when the organization revived itself in 1877, it reformed its charter to demand that the president consult all notables of the group before making appointments, a sure sign of past abuses that modern-day Mexicans would instantly recognize as *dedazo,* or rule by personal fiat.[60] The larger point is that an element of individual initiative helped mold and perpetuate the lay brotherhoods, as in fact it does with many other voluntary organizations both past and present. This personal ingredient resists quantification but, in the case of nineteenth-century Mexico, usually came from clerics or prestigious community leaders.

As in other parts of Mexico, Mérida society offered one particularly grand cathedral-based cofradía for the particularly high bourgeoisie, an *archicofradía* separate from the tiny, underfunded organizations of the city's artisans and Indians.[61] By the 1850s the wealthiest and most influential of all such peninsular institutions was the archicofradía of Santísimo Sacramento, already alluded to various times in the course of this work. Santísimo Sacramento's most critical base was Mérida but included important chapters in Campeche and secondary towns throughout the peninsula. For leadership (the office of mayordomo being the highest rung), it drew from prominent political figures, such as Francisco Martínez de Arredondo and Gerónimo Castillo; elections for offices traditionally took place on the eighth day of the June feast of Corpus Christi.[62] Similarly, the archicofradía selected as its members people of wealth; it required dues of one real per month, as well as the peer approval and leisure time necessary to participate in its many activities. Even more prohibitive were the graded entrance fees that ranged from three reales for those thirty years or younger to forty reales for the over-fifty set. There was even a touch of ancestor worship to the club in that members could inscribe their dead loved ones for a whopping fifty reales, though few appear to have done so. As with many other social clubs, it was best to join early and work your way up: the system encouraged young people to enter the adult world, learn the ropes, and prepare to carry on the traditions. Eventually, member-generated pressure to include their relatives became so great that in 1862 the archicofradía made a special one-time allowance whereby each cofrade could enlist one child or relative without charge.[63]

Despite the strong orientation toward prestige of Mérida's elite society, this body, too, suffered a troubled evolution. First founded in 1749, the archicofradía fell into abeyance three times, largely due to the problems inherent in voluntary organizations. Each time, a new bishop revived it with new hopes. Finally, the 1833 revival took root; aided by the conservative political coup of the following year, the organization embarked on a long period of growth and prosperity.[64] Indeed, the archicofradía enjoyed a remarkable boom in membership over the next few decades. In 1855 it had a mere 300 members; three years later that number grew to 520. By 1865, with imperial stability throughout the peninsula, there were now 902 cofrades. Nor does it appear to have declined with the return of liberal Mexican government, since by 1874 another 178 had joined. Over time the organization gradually came to admit members of Maya background. Originally a purely Spanish organization, by 1874 it included a 2 percent minority (22 people) of Maya surname; a few people of ethnically mixed background continued to find upward mobility in this race-conscious society.[65]

Perhaps the most significant feature of Mérida's archicofradía was its elaborate structure. In addition to a support network of some twenty to thirty priests, the organization entailed a parallel hierarchy of male and female cofrades, each governed by a set of officers (*hermanos mayores, capellanes,* and *celadores*). Their intricate seventy-article constitution provided detailed guidelines for such matters as how many times the church bell should be rung for the death of a member.[66]

At the bottom, the organization had three basic and related functions.

First, it catered to the spiritual needs of its members by offering the reassurance of action and ritual, here focused around the care and maintenance of a particular religious icon. Second, it served as an insurance program for potentially costly and catastrophic situations, such as an untimely death, allowing the members to provide for burial costs well in advance of the event. Third, it provided an outlet for the yearning to demonstrate one's social status. To these ends the archicofrades participated in a wide variety of religious processions and observances, particularly centering around the feasts of Corpus Christi and Holy Week. They also enjoyed special "visible" privileges, like having the santo carried to their houses in times of illness or death. Some archicofradía members enrolled in other pious organizations as well, while prestigious brotherhoods in Campeche could attract Mérida members, and vice versa.

The processions of the archicofradía must have stirred the hearts of nineteenth-century urbanites. The hermano mayor and the celador led the way, carrying above them the standards of the organization. Next came six cofrades with their santo, the bloodied body of Christ in its glass coffin. The remainder of the cofrades, each bearing a lit candle, marched in two parallel columns behind the symbolic bier; between them walked the clergy and the town's cabildo. All the while music punctuated their steps. Of even greater importance was the context of the march itself. The cofrades' restrained, disciplined, and measured procession took place against the riotous excesses of the town masses, with their shrieks and meanderings and Maya drumbeats. Order above chaos, hierarchy over hysteria: it was not hard to see who was important in this society, and why.[67]

Mérida's various *barrios,* or suburbs (Mejorada, San Cristóbal, Santa Ana, San Sebastián, and Santiago), had their own pious organizations. Their activities varied according to the socioeconomic character of the district. The relatively poor and ethnically mixed barrio of Santiago had a sodality, organized in 1868, that was 27 percent Maya; the history of these urban Mayas, like virtually everything else associated with barrio life, remains unwritten, but they clearly found the stiff one-peso entrance fee and the one-real monthly dues an acceptable tradeoff for the status the contributions bestowed.[68]

Barrio cofradías were based more on mutuality, particularly regarding burial assistance, than on prestigious spending for its own sake. Among the more intriguing and original cofradía plans we find the Asociación Católica of San Sebastian barrio. Devised in 1861, the Asociación operated on a sliding scale: people could buy into the organization at a level of their own choosing. The organizers hoped to create a pyramid similar to those of modern fundraising, with a few wealthy donors at the top and a large number of small donors at the bottom. The lowest monthly contribution was a mere medio real; the high-end remained open, but the planners calculated ten reales as an approximate guide. The overall idea was to attract enough cofrades for a monthly budget of one thousand reales, no small ambition in those uncertain times. The main attraction for would-be participants was the cofradía's burial plan. Major donors got a sendoff that would have satisfied kings and cardinals: high mass with the ecclesiastical cabildo in attendance, an army of priests and acolytes, fifteen masses sung before the bier, music, fifty candles, and a *gran tumba* (enormous tomb). On the low-end, the deceased children of those who paid the monthly medio were stretched out on a table with four candles and a wooden cross while an assistant cura said mass. Between these extremes were eight midrange options. The *sansebastianos* had hit upon a distinctly modern urban institution that incorporated a wide variety of social classes arranged according to their ability to pay, much like the modern baseball stadium with its combination of cheap seats and opulent skyboxes.[69]

Another interlinking of secular and clerical elites was the cofradía of Izamal. Perhaps the most famous of all Yucatecan cults, it was dedicated to the Virgin Mary. The cura and ministers of Izamal oversaw many of the cult's activities, but they also secured the appointment of the local *subdelegado,* or district governmental administrator, as mayordomo.[70] The arrangement was typical of the fusion of the Yucatecan clergy with the rural polity.

Urban cofradías also extended beyond the big city into smaller towns with their own fledgling bourgeoisie. One such case was that of the Hunucmá chapter of Santísimo Sacramento. Its extant hand-written charter provides a fascinating glimpse of the ordered life of these humble townsfolk. The cofradía admitted men of good repute, their applications (strictly voluntary) to be reviewed by standing members. As their principal function the cofrades attended mass every Thursday, all of Holy Week, and on various other religious feast days. Marching in columns of two with men clad in carnation tunics and wearing medallions of Christ, the cofrades, led by their standard-bearer, the hermano mayor, worked their way through the fourteen stations of the cross during the Lenten season. Like its Mérida counterpart, the Hunucmá cofradía included a parallel structure for women. They observed the same rules as men, down to the dues and election of an hermana mayor. However, their ceremonial tunics where black with white muslin trim, yet with the same medallions and yellow chains. Men and women apparently functioned in parallel structure, not as aggregates.[71]

Perhaps the most salient feature of the hermanos' charter is the degree to which the cofradía structured their lives. First, the organization placed them in a series of graded offices beginning with a presidency reserved for the cura or other local priest; after him came the hermano mayor, the secretary, the treasurer, the fiscal auditors, and their assistants. Second, the charter provided an elaborate guideline for payments: eight reales and a candle at admittance and twelve more annually—small enough to accommodate Hunucmá's well-to-do creoles but sufficient to keep out the rabble (Maya or otherwise). Third, cofrades prepared elaborate instructions for dealing with the illness, death, and perpetual commemoration of members, down to a refined system of bell strokes, the exact number of which corresponded to the status of the cofrade in question.[72] In sum, the minute twenty-eight-article charter satisfied a dual need for status and structure that lent meaning to life in the otherwise uneventful crossroads of Hunucmá. Santísimo Sacramento of Campeche was even more obsessive in its detailed procedure for carrying the consecrated host in processions or to the home of an ailing member, with instructions for who rang the church's various bells and how many times, who walked alongside the priest in his coach, who would hold the mule's rein and with which hand, and which musical instruments were to accompany the cofrades' stylized gestures.[73]

Somewhat farther down the social chain, the humble artisans of the cities and towns found expression for their religious and social sentiments in analogous organizations known as *gremios*. Little documentation of their activities survives, but it does appear that they functioned as smaller versions of the great archicofradías. By 1840 Mérida had ten registered gremios, for silversmiths, carpenters, saddle-makers, blacksmiths (by far the largest, with forty-one members), barbers, cobblers, sculptors and painters, tinsmiths, tanners, and shoemakers. These organizations included both Maya and Spanish members.[74] Mérida's *gremio de barberos* (barber's guild), founded in 1870, was clearly the reconstitution of such earlier associations. This organization dedicated itself to the veneration of Cristo de las Ampollas, or the Blistered Christ, a famous Yucatecan statue that had survived the fire in Ichmul many years before (the same fire commemorated in Rodríguez y Cantón's almanac) and that had been taken to Mérida as one of the more popular bourgeois religious icons. But the gremio's other function was as a kind of insurance policy: members paid a weekly medio real, with the funds divided between care of the santo and mutual aid for the contributors in times of sickness or death. The group admitted women as well as nonbarbers to its fold.[75] Apropos to a workingman's outfit, the cult's activities demanded far less time than the grander and more bourgeois archicofradías. There was also a merchant's gremio, although nothing is known about it, other than the fact that it, too, was dedicated to the Blistered Christ.[76] Southeast Mexican society was older and more organic than the mining societies emerging to the north, and its artisans, still autonomous, continued to rely on these essentially medieval forms of support for such needs as burial assistance.[77]

It is impossible to close on the subject of pious organizations without exploring the powerful attraction these bodies held for women. Indeed, concealed within the aggregate numbers of the urban cofradías we find a pronounced tendency toward feminization. The archicofradía of Mérida began as a predominantly male organization, but women gradually became the numerical majority. By 1865 female cofrades outnumbered male by nearly three to two. Urban piety remained very much a stronghold of women's roles.[78] An even more striking example was the cofradía of the Most Holy Virgin of Mount Carmel, founded in Temax in 1819 by Padre Manuel Pacheco. The organization began with 41 men and 195 women, hardly a model of gender parity. When reactivated in 1868, it contained only 5 men, and these dropped out altogether in the next ten years. By the 1870s the Temax cofradía was a strictly female organization dedicated to the most feminine of santos, with its own *patrona* and a hierarchy of female officers.[79] The same pattern holds true for Campeche's well-documented cofradía of Our Lady of Carmen, a large organization with one hundred women for every man; for that city's Archicofradía de Nuestra Señora de la Merced; and for the cofradía of the Sacred Heart of Mary.[80] Put simply, the cofradías were feminine gathering places.

Why was this? The answer touches on the complex relationship between feminine roles and the church in Hispanic society. From the very beginning the Catholic Church had found a strong constituency among females. Indeed, one of the distinct advantages of the church was that it offered a role for women, both Spanish and Maya. In Europe, the female pietistic tradition was already deeply entrenched by 1492. Spanish Catholic culture exalted motherhood, virginity, and the cults of Mary and other virgin saints—the opposite of the contempt and abuse rained on women deemed prostitutes. Given the limitations this could impose on male-female relationships, many women found a ready-made social world in the cultured and sexually unthreatening company of priests. Then as now, church-sponsored organizations provided a social structure that got women out of the house and allowed them to exercise creativity and leadership. Denied political power, women found an alternative in the moral and spiritual world. This combination was not unique to Yucatán, but it was no less important for its commonness.

Similarly, Maya women of the pueblos were indoctrinated at an early age into the ways of devotion. Take for example the Virgin cult of Izamal, where the priests organized processions of "upwards of four hundred Indian girls, clad in plain white cotton dresses, each carrying a lighted candle . . . In this the procession carried a figure of the Virgin, surrounded by all the symbols of the church upon a stage preceded by music, and heralded with occasional displays of fire-works."[81] Such behavior paralleled family life: from childhood females learned to be subordinate to men. Begun early and continually reinforced throughout childhood and adolescence, these sorts of roles became second nature by adulthood. Village men, by contrast, learned a form of *machismo,* including an ostensible impiety that enabled them to meet the challenges of life's evils: fighting the devil's fire with a fire of their own.[82] Even today, the reader will find few places with more pervasive *macho* attitudes than the rural village, where women provide the basis for family stability.

One common role available to the woman was that of the *beata,* the lay holy person. The beatas ranged from great to small; in its most common sense, the term simply referred to women of frequent and devout church attendance.[83] We know of no Yucatecan Rose of Lima, but certainly there were smaller versions of the same. Apolinar García y García lampooned the role in his 1861 essay "Las beatas," playing sardonically on their frequent confessions and their tendency to live in the church: "He would be spiritual indeed who would suggest that these women could go fifteen minutes without sinning."[84] While numbers have certainly diminished in the present day, the woman as locus of religious piety has by no means disappeared. They form the preponderance of modern church attendance and gremio maintenance, and the concern wives and mothers have about the pervasive alcoholism of rural life provides one of the main attractions of evangelical Protestantism, with its emphasis on abstinence, profound spiritual reform, and family responsibility.[85]

Women who developed close ties with the church also found that it opened economic opportunities. Urban women, particularly widows, had an important role as entrepreneurs, and their warm relations with the clergy permitted special access to one of the society's main sources of business information and loan capital. Raymundo Pérez's many loans to women are only one example of this. The most immediate evidence for church activities as the context of female economic activity comes from the notary papers of the times. Priests and bourgeois women appear to have crossed paths in numerous ways.

Priests made women the beneficiaries of their wills, particularly those caring for maiden sisters, cousins, or nieces. At times they also made them executors. These same wills, as well as numerous other documents, recorded the transactions between the priesthood and their female associates; peninsular priests customarily listed outstanding loans owed to them at the time of their deaths. Finally, in their own wills Yucatecan women tended to imitate priests in the habit of pardoning peon debts and bequeathing gifts to longtime servants, practices relatively uncommon in the testaments of creole men. All of the tendencies sketched above argue that female-clerical relations had economic as well as spiritual ramifications. The incentives of priestly company thus combined with early indoctrination, domestic responsibilities, and the quest for a fulfilling social niche to make urban women the Yucatecan cofrades *par excellence*.

For wealthy urban women, ostentatious piety provided the opportunity to shine, something into which they threw themselves without restraint. There are no better examples of big-spending feminine piety than the ongoing feud between two wealthy widows of Campeche, Josefa del Valle and María Josefa de la Fuente y Sarmiento. With their houses situated on opposing street corners, in the early 1800s the two began a competition as to who could erect the most lavish public altar on Corpus Christi, thereby making her house a key stopping point for processions. The rivalry became so rancorous that Bishop Estévez had to force the women to alternate the privilege each year. This rule in no way ended the feud, since each of the two rivals now had two years to concentrate on outspending the other. At last it looked as though Del Valle had triumphed, but De la Fuente secretly ordered the construction of a massive silver altar from Mexico City, something so extravagant that there was simply no topping it. She kept the whole affair hidden until the morning of Corpus. The citizens of Campeche awoke to discover that Del Valle's pretensions had been crushed once and for all, and the humiliated loser was forced to withdraw from future competition.[86] As the story suggests, urban piety was a high-stakes game that often had little to do with humility or charity and that held out grand prizes—but with terrible risks in the balance.

What one does not find here, or finds only rarely, is gender inversion. In early modern Europe, jokes, plays, drawings, and pageants that reversed male-female roles served as a way of momentarily calling attention to, and thereby questioning, the social order.[87] But at least in this particular subset of Hispanic culture, there appears to have been little tradition of Carnivalesque cross-dressing, women pretending to be men, and so forth. No doubt stereotypes of domineering wives and weak husbands did exist in popular lore, and certainly both rural and urban fiestas allowed women to be more sexually forward than on other occasions. One obscure case of gender reversal took place during the 1858 Carnival in Ixil, when the town's drunken magistrate got into a brawl. He happened to be dressed as a *mestiza* woman at the time, complete with *hipil* and petticoat (*piik* or *fustán*).[88] Nevertheless, public displays of explicit gender inversion failed to register significantly in what writings survive of the time, and if there were other cases of women on the symbolic top, I have failed to find them.[89] Hispanic culture seems to have been more thorough than many of its European counterparts in channeling feminine energies into religious activities and paternalistic family arrangements.

Urban feminine piety found its apotheosis in the nunnery. Mérida's only such institution, the Convent of Our Lady of Consolation, dates from 1596; according to legend, it began when a brokenhearted young noblewoman chose to withdraw from the world after her fiancé, the provincial governor's son, drowned in a shipwreck. Endowed through a multitude of gifts, legacies, and the dowries of the women themselves, the *concepcionistas,* as they came to be called, devoted themselves to educating young women in literature and the domestic arts. Maya peasants doubtless had no idea of these lofty goals, but they nevertheless subsidized the nunnery through a special tax known as the *holpatán.*[90]

Like other convents, the concepcionista establishment offered some distinct advantages to its residents. The nunnery provided an alternative life for women who had lost husbands or fiancés, who bore the stigma of unmarried pregnancy, or who simply sought a life more fulfilling and demanding than that of provincial daughter or housewife. The conceptionistas also constituted the only educational facility for women anywhere on the peninsula. Most important of all, the convent created a world for women only, and the nuns and novices apparently devoted much time and attention to the elaborate hierarchy that governed their cloistered lives, from the all-powerful abbess to the lowly *esclavas* (slaves), the first-year novices. Nor was life necessarily the hair shirt described in regulation manuals, since the nuns lived fairly comfortable lives with meals, servants, agreeable dormitories, and meaningful activities.

However, by the mid–nineteenth century this institution, too, was suffering a decline. Membership had peaked in 1762 with sixty-one members; by 1795 that number had fallen to forty-three, with a mere twenty remaining by the time of the convent's exclaustration in 1867.[91] The concepcionistas managed to evade their exclaustration several times: first after the original 1859 de-

cree went unheeded, then after the French occupation postponed Juárez's renewed 1863 initiative. It is clear, however, that for local women the institution
had an importance that far exceeded the monetary value of its capellanías. In
a last-ditch effort to avert exclaustration, some three hundred Mérida women,
including influential matrons such as Pilar Quijano de Barbachano (widow
of the late Governor Miguel Barbachano) and Catalina Machado (owner of
hacienda San Antonio Xocneceh, described in Chapter 5) sent a petition to
governor Manuel Cepeda Peraza in 1867. In some ways the document revealed
the limits of the new liberal ideology. Even if not *religiosas* themselves, and
increasingly disinclined to follow the rigorous path of the cloister, the women
saw the convent as a cornerstone to their own formation—many being former
students—and in turn to the health and well-being of elite urban society,
which they assumed to be synonymous with Mexico itself. The Liberal Party's
nationalist victory notwithstanding, the women's sympathies lay with the only
church institution that was of, by, and for women.[92]

Fiestas of the Cities and Towns

The impulse for public manifestations of piety inevitably brought urban *haute
couture* into contact with its cousin, the world of popular observance. Cofradías and gremios may have spoken of order, discipline, and hierarchy, but they
did so out of the whirlwind of the fiesta.[93] The details and even the larger
contours of Yucatán's fiestas and markets of the early decades remain poorly
understood. Given the paucity of documentary evidence, it seems probable
that we can only assemble a full picture from later, perhaps contemporary,
information. However, it is still possible to venture some observations.

The term *fiesta* normally suggests the Indian village, the closed corporate
community that redistributes its food and wealth in an event that reaffirms
some sort of collective consciousness.[94] But the fiestas described in this section
have a somewhat different nature. Regardless of origins, most involved significant planning and participation by urban elites. Maya peasants also came,
drank, and made merry, and the pueblo fiestas enjoyed the kind of ethnic and
historical layering found elsewhere in Mexican life. But by the 1840s the fiestas had a strong bourgeois component. They appear to have operated along
the principal of limited integration, with people of all races and social class
mixing at most parts (particularly at bullfights, street dances, and other open-
air functions), while elites contented themselves with reserving only selected
portions, such as a dance or private mixer, for themselves alone.[95] However,

the elements most visible in the written record—virtually the only such elements—come from creole planners and promoters, and for that reason I have chosen to analyze them under the rubric of urban piety.

Thus far we know little of the Yucatecan fiesta's colonial past. Some, like the cult of Izamal's Virgin, had been evolving for centuries. But not all fiestas had an ancient vintage. In 1824, for example, we find the ayuntamiento of Oxkutzcab applying to congress for the right to establish an annual fair of March 3–12, in commemoration of Mexican liberty. At the beginning of the nineteenth century, the easing of old colonial restrictions and the growth of the commercial economy stimulated fiesta activity. People traveled more, competition arose among towns, and there were more of the atomic particles of merriment—aguardiente, barbecue, bulls, and skyrockets—to give local fiestas a strong regional appeal.

The greatest of all peninsular fiestas was Mérida's Carnival. Like its cousin Mardi Gras, Carnival took place on the last week before Ash Wednesday, inaugurating the forty days of Lent (*cuaresma*), in which Catholics renounced certain luxuries, increased church attendance, and prepared generally for the Resurrection. The custom was declining in Mexico City and Chihuahua as a result of the Bourbon emphasis on order, but it remained stronger than ever in nineteenth-century Yucatán.[96] For the three days of Carnival the prohibited became the permitted, and boisterous behavior was the norm. The ayuntamiento tried unsuccessfully to reign in such behavior, sending out decrees against throwing "oranges, eggs, and any sort of noxious paints," limiting the celebrations to 9:00 P.M. ("el toque de las oraciones de la noche"), and outlawing the use of costumes and disguises that might offend local sensibilities.[97] For the most part these were decrees in the wind. Carnival rowdiness continued even during times of hardship, such as the cholera epidemic of the 1830s.[98] By 1845 the egg-throwing custom was momentarily on the wane, but people still liked to toss hollowed-out fruit skins filled with water, the equivalent of modern-day water balloons. Even today, the custom of *día de la batalla* (battle day) prevails on the Tuesday before Ash Wednesday, and the careless pedestrian is likely to be hit with a piece of refuse thrown straight from the nineteenth century.

As elsewhere in the Latin world, part of the appeal of Carnival lay in its momentary obliteration of social class. The leveling was most apparent to elites, who were hypersensitized to the distance their privileges normally accorded them. As one highly privileged participant wrote, "In those days we realize the fantastic illusion, the beautiful impossibility of living as republicans, with distinctions or classes which birth, education, blood, and the differences of social profession and money disappearing once and for all and as though by magic, because all enjoy themselves and all do so in the same way." Meridanos took to the streets by the thousands. There were musicians, bells, and shouting. At night, citizens could take their choice between dances, masked balls, or the ever-popular lottery. The final spectacle was a huge *piñata* ceremony on the following Sunday that marked the beginning of Lent.[99]

Some idea of how meridanos thought of the event comes from "A Scene of the Carnival." In this O. Henry–like vignette by Gerónimo Castillo, Felipe and Leonor are a storybook couple—young, beautiful, prosperous—who gradually lose touch with one another. Felipe begins an amorous flirtation with a captivating masked woman during Carnival season. Hoping to consummate the growing passion, he unmasks his intended lover, only to discover that she is none other than Leonor herself. Like the foolish young couple of "A Scene," carousers who attended Carnival could expect the incredible.[100]

But Mérida's inauguration of Lent was only one of many celebrations that punctuated urban daily life. Another well-documented fiesta was that of San Román, in 1851 and 1852. An ancient and multiethnic barrio of Campeche, San Román celebrated "the divine effigy of the Most Holy Christ" during the two weeks of September 14–26.[101] Clothes made the pious, and it was therefore critical to appear in the height of peninsular fashion. In 1851 women wore dresses of blue muslin with two embroidered ruffles. The ladies wrapped themselves in blue-and-white crepe shawls, while accessories of ribbon and white scarves completed the ensemble. For men, white frock coats were strictly out that year; the well-dressed *galán* preferred a multicolored alpaca jacket, vest, and gray denim or nankeen trousers. As the newspapers proudly noted, his black hat, with its broad ribbon and rakishly curled brim, followed "in the style of Louis Napoleon," at that moment the toast of bourgeois Europe.[102] The less affluent milled around in humbler outfits.

Beside signature clothing stood the matter of ceremonial order. There was hardly any point in organizing such affairs if they did not allow their directors to enact their visions of the world. One illustration of this point comes from the fiesta of San Román, one of the oldest in the peninsula. The annual celebration had diverse origins, but its most important inspiration was the statue of a black Christ (blackened by fire) popularly regarded as a patron of sailors.[103] During the annual fiesta of San Román, a different corporate body had charge of the Christ statue for each of the thirteen days. In chronological order, they were: the cofradía; *capitanes de indígenas* (leaders of

Maya units that served in the Yucatecan army during the Caste War); ship-builders; carpenters; tailors and seamstresses; farmers; cobblers, barbers, and butchers; "*imposición de D. Bartolo Barreyro*"; sailors; silversmiths, tinsmiths, and blacksmiths; "the ladies"; priests and cantors; and finally, employees of the maritime customs house.[104] The link between this rank ordering and the larger contours of social power was clear enough: the cofrades, together with the priests and customs officials, formed the bookends of the notables, with tradesmen, women, and Mayas shelved in between. San Román also cele-brated the Sacred Heart of Jesus and the Conception of Mary on Decem-ber 14, but despite the public procession this appears to have been a sec-ondary fiesta that failed to elicit the elaborate preparations of September's event.[105]

Processions provided one of the cornerstones of both urban and rural cele-brations. The yearning for these affairs ran deep, particularly during the Holy Week celebrations that marked the end of Lent: in 1848 when in Washington, D.C., lobbying for the annexation of Yucatán, Justo Sierra O'Reilly lamented having to pass Good Friday in a land where not even the Catholics took to the streets.[106] Campeche enjoyed one of the most prestigious of processions, based around a mammoth (supposedly fifteen hundred kilograms) mahogany sarcophagus that was created in 1728 out of the estate of a wealthy noble-woman, Margarita Guerra; the sarcophagus, known locally as the *urna,* can be seen today in Campeche's cathedral.[107]

Similar dynamics were to be found in smaller towns as well. José de los Aves Zetina's detailed account of Holy Week in Hecelchakán reveals a non-stop series of religious rituals, with parish priests traveling back and forth between the cabecera and its outlying *auxiliares* of Tinum and Tenabo sing-ing masses, preaching, blessing palms, leading novenas and processions, and reading from the Passion of Christ. Hecelchakán itself enjoyed the services of an orchestra, which performed between masses, while Tenabo's procession for Holy Saturday evening involved no fewer than five hundred candles.[108]

As with San Román's gremios, order in processions was paramount. The religious parades of Mérida enacted many of the old colonial values by assign-ing roles of dominance and servitude to the various participants. First came subservient Maya adults with long horns of tin and brass, followed by Maya boys drumming on the hollow logs knows as *tuunkules.* Next were official cus-todians of the cult and intermediaries with the divine—the priests—chanting and waving incense. Behind them walked a second body of Maya attendants playing drums and fifes and carrying a Virgin decorated with ornaments and flowers. The procession was "supported," just as the government itself was supported, by a company with fixed bayonets. The cult was a priesthood surrounded by Indian adherents, with a latent threat of coercion.[109]

One of the best descriptions of the rowdy popular behavior associated with processions comes from José María Oliver de Casares's remarkable *Noticia histórica* (1878–1880), an unpublished history of the Campeche chapter of Santísimo Sacramento.[110] Paraphrasing from a now-lost earlier memoir of that same organization, Oliver de Casares reported that at the beginning of the nineteenth century the processions still incorporated a great deal of public humor, role reversals, and social satire. Processions of Corpus Christi featured *gigantones,* the giant two-man costumes commonly associated with the Carnival of Veracruz; one of these, a man with two faces, was said to represent "the heretic Ecolampadio" (Johann Hausschein, 1482–1531, a Swiss theologian and partisan of Zwingli), "because when dealing with Catholics he led them to think he was Catholic, and if he spoke with Protestants, he acted like one of them."[111] The processions also included Maya tuunkul dancers and *sacatanes,* the latter of which has thus far resisted identification. However, the real stars of the show were the *diabletes* (devils), the virtually naked men who painted themselves from head to toe in black and yellow paint, wore horns, and carried large whips. These pranced their way through the parade, gyrating, leering, leaping, pouncing, and dealing out whiplashes to anyone who failed to remove his hat or who appeared insufficiently reverent, "so that they served as the policemen of the procession." This unusual turnaround of devil as policeman kept faith with a medieval Carnival pattern in which beggars ruled and rulers begged; by inverting social roles it called attention to, and satirically questioned, the pecking order of life in this late-colonial port city. Moreover, it also kept faith with existing folklore, which at times portrayed devils as the enforcers of social norms.

What exactly were these fiestas: religious? secular? hybrid? restrained? bacchanalian? Though ostensibly religious in nature, there is evidence of growing secular and even commercial trends.[112] The first indication of this was the tendency toward state regulation. The transition from the late Hapsburg to the early national Mexico involved many changes, but chief among them was an increasing state authority that superceded both local autonomy and religious custom. Oliver de Casares reported that for over two centuries the Campeche church, much like its counterpart in Mexico City, had tried to suppress these popular displays, but that civil authorities had always backed down in the face of public displeasure.[113] In the 1800s, however, official attitudes began to change. The gigantones finally disappeared in 1812, when independence-related squabbling virtually extinguished the cofradías that sponsored the parades; the diabletes pranced no more after 1827, and the Maya dancers departed two years thereafter.[114]

Or take once more the case of the Oxkutzcab fiesta established to commemorate Mexican independence. The Yucatecan congress imposed conditions that revealed growing state regulation. First, the local authorities were to maintain order and tranquility. Second, those selling cattle were to provide documents identifying both themselves and their animals, a check on Yucatán's ongoing cattle-theft problem. Third, "prohibited games" were not to be permitted, "being so harmful." Finally, the city government was to sell licenses for lots traditionally used for concession booths and apply the money for its municipal funds.[115] Ayuntamiento-licensed booths continued to be a source of sales tax receipts throughout the century.[116] Collectively, these stipulations portray a society in which new state builders were gradually rationalizing behavior in the countryside, trimming away at spontaneity and popular initiative and replacing them with guidelines intended to further state authority and local elite dominance.

A second clue to the increasingly bourgeois nature of fiestas was the rise of newspaper advertising to promote them. In the 1850s and 1860s it became increasingly common to place ads in the papers of Mérida and Campeche in an effort to lure travelers out to places like Espita and Ticul. (Some fiesta promoters distributed printed circulars, but no samples of these have survived.[117]) Such advertising worked not only for fiestas of pueblos but also for those of the larger cities themselves. The language of these advertisements merits attention insofar as it offers some hint of what people found desirable. Izamal, perhaps the best known and most popular of the out-of-town fiestas, made it clear that visitors could find lodging in the palatial house of local patriarch and attorney Pilar Canto Sosaya, directly adjacent to the plaza; any creature comfort of Mérida was available there.[118] A coach service (*diligencia*) whisked people from the capital in a reasonably comfortable six hours.[119] Not everyone could compete with affluent Izamal, but in some cases this served as an advantage. Tiny Cacalchén, for example, admitted that it could not provide the luxuries of its rivals; but *cacalcheños* managed to sell themselves on sincerity and down-home simplicity, much as small towns in the modern-day United States attract urban tourists through their nostalgic representation of a bygone America.[120]

Once at their destinations, travelers could expect a range of emotional experiences. On the devotional side, strict religious observations formed a nucleus to which the rest supposedly served as decoration. The watchword for this component was "solemn," (*solemne*); it implied a connection with something deep and eternal, a religious reorientation with the spiritual universe. Celebrants found their greatest solemnity during the *bajada,* or the removal of the santo from his place on the church wall, and during the all-important mass, conducted with the santo placed conspicuously before the altar. Hence, as part of its appeal, Izamal could promise that "the functions of the church will be very solemn. . . ."[121] Clearly, however, the language of solemnity concealed another dimension. Even in the ultrareligious fiesta of Izamal, the young folk of Yucatán's smart set threw decorum to the wind and indulged in frank flirting and sexual suggestion under the town's porticos. "Days of innocent pleasure, of love, of friendship, and of memories!" wrote one of the participants who, like some fifty thousand others, flocked to the holy city once a year.[122] A poem from an 1877 Izamal Carnival captured this same amorous ambience: "Epifanía Rodríguez is a beautiful creature/ A fresh flower that sways on the breezes of pleasure."[123]

The advertisements seldom spoke of shopping—because they didn't have to. Everyone knew that the *ferias,* particularly the larger ones, hosted vibrant folk markets, which Mexicans know as *tianguis.* Small vendors packed the plazas with their booths, amid which shoppers and animals alike wandered freely. Travelers to Izamal, for example, found "the palm fronds, mattresses, napkins, girdles, and bedspreads of the country," along with whistles, pin boxes, knickknacks, pottery, and a lively trade in votive candles. People short on cash could go to any of the innumerable pawnshops.[124] With or without money, people came prepared to shop.

Another item in the standard fiesta package was the *baile de mestizas.* Like the other features described here, the *baile,* or dance, has remained common in modern-day affairs. The dancers dressed in country finery: for the men, collarless white *filipina* shirts and straw hats, and for the women, embroidered *ternos* (an ensemble of embroidered huipil dresses and frilly underskirts), jewelry, and well-tressed hair. The stout heels of the white shoes known by their Maya name of *xanab k'eewel* were used for their percussive effect on the wooden platforms, much as cloggers use their shoes. It was common practice to hold the dance on or near the opening night, with a repeat performance the following morning. Concurrently the towns held *bailes serios* or *de etiqueta*—that is to say, more like balls in which all interested couples could take part.[125]

There was still one thing that nearly everyone offered: bulls, and plenty of them. Few activities had a more transcendent appeal for urbanites and peasants alike. People in Mérida knew that a bullfight was coming when four horsemen, their mounts jingling with rattles and bells, rode through town announcing the grand moment. Mobs of people then descended on the plaza; the empresarios sold seats whose qualities varied according to cost. The inconveniences of these often haphazardly organized spectacles failed to deter diehard fans like Manuel Barbachano:

> I confess that upon returning to my house, I am inclined to agree with foreigners who call the bullfight the barbarous entertainment of foreigners; but scarcely do I hear the *cascabeles* of the horses, the uproar of the people who run to the plaza, and the *voladores* [skyrockets] who announce that the moment has now arrived, and I forget the barbarism of the sport, the dangers of the stands, the boredom of the standard-bearers, the monotony of the function, the heat, the pushing and the crushing of feet, and I do what the foreigners do in such moments . . . I head for the bulls.[126]

The sentiment was universal. An ad for Mejorada's festivities thus spoke for the whole society when it observed that "there is nothing that animates a fiesta like *los toros,* except when they are animals of generally bad reputation." [127] "Most ferocious and well-proven bulls," promised Cansahcab, village of fair maidens.[128] In Tekanto, "The bulls are choice and the bullfighters the best in the region." [129] Ticuleños promised "bulls selected so as to leave nothing wanting." [130] The sport had other economic angles as well, since raising fighting bulls was highly profitable, while a percentage of the revenue accrued to the municipal funds.[131] It is clear that whatever their spiritual motives for attendance, fiesta-goers expected the sport of old Spain. Caste War refugees took the sport with them to non-Hispanic regions like Belize, and even the rebels of Chan Santa Cruz held bullfights, spiced up with drunken benders and the execution of prisoners, to celebrate successful raids.[132]

Finally, by the 1850s and 1860s there was the growing presence of fiesta entrepreneurs. We find several hints to this trend. Humble Cacalchén could still describe itself as the work of "the vecinos," but elsewhere specialization and hierarchy were setting in.[133] Peto, for example, had three prominent local creoles as *encargados.*[134] The same was true of Halachó, to take only one of many such mentions.[135] No evidence survives as to how these individuals were chosen, although most likely the alcalde or ayuntamiento selected respected and responsible men from among the creole elite. Others, however, explicitly identified themselves as empresarios; such was the case with barrios Santiago and Mejorada in 1864.[136] Doubtless this was the result of growing social complexity, of the problems inherent in managing mass demand. It is also true that these pressures had been building for some time; the search for the spontaneous fiesta, like the quest for pristine primitives, is probably a hopeless cause. However, what does remain clear is that the fiestas of Mérida and even of smaller rural towns had a significant strata of elite planning.

Meanwhile, a great deal of secular fiesta behavior broke from the bonds of piety and self-restraint. Like virtually everything else in this world, including politics and rebellion, public religiosity found its path lubricated by alcohol. Urban sophisticates had wine; the masses had their aguardiente. But in one way or another, drinking was part of the gaiety. Along the Sierra Alta, the markets had become major affairs. The *tiendas provisionales* that accompanied them became favorite tax items, as, for example, in the proposed municipal taxes of 1813, when towns such as Tekax, Oxkutzcab, and Dzitbalché planned to levy a two-real licensing fee. Several of these stores were designated explicitly as liquor stores, thus making the tax consonant with a long colonial pattern of taxing alcoholic beverages. Even the backwater Bacalar had *tendejones* where aguardiente was sold cheap and fast. In the annual fiesta of Corpus Christi in Dzitbalché, drunken disorder displaced religion altogether; with the parishioners on a rampage, there was nothing for the minister to do but sit knitting, while the cura dreamed of confining future observances to the interior of the church.[137]

The towns also contained other vices that prospered at fiesta time. Gambling was among the most pronounced of these, and it clearly emerged from a broader culture of betting and gaming that was prevalent even on average workdays. One of the more frequently repeated orders of the early national period was the decree to close up "prohibited games." [138] In fact, prosecutions for this same offense routinely crop up in Yucatán's nineteenth-century judicial archives.[139] Cards and dice were a mainstay of country entertainment, no less intense for the small stakes involved; more than one game ended like the blowup in Chichimilá in 1844, with Julián Fernández and the village priest in a fistfight over four reales lost in what began as a friendly roll of the bones.[140] Or, as John Lloyd Stephens found in Xul, "Everybody gambled, particularly in that village; they had no money, but they gambled corn and tobacco. . . ." [141] By 1823 billiard parlors were common in Mérida; the ayuntamiento struggled valiantly to eliminate roulette wheels, "more harmful than the other games because of the advantage which the house enjoys over the other players."[142] All of these activities intensified during fiesta time, when more people and more money circulated.

The largest and best organized of games was unquestionably the lottery. This venerable institution had enjoyed a great deal of promotion at the viceregal level during the Bourbon era; Mexican national governments, including the Juárez administration, continued to use lotteries as a way of coaxing funds out of a stagnant economy, while Mexico's lottery graphics became an art genre in and of themselves.[143] The southeast of Mexico was no exception, for during fiestas in larger cities like Mérida, the drawing houses represented one of the main attractions:

> In the lottery house, which is the general receptacle of all class of people, some silently attend to their cards, others eat and drink, others entertain themselves with sweet conversation, others shout, others bang on the table and all sweat by the ocean, because in such houses there are always more people than fit, and more heat than the human body can resist.[144]

The author of these lines, *costumbrista* writer Manuel Barbachano, knew what he was talking about, since his own brother, governor Miguel Barbachano, served as bonder for lottery contractors.[145] Operations had begun in 1844, with the original contract stipulating fifty *sorteos* (drawings) per year, with 2 percent of the revenues accruing to the state. By 1870 the number of yearly drawings had increased to three hundred, with special sorteos for events such as Carnival; the increasing volume of business allowed the state to lower its cut to 1 percent.[146]

For all the piety and decorum of an ostensibly religious feast day, games legal and otherwise abounded in other towns as well, a standard part of public gaiety.[147] Some idea of their importance comes from the case of Santa Ana, the northern barrio of old Mérida. The barrio's fiesta, dedicated to Our Lady of the Remedies, came to be one of the most popular by the mid–nineteenth century. However, the Caste War–related military governments of the early 1850s imposed strict prohibitions on the bullfights, lotteries, and card games, which, as its organizers noted, "attracted residents of surrounding villages in search of pastimes and recreation." As a result, Santa Ana's fiesta dwindled to virtual extinction, forcing barrio residents to demand an easing of restrictions. Gaming mattered, so much so that it continued beyond the grave. During wakes, Yucatecan exiles living in Belize in the 1860s were known to prop up their dead loved ones at the card table to enjoy one last hand with old friends.[148]

The huge and heterogeneous complex that was urban piety—the literature, the cofradías, the semipious and often impious public celebrations—formed a critical part of Mexican popular culture throughout the pre-Porfirian decades. It answered many needs, including those for social prestige, release of tensions, social opportunities, shopping, travel, sexual adventure, primitive insurance policies, and the need for an intellectual framework to govern human life. Urban piety also included important roles for women, roles that, like much of these cultural folkways, have not disappeared but simply changed form. Urban piety survived in part because it had integrated itself with popular fiestas and secular—even shocking—behavior. True, the state was emerging in part to regulate the expanding amount of travel and popular celebration. But the state was still embryonic, while the most critical transition, elite disengagement from popular culture—what Peter Burke described as "the withdrawal of the upper classes" during early modern Europe and what William Beezley identified as the key to understanding Porfirian cultural change—had yet to happen, or had made only partial headway.[149] With or without the gigantones, the classes and the masses could still find each other on a Mérida street corner on the day of Carnival. It is also important to note that piety remained an important part of popular culture despite the rise of nineteenth-century liberalism. This movement is normally seen as having its strongest support in the provinces, which resented the rule of the *capitalinos*—Juárez of Oaxaca, Ocampo of Michoacán—but in fact, liberalism coexisted with an older popular piety, as the case of Yucatán so decisively demonstrates.

Their hybrid nature makes it tricky to pin a definitive label on cultural manifestations like the early national fiestas. They gave evidence of increasing elite organization and bourgeois preference but still included the pandemonium of an earlier popular sentiment. Nor is it a simple matter to pick apart the sacred from the secular. Terms like "sacred" and "secular" present a false duality here. Or, at the very least, the division is the product of a modern age in which it has become virtually impossible to think the sacred. Early-nineteenth-century Mexicans assumed that being devout meant, at least for a large part of the time, feeling happy. If not, what was it good for? People came to fiestas for the same reason that they celebrated José María Flores's balloon flight over the city of Mérida in 1845; both were moments of transcendence, an "aerostatic journey" over the mundane, to borrow the words of Flores's anonymous reporter.[150] In all probability the sacred and secular had changing relationships: identical at some points, coexistent at others, opposed at still others. It is hard not to see a joyous worldliness in the pious traditions of old Mexico.

Later Urban Piety

A preliminary glance at the archicofradías, gremios, fiestas, novenas, and pious literature of Porfirian and postrevolutionary Yucatán suggests continuity, not radical change. The henequen boom of the late nineteenth century may have transformed urban life through tramways, water lines, electricity, and prisons, but it in no way eliminated a persistent past of lay brotherhoods and public religiosity.[151] On the contrary: although the peninsula had its anticlerical activists, Porfirian elites took their cue from the dictator and found it both expedient and reassuring to leave this facet of Mexico's traditional culture intact. Too much change all at once could lead to personal and perhaps even political conflict. Consequently, all of the early national period's hallmarks continued to play important roles in the later lives of meridanos and campechanos.

In the 1870s, then, bodies like the archicofradía of Mérida gave little hint of a tradition in decline. Beyond Santísimo Sacramento, Mérida now had some twenty other sodalities that had been active for at least a decade, some for far longer.[152] We also find several other such organizations forming in the early Porfirian years: cofradías dedicated to the Blessed Souls of Purgatory (1880), the Cord of San Francisco (1882), Our Lady of Carmen (1883), and Our Lady of Mercies (1883). There was, however, a modulation of tone. The two decades that followed the overthrow of the French Empire witnessed strong anticlerical sentiments on the part of peninsular liberals, at times forcing the lay churchmen into a lower profile and a more accommodating approach. At least in the case of these four, therefore, lay religious organizations imposed far lighter obligations upon members than had their historical counterparts. All economic contributions were to be voluntary, as was participation in special prayer sessions. San Francisco and Carmen merely involved wearing pious articles of clothing (a cord and a scapular, respectively), and not necessarily in a way visible to the public eye; in fact, their charters stressed that even these minimal obligations were mere custom, not an ironclad rule.[153] Like Raymundo Pérez in Hoctún, the lay organizations survived by learning to demand less.

Church archives document a similar high level of activity in Campeche-based associations in Porfirian times.[154] The brotherhood mentioned so often in this chapter, Santísimo Sacramento, was only one example of post-1876 cofradía revival. As before, these institutions provided security, fellowship, entertainment, and status for their members. They learned to circumvent liberal rules against corporate wealth by relying strictly on membership contributions, usually an *asiento,* or entrance fee, followed by periodic dues, *jornales.* This had been one form of cofradía maintenance prior to the reform, but by default it came to be universal practice thereafter. Levels of affluence defy generalization, but in some cases, at least, the revived organizations were clearly dealing in high numbers. By 1883 the cofradía del Señor of barrio San Román had a yearly income of over 1,400 pesos, most of which went toward church remodeling; operating with good kitchen economy, they scrupulously carried over remainders from year to year.[155] Our Lady of the Rosary, whose records survive for the somewhat earlier years 1860–1879, also shows generous surpluses of as much as 350 pesos annually, while the long-lived Our Lady of Carmen registered steady increases in revenue from 1873 onward.[156] A common denominator of these revived organizations is that they aimed primarily at piety and less at mutuality. This reflected the fact that with Porfirian economic growth the urban middle and upper-middle classes could see to themselves, while the financially debilitated church could not. We know virtually nothing of the contemporary *asociaciones de caridad,* or charitable associations, except that they existed; nor have I been able to unearth records of working-class gremios for the same period.[157]

As always, the secondary towns were not far behind the lead of their larger counterparts. Porfirian-era brotherhoods also sprung up in places such as Conkal and Temax, and presumably in other undocumented locations.[158] In the deep south, Peto continued to divide the responsibility for its period of Forty Hours' Devotion among the town's four principal gremios: artisans, merchants, farmers, and señoras.[159] These organizations apparently assumed far greater importance in community religious life than they had enjoyed in pre–Caste War days, when they fail even to register in the historical record of that earlier period.

The public fiestas of these small towns also survived relatively unchanged into the late Porfirian era. Their popular and religiously based celebrations persisted despite the implementation of the Liberal reform from 1859 onward. Places such as Izamal, Tekax, Ticul, Tizimín, and Valladolid held celebrations that drew crowds from large distances, as did smaller fairs in less prominent towns.[160] The devoted still gathered, the pious still read piously. With the

Liberal reform's new restrictions, the church now more than ever advanced its interests through clubs and associations of faithful laity. The Sociedad Católica de Mérida, closely linked with an umbrella organization founded in Mexico City in 1868, experienced significant growth in the 1870s.[161] Gremios based on trade, gender, or social status became more important than ever; the list included such categories as barbers, carpenters, students, señoras, and many others. The most durable of the lay organizations, *Acción Católica,* maintains a strong peninsular presence today, while the Secular Franciscans, far less prominent in historical literature, also enjoy an important role.[162] The very concept of the lay organization in fact formed an integral part of the evolving Catholic worldview in the late nineteenth century, a view that opposed both secular radicalism and individualistic capitalism in equal measure, in favor of a more organic society whose paternalistic leadership mediated between classes, genders, ethnicities, interest groups, and any other imaginable human divisions.[163]

The pious bourgeoisie lived on; what changed, however, was the world around them. Gradually Yucatán's elite society founded alternate avenues of civic association. From 1850 onward, for example, it was possible to join confraternities that promoted libraries and public instruction.[164] At the same time, private balls, or *tertulias,* allowed some degree of elite disengagement, while public celebrations like Carnival went through the wringer of Porfirian regimentation, acquiring *juntas directivas* and social clubs akin to the krewes of New Orleans' Mardi Gras.[165]

Devotional literature and lay confraternities still exist in this deeply conservative province. And yet they have fallen from their privileged, almost monopolistic position. Why? Certainly the Revolution of 1910 moderated the church's social influence, even if that point remains poorly understood in the context of Mexico's regions. Despite its failed attempt to replace the Catholic Church, the Revolution probably did contribute to making the average Mexican's Catholicism more nominal. However, one has to wonder if perhaps the real blow came with entertainment such as television, motion pictures, and the mass-marketed music industry. In modern times it takes a visit from the Pope himself to generate the kind of attendance common to Hollywood's summer blockbusters.[166] Finally, demographic changes played an important hand, since middle- and upper-class exodus to the suburbs spelled the virtual end of the archicofradía and its barrio counterparts. The affluent of today have other ways of advertising their good fortune, whether it be the cellular phone, the BMW, membership in the exclusive Club Campestre, or a trip to the Holy Land or Medjugorje. Their consumption is less quotidian and more costly. Perhaps the most accurate conclusion we can draw on the urban cofradías and processions is that they went from near monopolies of religion, prestige, and entertainment to competing structures in a world of electricity and motor travel, and finally to underfunded organizations of the poor and elderly struggling to survive in the materialist consumer culture that flourishes in many parts of modern-day Mexico.

Visual folklore, #1: The burro tuunich, *or stone donkey. It once carried children to a watery doom, but when its sorcerer-master was killed, it changed into the petrified curiosity found today in a field outside of Sudzal. Formerly erect, the burro tuunich now lies face down, head to the right. Photograph by author.*

Visual folklore, #2: Satan's hoofprint, in Tabi. The fiend had disguised himself as a horse to steal souls; when thwarted, he jumped into the cenote, leaving this reminder that spiritual dangers are real. Photograph by author, index finger courtesy of a local lad.

Few measured up to "the distinguished qualities of the late señor Dr. Don Raymundo Pérez," as one contemporary put it. Pastor, theologian, counselor, and one of the richest men in southeast Mexico, Pérez epitomized the high-end of religious culture but still maintained ties to the popular. From CAIHY, Retratos y biografía de yucatecos ilustres. *Photograph by Neil Rivas Vivas.*

The parish of San Miguel Hoctún went on without Raymundo Pérez; the main church is seen here on a lazy Sunday afternoon in the present day. Photograph by author.

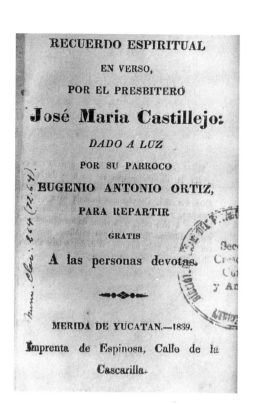

RECUERDO ESPIRITUAL

EN VERSO,

POR EL PRESBITERO

José Maria Castillejo:

DADO A LUZ

POR SU PARROCO

EUGENIO ANTONIO ORTIZ,

PARA REPARTIR

GRATIS

A las personas devotas.

MERIDA DE YUCATAN.—1839.

Imprenta de Espinosa, Calle de la Cascarilla.

Above: *Sample of popular pious literature. The first of these, "Recuerdo espiritual," was published in Mérida during the years of Conservative rule. From* CAIHY, Impresos, *III, 7, 1838. Photograph by Neil Rivas Vivas.*

Right: *"Crucified Christ, have mercy on us." Woodcut from an 1840 tract of popular piety entitled "Oración mental." From* CAIHY, Impresos, *III, 10. Photograph by Neil Rivas Vivas.*

Jesucristo crucifica-
do, tened misericordia
de nosotros.

The urna, *a three-thousand-pound artwork of silver and mahogany commissioned by doña Margarita Guerra in 1728, was a pinnacle of urban piety. It epitomized popular reverence for icons as well as the importance of women in the religious life of the age. Today the urna can be seen in the cathedral of Campeche.*
Photograph by José D. Beytia Arceo.

A tale of two communities: prosperous Sotuta, the parish cabecera *and the center of local political administration . . . and backward Tabi, a largely Maya village. Divided by class, ethnic composition, and locality, the two nevertheless shared rights to the Virgin of Tabi. Photographs by author.*

This portrait of San Antonio de Padua, formerly of hacienda San Antonio Xocneceh, was a key religious icon for the southern Sierra Alta region. Once taken by Caste War leader Jacinto Pat, the portrait hangs today in the church of Oxkutzcab. Photograph by author.

". . . we were shown San Antonio Xocnequej, the hacienda whose temple, as large as that of a regular town, is independent of the parish church and is a landmark of the estate to which it belongs." Like so many artifacts of the hacienda system, the chapel of Xocneceh now lies in ruins. Photograph by author.

Fr. Pepin de Misionero.

A sardonic view of the clergy by Yucatecan artist Gabriel Gahona ("Picheta"). Pepín ("Little Joe") the Missionary rides on the backs of Maya porters. From the 1847 journal D. Bullebulle. *Photograph courtesy of Michel Antochiw.*

Popular anticlericalism continued into the later nineteenth century, as seen in this illustration by Claudio Meex (Eduardo Urzaiz Rodríguez). "The wise bishop Don Crecencio Carrillo y Ancona was deeply concerned about the good behavior of his parish priests, especially those who occupied positions in the interior of the state. Having received various complaints regarding a certain Spanish priest, he requested a confidential opinion from General Don Teodocio Canto, who owned an hacienda close to the village where the pastor had his ministry. 'Well,' said the general, 'he's an even-tempered fellow: he gambles, falls in love, drinks heavily, and parties with us whenever the opportunity arises. . . . But even so, no matter how drunk he may be, at four in the morning he's in his church saying mass.'" From Reconstrucción de hechos: Anécdotas yucatecas illustradas, *Ediciones de la Universidad Autónoma de Yucatán, 1992. Courtesy of the Universidad Autónoma de Yucatán.*

Modesto Méndez, corregidor and all-around wise man of the Petén. He epitomized local values but also remained loyal to Mérida's religious polity. From CAIHY, Anales de la Sociedad de Geografía e Historia de Guatemala, XVI, (March 1940), 167. *Photograph by Neil Rivas Vivas.*

Popular piety outlived the protagonists of the Petén's 1858–1859 struggle over ecclesiastical authority; here, a religious procession in early twentieth-century Flores. From CAIHY, Anales de la Sociedad de Geografía e Historia de Guatemala XV, (September 1938), 46. *Photograph by Neil Rivas Vivas.*

CHAPTER
4

Spiritual Power, Worldly Possession

A History of Imágenes

I F MYSTERIOUS CROSSES were common in Campeche, then what happened in the countryside, where literacy and the influence of elite institutions were far weaker? Perhaps the most famous episode in Yucatán's religious history was the cult of the Speaking Cross. After the momentum of the Caste War began to turn against them in the spring of 1848, rebel Maya retreated to the forests of Quintana Roo; there they adopted a type of military theocracy in which the generals transmitted their commands through the voice of a speaking cross. Originally it spoke to its people by means of a ventriloquist. In later times the cross operated only through select scribes or prophets, or was believed to be hidden in trees, or even multiplied into several crosses in different villages. The cross cult functioned as a revitalization movement for the rebels, a ritual organization that strengthened resistance by demanding absolute and militant loyalty.[1]

The cross cult did not spring to life on its own. Rather, it enjoyed a long precedent involving both Spanish and Maya cultures. While the h-men, or shaman, remained important for country people, an equally important basis for religious authority was possession of an *imagen:* a religious icon, literally an image of a sacred figure such as a saint, the Virgin Mary, the cross, or Jesus. (A closely associated term, *santo,* could refer either to the spiritual being or to his iconic representation; while technically applied only to the Catholic saints, in popular usage *santo* also includes Jesus, Mary, and the cross.) Certain individuals enjoyed special religious privileges by controlling access to imágenes. This did not necessarily make them religious specialists; whatever their social advantages they continued to stand within the community and not above it. Nevertheless, possession of an important imagen did lend a degree of prestige and privilege not available to members of the general community, including the right to oversee the imagen's wealth. Indeed, few aspects of popular religious piety mattered more than icons. This was a time and place where many — not only Maya peasants — believed that statues of Jesus and the saints rose up at night and walked the land. Such beliefs in no way prevented the faithful from working as rational political actors, but it did throw certain peculiar hues over their way of seeing themselves and their world, particularly in matters that touched upon the sacred forces that conditioned human affairs.

The Roots of Iconography

Icons had an ancient history in both Maya and Spanish cultures. A complete review of pre-Columbian iconography would far exceed the scope of this chapter. Suffice it to say here that the Maya had always had iconic cults that extended from individualized worship of milpa gods to official state religions. In both classic and postclassic eras, state power was linked with deification of the nobility; the enormous monuments, or *stellae,* of these warrior princes shows them treading on their fallen enemies and communing with ancestors through the practice of ritualized bloodletting.[2] No visitor to places such as Chichén Itzá, Uxmal, or Chichanná fails to come away without a vivid sense of the cults of the rain god Cháak and the feathered serpent Kukul Kaan, maintained through strong elite power and, presumably, some degree of shared belief on the part of the masses. After the collapse of centralized power, religious orientation devolved to the local and household levels, where small statues continued to channel the spiritual energies of the faithful. Great or small, however, pre-Columbian icons carried a great psychological power because, like the village and the better-defined components of folk knowledge, they stood forth from the confusion and perpetual change of the monte.

The Spanish brought with them their own system of sacred beings — Jesus, the saints, the various manifestations of the Virgin Mary — each with his or her own conventions of representation. As it spread from Rome outward, the Catholic Church used both icons and holy relics to capture the imaginations of intended converts.[3] At various points in church history, some theologians objected that these devices threatened to become more important than the divine person of Jesus and the fundamental teachings of Christianity. Throughout its first fifteen centuries the church had wrestled with the issue of the power of icons, a contentious quarrel that ultimately contributed to the Roman/Orthodox schism of 1054, with Orthodox Catholics adhering to the view of icons as transcendent bridges to the spiritual kingdom.[4] Throughout the Middle Ages the Catholic prelates officially downplayed santos, but the mindset of a poor and mostly peasant Europe, always a mishmash of ancient local beliefs and official doctrine, kept the santos as popular as ever.

The convergence of the European and pre-Columbian iconographic traditions formed a cornerstone of Latin American folk Catholicism. In Yucatán as in other parts of Mexico, villages were assigned a patron saint (the *aj bolon pixan*) who took a special interest in community well-being and with whom the villagers observed a relationship of reciprocity quite similar to their relationship with the older gods. (Nineteenth- and twentieth-century towns continued the practice: the port of Progreso, for example, adopted San Telmo, "patron of navigators."[5] Even military barracks had their own santos, complete with special cofradías.[6]) As innumerable authors have pointed out, the imágenes themselves always had a syncretic identity, either because of certain points of similarity or because the Indians and friars both actively sought out and adapted the santos for their own purposes.[7] The manner of revering the santos fluctuated between European and Maya, a fact that did not necessarily imply rejection of Christianity on the part of the Indians themselves. Moreover, religion here mirrored basic political economy: the intermediary role of such miracle workers as San Baltasar and Santa Teresa paralleled that of the priests, officials, and native elites who brokered between indigenous communities and the greater outside powers.[8] The flexibility of the santo system allowed for a religion sufficiently orthodox for the priests but at least minimally responsive and satisfying to their native parishioners.

In the case of Yucatán, and probably throughout most of rural Mexico, part of the imágenes' appeal lay in their obtainability. Much of church regalia, objects such as relics, vestments, host presses, and religious officials and doctrine themselves, remained centrally allocated and controlled. Holy oils (*santos óleos*) were so restricted that only designated messengers carried them from Mérida to places as far away as Petén, Guatemala.[9] Religious sodalities, often dedicated to the care and adoration of a particular imagen, jealously guarded their treasures. In extremely rare cases, the object was kept locked away in the chapels of Europe; Izamal's chapter of the Third Order (the secular Franciscans) preened itself on the Rome chapter's possession of a small quantity of blood that had flowed from Christ's rib and that bubbled each year during its feast day.[10] But this level of elite control was hard to come by, for if the church wrote the cantos, it was usually people who carved the santos. The classic Yucatecan cross—two boards mounted on a pedestal and painted dark green—was the most accessible of all, given the simplicity of its construction. But even with more complex items, local craftsmen produced effigies of popular saints from the wood of the countryside, the preferred raw materials being soft Yucatecan cedar or imported cork.[11] For example, when Padre José María Domínguez of Ichmul decided to refurbish the altar at Uaymax, he hired sculptor Pio Bautista to redo the saints.[12] There were, of course, the exceptions: Bishop Guerra replaced the destroyed Virgin of Izamal in 1846 with a replica imported from special craftsmen in Guatemala.[13] But this was atypical and involved a distinctly urban Spanish cult.

At the same time, attitudes toward the imagen's physical integrity were inconsistent. Some clearly regarded the material construction of the imagen as an index of legitimacy. Take, for example, the case of the patron saint of Nolo, Our Lord of the Transfiguration. When the cura began what he intended as a minor repainting, he discovered that insects had plowed through its cork body. Fearing the effect that this news might have on parishioners, he commissioned a secret reconstruction "in order not to jeopardize the faith that they have in that Señor."[14] Even when the priest had the best intentions at heart, it was necessary to tread cautiously with a village santo's physical construction. The people of Tetiz approved when the cura arranged to refurbish their famous Virgin but became belligerent when the work led to aesthetic changes (reducing the base, moving her arms farther from her dress) that they considered an unwarranted tampering with the santo's very essence.[15] Quite to the contrary, however, the makeover of San Buenaventura of Sinanché was an open, well-publicized, and harmonious affair. When the santo's arm fell off one day, the parish mobilized with a collection drive. The reconstruction, repainting, and revarnishing does not seem to have shaken anyone's faith here, and San Buenaventura's reinauguration began with a mass and procession attended by parishioners of all ethnicities.[16] With santos as with just about everything else in popular culture, religious or otherwise: *no hay reglas fijas*— there are no fixed rules.

Not all imágenes were created equal. Maya peasants clearly favored certain figures over others, a point documented in both surviving records and modern fieldwork. The cross enjoyed enormous cachet for the simplicity of its design and construction, its overwhelming importance in Christian symbolism, and perhaps for certain indirect associations with pre-Hispanic cosmology. The standard Yucatecan cross was and is olive green, with standard motifs of the crucifixion, motifs known as the *atributos,* or attributes; these included Jesus' cloak, the Roman soldiers' dice, the tools of torture, and the rooster crowing at dawn. As William Christian pointed out in his study of sixteenth-century Spain, "generalist" santos, those with broad powers and purviews, tend to displace their specialist counterparts, since the faithful can credit them with a wider range of miracles, cures, and benevolent intercessions.[17] Doubtless this had much to do with the cross's ongoing influence. However, certain specialist santos retained powerful reputations. Among the people of the eastern Yuca-tán, the Three Wise Men of Tizimín, whose selection and ongoing appeal as aj bolon pixan probably related to the town's organization around the three cenotes of *boox ch'e'en* (black well), *siis ch'e'en* (cold well), and *jok ch'e'en* (fishing well), promised spiritual protection and guidance.[18] San Antonio remained enormously popular for his ability to bring sweethearts together and because rural cultivators considered his feast day, June 13, to be the last possible day for rains and hence the last hope for successful plantings. His ascendancy also owed to the fact that Franciscans had heavily promoted his cult for several centuries. Key santos also included San Diego, prominent in Tekax; and San Isidro, the patron of agriculture, whose own feast day of May 15 coincided ap-proximately with the spring rains.[19] Standard iconography represents San Isi-dro as a farmer wandering the monte with his satchel, his staff, and his faithful pup. San Isidro's association with agriculture made him a likely hero through-out Mexico, a fact evidenced by his appearance in the folklore of Veracruz, among other places.[20]

In the nineteenth century, Mary does not appear to have been the all-important patroness suggested by the modern-day devotion to the Virgin of Guadalupe or other Marian manifestations.[21] There were exceptions, however. The most famous, the Virgin of Izamal, began with a statue that the Francis-can missionary Diego de Landa commissioned from a prominent Guatemalan sculptor and whose cult he then imposed in a location anciently devoted to the sky god Itzamná.[22] Her fame supposedly took root when a devout Spanish woman used pieces of paper that had wrapped the Virgin in her packing crate to cure a Maya servant who had fallen off the roof. More wonders followed; among other things, the Virgin healed the lame, relieved constipation, rescued sailors from storms, and restored tongues cut out by pirates.[23] Certainly the

Virgin achieved her greatest fame in connection with colonial Yucatán's many plagues, for beginning in 1648 meridanos began the practice of bringing her to the provincial capitol to fight off smallpox, cholera, and other epidemics.[24] These plague-related processions continued in the early nineteenth century. The cult entered a profound decline when fire destroyed the original Virgin in the early 1840s, but it survived the crisis and continued into the twentieth century.[25] The nineteenth-century history of other peninsular Marian cults, such as those of the Virgin of Tabi (discussed below), the Virgin of Tetiz, the Virgin of Tekax, the Madre Santísima of Campeche, or the Candelaria Virgin of Tibolón, have thus far received little attention.[26] However, they clearly enjoyed prominent reputations in the nineteenth century; in 1855, for example, army deserters from the Caste War were able to make a living selling stolen candles to pilgrims outside the church at Tetiz.[27]

Iconography may have been a part of the pre-Conquest religious complex, but the Spanish nevertheless introduced certain key changes that contributed to the later santo cults. First, they imposed their own iconography upon Maya beliefs. If nothing else, the experience of persecution, terror, and torture under Landa and the Franciscans taught the Maya that it was impossible to speak openly of pre-Columbian deities. Through forced acculturation the Maya adapted their own religious system into the vocabulary and representation provided by the conquerors. The roles of the four cháaks thus fell to various saints, while the idea of an overarching and omnipotent god remained a matter of lesser certainty and importance.[28] The Maya also made unusual adaptations of the Spanish devil. Whereas Satan was presented to them as a Manichaean entity, an evil force precisely because it opposed the Spanish social order and its ideological structure, the Maya transferred the devil identity to numerous other spirits who opposed the violation of traditional norms. The most conspicuous of these was Juan del Monte; as the owner of forest lands, this spirit permitted a reasonable degree of exploitation. But if an individual took too much, other Maya assumed that he had exchanged his soul for this privilege and that Juan del Monte would extract a price, usually a gruesome death or some Elizabethan reversal of fortune. At other times, the devil figure had striking associations with Spanish-imposed labor discipline. It was popularly believed, for example, that the devil, in the form of a little boy wearing only a hat, turned the wheels of the sugar mill at night.[29] But as seen in the folktales, the devil was not always entirely bad, and, if properly approached, might help out the poor milpero with a tidbit of information. In fact, virtually all santos had an ambivalent streak, and surviving folktales often touch on their pride, stubbornness, or lack of judgment.[30] As Margaret Park Redfield observed in her analysis of rural Mexican folklore, "*santos* by their very nature are entitled, it appears, to a certain freedom of behavior."[31]

Second, the Spanish codified the rules of private property. The pre-Conquest Mayas, to be certain, had practiced some degree of private ownership; here as elsewhere, the old reading of peasants as primitive socialists looks increasingly dubious.[32] The Maya nobility had enjoyed private land and riches. But under Spanish domination the rules began to tighten. The Spanish recodified the domain of private property, simultaneously introducing a system of written and notarized record that took the power of sanction from indigenous communities and placed it in the hands of state officials. Spanish law sanctioned female as well as male property rights. The Spanish replaced primitive barter and cacao beans with money, a universal medium for exchange of property. Finally, the new laws of private property came to apply to virtually all material objects—food, livestock, clothing, and so forth—as well as to land. Certain factors limited accumulation of private property among the rural Mayas; they were simply poorer, and their wealth had always been grounded in family and household, a point reflected in the nineteenth-century Mayas' practice of partible inheritance, while the intense suspicions and jealousies of village life provided a certain minimal control over the decisions and activities of more prosperous villagers.[33] Nevertheless, the Spanish-imposed vision of private property did penetrate to a considerable degree into the daily lives of the Mayas.

These tendencies converged in an obscure dimension of rural political economy: icon wealth, the possession of crucifixes, rosaries, altar tableaus, and the all-important imágenes. Icons such as santos were more than mere church decoration. Rather, they lived in a peculiar world between spiritual essence and worldly property, one that has no ready correlate in the minds of secular moderns. Faith in the literal powers and personal identity of the object bridged Maya and Spanish culture, particularly among the poor. At the same time, however, they were material possessions that Yucatecans bought, sold, traded, stole, borrowed, and bequeathed. In the wills of the state's notarial archives, these icons and religious decorations rank as one of the more frequently mentioned forms of property, along with land, houses, debts, livestock, and moveable goods.[34] These items typically passed from generation to generation. Sometimes they provided careful individual descriptions, as in the case of Nasario Encalada's gold-decorated statue of Jesus,[35] or Padre Jacobo Machado's nativity scene,[36] or the extensive list of icons and religious writings indexed among the estate of the deceased Padre Julian Acevedo,[37] or the pearl rosary that Rita Mugártegui of Opichen willed to her servant Juliana Tuyú.[38] At other times the reference was generic, as with the "sacred ornaments and vessels" of Gregorio Domínguez, cura of Kopomá.[39] Hacienda inventories, too, sometimes included detailed lists of imagen possessions. In some cases this consisted of no more than a handful of crucifixes and santos. But more developed properties, such as San Antonio Xocneceh near Yotholim (see Chapter 5), used built-in chapels and oratories as an attraction to the labor force, duplicating the amenities of town life. The hacienda San Antonio outside Kopomá had an equally elaborate oratory complete with "six reliquaries of the various saints." [40]

Mayas also passed on their icons as family heirlooms. One of the more intriguing notarial documents in this respect is the will of Gregorio May, the batab of Umán, who, condemned to death for purported complicity in the Caste War uprising, bequeathed his santos of Christ and San Antonio, together with instructions for their care and veneration, to his four daughters. The icons had come to him in similar manner from his grandfather Juan de Dios May.[41] The imágenes of Santiago Pacab, batab of barrio Santiago, passed first to his widow, Marcela Cen, then, since the couple was without issue, to her cousin Feliciana Cen.[42] All available evidence suggests that the practice had come to be universal: legally documented among Maya elites but carried on without documentational formality by the rural masses, as some of the cases described below illustrate.

The sum of these dynamics was simple: the Mayas lost possession of their old idols — or at least the more visible ones — but over the course of the colonial era, various peasants acquired new and in some ways better ones. Even poor peasants now had legally permissible santos that they passed from generation to generation. The net effect was to encourage small local cults under the control of individual Maya peasants of both sexes.[43] Imágenes were half-property in a world where things communal were gradually losing out to things owned. As such, they drew people as a common meeting ground, but that very ambiguity carried the potential for making them points of contention.

Icon wealth incorporated diverse concepts and reflected the hybrid nature of Yucatán's economy and society. The icon was a form of wealth partly akin to money in deriving value from its substance, the arbitrarily valuable metals of silver and gold. Icons were also at times stolen, just like other forms of valuable property; we find at least one report of this, when certain santos disappeared from the church of Chablekal in 1845.[44] However, like jewelry (*alha-*

jas), the icon derived its value in no small measure from the shape it took, from the added value of specific silverwork, gem cutting, and so forth, refinements that lacked the easily quantified value of monetary sums. As such, the imagen embodied the work of skilled artisans still operating on a craft basis. While drawing in prestige, like the ostentatious wealth of the landed estate, it also enjoyed a religious and symbolic power those other forms of wealth could never possess.

At the same time, the imagen's ability to function according to the rules of money or the hard dictates of land was circumscribed by the social rights and obligations invested in it. Owners occasionally sold access to their santos, but they also found themselves under long-understood restrictions that recall precapitalist restrictions on land usage. In difficult times (drought, epidemics, and so forth) the proprietors of imágenes had no choice but to lend the services of their santo for the benefit of the community, just as in times of economic hardship the tributary overlord or the wealthy peasant was to redistribute some of his reserves back into the community. The imagen was at once owned and not owned, a remnant and mirror of the colonial order of tribute. It possessed much of the motivating power of money but only part of its autonomy. Most importantly, it provided an outlet for the innumerable personal problems and anxieties that beset the human race and provided important glimmers of transcendence in lives that were often monotonous and mundane.

Community imágenes usually came with what we might call "validating stories," which proved that the santo had somehow chosen the church or chapel as its place of residence. Validating stories normally boil down to one of two versions, each revolving around attempts to move the santo to a new location. In the first, the locals discover that the santo has made himself so heavy that they can't budge him an inch. In the second, the locals do relocate the santo without difficulties, but the imagen continues to return, by its own mysterious power, to its original home. The story typically ends with a familiar trope: "So they knew that this is where he wanted to stay." [45] Parsons reported a similar Zapotec tale in the 1930s. [46] People understood that santos had a certain orneriness that defied control, and through this construct the rural folk interpreted ownership, whether by a community or an individual, as the santo's own choice.

In other instances the rise of certain imágenes at times related to apparitions, fleeting and subjective glimpses of spiritual beings that served to confirm faith or resolve crisis. Belief in the reality of apparitions kept people on their spiritual toes by allowing laymen to feel that they were taking part in the lookout for important messages. Apparitions form a familiar part of popular Catholicism in Europe, Latin America, and elsewhere; in Mexico, the most important has been the apocryphal story of Juan Diego and the Virgin of Guadalupe, but there are dozens of small cases that occur in Mexico each year, episodes much like the kindling crosses and the numerous if unspecified precursors to which Padre Solís alluded in his investigation. Apparitions have the advantage of bypassing hierarchies and experts as they connect individuals directly with vast and benevolent spiritual forces. The right to see them has always been an unwritten tenet of Catholicism. They function as safety valves for individual and perhaps even collective energies in otherwise hierarchical religious and political structures. (Similarly, evangelicals receive divine revelations, while modern seculars look to miracle technology or extraterrestrial visitations.) Loosely associated with personal dilemmas or pressing social conditions, they may lead to solitary veneration of an imagen, perhaps in a small altar in the corner of the house, but when the circumstances are right they can blossom into full-fledged cults. As with the messages received during spirit possession in the syncretized African religions of the Caribbean and Brazil, the apparition often imparts a message that the witness wants to hear. Sometimes the message is one of hope and inspiration, at other times a prophecy of impending doom or judgment, at still other times an implied warning, such as the voice of tortured souls in purgatory calling for water. In all of these variations, however, the larger message is positive, since apocalyptic versions emphasize that the wicked (who usually happen to be the powerful) are about to be brought down, while all confirm the existence of superhuman agency. The appeal of apparitions was illustrated in July 1997 when the Universidad Autónoma de Yucatán hosted an international congress on the Caste War. The event received a great deal of coverage in the local newspapers, but in terms of galvanizing popular attention it failed to compete with a sighting of the Virgin Mary on the wall of a home in one of Mérida's poorest barrios.[47] The residents of the city's down-and-out south end clearly had a motive for miracle that was lacking among university researchers.

At the same time, the popular ferment sparked by religious wonders could easily get out of hand, particularly when times were bad. Apparitions, prophets, and healers promise a better way for mankind, but in so doing they indirectly condemn the way things are. Some of Europe's greatest apparitions—including Lourdes, Fatima, and Medjugorje—happened during times of particularly acute social anxieties.[48] Mexico and Latin America have had more than their share of the same. For the poor the only hope often lies in the miraculous, which they in turn know and speak through the vocabulary of religion. Chiapas, for example, has the Tzeltal revolt of 1719;[49] in late-nineteenth-century Chihuahua, devotion inspired by the healings of young Teresa Urrea seemed to offer an escape from local grievances and oppressive Porfirian policies.[50] In northeastern Brazil, the Bangladesh of the western hemisphere, Padre Cicero won the allegiance of thousands in his struggle to verify certain miracles of his parish and later to establish a degree of political autonomy in the São Paulo–dominated republic.[51] This same region witnessed the rise and cataclysmic fall of the holy man Antônio Conselheiro and his separatist city, Canudos, while Antônio's southern counterpart, the wandering prophet José Maria, began a movement among the underclasses of Santa Catarina that eventually evolved in the Contestado rebellion.[52] Religious wonders could lend voice to popular discontents, class hatreds, and personal ambitions, and for that reason it is hardly surprising that authorities themselves remained leery. Churchmen were more educated than most of their parishioners, and the propensity to see wonders tended to decline among the more learned and prosperous. Moreover, popular contact with divine forces bypassed the normal church bureaucracy. Nineteenth-century prefects and prelates handled wonders with extreme caution, downplaying the small ones and co-opting or suppressing the more intractable cases.

With or without apparitions, most imágenes underwent a formal rite of sanctification that inaugurated their careers as holy objects and benefactors. As with many other rites, this was the responsibility of the priest. We find letters like that of Padre Juan de la Cruz Camal of Halachó asking that the bishop extend his license to allow him to revalidate marriages, to rehabilitate the incestuous, and to bless imágenes.[53] Such benediction, however, did not in and of itself establish the imagen's reputation as a powerful santo; rather, it required a period of time in which the santo proved himself through healing and miracles. Like the elect status of the seventeenth-century Calvinist bourgeois, a santo's holiness was reflected by the demonstrable prosperity that followed him. Lavish festivals served, in a circular sort of reasoning, as proof that a particular santo was the genuine article. And just as icons and their cults enjoyed a specific genesis, so too did they at times suffer sudden reversals. The cult of the Virgin at Izamal, which had commanded such reverence during the colonial age and was recently visited by Pope John Paul II, had lost much of its power by the early 1840s. In part this was due to demographic changes, for the greater part of the population had moved toward the southern interior, causing the numbers located in the old colonial cities to decline in the overall percentages. By March 1841, Izamal, which was a much larger religious organization than most rural parishes and required considerable overhead, was teetering on the brink of insolvency.[54] The decline related to the anticlerical Imán revolt of 1839–1840, which cut deeply into church revenues, but it also reflected the fact that Izamal's Virgin had perished in a fire. The effect of a santo's physical destruction on its worldly prestige should not be underestimated, particularly by modern observers who tend to locate spirituality in transcendent and sharply antimaterialist terms. Certainly the mayordomo of the cult had some understanding of these affairs when he wrote his own gloomy analysis:

> As Your Holiness knows, since the burning of the Virgin her funds have decayed, reduced at the present to almost 600 annual pesos, of which over 400 are invested each year in regular costs, apart from the extraordinary cost of repairing buildings and other matters which always arise . . .[55]

A santo's physical integrity and sheer good luck, no less than the economic prosperity that attended its village, affected the imagen's influence among the people.

Imágenes could also fall casualty when different factions of the creole elite quarreled. In such instances, physical control of the santos came to symbolize the legitimacy of one's political authority. One such incident took place in October 1836 in the northern coastal city of Telchac. Reeling under the effects of a drought, the cura and ayuntamiento decided to organize a novena using a special statue of San Antonio that was the private property of a certain José Ortega. With his permission they carried the santo to the church and placed it in the niche ordinarily used to house the church's Virgin Mary. On the day of the third mass, however, the Virgin's patrón, Félix de León, returned to town; finding his own particular santo dispossessed, De León carried off San Antonio to his own house. De León and Telchac's minister fell into a heated argument that almost came to blows, but the patrón refused to release the captive santo, which the vecinos had dared to place above his own special imagen.[56] In another episode of that same year, the alcalde of Nohcacab "arrested" the imagen known as Jesucristo Mankantún when it made its annual pilgrimage to rancho Chac in December. Soldiers took away the mayordomo as well, and although they released him a week later, the imagen remained in custody of a local vecino. In this case the underlying issue was priests collecting money on private ranchos, something that irritated the property owners, who tended to dominate municipal governments. Although Padre Antonio Fernández of Bolonchén could appeal to ancient custom, the impatient alcalde declared Jesucristo Mankantún to be "a vagabond" and refused to return it.[57] In both of these cases, the imagen became a lightning rod for quarrels that had mainly to do with local power.

There were other issues surrounding this problematic form of property, issues such as rights of access and usage. Did those rights belong to the cura who tended the parish? Or were the imagen's powers rooted in its place of residence and in those pilgrimages that had been established by custom and usage? The question became one of elite authority versus peasant rights. In this world most people still seemed ready to acknowledge that local custom and usage enjoyed some primacy over unrestricted property ownership. When the cura of Chicbul removed church ornaments to decorate an *hermanito* in Mérida, using the república de indígenas to oversee their transportation, the event provoked outrage from Chicbul's Maya sacristans.[58] To the mass of rural Mexicans, religion was local and concerned the immediate problems and practices of the day, not questions of theology or hierarchy.

Peasant Imagen Cults: Some Cases

Imágenes mirrored more familiar forms of wealth in other ways. Though largely the property of elites, they also found their way to a handful of peasant families and peasant entrepreneurs. Such ownership complicated role divisions within the Maya community: a h-men might possess imágenes, but so could an average, if perhaps lucky, peasant. They existed more or less hidden in family chests and household niches, emerging into the historical record only in times of scandal and controversy, and it is to these cases that we now turn.

Peasant cults dedicated to santos grew out of, or alongside of, a larger religious complex that emphasized sacrifice to the spirits of the field and the monte. This complex has already attracted an extensive literature and here requires only brief review. Maya folk religion manifested less social hierarchy than ecclesiastical cults; power in rituals depended on communal participation or communally understood actions.[59] The most important religious figure of the Maya community was the h-men, or "he who does." This figure has already been well described by Redfield, Villa Rojas, Farriss, Bartolomé, and others.[60] A classic shaman, the h-men adopted his practice not because of institutionalized selection and training but because he felt a personal calling to work in supernatural matters. Even though he served as an apprentice to an older h-men (often his father), he qualified for that training by reason of his inner orientation. He was both a part of and apart from his people. Unlike either the batab or the more-domesticated church assistants, the h-men retained a mystique of the uncanny. This figure was apparently a perpetuation of the pre-Columbian shamanic tradition of the *aj k'iin,* or tribal priest, and unlike the *maestro cantor,* or church singer, he stood outside the Christian realm. In terms of his dealings with the Maya community, he provided a fairly standard repertoire of ritual services; most of these concerned fertility rituals linked to the agricultural season, but they also included incidental care against illness and witchcraft, closely identified in the Maya understanding of things. His powers were strong, but his slightly uncanny aura could also serve to intimidate and divide villagers.[61]

It was a man's role, but there is some evidence that women also participated in a less formalized practice of magic. Modern ethnographers, particularly Redfield, left the impression that Maya religious practices fell primarily within the male sphere, while women saw to the performance of more orthodox Christian observances.[62] However, this seems a bit simplistic and at times runs counter to historical evidence. In 1815, for example, we find Hermenegilda Poot of Dzidzantún imprisoned for being an *hechicera,* or witch. Bernardo Rodríguez, assigned to investigate, reported: "I have found her to have made an implicit and explicit pact with the Devil, and that she did not know how to conclude the evil business, and I have spent two months and fourteen additional days in prison, performing the doctrina and the Mass, with a lit candle, as penitence."[63] We know nothing of Poot's alleged witchcraft. Interpretations of indigenous female magic tend to vary; perhaps, as suggested in recent work on Andean culture, Maya women were accommodating themselves to one of the few paths of social activity allowed them by the colonial regime.[64] But low-level female magic had probably been a long-standing feature not only among Mayas but among most indigenous peoples of Mexico, particularly in matters of the household and the heart. The authorities often suspected (accurately enough) that rural Indian women were dabbling in low-level sexual magic—ensorcelling wayward lovers, and so forth—but they considered these activities too trivial to prosecute.[65]

The h-men's chief ritual responsibility was the *u janli kol* (dinner of the milpa), also known as the *wajil kol* (bread of the milpa). This was the chief offering to the rain gods (cháaks) and the milpa gods (balams), made at the onset of the planting season. To discharge a promise to a saint for services rendered, the Maya held novenas, usually sponsored on an individual basis and involving communal eating and drinking. At least in their modern versions, these occasionally involve the services of the maestro cantor. However, the chief ritual ceremonies, as well as the special acts of healing and protection from witchcraft, were and are the responsibility of the h-men.[66] Prayers from such ceremonies, incidentally, borrow closely from the appositive construction of the novenarios described in Chapter 3; the h-men chants out an invocation that combines the cháaks with the figures of the cross, the Holy Trinity, Mary, and the Christian saints, celebrating their aspects and seeking their interventions in a constantly evolving series of different wordings and formulas.[67]

Another ritual, known as the *tich'*, used the same process of reciprocity for purposes of ensuring a fruitful harvest. One case of this highly elusive ceremony appears in church records from Panabá, along Yucatán's northeastern coast, in the year 1816. For reasons unknown, a mulatto woman named Tomasa Camejo had walked through a milpa partially undressed one evening, thus incurring the balam's wrath in the form of an illness. Seeking a cure, Camejo contacted a local h-men by the name of Bernardo Tsahe, who imposed the following remedy: Tsahe, Camejo, her son, and three other villagers met in the bush, where the woman offered the balam a meal of tortillas, frijoles, and balche. Unfortunately, a priest raided the ceremony, and though the h-men and his assistant were able to escape, Camejo and the others were placed under arrest. The priest reported, "I have given them 99 lashes over three successive days and did not continue since the notary happened to be absent, and because it was necessary for me to leave the village to celebrate the nativity of the Virgin."[68] Despite long familiarity with the Maya peasantry, the rural curas, perhaps by choice, seemed to have possessed little information about the details of Maya beliefs. "None of them were able to explain who this Balam was," he remarked.

Another ritual involving the h-men was the *kuuch*. "We all know of the *kuuch*," wrote gentleman ethnographer Gerónimo Castillo in 1845 regarding this most popular of folk ceremonies, his assumed familiarity unfortunately causing him to omit details. The name literally means "burden," like the cargo of the highland Maya, apparently in reference to the burden the sponsor assumed in providing food and drink for the participants. Though individual Maya did assume responsibility for financing the ritual, the culture as a whole never adopted the type of all-encompassing cargo system characteristic of Chiapas or of highland Guatemala. Certainly the practice had been in use since the conquest. The kuuch ceremony was troubling to the religious authorities, both for its excesses of drinking and its resistance to elite control. A highly decentralized religious observance, it was impossible to remove it by controlling a cult center or authority. The cura of Chancenote found kuuches particularly bothersome during the constitutional crisis, when Maya peasants shed all inhibitions in the observance of these ceremonies:

> The *kuuches* continue in the cabecera, auxiliar, ranchos and estancias, all amounting to little more than the slaughter of pigs, *pitarillas* [a kind of beer], and sales of liquor with which the Indians become drunk. And those who are not drunk have no respect for God himself, insensitively entering the church as if they were entering a den of thieves . . .[69]

Kuuch ceremonies involved borrowing the church santo and transporting him to one of the local Maya houses for the celebration. In these ceremonies the h-men interceded between god and human. The *wajil kol, ch'a'-cháak,* and other rites persisted through the duration of the colonial era and in the 170 years that followed. Despite repeated attempts, the curas were unable to put an end to the practice. Many had tried to suppress them with beatings ("nor does there seem to me to be a more effective means," one affirmed). But the knowledge that the ceremonies continued in secret remained an ongoing source of rural tension.[70]

Should rains fail to appear, the Maya resorted to a ceremony called the *ch'a'-cháak.* It involved extensive offerings to the gods as well as a communal dinner. In the case of the ch'a'-cháak, the participants used various forms of sympathetic magic to bring rain. Small children crouched around the altar imitating the frogs associated with wells and cenotes. (Urban creoles, incidentally, had their own version: in 1821, Mérida's ayuntamiento was still paying thirty pesos annually for novenas to bring rainfall.[71]) An unusually well-documented ch'a'-cháak ceremony in August 1845 in the parish of Conkal throws light on the social conditions surrounding these cults. Faced with drought conditions, a local peasant had contracted a h-men named Gregorio Matu "to come to his milpa and make the sacrifice for the purpose of bringing rain, because the corn was dying." The report by the morally indignant cura (the elderly José Gregorio del Canto) highlights some of the key features of ceremonies conducted by "false or deceiving priests" during his fifteen-year tenure in the parish:

> . . . it has not been possible to extinguish these practices. This type of sacrifice comes down to a hodgepodge in this form, namely: They take turkeys or ani-

mals which they have selected and carry them to remote parts of the milpa or the lot where the maestro is getting ready with copal and tree bark for wine. Tying up the animal or bird they cut out the tongue. They take it and fill it with the wine made of the tree bark, pitarrilla. They squeeze it by the neck and strangle it amid the smoke of the copal, which serves them for light. The minister, kneeling, says his prayers, and later the dead animal serves to make them a poorly seasoned meal, accompanied by the ceremonies which we use in the baptismal blessing . . . scattering the food in the form of the cross, and the wine and smoke in the same fashion. And with the ceremonies concluded the food is distributed according to their order; and they conclude by a dance performed with grasses to take their leave of their gods, who are the fields and the winds.[72]

Del Canto also recorded a brief, garbled version of the Maya incantation as reported to him, an incantation bearing the usual mixture of Christian and Mayan deities: "In the name of God the Father, God the Son, God the Holy Spirit, the Red Rain God [*pajajtun*], the White Rain God."[73]

The case of Conkal points toward the often conflicting social dynamics associated with religious syncretism and the survival of pre-Conquest Maya practices. On one hand, the ceremonial system had broad appeal; it gave the rural folk a sense of security and may have helped to bridge social gaps in the community. As the anonymous peasant farmer argued in his own defense, he was simply doing what he and other farmers always did when they needed rain. Even locals with such non-Maya patronymics as Aguilar and Villalobos employed Matu for the ch'a'-cháak. At the same time, however, the folk religious complex did not necessarily mitigate the feuds and factions that lurked within rural communities. Beyond the more obvious hostility of the cura, some villagers opposed Matu for more personal reasons. Authorities only learned of the affair because a local Maya woman, Petrona Chi, had decided that Matu was casting a spell over her and decided to expose him (ch'a'-cháaks are men-only affairs). If the h-men enjoyed the power to neutralize hostile spirits, he was also capable of directing those spirits to malicious acts. These hostilities—and their supernatural projection into witchcraft—survived in spite of shared folk understandings. Peasant communities remained the scene of deeply seated jealousies, feuds, and contentions whose true extent we can only begin to gather from fragmentary documentation such as this.

Del Canto's efforts notwithstanding, the quest for secret Maya practices made little impression on the written record of the nineteenth century. (I review the handful of extant cases in the course of this book.) But there can be little doubt that these innocuous field ceremonies went on everywhere in the nineteenth century; Manuel Barbachano's prewar *costumbrista* essay on provincial life mentions them as the object of humor, the harmless eccentricities of country people.[74] They are commonplace today. Many Yucatecan towns still have h-men; a good one, a seasoned practitioner with a talent for battling secret enemies, can expect to draw clients from as far away as Mérida and even Mexico City. What then of their archival absence? The lack of documentary evidence may simply mean that most rural priests preferred to keep such matters under wraps. More important, however, was the decline of the nineteenth-century church's inquisitional zeal. The nineteenth-century priesthood increasingly drew its members from lower social classes, who were less scandalized by popular wonders than their upper-class predecessors had been. Furthermore, by 1850 the Mexican Catholic Church had to focus most of its attention on economic and political survival. With the sugar boom, Mexico's ongoing political strife, the Caste War, and subsequent Liberal reform, the clergy simply had bigger things to worry about. The cases that do survive probably reflect the inflexibility of an individual cura or the degree to which a particular cult was stirring up the parishioners. But in the larger picture, the church's days as an extirpator of idols were receding into memory.[75]

To repeat, then, peasant cults only drew attention when they became too powerful and began to detract from allegiance to the local church. At that point the peasant suffered confiscation of his property. In this sense, the imagen retained social practices far more ancient than those associated with nineteenth-century landholding. These cults manifested local peasant anxieties, most of which never passed beyond the confines of the village and consequently remain unknown to history. Only when peasant cults came into conflict with the local authorities did they enter the written record. One poorly documented 1823 case in Maxcanú involved the confiscation of a statue of San Antonio from a certain Pedro May. In this instance the complaints of the Maya patrón reached as far as the state congress, resulting in a series of investigations whose results are not extant.[76] The story is unsurprising except in the degree to which May managed to take the matter.

A better-documented case concerns the San Diego cult of Sahcabchén, a small village halfway between Mérida and Campeche. Sahcabchén was a pueblo that had formed shortly before 1820 within the parish of Calkiní. This cabecera was one of the larger Maya communities and was also a place well acquainted with the ways of Hispanics, for many of the locals took part in the regular trade and travel between the peninsula's two leading cities. In this instance the popularity of unorthodox cults surfaced against a background of conflicts on the cura's nearby estate. In the last decade of Spanish rule, Hurtado had been able to expand his hacienda by absorbing adjacent properties of local peasants. As he expanded production, Padre Pedro José Hurtado drew from the local community Maya peasants for his work force. These practices sparked rancorous litigation, and although the results are unknown, the surviving documents make it clear that Hurtado operated as an *hacendado* within the confines of his own parish, that his operations there provoked the peasants, and that Hurtado enjoyed consistent support from local officials.[77]

Trouble began with the death of a certain peasant called Tun, first name unknown. To his widow and children, Tun bequeathed little in the way of real worth. But he did leave something that would prove to be the key to their fortunes: a statue of San Diego, complete with cross, crown of silver, assorted ornaments, and its own tabernacle. This figure had enjoyed a certain fame during Tun's lifetime; his widow, Catalina Pan, however, managed to develop it into the most popular cult in the region, rivaling even the parish church itself. (Despite the fact that the name of Pan's son, Dionicio Tun, appears on many of the documents, Pan herself was considered the founder of the cult.)

Success was immediate. The Pan-Tun family began as peons on the hacienda San José. Their effigy of San Diego began to make pilgrimages to local haciendas and ranchos, each time returning with a contribution to Catalina Pan and her sons. Initially the indigenous religious practices were able to co-exist with the parish church. Peasants would bring San Diego to mass, but when that was over, they whisked him off to a private house where they celebrated with music and "an abundance of aguardiente, corn, and other foods." The Pan-Tun family imposed no limits on attendance but welcomed peasants both male and female and of all ages. Their cult became so profitable that they gave up farming altogether.[78]

These practices eventually antagonized local church authorities, prompting Hurtado to confiscate the statue. Catalina Pan responded with a series of protests now lost to the historical record. She succeeded, for within a few days the cura returned San Diego to his old proprietors, apparently believing that his show of force had been sufficient. He specified, however, that in the future all religious activities of the cult were to be confined to the church "as the true house of adoration." But such warnings had little effect. As soon as Hurtado set foot outside the village, Pan relocated her activities to a remote house, where, free from clerical scrutiny, the process began all over again. But the cult's popularity made it difficult to conceal. On Friday, April 9, when the faithful peasants paid Hurtado's minister to say a mass for the santo in Nunkiní, the minister took the opportunity to caution against further ceremonies. Undeterred, Catalina Pan returned the statue to her new home for a round of drinking and folk veneration. Hurtado returned that evening; apprised of what was afoot, he raided the house, where he found "more than three hundred persons of both sexes who were gathered together with musicians, clamoring, and drunkenness." This time the crackdown was final. Hurtado confiscated the statue and placed it under lock and key at the church in Bécal. Dionicio Tun appealed directly to the bishop for return of his property, but in vain.

The scandals of Sahcabchén soon repeated themselves in Chableckal, a hamlet just north of Mérida. As with Sahcabchén, there was a history of conflict here between Maya parishioners and the cura, who in concert with the local magistrate used unpaid church taxes as the basis of a system of forced labor, of which they themselves were the chief beneficiaries.[79] The background of the peasant cult also bore similarities. Here a certain Santiago Kantún possessed a miraculous imagen of the most popular of Maya santos, Antonio de Padua. This silver-crowned statue had passed to Santiago Kantún from his mother upon her death in 1817 and was so important to local peasants that the curas of Conkal had been allowed to see it only twice. First, Santiago Kantún and his wife, who was apparently integral to the cult, told local peasants that the santo inhabited a log of *ciruela,* or figwood. This log remained perpetually and miraculously filled with a water the Kantúns sold as medicine. The cult featured evening devotionals at the Kantúns' home. Ceremonies included a rosary service and ritual drinking. As in Sahcabchén, the peasants of Chablekal realized that their cult overstepped certain official boundaries, and they took measures to conceal or disguise its true nature. When dealing with the authorities, Kantún circumspectly referred to his statue as "San Antonio de Padua," but local peasants used the name "San Antonio Abal" (San Antonio of the Ciruela) when speaking among themselves.[80]

The cult caught the attention of the local powers only when it began to attract peasants from outside the village. When a body of Mayas from Suma (fifty miles away) made a pilgrimage to the santo, the cura of Conkal, a certain Padre Quijano, decided that San Antonio of the Ciruela was threatening to become a rival religious organization—and, in fairness, the padre had a point. As in larger Mexico, the history of Yucatán had shown that wonder-workers and miraculous cults could quickly get out of hand. Some sixty years earlier a divinely inspired prophet who took the name Jacinto Canek had raised a rebellion that attracted Mayas from villages in the south-central region. Among other things, Canek ate jasmine flowers, preached the extermination of pigs, and offered a mysterious potion made of honey and squash. Conflicts between his followers and Spanish authorities resulted in over five hundred deaths.[81] Quijano suspected that a direct confrontation in this situation might result in similar violence, so he convinced Kantún to allow him to take the imagen in order to say a special mass; once he had it in his possession, he locked up the santo and refused to return it. Kantún was illiterate, but acting through a local scribe he filed a petition for restitution to the bishop. Quijano justified his action by describing the activities of the cult, and there the story of San Antonio Abal—or at least our knowledge of it—ends.[82]

The two stories provide a primer in the themes and dilemmas of peasant santo cults. Such cults did not take place within a hermetically sealed Maya culture; nor was their broader significance intended for the peasantry alone. They represented a form of religious activity in which peasants actively competed with the official church for prestige, power, and resources. This competition was possible only because of the ambiguous nature of the imágenes. The Pan and Kantún families operated their cults through rules of property ownership that had been imposed or at least modified by colonial Spanish culture. The cults also operated on a symbolic language that was to some degree shared; Maya folk practices borrowed heavily from conventional Catholicism. But shared symbolism did not always translate into an identical viewpoint, for at times the meanings and activities the church sanctioned for the imágenes failed to contain peasant energies; in fact, they opened space for resistance and social protest.[83] In part the cults appealed to peasants (and infuriated the curas) because they invoked miraculous and amorphous powers. The two imágenes discussed were associated with miracles, and in the case of San Antonio Abal, with healing.

Perhaps the most persistent subtext of the santo cults was usurpation. The peasants' interaction with the local church hierarchy advanced a subtle inversion of rural social power. The Maya-controlled cults stressed miraculous folk healing, communal drinking rituals, and village pilgrimages, all officiated by peasants themselves. The structure of religious participation muted the authoritarian style in which the priest administered sacraments and proclaimed the liturgy to an audience of passive receptors. Peasants occasionally used priests to sanctify the icons but still succeeded in keeping them at arm's distance. Given the inescapable fact of the church's presence, the Maya peasantry sought to limit their ministers' authority (to blessing images, saying masses, etcetera), and to put them under the control of the peasants themselves, who were more in tune with local needs and aspirations. Correspondingly, it reduced the priest to a mere functionary in the religious process; his role extended no further than saying an hour of mass, while the full scope of cult activities extended over whole days and nights and involved a range of unknown and unauthorized activities. Priest and peasant underwent a symbolic power inversion.

These messages of secret overthrow were not lost on the priests. Their reports betrayed an indignation regarding the santos and their cults. Quijano repeatedly charged that the Kantúns were imposters making a living purely on their mediation of a religious cult, a peasant imitation of the church that he found disconcerting. Furthermore, he always referred to the money drawn by the Kantúns as *limosnas,* a word that means "alms" but that was also applied to the church tax paid by Yucatecan peasants. Such word choice underscored the parallels between peasant and official cults. It also illustrates why church authorities could not allow peasant cults to continue: money normally destined for the church was circulating back into peasant communities.

Simultaneously, however, these case studies point to a certain predictable fragmentation within the peasantry. The two cults were not community organizations; despite egalitarian dimensions, they took place at a subcommunal level and enhanced the status and mobility of only a few. This mobility took place at the expense of traditional Maya elites like the batab and h-men, neither of whom figured in the cults.[84] This egalitarian emphasis can be seen in drinking privileges. The two cults, together with the Speaking Cross and virtually every other recorded incident of Maya folk religion, involved certain standard features of ceremony and festivity, most obviously the consumption of alcohol. The Maya may have found these colonial resistance cults more appealing than those of their pre-Hispanic predecessors, for it appears that earlier debaucheries were reserved for the nobility whereas these ceremonies drew Maya peasants by the hundreds.[85]

We also find women actively participating in both cults. In the case of Sahcabchén, Catalina Pan served as the matron of the cult, while Santiago Kantún's wife acted as partner in officiating the Chablekal cult. Peasant cults blurred gender distinctions, which had long been integral to the imposed colonial structure. Maya women derived more participation and personal empowerment in the santo cults than in either formalized Mayan practices or in extremely orthodox practices such as the cofradía. As previously noted, men tended to dominate in both instances, either as h-men in the former or as co-frades in the latter. The ability to own an imagen, however, provided women such as Catalina Pan with the conditions for both economic opportunity and community prestige. In sum, the santo cults were part of a larger dialogue between peasants and nonpeasants. Each side argued endlessly, in word or deed, over the meaning of religious symbols and rites, over who had the power to control them, and over what they meant, and for whom.

The Virgin of Tabi

Sahcabchén and Chablekal shared an almost outlaw quality. No one authorized these cults; curas closely watched the imágenes' followers. Similarly, the conjurings of a h-men, common though they were, were an idolatry carried on in secret clearings of the woods. But in other instances folk religion operated within officially sanctioned vehicles—village fiesta systems, cofradías, and other, more acceptable channels for peasant piety. This did not mean that the social conflicts had ended. Rather, tensions between peasants and rural elites were simply internalized within those channels.

One episode of intracult rivalry involved a struggle for land and power in the parish of Sotuta. Sotuta's relationship with nearby Tabi was a tale of two worlds: the former a prosperous *cabecera,* or head town, the latter a tiny and squalid hamlet. Throughout the 1820s and 1830s a cohesive local elite had helped Sotuta dominate both the economy and politics of its outlying communities. The nearest comparable town, Yaxcabá, struggled to hold its own against Sotuta in a rivalry that endured beyond the Caste War itself.[86] Sotuta's cura in particular, José Manuel Pardío, was a powerful man. He owned multiple estates, including the hacienda Kalil, two leagues to the south of Sotuta; Chacontel, two-and-a-half leagues in the direction of Cantamayec; Xmah, three leagues to the north of Sotuta; and San Francisco Tsitsilche', two leagues to the northwest. These estates alone had a combined value of over fifteen thousand pesos, making Pardío not only a prominent churchman but also one of the country's prosperous hacendados.[87] In addition to the usual complex of corn, cattle, and beehives, Pardío had also managed to take control of a sizeable salt flat named Xcan-ocon ("where the serpent sits"), near Chicxulub, along the Gulf Coast. These properties are among the best inventoried in all of Yucatán's documentary record. Pardío also owned estates as far south as Tekax, where his cattle production raised the hackles of local peasants.[88] The padre's economic success, together with his warm ties with the town's leading citizens, provide a classic example of clergy adapting themselves into the local bourgeoisie in part through the shared interest of estate ownership.

Tabi—or Bolon-Tabi, as people often called it in those days—was poor. But it held a special advantage in dealing with the pervasive Sotutan influence, for its church was the home of a Virgin that enjoyed regional popularity.[89] Tabi's role as a religious center apparently predated the coming of Christianity. Its sacred character related more to its cenote, which "had been the scene of some miracle, the particulars of which we were unable to learn," reported the traveler B. A. Norman in 1843. One miracle that eluded Norman in fact does survive in the folktale of a ranch hand who learned to ride a *wáay-tsíimin,* or phantom horse; the wáay was about to carry him into the cenote, but at the last possible moment the cowboy jumped off; in his fury, the devil left a horseshoe impression in the rock at the cenote's rim.[90] Also potent were the spiritual properties of the great mamey tree that grew nearby, issuing from what appeared to be solid rock.[91] Whatever Tabi's pre-Conquest spiritual co-ordinates, they transferred easily to the colonial religion, so the village was "held in much reverence by the Indians." The community was heavily Maya and extremely poor; aside from the chapel, which bordered the cenote, it contained not a single masonry building. The cura, a certain José de la Cámara, was kept under close scrutiny by Pardío and gave only a token presence in the village, particularly in the years leading up to the war. As early as 1843 the locals complained that his ill health was resulting in almost total church neglect, including infrequent church hours and neglect of the town's celebrated Virgin cult.[92]

Conflict erupted in 1827 over labor practices at Pardío's hacienda Nohitzá. This estate utilized workers from Tabi, but Pardío had fallen into arrears in paying their salaries. Moreover, the hacienda's expansion had raised land disputes by absorbing several banana and fruit groves the Tabi peasants believed to belong to them. Pardío insisted that if the peasants continued to work the fruit groves they would have to pay rent. When they refused, he had the local alcalde jail them. The Tabi peasants immediately responded with a protest to the bishop. They forwarded a detailed exposé of the cura's practices and for good measure threw in allegations that Pardío's religious services in Tabi were lacking.[93] After an investigation, Pardío was ordered to pay the workers, to stop harassing the locals of Tabi, and to produce all his land titles. The issue of whether or not he owned the fruit groves remained unresolved.[94]

Their initial success encouraged the Tabi peasants to keep the quarrel going. On August 12, the Tabi república (bypassing their batab, whom they considered a Sotutan operative) petitioned the bishop to put an end to the Virgin's annual pilgrimage to Sotuta. They argued that the deteriorated condition of the road was causing unusual wear and tear on the statue, that the pedestal and attached figurines of angels were falling apart, and that the sun was cracking the Virgin's painted face.[95] The Virgin of Tabi, they insisted, would travel no more. This declaration was a serious matter in a time and place where ritualized peregrination of imágenes formed an integral feature of the spiritual landscape. The physical absence of an imagen like the Virgin of Tabi, punctuated by an annual return, symbolically reenacted the underlying beliefs of Christian resurrection and the renewal of life on earth.

These tactics also struck at the heart of Sotutan self-image. Indeed, it was a grand day when the Virgin of Tabi entered Sotuta, grand in particular for the town's elites. The annual procession provided an opportunity for creole townsmen to enact their social superiority over the inhabitants of the Indian hamlet. Tabi's own festival ended on August 15, and the following day the Virgin of the Immaculate Conception made her procession to the cabecera to inaugurate festivities that would last until the first Sunday in September. The streets were specially cleaned not only in Sotuta proper but for several miles in the direction of Tabi, exactly to the midpoint of the two villages, leaving no doubt that the Virgin was passing from a land of squalor to one of culture and affluence. On the morning of the procession, the town of Sotuta was evacuated as whole families embarked to escort the Virgin to her new abode. Only the crippled and infirm remained behind along the streets and in the doorways of the church. At last the long-awaited procession wound its way into the town. Prominent in this display of piety were members of the local brotherhood, well-to-do Sotutans like José Monforte and José Florentino del Canto. Behind the Virgin herself walked the minister, upholding her sacred blue cape and singing *salves*. Branches and decorative arches graced the entire distance, and as the procession advanced, musicians played while the faithful sang, prayed, wept, and called out praises to the Holy Mother. Once safely installed in Sotuta, the Virgin presided over a two-week fiesta. The villagers enjoyed masses, novenas, food, drink, music, and fireworks. This was the transcendent moment in Sotuta's annual cycle of life, when children ate candies, old men poured another cup of aguardiente, the lame dreamt of being healed and the poor dreamt of riches, and the great men of the town conspicuously reaffirmed their own exalted position in the social order.[96]

Whatever else they may have accomplished, the Tabi peasants succeeded in getting the goat of their more powerful neighbors. In their response the

Sotutans outdid themselves in summoning the synonyms of treachery and slander. Pardío argued that the Indian's impunity from physical beatings had resulted in their practice of making all sorts of baseless accusations against the local priests. The peasant's strategy also provoked the local confraternity of lay vecinos, leading creoles who prided themselves on being the Virgin's temporary custodians. Sotuta's annual procession causing damage to the icon? "Horrendous slanders vomiting from the coryphaei of Satan, with the malignant purpose of falsifying the cult of Mary!"[97]

The Tabi case illustrates the give-and-take involved as entrepreneurs, prosperous townsfolk, and indigenous peasants worked out the tensions associated with the agrarian transformations of Mexico's nineteenth century. Tabi remained a source of tax money and labor for Sotuta, and the available evidence suggests a gradual erosion of their land base. Despite their relative weakness, the peasants still enjoyed certain rights that had evolved over long years. Complaints regarding the violation of labor and land practices found a certain sympathy within the state bureaucracy of their day. More importantly, however, the Mayas of Tabi wielded a measure of control over Sotutan creoles' chief symbol of prestige, the icon of the local Virgin cult. Any attempt to limit access to the imagen threatened the Sotuta elite in the most elemental fashion. Moreover, the church bureaucracy of Mérida, informed by paternalistic values, tended to support parishioners against the curas and ministers who were often an integral part of local polity.

As with so many other episodes of conflict in this period, we do not know the outcome, but we may surmise that town and pueblo reached some understanding, adequate if not quite amicable, for the controversy died then and there. Eight years later Pardío rose to become provisor of the cathedral and spent the remainder of his life in a series of unsuccessful intrigues to become bishop (see Chapter 7).[98] Shortly before that, he had enjoyed the last laugh over the peasants when he acquired the hacienda property that had once belonged to Tabi's cofradía, originally sold in public auction in 1831.[99] However, Tabi remained a scene of regional hostilities in later years, and the violence that erupted there in January 1847 helped provoke the Caste War.[100] But throughout the war the imagen lived up to its miraculous reputation. Contrary to popular legend, the Virgin of Tabi was not abducted by rebels or thrown into the town's cenote; rather, a village priest managed to take it to Sotuta before Tabi was overrun in 1848. It made yet another hairbreadth escape when a raiding party from Chan Santa Cruz overran the pueblo suddenly and without warning in December 1858. The cura grabbed it and ran for Sotuta, but the imagen was so heavy that he had to hide it in the woods and return for it a few days later.[101] Only in 1859 did the silver decorations and halo of the prewar Virgin finally turn up in the hands of a man living in Tixkokob.[102] The cult continued to generate quarrels over management issues and was still making the journey from Tabi to Sotuta as late as 1879, after which point I have been unable to follow its historical thread.[103]

Meanwhile, the Caste War in no way ended the power struggles that were written into imagen cults. Certainly the Speaking Cross of Chan Santa Cruz enjoyed the greatest organized support, but individual ownership of particular santos not integral to the cross cult persisted in the east and remained an important practice into the twentieth century.[104] Finally, the earlier prestige and power of the Speaking Cross was insufficient to prevent divisions in later rebel society; discontented factions broke off to form their own communities, each built around its own cross.[105] Significantly, however, the cross encountered some of the same problems that had dogged the colonial Catholic Church. For all its powers, the Speaking Cross never enjoyed an absolute monopoly on supernatural authority. Devotion tended to follow political-military allegiances, with wayward generals remaining skeptics. We know, for example, that Bonifacio Novelo, a mestizo who played a key role in fomenting the war and who eventually rose to become patrón of the cross, had earlier tried to encourage his own rival cult dedicated to the Virgin, but without success.[106] Nor was José María Barrera, the cross's presumed founder, able to bring militarily independent commanders of the south, men such as Florentino Chan, into the cult.[107] Some of these generals had their own santos, for the most part taken from plundered churches. In Mesapich, for example, General José Tiburcio Briceño maintained his own Señora de la Concepción, an imagen that was the gift of no less a person than the bishop of Yucatán, José María Guerra.[108] As late as 1869, pacífico General Eugenio Arana of Xcanhá threatened war with Petén, Guatemala, unless the authorities there returned his potent icon of Santa Rita, carried off by war-weary deserters.[109] The struggle for central versus decentralized religious power thus continued in different forms throughout the 1850s and 1860s.

There was also the matter of the cross's influence over the masses. This was clearly enormous. Individual officers wrote to Chan Santa Cruz asking for pieces of the melted wax of candles lit in the cross's honor; even these thirdhand fragments of the divinity held sway among the masses.[110] At various times the cross, or at least the strategic conditions under which it flourished, attracted anywhere from twenty-five to fifty thousand people. (Like the santo owned by the Kantúns, the spirit of the later Speaking Cross was also known to reside from time to time in trees.[111]) However, even here the peasant masses demonstrated the kind of foot-dragging and unorthodox ideological adaptations that they had previously applied to officials of the Yucatecan church and state. In 1851, when the eastern rebels were reeling under famine and military defeat, numerous Maya soldiers took advantage of amnesty offers by claiming that the cross had in fact instructed them to surrender.[112] Like the radical sects during the English civil war, these foot soldiers of the cause found that God spoke directly to them as well.[113] Individual ownership of particular santos not integral to the cross cult persisted in the east; the practice was alive and well in the twentieth century.[114]

Big Icons: The Churches

The greatest of all icons were the churches themselves, the houses of all other imágenes. Even today, there is not a single Yucatecan town, Mérida and Campeche included, with an architectural structure rivaling the local church in size and magnificence. Put simply, nothing stood forth like these sacred constructions. They were visible centers of power, knowledge, and authority, setting boundaries in an overgrown and irregularly populated landscape, but at the same time they shared many of the functions of their portable counterparts.

Like the statues of santos, the village church had an uncertain status. It was at once institutional property, communal property, and domain of the resident cura. At the bottom, however, churches had two broad sets of functions in the communities. First, they served as elements of prestige and organization. Far more than the plaza or the later ayuntamiento house, the church established the village's center. It announced that the village was civilized, that it had wealth, that its people worked together, that they maintained a community life. No other edifice features as commonly in documents of peace and war in the pueblos than these structures. The churches symbolized human presence and initiative, the triumph of human permanence in a land where the monte threatened to devour everything.

Villagers of whatever ethnic background had little patience with curas who failed to keep the physical structure in good repair (see Chapter 6). Pride in village churches continued in later times as well. Beyond feeding community self-image, the building itself had enormous economic ramifications. The construction and physical care of the churches generated much employment in the towns, just as ceremonial construction had done in the classic Maya cities or as defense installations and highways do in the modern United States. This mixture of cosmic self-assertion and jobs in no way suggested the profane to village parishioners. On the contrary, it deepened the bonds of reciprocity between a colonialized people and their powerful overlords. Priests gained status by building and furnishing churches, just as Antonio Conselhiero and other beatos of the Brazilian *sertão* would earn their reputations of holiness by refurbishing churches and cemeteries.[115]

Building churches had always been a part of the colonial system here, but as in central Mexico, the economic growth of the eighteenth century had brought with it a boom in religious construction. Indeed, most of the venerable old churches the tourist sees today actually date from the second half of the colonial era. Curas undertook at least thirty major construction or remodeling projects from the late 1600s to the end of the eighteenth century.[116] But the trend slackened considerably with the economic and political instabilities of the early 1800s. New construction was replaced by remodeling and repair, although these projects were neither as prolonged or as labor-intensive. Reconstruction in part derived from the curas' desire to make their vocational mark on the community. But there were also emergency cases, since church buildings suffered occasional destruction through human accidents and by the forces of nature. Within the dates of this study alone we know of several major church catastrophes. In August 1838 a hurricane flattened the church of remote Chunhuhub, forcing parish operations to relocate to Tituc.[117] Earlier in that same year, the church of Kopomá burned as the result of a thunderbolt.[118] The great church of Tihosuco, later to be damaged during a late stage of the Caste War (1866), collapsed in 1835 as a result of simple deterioration; nor could its cura Antonio Mais rebuild immediately, for most Maya villagers had fled to the backlands to escape cholera.[119] In March 1841 the church of Sahcabchén burned to the ground. All that was salvaged was assorted furniture and a violin. The fire was apparently the result of votive candles left burning by Mayas of the nearby rancho Santa Cruz.[120] In 1846 the church of Pixoy (Campeche) was lost to a fire, destroying its highly venerated reproduction of the Virgin of Guadalupe; most men were off in their milpas, and only the quick work of the village women saved the other icons.[121] A misdirected skyrocket set fire to and destroyed the church roof at Chablekal during the fiesta to village patroness Saint Ursula, a mere seven days after an anonymous bandit had stolen the santo's emerald chain.[122]

Even the great urban cathedrals suffered the same problems, as demonstrated in 1886 when a bolt of lightning decimated one of the twin church towers of Campeche before the eyes of astonished burghers.[123] Campeche's barrio church of San Román had suffered the same fate only six years earlier: "The temples of the infidels have more decency and grandeur than this one of San Román, of universal fame," lamented the cura after lightning opened an inch-wide crack in the side.[124] Whatever their strength, the majestic Yucatecan churches were not immune to sudden destruction.

There is no evidence that the people saw these catastrophes as some sort of divine wrath. Nor, on the other extreme, did they rejoice at the creation of jobs. Human belief has far too many compartments to allow these kinds of simplistic readings. What is certain, however, is that the boom in massive religious construction had ended by 1800. The principal exception was the building of a church at Becanchén, the sugar-boom town that mushroomed into existence south of Tekax after 1821; the cura of Tekax had only begun church construction in 1838 when the Imán revolt suddenly brought his project to a halt.[125] (Those who visit Becanchén today will find a church that looks like it was partially reconstructed after a bomb blast; it is hard to say to what degree the present-day structure resembles the original building.) The end of new churches in some ways marked an end to one important aspect of church patronage. Doubtless there would have been problems with the community issue of church maintenance even without the Caste War.

As a concluding postscript to this matter, it is worth mentioning that church destruction during the Caste War has been exaggerated. These buildings were neither the principal targets of the rebels, nor was the destruction that did take place necessarily a conscious attack on the spiritual *ancien regime*. The best example is the most famous one: Tihosuco. No one who visits modern-day Tihosuco can fail to be impressed by the jagged remains of the church's facade—in some ways the most arresting scene of the entire peninsula. But we know beyond doubt that the early rebels left this building intact. In the words of a priest who reentered Tihosuco with the army in late 1848, "The church as well as the convent were found to be in the best possible state."[126] The destruction seen today apparently took place in 1867 as part of the rebels' scorched-earth tactic to create a buffer between Yucatán and Chan Santa Cruz.[127] In an earlier publication, I, too, have suggested Tihosuco as Yucatán's Bastille, but after further investigation I am inclined to think that it reflected mere military necessity, not symbolic revolution.[128] In fact, I have found no cases of the kind of calculated religious defilement described for the Tepeuano revolt of 1616 or the Pueblo revolt of 1680—broken crucifixes, altars smeared with feces, and so forth.[129] Churches were looted during the war, but so was everything else; these august buildings were merely the most obvious targets, and also the best documented. In 1848 the Yucatecan state sold off many (though by no means all) of the churches' interior decorations to finance the Caste War, an act that greatly contributed to their present-day look of austerity. In other cases, church deterioration derived only indirectly from the war: with the collapse of political authority and the dispersal of populations, physical maintenance became irregular and insufficient in a part of the world where the salt air, humidity, and insistent vegetation cause buildings to deteriorate rapidly. Whatever their tensions with village priests, Maya rebels by no means tried to wipe away the architectural presence of Catholicism during their half century of rebellion; rather, they imitated it point for point in their laborious and prolonged construction of a whole new church, in traditional style, in Chan Santa Cruz.

The Santos of Today

The complex of behavior surrounding imágenes, like that of urban cofradías and village fiestas, has proven one of the most durable features of Mexican popular piety. Struggles between towns and haciendas over the control of specific imágenes continued into the Porfirian era, as seen in the case of San Román of Abalá, analyzed by Franco Savarino.[130] The two main peninsular newspapers—Por Esto! and Diario de Yucatán—carry periodic features regarding their histories and lore.[131] Santos such as the Three Wise Men of Tizimín draw enormous crowds who line up for blocks to touch the three statues with sprigs of rosemary, an action the faithful believe will predispose Melchor, Gaspar, and Baltazar toward their requests.[132] But these are simply the celebrity santos. Interested parties can buy their own in commercial bulk, while the discriminating collector can acquire pricey antiques or else order special creations from rural artisans. Many a house in Yucatán has its figurines of Jesus or the Virgin Mary, or posters of Pope John Paul II. More traditional households may include tiny oratorios with candles, photographs of loved ones, and a cross adorned with its sudario, an embroidered cloth stole. This, one of the most critical features of Mexico's folk Catholicism, has outlived henequen, haciendas, bishops, powerful priests, socialist parties, and the visions of an independent Yucatán, adapting itself to a society that is increasingly drawn into a web of international production and exchange. There seems to be little doubt that imágenes will continue to draw adherents in the twenty-first century.

Official Cult and Peasant Protocol

Rural Cofradías
and the History of San Antonio Xocneceh

THE EMERGENCE OF independent Latin American nations involved social transformations that are still poorly understood in terms of rural and local culture. Initial attempts to come to grips with that culture tended to rely on categories: the closed Indian village, the hacienda, and so forth. While studies oriented toward these institutions have been rewarding, they often result in an excessively structural vision of impermeable historical entities that existed with little relation to other impermeables save for a fundamental distrust and opposition. Integral to these views has been the tendency to assign certain essential identities—peasant, nonpeasant, Christian, syncretic—after which no further exploration seemed necessary.

But structures can hide as much as they reveal. Seldom has that been truer than in the case of the rural cofradías, the lay religious organizations long considered a defining feature of peasant village life. Between the advent of the Bourbon reforms and the triumph of liberalism in the mid- to late 1800s, indigenous communities found their lay brotherhoods caught between tradition and modernization, between the colonial protections of the past and the new impulses toward profit and commercial use. The quest to define these rural cofradías has already generated an extensive literature. An earlier interpretive strain, heavily based on Chiapas and highland Guatemala, saw these as communal and redistributive, a cornerstone of Eric Wolf's closed corporate village.[1] The reaction came in an antifunctionalist assault that reinterpreted cofradía behavior as a consequence of exclusion from wider economic circles, something that declined when those same opportunities became more accessible.[2] Many studies now stress the interaction of essential cultural features and historical pressures in the rural highland cofradías, arguing that most of the twentieth-century studies were based on a form of fiesta behavior that was relatively recent in appearance and is rapidly disappearing.[3]

But the changes of the early national period raise new questions. This was an era that saw the decline of Spanish imperial stability, an increasing non-Indian presence in the countryside, and the opening of Mexican society to new ideas and influences. How then do we read cofradías when they ceased to be pure peasant institutions (if such they ever were) and became explicitly "mixed" institutions?[4] In reality, those Yucatecan cofradías that survived into the mid- to late nineteenth century did so by internalizing themselves in the hacienda system, something that gave them confused, overlapping jurisdictions and constituencies. There is no reason to dismiss them as mere social controls: we would not, for example, describe family structure as merely a form of social control, even though in part it is. This chapter argues that the picture was not entirely declensional, and the later fortunes of Yucatán's fiesta systems offer a means of gauging peasant involvement in and responses to larger changes during the first decades of independence, responses deeply grounded in the popular cultural expectations of country life.

Rural Cofradías in Yucatán

We have already seen something of cofradías in the city. But the lay brotherhoods, whose roots lay in urban medieval Europe, became a fixture of rural Latin America soon after the conquest. Once transplanted among the peasantry, the institution took on a whole new foliage. Participation centered around production of various cash commodities, principally corn, cattle, and honey, the proceeds of which would then apply to fiestas and religious ceremonies in honor of the village's patron saint. The properties and resources of the cofradía were registered as belonging to a patron saint, who served, in effect, as a legal fiction for corporate ownership.[5] Documents well into the post–Caste War period continue to identify the santo as an owner of goods and loan money.

A handful of case studies now permit us some idea of the history and workings of these institutions.[6] Sixteenth- and seventeenth-century activity remains unclear, but by the year 1700 the cofradías had begun to sell corn in nearby urban markets. Around 1750 the corn market reached saturation, and in a departure from their usual economic roles, the Maya cofrades themselves moved into commercial cattle production. Despite a resurgence of the corn market after 1770, livestock, above all cattle, formed the basis of the cofradía's revenues.[7] Like their counterparts, the cattle haciendas, the cofradía estancias also turned out a certain amount of honey, while the wax from the honeycombs provided candles for the peninsula. There were other items grown here—produce such as vegetables, fruits, and even coconuts—but they provided only a small portion of the tally, and their production, as well as pig and goat raising, tended to lessen as commercial cattle ranching occupied more and more of the total picture.[8]

The cofradía estancia mimicked the hacienda in labor structure as well. There was a figure known as the *mayorcol* who supervised farming activities, and a staff of vaqueros who looked after the herd. In addition, the cofradía employed a number of specialists, such as the waterwheel operator (*noriero*) and the beekeeper (*colmenero*). After 1750, a large amount of the cofradía's corn went to feed local workers.[9] Unfortunately, our understanding of these labor structures is lacking in many ways. We know that workers came to live on these properties and that they accumulated debts, but we cannot separate either point from their role in the cofradía. For example, was employment in such an arrangement more flexible and desirable than work on the hacienda? The only answers are conjectural.

Details regarding the cofradía's social organization are somewhat clearer. At the top, a non-Indian patrón, often the local cura, kept record books for periodic inspection by the bishop's office. The mayordomo held responsibility for the internal management of the cofradías, the work assignments of its members, and so forth. Beneath him, a team of *priostes,* or internal auditors, certified the acts of the organization. Dovetailing this were sundry other offices, including *comisario, teniente de comisario, mayordomo, secretario,* and, at least in some cases, the *mayordomo de hachas.* (This last officer took care of the enormous candles known as *hachas,* or "hatchets.")[10] The exact number and duties of the offices probably varied over locations, but the general pattern was an upper tier of management that connected with the outside world, with lower and more elaborate tiers handling internal activities. The former group was more likely to include non-Mayas, while the latter was entirely Maya and involved some degree of selection by rank-and-file members. Cofradías therefore had a culturally and ethnically mixed composition from an early date.

The bulk of the organization's revenues went to subsidize local church activity. Most importantly, cofradía money paid a priest to say masses for the santo. In the case of Euán, for example, the cofradía's constitution designated an annual group contribution of fifteen pesos toward religious services associated with the Feast of the Immaculate Conception (December 8), and an additional three pesos for rites on Day of the Dead (November 1); all other feast-day masses ran at one peso, as did a cofrade's funeral. Cofradías also purchased candles for devotion, despite the fact that the bishop cautioned against such excesses as "the cause of the demise of such brotherhoods and cofradías." Because of its commercial activities, the cofradía lost its exemption to church tithes; thus evidence of the contributions of some of these organizations still exist among the fragmentary tithe records of the eighteenth century. In spite of tithing, the cofradía paid the yearly obvention as though it were a single person, and its individual members enjoyed no exemption on this score. Finally, if the patrón was a non-Maya, whether the local cura or some other appointee, then this also fell to the church's benefit, for it allowed the church to provide someone a ceremonial title and nominal salary.[11]

As the foregoing information hints, a certain ambiguity dogged cofradías from the beginning. This was an institution by and for whom? The peasants who were its laborers and supposed beneficiaries, or the priests and other local creoles who served as its patrons, managers, and clients? Were these institutions property of the church, social property of a larger community, or the private concerns of the hacendados who availed themselves of cofradía funds and to whose estates cofradía behavior was later transplanted? Doubtless the answers were as unclear to historical participants as they have remained to later scholars; custom and usage of daily behavior usually papered over the ambiguities. Nevertheless, cofradía-related controversy would continue to surface occasionally throughout peninsular history, even into the national era, when the "classic" Yucatecan cofradías had entered a state of change.

This latter process began in the 1780s, when the Yucatecan church began to sell off its cofradía properties. The move came as part of the Bourbon administration's campaigns to centralize political authority while reinvigorating an economy that had stagnated under Hapsburg rule. The church auctioned off some two-thirds of these properties, with the proceeds going to form a church loan reservoir known as the *fondo de cofradías,* still active into the 1850s.[12] But by 1821 two-thirds of Yucatán's cofradías had been sold; the remainder, which numbered somewhere around fifty, gradually fell prey to privatization decrees.[13] In August 1823, for example, a tax administrator for the region of

Ichmul reported that there was only one cofradía left in the entire area, the brotherhood of Telá in Chikintsonot.[14] Elsewhere the story was similar, with the handful of remaining organizations making only a fleeting appearance in the existing documents, such as the loans from organizations in Baca, Teya, and Tekantó.[15] After independence many favored completing the policy of liquidation. The test case came in 1821, when the *jefe político* of Tixkokob tried to sell off the cofradía Misercordia, a move that provoked furor from creoles and Mayas alike. The case went before various commissions, which found the cofradía's arguments so convincing that they not only scotched Misercordia's sale but drafted a bill mandating the restoration of those cofradía properties already sold. But the Yucatecan government aborted this plan, which would have had the effect of restoring control of land to peasants.[16]

We know little of who received cofradía properties. In some cases, at least, the beneficiaries were the local clergy or their friends and family. Cura Baltasar Larena acquired the cofradía Tsabcan of Chuburná village, today a slightly deteriorated neighborhood of northwest Mérida.[17] When Ignacio Manzanilla took charge of liquidating four cofradías in the parish of Umán (Kuchel, Cumpich, Cancahcán, and Oxbolom), the livestock went to local ranchers and meat sellers, including his brother Simón.[18] The combined value of their animals totaled 181 pesos. In other cases, returns of cofradía sales proved hard to collect. Those responsible for the sales simply pocketed the money and dragged their feet when asked to produce it.[19] Gauging peasant reaction to this change is also difficult. In the case of Kuchel, at least, the peasants did not go quietly, since two years after the cofradía's legal liquidation the former cofrades were still protesting. Their insistence derived in large part from the fact that they used the cofradía property as their place of residence. Kuchel had thus passed from being a lay institution to a community in itself to a private property.[20] We should not automatically conclude, however, that alienation of cofradía lands produced smoldering rage among the peasantry. Kuchel is very much the exception in nineteenth-century documents. At least during the first half of the 1800s, complaints regarding cofradía losses were rare, and peasants were not reluctant to complain. There seems to be little evidence to support assertions that cofradía alienation contributed to a "hatred toward the usurping invader," or that the Caste War stemmed from peasant fury over the sale of cofradía lands.[21] By the 1840s cofradías were simply not a primary or even secondary issue. One likely explanation for this is that religious culture was already in a transition to other forms that satisfied peasant needs. It is not that one single institution replaced the cofradía, but rather that a variety did, almost all of which we have tended to dismiss as diluted, corrupted, or manipulated versions of some more pristine world.

If anything, the policy struck at the power and prerogatives of local clergy, who were accustomed to directing cofradía operations, brokering loans, and drawing service fees for their own involvement. It fit neatly within the larger contours of Bourbon policy: to liberate goods and resources from their medieval restrictions, to increase economic activity, and to push colonial society toward a centralized and secular state.[22] But with the dissolution of corporate properties, rural priests nevertheless attempted to continue cofradía activities in somewhat disguised arrangements. As seen in Chapter 2, Raymundo Pérez reorganized the parish cofradías into seven different investment funds under his own management.[23] Another case comes from Sacalaca, where a certain Juan Tomás Brito purchased a stretch of land during his ministry there in the early 1800s. He developed this into the hacienda San Antonio and operated it exactly like a cofradía, using the returns on its cattle sales to finance the annual fiesta. Although Brito eventually transferred out, he continued to operate San Antonio through a mayordomo (apparently non-Maya) named José García. In his 1816 will he specifically requested that his executors maintain San Antonio to the profit of "the divine cult."[24] But even when a formal estate was lacking, some rural priests carried on the funding process, either through a sense of *noblesse oblige* or simply in order to make ends meet in the parish budget. As late as February 1829 José Bartolomé Baeza of Yaxcabá made private loans whose interest payments were used to fund village fiesta activities formerly financed by the cofradía Xiat.[25] Though many of the functions of the cofradía persisted, they did so with a priest as formal owner and director.

The land-based cofradía's considerable external control may have been another factor that helped make the liquidations easier for peasants to bear. One example of peasant ambivalence or downright hostility to cofradía business comes from Chancenote during the final years of Spanish rule. When Padre José María Torrens became cura here in 1819, he was shocked by the lack of reverence for the local cult. Torrens discovered that the supposedly devout peasants of this Yucatecan parish had not only sold off the cattle and horses that belonged to their cofradía, but they were also in the process of liquidating the cofradía property itself. Dissatisfaction stemmed from the fact that the previous pastor, Tomás Gutiérrez, had operated the organization as his private business venture. Torrens was unable to convince his new parishioners to change their minds—perhaps because he spoke not a word of Maya—and had to appeal to the bishop for a decree to reestablish fraternal operations.[26]

With or without land, however, organized rural religious piety continued in a variety of forms after 1821. In 1841 the traveler John Lloyd Stephens observed fiesta activities in the town of Nohcacab.[27] Abalá's cofradía continued to sponsor five annual fiestas even into the time of the Caste War (although it is not clear whether this was a peasant organization, a bourgeois fraternity, or some combination of the two).[28] Anthropologists of the 1930s found at least two types of cofradía activity among Yucatec Mayas: a highly ritualized variation among rebel holdouts in Quintana Roo and a much more informal, at times even reluctant, participation among the more pacific Mayas of Chan Kom.[29] Meanwhile, many present-day villages still have religious guilds known as *gremios*. The earliest date for these is uncertain, but some, such as Chuburná's Gremio of Faith, Hope, and Charity, have operated since 1926.[30] The gremio is essentially a landless cofradía in which participants dedicate themselves to venerating a particular santo. They usually associate themselves by profession: hunters, farmers, fishers, and so forth. The practice is widespread today and enjoys a modest corpus of descriptive literature.[31]

Cofradía behavior also survived by insinuating itself into the private estates of the later henequen era. During the Porfirian age of the great haciendas, the owners frequently built chapels and encouraged or at least allowed ritual organizations; we find frequent petitions from hacendados requesting church permission to construct oratories.[32] As Savarino noted in his 1997 study of the Porfirian era, the continuation of preexisting forms of religious practice eased the transition from village- to hacienda-based life for thousands of peasants.[33] Even Yucatecan creoles and Mayas who fled to Belize during the Caste War still maintained fiesta activities in the 1860s, often to the disgust of censorious (and non-Catholic) British officials.[34]

Finally, it is clear that the death of what might be called "classic" cofradías has been exaggerated. In some villages the same practices continued, except that instead of referring to them as cofradías per se, locals simply described them as "a plot of land with cattle whose revenues support the village saint," or some similar formula. These activities were collective and in some cases had Maya mayordomos or patrons. They begin to turn up in the documents during the late 1840s and throughout the 1850s, after the Caste War had ceased to threaten northwestern towns in any significant fashion and the parish churches began looking around for ways of financing their reconstruction. Such organizations appear in Dzitbalché, Maní, Telchac, Nolo, Sotuta, Mocochá, and Hool.[35] The pattern makes sense for rural Mexican history, where cultural norms and long-standing practices, when officially suppressed, often had a way of reasserting themselves in somewhat altered form.

In all these cases there is reason to believe that ritual structure did not represent chimerical pristine forms but rather were products of historical experience before, during, and after the Caste War.[36] Nevertheless, they reveal the tendency of cultural folkways to persist beneath the official level. The cumulative evidence also suggests that the elimination of cofradías was not a crushing blow to rural peasants. Or, at the most, it was a blow from which they had recovered by the time of independence. The change eliminated certain economic practices associated with popular piety, but thereafter peasants found new channels and new means of expression for those same impulses. In this sense, cofradía behavior provides a microcosm of peasant reaction to change throughout nineteenth-century Mexico.

The Cult of San Antonio Xocneceh

The remainder of this chapter focuses on the transitions of a single institution: the hacienda cult. This was perhaps the most interesting of all, for, given its hybrid nature, the hacienda served as an ethnic and cultural crossroads. It is seldom possible to explore hacienda cults in detail, for the patchy records of the nineteenth century afford little more than brief glimpses into the popular piety on the great estates. But in one case, that of a Yucatecan lay-religious brotherhood named San Antonio Xocneceh (pronounced shok-ne-KE), the surviving documents allow us to reconstruct a more extensive account of such affairs. Xocneceh suggests no simple peasant role in religious change but rather a more complex pattern of engagement, initiative, and resistance.

The exquisitely picturesque remains of what was once hacienda San Antonio Xocneceh lie approximately ten miles to the northwest of Oxkutzcab, in the Sierra Alta region of southern Yucatán. Although the hacienda and its cofradía began in the colonial era, the location had a pre-Columbian identity; the *Chilam Balam of Chumayel,* a Maya-language compilation of history, myth, and prophesy, refers to it as a way station for southbound religious pilgrims: "Then they went to Xocneceh; the deer was their familiar spirit when they arrived."[37] The word *xook* means "to count, read, or study," while *nej kéej* means "tail of a deer." *Xocneceh* therefore translates into "count of deer tails," suggesting a place where deer were abundant and the living was easy. At the same time, the reference in *Chilam Balam* hints at a totemic association, and although it is impossible to prove that the later cult drew upon Xocneceh's pre-Columbian religious status, remains of an enormous pyramid can still be seen only a short distance from the main house of the hacienda. Xocneceh apparently continued as a settlement throughout the seventeenth century.[38] Thereafter, however, it underwent what was a fairly common evolution from pueblo to cattle estancia to hacienda. During the late colonial period, haciendas such as Xocneceh began to establish their own religious cults in order to attract workers, to cultivate their own prestige, and to carve out a greater autonomy from the towns.[39] The object of this particular cult's veneration was a canvas portrait of San Antonio de Padua. How it came to the area of Oxkutzcab, or whether it was the product of some local artist, we cannot say. But we do know that a certain Juan Burgos, "one of the ancient *devotos* of that village," founded both chapel and cofradía in 1767, so we may plausibly date the icon from this year as well.[40] Small reproductions of the Xocneceh portrait apparently circulated as well, such as the one that turned up in the will of Anastacia Ramírez in 1854.[41]

The historical San Antonio was a thirteenth-century Franciscan mystic from the city of Lisbon. Hoping to be martyred by infidels, Antonio sailed for Morocco in 1221, but ill health forced him to shelve these plans and return to Europe. He instead spent the remainder of his life in a convent near Bologna, earning fame as a teacher and miracle worker and dying at the age of thirty-six. To the mass of rural nineteenth-century Mexicans, however, the relevant passages of San Antonio's life took place in Origin Time. For example, the saint was famous for preaching to fishes of the sea when humans refused to listen. Regarding his more celebrated exploits, one hagiographer reports: "He was staying in the house of a man of rank in Limousin; the gentleman was curious to watch him in private, and through a chink in the wall saw the saint holding converse with, and embracing, the infant Savior." [42] The scene of San Antonio with the infant Christ became the saint's traditional iconographic representation; it is what the folk remembered, and it is what Burgos selected for his canvas. In the rural imagination of Yucatán, San Antonio favors his adherents by bringing them sweethearts and spouses. But equally important is his association with rain. San Antonio's feast day, June 13, is considered to be the last possible day for the spring planting rains. For this reason Maya peasants subject the santo to an intense lobbying campaign in the dry months of April and May. San Antonio therefore functions as a fertility santo, promoting social bonds within the community while ensuring the yearly waters on which Yucatecan life depends.

We do not possess comprehensive records of Xocneceh's owners, but the estate's first known appearance in the notarial records occurs in 1760 when its owner, doña María del Castillo, a widow living in Mérida, sold it to her daugh-

OFFICIAL CULT AND PEASANT PROTOCOL

151

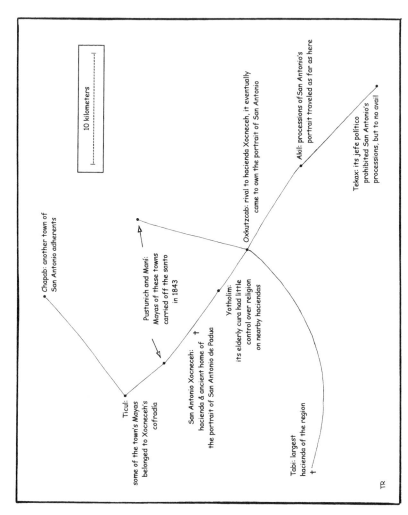

Map 3. The hacienda San Antonio Xocneceh and surrounding communities.

Chapab: another town of
San Antonio adherents

Pustunich and Maní:
Mayas of these towns
carried off the santo
in 1843

Ticul:
some of the town's Mayas
belonged to Xocneceh's
cofradía

San Antonio Xocneceh:
hacienda & ancient home of
the portrait of San Antonio de Padua

Yotholim:
its elderly cura had little
control over religion
on nearby haciendas

Oxkutzcab: rival to hacienda Xocneceh, it eventually
came to own the portrait of San Antonio

Akil: processions of San Antonio's
portrait traveled as far as here

Tabi: largest
hacienda of the region

Tekax: its jefe político
prohibited San Antonio's
processions, but to no avail

10 kilometers

TR

ter Patrona de Solís y Castillo. The price of 9,989 pesos placed it among the more valuable properties of its day and time.[43] Xocneceh then carried a two-thousand-peso mortgage drawn from the capellanía founded by Diego de la Cámara; according to the usual custom, the priest who owned it was to say masses to Cámara's soul. Family relationships almost always interpenetrated economic dealings, and it is no surprise to find Petrona's brother Antonio de Solís serving as the capellanía's beneficiary. Links with the property, its owners, and the church thus began from the hacienda's earliest days. Josefa Zaválegui owned it until her death shortly before March 1831, at which time it passed briefly into the hands of José Ignacio Machado of Ticul.[44] However, for the main period of this study—the 1840s and 1850s—the proprietor was a certain José Concepción Cáceres. Cáceres appears to have been an absentee landlord; an 1847 newspaper advertised him as a bookseller in Mérida, and when he sold the hacienda in 1855 he listed that city as his place of residence.[45] This would explain his relative absence from documents concerning daily events of San Antonio Xocneceh. He married a woman named Catalina Machado and eventually brought members of the Ticul-based Machado clan into the management of the cofradía.

Judging from the surviving ruins and inventories, San Antonio's chapel must have presented a stunning sight. The building itself was a rubble-masonry construction with five arches and a vaulted ceiling.[46] Internal passageways along the high upper ceiling (known as *gallinas ciegas,* the Spanish equivalent of blind man's bluff) lent the appearance of a fortress.[47] The chapel enjoyed lamps and bells mounted in a type of wheel mechanism for ringing. Decorations for the santo included gold stars, crucifixes, a crown of thorns, silver candlestick holders in gold cases, a reliquary, assorted devotional wax figures, white cotton altar cloth, as well as at least six different glass cases with curtains for the painting itself. This inventory is only partial, since it fails to include decorations seized by Maya rebels in 1848.[48] The glass cases were used only as travel equippage, for when at home San Antonio resided in a special niche with serrated metal edgework. By 1845 the elegant chapel had become a landmark in the region. For example, an anonymous memoir of travel through the Sierra Alta reported: "When we departed from Pustunich, at a brief distance we were shown San Antonio Xocnequej, the hacienda whose temple, as large as that of a regular town, is independent of the *fábrica* [parish church] and is a landmark of the estate to which it belongs."[49]

We know less about the hacienda itself. It is clear that Xocneceh began its life as a corn and livestock hacienda, with the usual beehives and servants' debts.[50] However, it took a tentative step into the sugar business after the market expanded in 1821. One clue to Xocneceh's original layout is a document reporting that a two-story, eleven-room main house sat at "una cuadra," or one block's distance, from the chapel.[51] Finally, we know that the estate contained temporary accommodations for pilgrims, since one of the mayordomos was accused of failing to maintain these houses in good repair.[52] Maya villagers from Ticul and probably other surrounding hamlets took part in observing the santo's fiestas.

The portrait itself traveled according to a series of fiestas throughout the Sierra Alta, events that involved the towns of Ticul, Yotholim, Oxkutzcab, Akil, and more. Although regional markets and fairs were apparently not a major aspect of Maya life at the time of European contact (a fact reflecting the political chaos after the collapse of the Yucatec Mayas' last intercity alliance, from 1441 onward), such markets gradually developed throughout the colonial period. By the 1820s the fairs of the Sierra Alta had become significant events in which creoles and peasants alike sold corn, liquor, cattle, and other merchandise. As early as 1813 the booths of these fairs were attracting interest as possible tax sources. Cofrades—and indeed, the entire secular and religious community around them—had good reason to worry over the upkeep of shrines related to the fairs. The church sold candles and devotionals, the locals sold food and traded commodities. The fairs were the great bazaars of their time and place, and they made the difference between a rude collection of huts and a viable, even prosperous, peasant community. The emphasis on regional markets reflected the increasing commercial growth in the form of cattle and sugar estates that had penetrated the countryside.[53] Shrines in turn required sanctuaries that were clean, well maintained, and conspicuously decorated. As members of another cofradía had remarked when faced with problems of neglect, there was the danger that the mayordomo would let things deteriorate "to the point that the faithfuls' devotion to such a miraculous image will end altogether."[54] Clearly, pictistic neatness mattered.

Unlike the cofradías described for the eighteenth century, Xocneceh operated principally on revenues from beekeeping and loan capital. Viewed from an extremely narrow perspective, it was little more than a candle factory operating within the hacienda on a system of volunteer and paid labor.[55] In the only documented years—November 1845 and October 1846—the cofradía produced nearly 168 pounds of wax. This far exceeded the output of the Hecelchakán cofradía, whose highest recorded production (in 1742) was a mere 14 pounds.[56] However, the larger source of revenue for the cult was the interest that it received on loans. This source accounted for slightly over 50 percent of total revenues.[57]

Xocneceh's management remained within a tight circle of creoles. The cult and chapel functioned on the private property of the hacendado, and it appears that he had a hand in appointing mayordomos. Management also required the cooperation of the ecclesiastics of Yotholim and Oxkutzcab, for they communicated with the bishop's office regarding the cofradía. The hacienda lay within the parish of Yotholim, where the cura kept the cult's liquid capital under lock and key in the church. Nevertheless, Xocneceh's ties with Oxkutzcab remained strong. Care for outlying communities typically fell to parish assistants, and consequently we find that the Oxkutzcab priest most concerned with Xocneceh was not the cura, José Lenard, but his minister, José Leocadio Espinosa. In contrast to Espinosa's constant meddling, the bishop's office was restrained in its dealings with Xocneceh and intervened only when complaints got out of hand.[58] In Oxkutzcab as elsewhere, the rural church remained a highly decentralized institution, with much of its character depending on the initiative, personality, and relative affluence of the local cura.

The issue of selecting a mayordomo was sensitive and political. It was he who balanced the many interests of a hacienda-based cofradía. He bore the simultaneous responsibilities of overseeing cult activities, placating Indian cofrades, keeping local priests involved, and making sure that the cathedral received its share of revenues. At the same time he also had to manage his own financial affairs, for as with colonial officials, no one seriously expected the mayordomo to live off the proceeds of this largely ceremonial office. Since this was a hacienda, the ancient system of Indian repúblicas had little influence, and creoles were able to assume more authority in making decisions that affected the various sectors. Still, the mayordomo, like the batab who collected taxes but also had to represent village interests, worked a delicate balancing act or else risked attack from any of the various interests involved. For the most part, Xocneceh's mayordomía followed a pattern of in-group participation. The cult's first known mayordomo was Juan José Dorantes, who died in 1819 or shortly thereafter. His son Juan Nepomuceno Dorantes inherited the office but abandoned it before 1829. He was succeeded by José Ignacio Machado (in-law to owner José Concepción Cáceres), who in turn handed the office to Feliciano Martínez in 1835. In 1842 Martínez himself resigned in favor of Dario Ascencio Machado (another in-law), of whom we shall say more presently.[59]

Like its management personnel, Xocneceh's loan portfolio remained within a closed circle. In 1829 the younger Dorantes, now ex-mayordomo, contracted a 783-peso mortgage from Xocneceh on his nearby hacienda, Santa Rita Komak, on the standard terms of four years at 5 percent. Dorantes died within six years of this contract, for in 1836 we find his widow, Isabel Romero of Oxkutzcab, procuring an additional 382-peso loan from Xocneceh and putting up a stone house located in Oxkutzcab. In 1841 Señora Romero sold Santa Rita to Bernardo Cetina; on the title of transfer, the hacienda was still listed as collateral mortgaged to Xocneceh, and Cetina himself took over the mortgage payments. Other loans went to relatives of the local priests. Odd loans occasionally did go out; for example, when Juan Andrés Liborio de Herrera made out his will in 1837, he left forty-nine pesos to the cult of Xocneceh "in order to ease my conscience." But on the whole it appears that access to San Antonio Xocneceh's loan capital depended on the lendee being part of a small network of family and business connections. The lack of organized banking institutions, together with the need for constant finance capital, explains why creoles found it necessary to employ these small "private banks" and why these same creoles occasionally rose to defend institutions that offered some economic and cultural dividends to peasants.[60]

The Town and the Hacienda

One key to San Antonio Xocneceh's history was the continued rivalry between the hacienda and the church at Oxkutzcab. The citizens and pastor of Oxkutzcab always claimed that the santo was theirs by right, that the ancient founder Juan Burgos was himself of the town, and that the hacienda held their birthright in a sort of gilded captivity. To mollify their demands the santo traveled periodically to the church at Oxkutzcab, alternating homes like a rural Persephone. The hacienda made San Antonio available for many local fiestas, but the trip to Oxkutzcab was the most important and would occasion the most controversy.

Deeper conflicts underlay this rivalry: specifically, the social realignments and demographic shifts created by the commercialization of agriculture in the eighteenth century.[61] The period between 1590 and 1730 had constituted a colonial status quo; Spaniards, whether secular or clerical, drew off wealth mainly by tribute, while the native Maya population hovered at around two hundred thousand.[62] Thereafter, Yucatán began to grow both demographically and economically. Estate owners wanted labor for cash crops; landless

Mayas sought milpa work, a measure of economic security and the perpetuation of certain reciprocal relationships now located in the mutual obligations existing between hacendado and peon. The hacienda to some extent reconciled these goals. The emergence of this social formation favored outlying regions, since the opening of new estates either lured away town-based Mayas or drove them farther outward in search of independent milpa lands. This in turn meant trouble for town churches, whose strategy had always been to congregate Mayas in settlements where they would be more available for taxes, labor, and religious indoctrination. Growth of both haciendas and the smaller ranchos proved decongregational.[63]

Oxkutzcab and its outlying settlements typified these tendencies. In 1806 the parish of Oxkutzcab was fairly large, including Oxkutzcab itself (the cabecera, or administrative head town), Yotholim, Xocneceh, and Xul, as well as numerous other small settlements clustered around them. The cabecera clearly dominated; not only was it by far the largest community in the parish, but it was also nearly half Spanish: 84 percent of all Spaniards in the parish lived in Oxkutzcab proper. Not surprisingly, the total parish was 75 percent Maya, most of whom (9,093, or 71.6 percent) lived either in the smaller surrounding communities or on haciendas and outlying settlements known as *ranchos*. This racial division between town and country was and is fairly typical for Yucatán. In late colonial days the abundance of Mayas provided Oxkutzcab with a moderate yearly revenue of two thousand pesos in church taxes.[64]

In 1821 church authorities redistricted the parish, with Yotholim and Xul each becoming separate entities. The former carried with it four ranchos and four haciendas (including Xocneceh); the latter took one hacienda, one additional town, and fourteen small commercial properties known as *sitios*. Initially the pastor of Oxkutzcab could afford to bear these losses philosophically. In 1828 the cabecera grossed nearly 18,000 pesos, compared to Yotholim's and Xul's combined total of 3,187 pesos. But time would undo Oxkutzcab's favored position. For although the parish registered some growth between 1806 and 1821, it appears to have fallen by 1845. At the same time, Yotholim more than doubled between 1806 and 1845. Xul expanded even more dramatically, rising from 1,299 in 1806 to 13,580 in 1845. Growth in the cabecera had slowed because the less-developed rural surroundings, especially in the far south, were drawing away the population. Akil remained a mere way station between Oxkutzcab and Tekax, with a population that hovered constant at approximately two thousand.[65]

The hacienda Xocneceh participated in this growth. By 1841 it was the home of ninety-eight workers, mostly young laborers and their families.[66] Its chapel and cofradía served in part to draw in ancillary church revenues from an outlying hacienda. But the situation changed as Mayas increasingly fled the parish center. The hacendado and cofrades of Xocneceh gradually found themselves in control of the one symbolic force that unified the entire region through its link to the annual fiesta cycle. A dramatic destabilization of church taxes in 1841 turned matters for the worse, and the years that followed witnessed an eruption of ancient grudges and town-country bickerings.

The Mayas of Xocneceh

Tracking the Mayas who formed the numerical majority of the hacienda and its cult is no easy task. They left relatively few papers, and local memory of the nineteenth century has all but vanished. However, the estate's Maya workers do appear in some of the inventories and financial statements that constitute most of the surviving documents. They also feature in certain records of social conflict surrounding the cult, when peasant grievances meshed with the interests of local church figures dissatisfied with the cofradía's management.

One such episode was the abduction of the santo. On June 3, 1843, the santo of Xocneceh was scheduled to make his annual journey to Oxkutzcab. In anticipation of this passage, a large crowd of peasants from the nearby towns of Oxkutzcab, Maní, Chapab, Yotholim, and Pustunich had gathered at the hacienda. Espinosa was on hand to conduct the traditional religious ceremonies and to oversee the novenas that had always been associated with San Antonio's travels. But this year was to be different. Leaders of Yucatán's recent political conflicts, including a defense against invading Mexican soldiers, had armed many of the peasants and had acquainted them with certain basic military skills; political violence was becoming increasingly common throughout the rural towns.[67] Consequently, the local officials had become wary of peasant masses wandering from town to town. At midnight on Friday, June 2, the jefe político of Tekax notified Espinosa that there would be no procession that year.[68]

The next morning Espinosa celebrated a predawn mass. What he said remains a mystery, but by six o'clock he was taking chocolate with prominent creoles in the main house when the prioste burst in to report that a mob of Mayas had abducted San Antonio. This mob consisted of "more than a thousand persons, almost all women." Asked for advice, Espinosa casually replied that he did not involve himself in such affairs, and that concerned parties should speak with the cult's patrón. Subsequent investigation revealed nothing. Witnesses claimed they could not identify the thousand women who had perpetrated the crime. Those who lived along the main street of Oxkutzcab, and by whose house the procession had passed, simply explained that they did not recognize the processants, "since they had come from other towns." Investigators pressed the jefe político of Tekax, Simón de Vargas, but he had little patience with the business. Vargas had written the original order canceling the procession, and though he may have bridled at the thought of peasants violating his command, he had even less patience with church investigators. Vargas therefore rebuffed the inquiry with a curt letter, and on that note the matter ended.

The abduction reflected several features of the society. We notice that peasants had their own ways of dealing with creoles who acted as officers in cults that they, the peasants, perceived in some way to be theirs. Indeed, it is difficult not to pick up on hostility toward Machado, the cult's new mayordomo, who had been kept in the dark about the affair. Machado had in fact grown disenchanted with the ceremonial power of mayordomía; the following October he submitted his resignation, arguing that the responsibilities of executing his late father's will left him no time for Xocneceh. The bishop approved, but for reasons unknown Machado stayed on another year, a half-hearted presence that invited controversy and direct community action.[69]

The hostility toward Machado that had been simmering throughout 1843 and 1844 soon erupted once more. In May 1845, villagers of Ticul who identified themselves as cofrades of Xocneceh and who enjoyed the support of the elderly Padre Méndez complained that Machado's indifference was causing the downfall of the cult.[70] Complaints focused on four points. First, Machado neglected care of the sanctuary and spent all his time engrossed in his own affairs. If repairs were in order, he sent his son to handle them. That a child should attend the santo scandalized the cofrades, conservative peasants to whom any link with the santo implied a prestigious role in the community. Second, and related to this same fastidious attention to prestige, Machado had failed to maintain the cofrades' schedule for attending mass. During and before a fiesta, past mayordomos had always prepared a schedule for members, seeing to it that a certain number attended each service; he then distributed tickets among the *cofrades* to remind them of their assigned days. But Machado had simply abandoned the practice. He had initially distributed the tickets "with repugnance," then stopped altogether, dismissing the whole matter as inconsequential. Third, Machado had allowed the pilgrimage houses to fall into disrepair and had even decorated his home with the santo's regalia.[71] The last offense was the most heinous of all: Machado had dared to smoke a cigar while leading the procession of San Antonio![72]

These episodes highlight certain facts about rural life. Most importantly, traditional rights and peasant protocols had embedded themselves in cults supposedly dominated by creole elites. Popular celebrations could reassert themselves in the face of official prohibition: rain and sweethearts mattered too much to be left in the hands of a jefe político. The interpenetration of town privileges and traditions into the cult, the direct relationship between the santo and the people, gave these Maya peasants a notion of their right to intervene in decisions regarding the santo himself. Mayordomos and jefes políticos therefore could not infringe on processions and access to the santo without provoking stiff resistance.

The patterns of peasant self-assertion are revealing as well. Intervillage action was still possible, at least in cases as important as the procession of a santo. San Antonio Xocneceh still managed to draw people out of their highly parochial allegiances and into regional cooperation. At the same time, religious activities such as processions and the veneration of santos provided an important role for the energies and attentions of village women, who appear to have taken a leading role in the abduction. But there were also real limitations to peasant action. Their methods usually involved a patrón. Peasants sought out elite factions that were willing to support their claims. During the abduction, peasants had the help of Espinosa, who obviously despised Machado. Moreover, the priest had every interest in publicly discrediting hacienda control of the cult while strengthening the hand of Oxkutzcab's church by stressing San Antonio Xocneceh as a regional and communal affair, not hacienda property. In the second episode, peasants made use of Padre Méndez, who was distressed to see that a man supposedly in charge of a prominent cofradía would spend all his time in "his own commerce."[73] Despite initiatives from below, rural Yucatán remained very much a world of patron-client relationships.

These sorts of Maya initiatives were not unique. Indeed, the revolt against Machado had a close parallel in another santo cult popular at the time, the Virgin of Hool, a tiny village in what is now Campeche state. Like hacienda Xocneceh, Hool was an essentially Maya peasant community with a santo that bound together a region through pilgrimages and processions. This particular cult was founded in 1813, a time when the church needed to rally the faithful in the face of Spain's liberal constitution and the grass-roots noncompliance that document had facilitated throughout the peninsula.[74] The faithful who came here to confess themselves and seek favors found themselves dazzled by Hool's lavishly appointed chapel. Here, too, the cura selected a prominent local creole mayordomo to collect revenues, keep inventories, and organize the cult's activities. Cofrades carried the Virgin, suitably accommodated in a glass case, to the houses of the sick when necessary and to bless the opening of new ranchos in the monte. Each lay brother was expected to provide wax each Sunday, with two *arrobas* (about fifty pounds) more for when the cofradía sponsored a novena.[75] As with its counterpart in Tabi-Sotuta, the Virgin of Hool made a special pilgrimage each year to the far more sophisticated barrio San Román of Campeche; here, too, the act of ritualized travel carved spacial meanings out of the monte and bestowed immense prestige on the imagen in question.[76] And, like peasants of the Sierra Alta, local Maya cofrades rebelled when the church-appointed creole mayordomo failed to maintain the cult.[77] Devotion sagged in the 1870s; contributions declined, while a freak fireworks accident killed several fiesta-goers in 1882.[78] But the cult somehow survived into the twentieth century. Taken together, the examples of Hool and Xocneceh argue that Maya peasants had fairly strong opinions on how things ought to be, and they still had ways of negotiating for what they wanted.

Xocneceh after 1845

Machado's replacement turned out to be a thoroughgoing manager and bookkeeper. Retired military officer Juan Pablo Talavera had occupied numerous political offices in Maxcanú and Tekax in the 1830s; what brought him to Xocneceh remains a mystery, but his accounts for the year 1846 leave a precise picture of the cofradía's activities.[79] It is from his administrative papers that we take much of what we know about the cult's activities.

But Talavera's term in office was destined to be brief. While he was busy straightening accounts, a factional revolt of November 1846 not only dislodged the government but seriously destabilized the peninsula. By this time the rural peasantry had already become deeply embittered by the various social and economic changes since 1840.[80] Batabs in the string of villages from Valladolid to Tihosuco had led peasant mobilizations during this conflict; alarmed by their deteriorating social and economic position, the batabs Jacinto Pat and Cecilio Chi used their newly acquired skills to mobilize peasant masses on the promise of eradicating both civil and religious taxes. The ensuing conflict, known to history as the Caste War, first erupted in the eastern village of

Tepich in the early morning hours of July 30, 1847, and gradually spread to adjacent regions.[81]

The war took half a year to reach the area of Xocneceh. Not until Christmas had the situation grown sufficiently alarming to make the Ticul schoolmaster leave town. Even then, some were still optimistic. Government troops still held the *sierra,* peace initiatives were underway, and Talavera was running ads in the Mérida newspapers soliciting a replacement teacher. But the sudden collapse of negotiations and the fall of Oxkutzcab exposed Xocneceh to imminent attack. Maya recruits from local ranchos and haciendas were swelling rebel forces daily. At the last minute Talavera managed to pack up the cult's valuables and send them to Mérida. Ever the perfectionist, he drew out a list of the salvaged items. On May 27, 1848, the army, together with the batab and Mayas of Ticul, withdrew from the town and marched north. The Sierra Alta was now in rebel hands.

Inexplicably, one item Talavera did *not* save was San Antonio himself. When creoles retreated from the hacienda amid sniper fire, they abandoned the portrait to the rebels. Jacinto Pat, the Maya leader who occupied San Antonio Xocneceh, immediately made off with the portrait and anything else his men could carry. But San Antonio was not destined to disappear into the wilds of the eastern rainforest. Xocneceh was actually the scene of an important but uncommemorated battle of the war, one of the first losses by rebel forces in the great reversal of the spring of 1848. Pat retreated from Pustunich, the point of his farthest advance; his forces dug in at Xocneceh to resist troops advancing from Ticul. A column of five hundred Yucatecan soldiers under the command of Felipe Pren succeeded in dislodging the insurgents on April 11, and Pat moved farther to the southeast, in the process abandoning the portrait.

Although the army had retaken the territory, Talavera prudently resigned his office as mayordomo and retired to Campeche. His successors spent the next four years tracking down crates and secret caches throughout Yucatán in order to restore the temple of San Antonio de Padua to its former glory. But the most difficult item to recover was the santo. Pren's officers had placed the canvas in the church of Oxkutzcab for safekeeping, with the intention of restoring it to its owner in due time. The war, however, drew Pren's soldiers farther into the interior, and the portrait stayed put, much to the satisfaction of those citizens of Oxkutzcab who had coveted it for so long. In this and in other ways, the postwar period allowed Oxkutzcab to regain ascendancy over the cult. Oxkutzcab's cura was now Miguel Méndez, formerly of Yotholim; old and nearly blind, he represented no challenge to the initiatives of

José Leocadio Espinosa, who effectively managed the parish. When Méndez died of dysentery in 1852, Espinosa rose to interim cura, making his authority nearly complete.[82] Espinosa now designated a succession of longtime cronies, including his own nephew, as mayordomos. Moreover, with money scarce and the canvas now in his own hands, he wasted no time in loaning himself money from its cofradía funds as well as gaining title to the cofradía's longtime beneficiary, the hacienda Santa Rita Komak.[83] Control had passed from the hacienda back to the town.

The hacienda changed owners as well. Like many surrounding properties, Xocneceh suffered mightily during the war; by 1855 its resident population fell by 13–30 percent, to a mere seventeen families.[84] Not a single worker from the 1841 census still remained, one hint to the degree of dislocation that the war had caused. As a result of these difficulties, or perhaps because of his advanced age, José Concepción Cáceres sold San Antonio Xocneceh to satisfy his debt to the estate of a Tekax oligarch, the late Pablo Luján.[85] It cost 1,578 pesos, 20–40 percent of its value in more stable times.[86] Even this transaction illustrated the closed quality of rural elite networks. The new owner was Gregoria González, widow of Pablo Luján, who himself had been the attorney of Cáceres's wife, Catalina Machado.[87] Nevertheless, Xocneceh remained a diminished version of its former splendor, with a mere sixty-seven inhabitants in 1862, including its new mayordomo, González's son Benjamín Luján.[88] Within fifteen years that number declined to thirty-eight.[89]

The last documented episode of this story took place during the years immediately before the coming of the French Empire in Yucatán. Between 1857 and 1863 the state roiled in profound political instability. Ostensibly the result of ambitious generals and politicians, the innumerable coups gained popular support from the resentment over the prolonged Caste War; the incessant conscription of peons and other rural laborers generated considerable opposition among the rural folk, pitting them against the factions of town jefes políticos, whose responsibility it was to round out the army rosters.[90] These uprisings divided rural property owners, including González, from Oxkutzcab. In order to buy the loyalty of the oxkutzcabeños during the uprising of Pantaleón Barrera in the summer of 1859, Governor Agustín Acereto granted them the portrait they had so long coveted. Gregoria González spent more than four years petitioning for its return; the bishop complied, ordering its return, but in the best Spanish tradition, the citizens of Oxkutzcab managed to obey without complying.[91] Padre Espinosa continued to allow the portrait to travel to other parishes in the vicinity but stipulated that the revenues for all masses sung before it accrue to Oxkutzcab, not to the host parish.[92] The story itself illustrates the conflicts and rivalries that characterized rural society, in which the symbols of piety and power represented the control of human and material resources.

For Yucatecans, two decades of turmoil still lay ahead, but by the early 1860s there were already subtle hints of the growing bourgeois culture commonly associated with the later henequen boom. Travel through the peninsula resumed, and local santo-based fiestas once more began to advertise themselves in the Mérida newspapers. From Oxkutzcab, Leocadio Espinosa posted an announcement in 1861 for that year's fiesta of San Antonio Xocneceh; he promised a mass, a ball, bullfights, a dance of mestiza women, and dazzling displays of lariat skills by "the young and dexterous vaqueros of Maní, Tekax, and Ticul."[93] What gentleman of leisure could resist? Like other townsfolk, the faithful of Xocneceh were inching ever so slightly closer to selling their santo as entertainment.

Xocneceh illustrates some of the dynamics associated with postclassic cofradías—that is, cofradía activity after the great liquidations of the Bourbon era. First, cofradía behavior never really disappeared; it simply assumed new forms. In this case, cult activities were internalized in the haciendas. Second, Xocneceh never entirely overcame the struggle between local private property and a broader public ownership. It also became the focal point of conflicts between legal administrative authority and popular custom, between prewar property rights and revolutionary expropriation. Like so much of the wealth and status of this society, the portrait of San Antonio found itself shifted to new hands.

More important than these, however, is the case's larger implications for Mexico's early national period. As a result of the Caste War and similar peasant rebellions, we have tended to paint the era in darkly declensional tones: the crisis of the cosmos, the unraveling of the Maya world, the liberal assault, and so forth.[94] We draw lines in the sand of history, branding anyone who dares to cross a betrayer of time-honored moral economies. But in reality things were not so simple. When one world replaces another—and seldom is the transition uniform or complete—there are normally attractions as well as coercions. More to the point, things presumed to be lost often return in modified forms. What persisted on the hacienda San Antonio Xocneceh were certain norms and protocols of peasant piety, certain community rights that occasionally overrode the cudgel of private property. This persistent past helped mediate the changes that were underway for Maya peasants and ensured that some of the most important features of late-colonial popular culture would be internalized to the emerging hacienda structure. All was not lost, and all change was not an earthquake.

Xocneceh to the Present

After exploring this case for so long, it is worth a moment to follow its traceable threads to the present. When Gregoria González died, her son Benjamín Luján inherited Xocneceh. He did manage to have the portrait returned to the hacienda, but he was unable to restore the estate to its old economic vigor. By the time of his death in 1898 San Antonio Xocneceh had fallen into decrepitude. The fertility of the soil sustained the estate's relatively strong market value—5,979 pesos—but Xocneceh itself had little more than a handful of cattle and a "small, antiquated mill," some tattered furniture, and a clock that no longer kept time. In fact, the only item of property that stood out for its value was the portrait itself, worth one hundred pesos.[95]

By the time of the Mexican Revolution of 1910, the hacienda San Antonio Xocneceh had passed into the hands of Francisco "Pancho" Cantón, a member of one of Yucatán's wealthiest families and the most stalwart of religious conservatives.[96] Cantón eventually served as governor during the time that Porfirio Díaz carved out the national territory of Quintana Roo; the former was so famous for his religious devotion that popular folklore attributed his military successes to the interventions of Santa Inez, who appeared beside him in battle.[97] The temptation is to believe that he purchased the hacienda out of religious piety, since even before the French Empire had fallen, complaints had surfaced about the ongoing decline of the cult.[98] At the same time, the huge henequen plantations of the north now dwarfed San Antonio Xocneceh as an economic power.[99] Indeed, Cantón's property often did little more than supply corn for the larger and economically more dynamic hacienda Tabi, some twelve miles away.[100] Xocneceh was passing into quaintness. Nevertheless, the hacienda and chapel continued their operations well past the "first spark of the Revolution," only to be broken up in the 1940s following President Lázaro Cárdenas's (1934–1940) imposition of agrarian reform in the peninsula. Part of the estate became ejido land; the chapel, the corral, and some seventy hectares remained private property but lay in disuse for decades. The company that held Cantón's mortgage, Agustín Vales and Sons, retained control of the hacienda's nucleus, and it has remained in the hands of the Vales family ever since.[101] Signs of life have recently returned, for Xocneceh's current owner is redeveloping the property to produce Italian lemons for sale to the Coca-Cola company, while a son-in-law of the current governor (Victor Manuel Cervera Pacheco) has purchased the house and chapel as possible tourist attractions.[102]

But the Yucatecan past survives in obscure corners. Today the somber portrait of San Antonio de Padua de Xocneceh—alternately the property of José Concepción Cáceres, of Jacinto Pat, of Gregoria González, of Governor Cantón—hangs today in the church of Oxkutzcab. The saint faces the right side of the canvas. Before him stands a table with the Bible laid upon it; above the Bible hovers a cloud bearing the Christ child and a rose bush with three red blooms. This canvas rests within the innermost panel of a triptych suspended from the southern wall. Below appears the following inscription:

PROMESA TO SEÑOR SAN ANTONIO DE PADUA
OXKUTZCAB, 26 APRIL 1948
SEÑORA CARMELA AVILA DE L.

Other continuities surround the cult. Today a local group, the *Gremio de Agricultores,* has the responsibility of managing the saint's fiesta every June 13. Each year the gremio selects a patrón to be responsible for organizing a fiesta. Although a man serves as patrón, the members themselves are all women of various ages; they decorate the church with ribbons and paper streamers, together with elaborately woven banners called *ex votos,* which announce that the work was done in exchange for the supernatural services of the santo. At the time of writing (1995–1999), the June 13 sermon still commemorates the deeds of the santo, especially his celebrated conversation. After mass, the gremio members parade San Antonio through the streets to the accompaniment of drums and saxophone. Others send up skyrockets. In the face of the santo the faithful still identify the unfulfilled longings of a thousand years.[103]

But old-time religion here is in patent decline. The fifty to sixty participants of the gremio are a far cry from the hundreds of men and women who abducted San Antonio in the time of Padre Espinosa. In fact, few men seem to pay much attention to the cult. Many are unemployed; despite its citrus industry, Oxkutzcab, like other parts of Yucatán, is staggering under the collapse of henequen and the nonappearance of a successor. Some men have become evangelicals. Although a man invariably serves as the patrón of San Antonio's annual fiesta (offering tortillas, *relleno negro,* Coca-Cola, and beer), village men see the event as a woman's affair and for the most part stay away, or else stick to themselves in a safely segregated masculine corner. Like the urban cofrades of the nineteenth century, they have yielded leadership and participation to their wives, whom they refer to as *las viejitas*.

And the chapel? Informants in Yotholim report that San Antonio still makes an annual visit to their village; furthermore, the santo himself was once accustomed to spending two days each year in his ancient home of Xocneceh, but the church there has fallen into such disrepair (the roof collapsed over twenty years ago) that this is no longer possible. A visit to Xocneceh readily confirms these accounts, for, as the *Catalogue of Religious Constructions of the State of Yucatán* (1945) notes, with understatement, "Its state of preservation is quite poor." The *Catalogue* also reports that a carved stone image of San Antonio that once graced its facade was removed to Mérida's Archaeological Museum during the revolutionary regime of General Salvador Alvarado (1915–1918), when religious iconography once more became a controversial issue.[104] The current whereabouts of this other San Antonio are anyone's guess.

CHAPTER 6

A Culture of Conflict

*Anticlericalism, Parish Problems,
and Alternative Beliefs*

SOME MEN HATED priests. Even though they may have considered themselves Christians and believers, they nonetheless disdained the clerics who were the backbone of the church. This fact colored life in the rural towns, and it also had a great deal to do with the revolutions of the 1840s. Yucatán's Caste War came into existence in part because local caudillos and Maya peasants agreed that they disliked priests, or at least the taxes priests charged. In spite of an established church with deep folkloric roots, then, the half century after independence included a culture of religious conflict as well as consensus. Consequently, both this and the succeeding chapter explore upheavals, hatreds, accusations, and ideological dissidence in order to answer a simple question: Why the rancor in a land where everyone was Catholic?

Anticlericalism and parish conflicts were facts of provincial life, but they also reached beyond state boundaries and into one of Mexico's most important nineteenth-century movements: liberalism. From a top-down perspective, liberalism was an attempt to impose a laissez-faire capitalism based on both social and economic individualism with a particular animus toward the corporate wealth and privileges of the Catholic Church and the traditionalistic, communally based Indian village.[1] But recent work argues that liberalism was as potent in its "folk" versions as in its official doctrine; these included a demand for greater autonomy (individual or municipal), lighter taxes, broader political participation, and vaguely defined notions of progress.[2] As I hope to show here, folk liberalism also included a stubborn streak of anticlericalism based on a resentment of the parish priest's social influence, personal prestige, and economic advantage. Anticlerical quarrels of the pre-reform years help to explain how people experienced these issues at a local level, what they expected of priests, and why they gravitated away from the pre-Bourbon vision of a parish-based community life. Finally, this look at a culture of religious conflict examines the emergence of the first coherent, alternative religious ideology—spiritualism—to see how it provided a transition from traditional Catholic teachings to such new systems of belief as liberalism and Protestantism.

The Roots of Popular Anticlericalism

The Catholic religion may have had no rivals to official power, but hegemonies breed counterhegemonies. This, I think, explains why some parishioners, whether rural or urban, demonstrated such a persistent streak of hostility to the institution and its servants. In a sense the early postcolonial church cornered itself by its own absolutism. Catholicism functioned as the established, official religion until the 1856 reform laws; even then, Protestant sects remained virtually unknown on the peninsula until the first Presbyterian mission there in 1877.[3] The upshot was that in Mexico, as in other nations where Catholicism has enjoyed a virtual monopoly, dissenters found no alternative religions to which to gravitate.[4]

Spain offers a case in point. A Catholic nation if ever there was one, it also harbored some of the most bitterly anti-Catholic feelings of all of Europe. The national folklore is replete with motifs such as the fat, licentious friar, while anticlerical rumors, or *bules,* punctuated the nineteenth century. (Example: Jesuits began the 1834 cholera epidemic.[5]) Between 1812 and 1860 Spanish liberals fought their own war of reform against the privileges of the Spanish Catholic Church, gradually stripping it of its lands and making it dependent on state funding.[6] Finally, all of Spain's latent anticlerical tendencies came to a head during the early months of the civil war, when violence against priests and nuns erupted throughout the country.[7] As with the persecution of Jews in eastern Europe, it is impossible to explain these events solely as the machinations of a handful of powerful men; rather, anticlerical agitations spoke to something deep in the Spanish psyche. In both Spain and Mexico, anti-Catholicism became a kind of creed in itself: an attitude of disbelief in which the individual defined himself through a negative posture toward the church, its doctrines, its regalia, and, above all, its priests. Hence the anticlerical mood, not only of Yucatán but of most of the nineteenth-century Hispanic world.

In some parts of the world, perhaps, this mood stemmed from the church's reluctance to adapt itself to a changing scientific worldview. But it is doubtful that scientific paradigms weighed much on the minds of townsfolk in Peto or Pustunich. Rather, economic growth, increasing competition, and widespread demographic realignments were helping to break down older colonial norms. These changes fueled a growing individualism in both social and economic matters, heightened resentment toward traditional prestige and social power, and made it easier to be skeptical about the church's rights and ideological foundations. Curas had privileged access to peasant taxes, an institutional advantage as accumulators of loan capital, and a degree of literacy and legal ability usually superior to that of the average creole, facts that did not always endear the padres to their congregations.

Other key historical changes were also at work. Between 1800 and 1847 several related dynamics were operating upon the clergy. More affluent curas like Raymundo Pérez had blended into the rural bourgeoisie, acquiring properties and contracting mortgages at a steady rate. The church may have been declining as a political institution, but at the same time key members came to enjoy great importance in secular business and politics. With their education and broad discretionary powers, the curas provided important nuclei for town politics and factions. The priest's importance may have depended on himself as individual, but it was also true that his wealth and power had been accumulated through the institutional devices that had always been the lifeblood of church economics.

Simultaneously, however, the overall quality of the priesthood deteriorated. In part this had to do with the near-total disappearance of the regular orders, historically characterized by greater discipline and motivation than the seculars.[8] A military governor in the 1850s spoke accurately when he observed that "the Indians respect [friars] much more than the secular ecclesiastics."[9] Moreover, and beginning with the bishopric of Agustín Estévez y Ugarte (1797–1827), the secular church recruited more than ever from the middle and lower classes, poorer, less polished, and less educated than their patrician predecessors; seminary training remained the exception, not the rule, and therefore failed to counteract their lack of preparation as leaders of the old parish system.[10] Lack of family means forced them to grub for whatever could be gotten out of parish work. These changes contributed to a polarization of wealth and power, with better-positioned members continuing to wield their accustomed influence in the society; disadvantaged members lost out, working as temporary help or else abandoning their vocations for other pastures.

It is perhaps not surprising, then, that their numbers were shrinking. The overall size of the Mexican church had been declining since the eighteenth century as Bourbon reformers restricted the regular orders, forbade the establishment of new convents, and reactivated the *patronato real,* or crown right to approve new clerical appointments to the Americas.[11] Southeast Mexico was no exception to the trend. The French traveler Federick de Waldeck, whose sources are unknown, reported that Yucatán's ecclesiastical numbers declined by 20 percent between 1830 and 1834, part of an overall trend of dwindling priests in Mexico.[12] Decline in friars, nuns, and convented children was even more precipitous. This report finds confirmation in other accounts of a decline in church support, a trend beginning well before independence. At least in the case of Yucatán, the higher functionaries of the cathedral were reluctant to impose too much discipline on a priesthood that was undertrained, undermanned, underfunded, and underappreciated.[13]

Another change involved the political liberalizations that followed independence, particularly regarding contact with foreign countries. Independence had much to do with the creoles' desire for freer trade, and with that trade came a livelier flow of ideas and opinions. Visits to and from the United States increased, a point well documented by the numerous legal disputes of Yankee sea captains in the state's notarial archives.[14] At least two of the more prominent foreign visitors, Waldeck and the New Orleans book dealer B. A. Norman, left blistering accounts of the clergy. These writers certainly did not cause anticlericalism; in fact, they emerged from two separate traditions of anti-Catholic hostility, the former an enlightenment skeptic, the latter a Protestant disdainful of Mexico's religious traditions. But they were read in the peninsula, and their words spoke to a set of values and beliefs—or, better said, disbeliefs—that had been maturing in Mexico since the early eighteenth century. The Bourbon administrators who arrived in Madrid brought with them the French secular state's struggle to limit the church, particularly in the colonies. This resulted in an increasing administrative hostility to the church, something of which peasants and vecinos were well aware: they could now attack the village priest and get away with it.

These changes took their collective toll on the aura of prestige and inviolability the colonial friars had enjoyed. Without regressing to an earlier underestimation of the priest's social importance in peninsular Mexico, we can still safely admit that clerical legitimacy deteriorated in the nineteenth century.[15] Certainly the Catholic organization emerged bruised from the brief years of the Spanish constitution. Additional factors included the secularization of the Franciscans, the participation of priests in the increasingly rough-and-tumble politics of the time, and the curas' integral (and privileged) role in the expanding commercial economy. Beyond this lay a broad category of problems that cast dispersions on the clergy and made it less attractive as a source of social leadership. These problems involved incompetence, secularism, moral laxity, and institutional infighting.

Who were the anticlerics? Jean Meyer's massive study of Mexican anticlericalism has left the impression that such sentiments were the imposition of a handful of elites, mostly northerners, over an otherwise intensely devout people.[16] Although accurate in some regards, this reading tends to simplify and distort. Hostility toward the church and its servants emanated from a far broader base than Meyer was willing to acknowledge. In fact, as nearly as can be determined, the anticlerical mood of the early national period did not always find its most strident voice among prominent oligarchs and landowners. Such men had intimate family and economic relations with the church and consequently found little reason to rain blasphemies on the land. The best and perhaps most ironic example was also the most prominent: Santiago Imán, the forty-year-old Tizimín merchant and military officer who launched a successful break with Mexico in 1839 by promising his peasant recruits that he would abolish their church taxes. Imán's family had long connections with the church; his father had made much of his wealth by taking contracts as a tithe collector for the church, while Santiago Imán himself remained on good terms with numerous priests (including his own nephew) after the revolt. The caudillo of Tizimín appears only to have adopted his anticlerical platform from sheer expediency.[17] Similarly, his even more powerful counterpart in Valladolid, the patriarch Agustín Acereto, enjoyed close relations with the local clergy.[18] Social conservatism suited these men, a point Imán made clear in his own writings.

Rather, it would be a secondary level of creoles and mestizos who provided shock troops for the anticlerical assault. They were less likely to be connected with the church through family ties, since upward mobility into the priesthood was limited.[19] Although there is little available research on the matter, it seems reasonable to assume that humble artisans and rancheros had less stable home lives than did the patriarchs, were more prone to common-law marriages, and had less motive for upholding church prescriptions for public morality. Historically excluded from the clergy, they had never been the main focus of colonial church activity, and they associated deference toward clergy with their ethnic inferiors, the Maya peasantry.[20] Above all they were ambitious. Such men dreamed of opportunity regardless of the social cost. Less propertied and less scrupulous than the great patriarchs, they resented the privileged position that priests enjoyed in municipal life, and they found that peasants, while otherwise devout Catholics of the folk variety, responded to demagogy against clerical authority and church taxes. A Belizean official who met one of the more important of Imán's lieutenants (the smuggler Vito Pacheco) in 1849 during the height of the Caste War dryly remarked that he "does not appear to be very partial to padres in general."[21] Lucas Polanco, the creole who tried to end the urban cofradía of Chocholá (see Chapter 3), was in fact illiterate.[22] Although social elites may have set the tone in some matters, in this case it seems more likely that certain attitudes simmered among the mestizos and lesser creoles, eventually bubbling up to men like Imán and, by extension, into state political life.

To a large extent Mayas filled out the anticlerical ranks. The matter of Maya-priest relationships is one of the most complex of all Caste War–related problems. On one hand, there is little real evidence that the war was motivated by peasant outrage over lack of church piety; clear-cut material factors such as land, taxes, subregional separatism, and growing political violence at the municipal level played a demonstrably greater role, while approximately identical pastoral conditions failed to provoke violence or revolt in areas outside the rebellious east. Moreover, peasant relationships with priests were often political in nature, each side working to get what it wanted from the arrangement. Priests and Mayas continued to associate once the war began. The prickly separatists of Chan Santa Cruz allowed priests to enter from time to time, albeit under highly controlled circumstances. The *pacíficos del sur,* a largely autonomous group of deserters and refugees, were even more well disposed to visiting clergy; the 1863 mission of José Dolores Crespo and the 1865–1866 mission of Juan de la Cruz Camal and Juan Bautista Aguilar resulted in hundreds of well-documented baptisms and marriages.[23] Though suspicious of outsiders, this group—ethnically and even nationally mixed, though predominantly Maya—was accommodating enough with the Catholic clergy. There was never any irreparable breach between priest and peasant in the nineteenth century, at least when taking the society as a whole.

On the other hand, there were enough problems to guarantee a steady undercurrent of hostilities. This was particularly true from the eighteenth century onward. As Robert Haskett pointed out about the Cuernavaca and Taxco regions, the rebounding indigenous population made it difficult to maintain earlier levels of service to parishioners.[24] Moreover, anticlerical Bourbon tendencies began to filter into southeast Mexico at this same time, teaching peasants that they could stand up to the church with impunity. In Chikintsonot, for example, Padre José Escalante found himself menaced by Melchor Yama, a Maya who had served in the recently abolished ayuntamiento under the 1812–1814 constitution; Yama took to stalking Escalante through the local cemetery—disguised, shirtless, knife in hand. This was a far cry from the hand-kissing peasant subordinates of legend.[25] Incidents of peasants confronting their spiritual shepherds were common; popular opposition to church taxes was usually the underlying issue, and under the right circumstances, such as those that surrounded the outbreak of the war in 1847, peasant-priest hostilities could boil over into violence.[26]

Mexican folklore captures this ambiguous relationship. Curas often function as benefactors, as in "The Mare's Son," the tale of a girl whose wicked stepmother causes her to give birth to a horse by slipping horse urine into her chocolate; the father disowns the poor girl until a local cura discovers the witchcraft and puts things right.[27] Similarly, in the story "Dámaso and the Demon," when the townsfolk discover a bush enchanted by the devil, they burn it and call in the local priest to bless the ground.[28] Or when stalking the wáay-chivo, even if the hunter had already cut a cross into his bullets and rubbed them in salt, he might still call upon a priest to bless them.[29] Finally, in a folktale collected from a Puebla informant (around 1929), the boy who kills a kindly priest is unable to escape the telltale evidence of his victim's ghostly head.[30] In all four instances, what is of value is the priest's ability to counteract spells, malevolent forces, and evil deeds. But the curas could also be the butt of cruel jokes. "The Man with a Tiny Penis," collected near Chichén Itzá in 1930, provides the best example of this countercurrent. In this ribald story an underendowed Maya procures a magic ring that causes his penis to grow whenever he raises his hand. One day by mishap the ring ends up with the cura, and as he lifts his hand to say mass his member grows uncontrollably, until it has to be cut off.[31] The story plays upon tension between the priest's vocational asexuality and his nonetheless real male identity.

Gender also played a hand, since anticlerics were overwhelmingly male; I have seen no evidence of explicit female anticlericalism, although there were certainly enough cases in which friction erupted with women, Maya peasant women in particular, over specific personalities and practices. The situation resembled that of overwhelmingly Catholic nations such as nineteenth-century France, where "in many regions practically no man except the priest set foot in church."[32] Men had less tolerance of supervision—whether economic, political, or social—by other men. They often viewed the priest as a *metiche,* or intrusive busybody, who was always checking up on other people's morals. The public sphere was reserved for them alone, and they resented privileged roles occupied by clerics. They also had less interest in the company of non-threatening males, less commitment to domestic values, and little need for the church as a framework for their public activities.[33] Finally, anticlerical tendencies in the Americas dated back to fundamental competitions between the friars and the male *encomenderos* over control of the Indians. Their competition had continued in various forms over the centuries but erupted with new virulence once the restraining hand of Spain was gone. This gender difference regarding piety is captured in a Veracruzan folksong, "*La paloma*": "The she-dove and the he-dove went to mass/ The she-dove prayed and the he-dove laughed."[34]

Another distinguishing characteristic is that these men usually did not live in Mérida or Campeche. They tended to come from rural towns, particularly from the backwoods and the wild, dusty streets of the *oriente,* the peninsula's eastern half. The church's systems of ideological reproduction were weak here. Newspapers were few, the locals were far removed from the scrutinies of the cathedral, and bourgeois forms of reverence and decorum meant less than in the city. As with the poor northeast of nineteenth-century Brazil, people were freer to carry religious sentiments, or lack of them, to new limits.[35]

For precisely the same reasons, anticlerics kept a lower profile in the capital. One evidence of this was newspaper and literary production of the prereform years. As previously discussed, most of the newspapers and literary journals were either conservative or else relatively circumspect. True, there were cases in which anticlericalism did indeed inform the peninsula's ideological production. Raymundo Pérez's 1813 polemical exchange was one. *El yucateco*'s 1824 exposé on church tax irregularities in Peto was another.[36] Silvestre Antonio Dondé of Tekax was severely attacked in 1841 after the Imán revolt opened new paths of permissibility.[37] But these hotly anticlerical writings avoided criticizing the underlying assumptions of religion: the soul, the afterlife, the importance of a spiritual institution. Whether they really thought or cared about such theological matters is not always clear; what is certain is that the literary device of the good priest was useful for bludgeoning real priests who stood in their way. The reader has to go all the way to 1861, to Apolinar García y García's *El mus,* to find a journal with out-and-out ridicule of the church; and even García always insisted, perhaps ingenuously, that he fought against abuses, not against the institution itself.[38]

But the anticlerical tendency began long before Yucatecans printed their first newspaper. It probably traced back to the Middle Ages, when the church was gaining ascendancy throughout southern Europe. It was certainly well developed by the time of the conquest: the most notorious incident of sixteenth-century peninsular society was Bishop Diego de Landa's inquisitional trials (1562) for suspected Maya "heretics." The investigations quickly degenerated into torture sessions that put Landa in conflict with secular vecinos dependant on Maya tribute.[39] Church-vecino quarrels continued for the next quarter century. They were exacerbated by internal church quarrels (the problem of Franciscans) and by the dawning commercialization of the eighteenth century. Before independence Yucatán witnessed two significant outbreaks of anticlericalism. The first was the constitutional crisis of 1812–1814, which momentarily lifted the traditional controls of the countryside. The second was the secularization of the Franciscans on January 1, 1821: a joyous moment for liberals but a sad day for historians, as it witnessed the destruction of a large quantity of the order's books and manuscripts. What took place after 1821, therefore, had long antecedents in this dry land.

Complaints

There is abundant evidence of problems with priests in documents of the nineteenth century.[40] In addition to skepticism, we find unseemly public brawls and lawsuits among vecinos and clergy that not only questioned the sanctity of the church as an institution but also drew in the local Mayas as witnesses and partisans. These quarrels erupted over a wide variety of issues, many of them discussed in the preceding chapter. In most cases, however, disputes boiled down to the fact that some faction of the rural community resented what they perceived to be clerical privilege in social and economic matters on the local stage. It is never entirely clear whether the complaints resulted from a deep-seated hatred of priests or from parishioners' discontent with the way a particular priest was doing his job. Most seem to have involved a combination of both: anticlerics and an unpoliticized, generally devout majority saw the same priestly misbehavior, and though discontents led the complaint, most of the community simply wanted to rectify a problem.

The majority of the cases found in the Mexico City and Mérida archives have to do with some form of clerical mismanagement. There were clear reasons for this. Priests bore enormous administrative responsibilities in a system that bridged Maya and Spaniard, tributary and capitalist economies, personal and institutional wealth, all with minimal infrastructure and the most primitive of records keeping. It is hardly surprising, then, to find conflicts of finance and administration at center stage.

One underlying problem was the increasing poverty of parishes, something that had been growing serious since the 1830s. First came the end of tithes (1834), then the reduction of obventions after the Imán revolt (1840), their further reduction following the eruption of the Caste War (1847), and the complete abolition of all funding, excluding fees for services such as baptisms and weddings (1859). Priests found themselves trying to reconcile contradictory desires of their people: maximum religious service with minimal funding. The dilemma forced them into difficult and at times unsavory choices. In restoring the church of Opichén, for example, Silvestre Barbosa cannibalized the doors and windows of the abandoned convent at Kopomá. This latter town was itself poor and unkempt as a result of demographic shifts and prolonged war, and rumor immediately arose that Barbosa had taken the objects for his own personal use.[41] In another case, Padre Antonio Acosta of Cholul converted the unused convent behind the church into a general store.[42] In the worst cases, curas simply had to lay off their assistant ministers until political and economic times improved.[43]

Mismanagement also involved fundamental questions of *how* to manage. One quarrel of long standing was the right to collect church taxes of peons, something the hacendado supposedly handled. Prior to the reform laws, curas often looked at the haciendas as tax shelters for peasants, since the obligation of payment devolved to the hacendado, who might refuse to pay or even to allow the priest or his collectors onto the property. Hacendados in turn accused the fathers of overstepping their jurisdiction by intruding in hacienda affairs. This conflict turned up in Sacalum, for example, where Padre José León García accused Felipe Peón of harboring peasants on his property, San Antonio. But Peón was no mere citizen; the political prefect of Ticul and one of the biggest property owners on the peninsula, he reversed the direction of the case, which ended in a reprimand of García.[44]

Mayas and vecinos alike often complained of poor religious service, particularly of extreme unction or the spiritual absolution of those about to die. It was the easy accusation because it was often true: the great distances and poor transportation of rural society, together with the occasionally sudden nature of death, made it difficult to deliver the sacrament in a timely fashion. However, many of these cases appear to be contrived, or at least utilized, for political ends. Complaints of poor service also related to one of the most fundamental conflicts of rural society. Outlying villages and estates paid taxes to larger urban centers but received only a fraction of the services. Rather than repeat the work of previous studies, suffice it to say that the quest for municipal autonomy was a locomotive of political change in the region, perhaps in all of Mexico, and that complaints of poor clerical service were one of its telltale signs.[45]

Conflicts with the peasantry were also rooted in the priest's multiple roles. Being the village's main public servant deepened social bonds, but the priest's simultaneous demands as hacendado and employer could also lead to misunderstandings and hard feelings. Probably the best case study of this was Pedro José Hurtado, longtime priest of Bécal and a clergyman in many ways as interesting as Raymundo Pérez. Hurtado was a *malagueño* by birth and had vigorously opposed independence; his name appears on an 1822 broadside advertising the names of peninsular reactionaries and urging concerned parties not to employ them.[46] But despite the initial anti-Spanish hysteria of the early 1820s, Hurtado adjusted well enough to life in the new nation. Although he never learned to speak Maya with much fluency, Hurtado did have a flair for business and like many curas went on to develop haciendas within the confines of his own parish.[47] Moreover, he also acted as the legal agent of Felipe Peón in connection with the latter's sugar hacienda, Tabí, in the Sierra Alta, one of the largest of all Yucatecan estates.[48] In 1845 the padre joined the rush for public lands by denouncing two different properties. The first consisted of five square miles in the nearby town of Muna, immediately to the south of Mérida. The other consisted of a slightly larger property in his own parish of Nunkiní. In the latter instance, the grant title specifically described the padre's new property as bordering on village lands. Hurtado was in fact one of the few individuals to file multiple denuncias.[49]

From the cura's point of view, these enterprises were not merely lucrative but essential to parish life. They provided the priest with a reliable source of income in otherwise uncertain times and allowed him to cover the often considerable costs of parish maintenance. However, they also led to a confusion of roles that in turn generated quarrels with peasants who worked on his haciendas; Hurtado chose to see them as laborers who had contractual obligations, while they emphasized that they were parishioners who deserved special consideration. This interpretive conflict operated, for example, in the 1822 lawsuit that Feliciano Pat and Francisco Kantún filed against Hurtado. The plaintiffs, peasants of Nunkiní, argued that six years earlier Hurtado had confiscated the papers documenting the founding of their sitios, Ib and Hambul, and had annexed the properties to his own estate. In April of 1822, six laborers sent repeated complaints to the bishop, charging that Hurtado refused to present them with the documents that would allow them to leave. The six stressed that they were independent masons and free villagers and that Hurtado was continuing to charge them obventions (for which he, as hacendado, was technically liable) while at the same time falling into arrears on their salaries. Hurtado countered with the testimony of two alcaldes who swore that the workers in question were not masons as they had claimed but simple peons who had failed to fulfill their contracts.[50] The peasants' complaints were eventually pushed aside, even though Hurtado continued to have problems with both peasant parishioners (witness Catalina Pan's cult of San Diego) and with creoles.

Mismanagement problems, then, stemmed from two related sources. The first and most fundamental was the declining base of parish revenues that drove priests to unpalatable decisions or even vocational apathy. The second concerned the multiplicity of roles that curas tended to occupy, especially when curas were hacendados within the confines of their own parishes. Seen in the long view, the second stemmed from the first, since Yucatecan curas entered into the hacienda business to find security in a poor and insecure rural province. The success of men like Hurtado and Raymundo Pérez, however, tended to compromise their spiritual activities and left them open to criticisms and attacks.

Sexual indiscretion was a less common but highly sensitive complaint, all the more unique given the priest's universally known vow of celibacy. Much has been written about the problem, usually drawing upon John Lloyd Stephens's wry observation that "in Yucatan the burden [of celibacy] was found too heavy to be borne."[51] A self-described admirer of the padres, who aided him inestimably with his research and travel, Stephens nonetheless perceived clerical common-law marriages to be the norm. But there has never been systematic investigation of the matter. The fact is that in its day and time the issue defied simple responses but, rather, depended on a matrix of conditions. Parishioners tolerated priests' relationships with women when the individuals in question were mature and responsible and the relationship carried on with discretion. Extant evidence suggests that sexual relations were usually consensual. Moreover, country people understood the importance of the household as a way of life and were apt to forgive when the priest found ways to make his life more comfortable. (Miguel Hidalgo's robust carryings-on do not seem to have bothered anyone but his superiors.) But morality issues went arm in arm with questions of local ecclesiastical authority. When one person—priest, official, or hacendado—trespassed into someone else's baili-wick, he risked having his dirty laundry brought up before the authorities in Mérida. Similarly, townsfolk grew indignant when the affair in question be-came scandalous or violent. One way or the other, such relationships were a part of rural life, and while many of the allegations were mere embellishment, they often contained a core of truth revealed in subsequent investigations.

This was the case with Ignacio Romero. A Franciscan, Romero had been turned out of his monastery during the secularization of January 1821. As a livelihood he began to freelance the sacraments in the vicinity of Tzucacab, Ticum, and Peto, and with some success, since he was able to win a follow-ing among the Maya sacristans and even enjoyed the support of Tzucacab's alcalde. Romero made himself vulnerable, however, by taking up with a Baca-lar woman named Guadalupe González, with whom he fathered a child. All of this infuriated the cura of Peto, Miguel Pacheco, who was able to use the charge of *concubinato* (concubinage) to discredit his interloping rival. Romero admitted to his illicit relationship but pleaded hardship. He had been thrown out of the monastery: how else was he to make ends meet? Doubtless the affair had more emotional links than Romero cared to admit, but in the end they failed to save him: Romero suffered two months suspension, while Guadalupe González ran away to Mérida with another man.[52] This case of the freelance minister throws out tantalizing hints about rural life. Clearly, fees for inci-dental services offered priests one of the few ways to make a livelihood out of a peasant society, and curas quite understandably guarded their territory against interlopers. At the same time, we should note that Romero's mistress and his lack of official appointment did not in themselves alienate him from peasants or vecinos; popular definitions of the clerical role proved highly tol-erant. Romero offered expanded religious services to meet local demand and in so doing provided an alternative to the official church authority. His love life, however, fell to casualty in the process.

One of the more elaborate cases of illicit sexual relations concerned Manuel Matías Mendoza, the minister of Acanceh. In 1851 (not everyone was worrying about the Caste War) the thirty-four-year-old Mendoza conceived a mad pas-sion for a certain Egidia Cetina, a local woman thirteen years his junior. She reciprocated and ran away with him to his parents' house for several months, and even though she eventually returned home, Egidia gave birth to his two children over the next three years. This much the family could forgive, apparently. But trouble erupted once more when Mendoza, always profoundly jealous, fixed his suspicions on Juan Nepomuceno López, the brother of one of Egidia's close friends. Mendoza staged embarrassing public rows, even threatening López and other supposed rivals with a knife. In the late evenings Mendoza disguised himself as a vaquero in order to follow López's movements. Owing to Mendoza's increasing belligerence, Egidia's father ordered a separation, and a complex struggle ensued. The father tried to keep Mendoza away, Egidia tried to get Mendoza to return, and the priest himself continued his jealous vendetta against López. In the end it was Egidia's own love that brought matters to a head; hoping to rekindle Mendoza's amorous visits, she misguidedly informed the cura of Izamal (José Canuto Vela, a priest who had once negotiated with the Caste War rebels) of the situation when he passed through town in late 1854. Testimony against Mendoza was massive and consistent: some 108 pages of interviews with all of the principals, many of the local townsfolk, and even the batab and república de indígenas. For all of this, Mendoza received eight days' suspension and the court costs of sixty-two pesos. This sort of treatment was indicative of the lenient sentences the ecclesiastical courts meted out to priests accused of wrongdoing. Egidia, meanwhile, was forgotten.

Somewhat similar dynamics run through the story of Candelaria Tukuch, the only case I have been able to find of a Maya woman advancing a paternity suit against a priest. In 1858 Candelaria Tukuch accused Padre Jacobo Machado of having seduced her six years earlier "with gifts and shows of affection." Tukuch eventually became pregnant; Machado purchased the family a house and gave his lover money when the child was born. But "unfounded suspicions" caused him to break off the affair. Here, too, there was at least some degree of consent. Tukuch's explanation for the affair alternated between pleas of poverty and suggestions of real attraction. She only sought five hundred pesos in damages after the relationship had gone sour.[53]

As with mistreatment of peasants, sexual improprieties were less tolerable when the woman was married or when powerful rivalries were involved—when a priest vied with an official or influential local creole for the woman in question. In such cases, the bishop was certain to get an earful of angry complaints. In 1815, for example, the cura of remote Polyuc, a certain Francisco Brito, fell in love with the wife of the town's *juez de paz* (magistrate). The jealous husband responded by beating the woman and threatening to shoot the priest, but the liaisons continued nevertheless. The contest between the men grew so heated that Polyuc's juez eventually had to write to have Brito recalled before "an altogether fatal disaster" should happen.[54] Similarly, the cura of Hopelchén had to step in and negotiate a peaceful resolution when Miguel Cabañas, a priest and sugar entrepreneur of Hopelchén, developed a relationship with Hipólita Maldonado, a woman with a husband and two children.[55] Far stranger, however, was the case of Padre José Antonio Acosta of Conkal. Acosta had become friendly with the family of a certain Santiago Aguilar when he fell into a passionate affair with the man's sixteen-year-old daughter. The girl had in fact left her home and gone to live with Acosta. When Aguilar made efforts to force her return, Acosta told Aguilar's wife (rightly or otherwise) that Aguilar himself was carrying on an affair with another woman, "as a result of which he lives in a state of continual warfare." The town's magistrate, himself "no enemy of the clergy," found himself in the delicate position of explaining the situation to the bishop. The church's response was to relocate Acosta to an outlying town of the parish, with the understanding that he must stay out of Conkal.[56]

Sexual relations in all these instances where consensual. Egidia Cetina only made her decision to inform on her lover in a misguided effort to force his return; reciprocated affection was common to the other cases as well. Candelaria Tukuch abided the situation with Padre Machado as long as it appeared that the two still shared an emotional bond. It was far more likely that a third party would intervene, as happened when the mother of Florentina Cervera tried to put an end to the love affair between her married daughter and the minister of Sotuta.[57] The only documented case of what today would be called sexual harassment occurred in Yaxcabá, where José Bartolomé del Granado Baeza presided for many years. One day a girl of the village accused his minister, Alexo del Castillo, of unwanted advances. Accosting her down by the town's enormous cenote, he placed his hand on her pubis and told her not to be afraid, that "it is not a sin" ("*no seas tonta, no es pecado*"). Other victims soon came forward. The outraged Baeza banished Castillo forever from Yaxcabá, "for I do not want a wolf in sheep's clothing."[58] Yaxcabá aside, however, sexual harassment does not form a running litany in surviving correspondence of the church and its female members. When peasant women complained, it was more likely to do with more practical matters, as when twenty-five Maya widows of Tixcacaltuyú petitioned that their cura had locked them in a house to force their long-delinquent payment of church taxes.[59]

Padre Castillo notwithstanding, the lore of priestly impropriety does not always coexist easily with a provable past. Current folklore in Quintana Roo's Caste War towns insists that the war erupted when the batab Cecilio Chi discovered that the local priest had violated his daughter, or in more elaborate versions was keeping local Maya damsels captive in a harem underneath the church.[60] I have found no documentary evidence to suggest such a relationship; this kind of sexual dominance flies in the face of what we know about nineteenth-century priests and their far-from-submissive Maya parishioners, while the story's underlying motif resembles the widely known story of how Pancho Villa began his life of banditry after murdering a property owner who had raped his sister. But the harem's value as lore is indisputable. On one hand, the avenging of wronged family honor is something that an audience understands in its gut, an undeniable provocation. On the other, the story encapsulates peasant resentments toward local elites, here embodied in the anonymous but lusty priest.

Despite its distinctly gentle punishments, the church appears to have dealt energetically with complaints of gross sexual misconduct. Of the ten cases I have been able to find, only three ended in clear admissions of guilt. What remains is a percentage in which sexual accusations formed part of the anticlerical arsenal, largely because they were both easy and potent. In the end the sexual behavior of priests brings us to the limits of documentable knowledge. It is impossible to say how common intimate relations were, and we exaggerate if we accept the old anticlerical quip that "parishioners only accepted a priest who had settled down with one woman."[61] Petitions against priests often started with accusations of concubinage, often a kind of warm-up for the real complaint. It is impossible to tell whether these charges were true or false or whether priest-woman relationships were simply a fact that did not become an issue until a larger rift developed in the community, at which point they became convenient charges. What is clear, however, is the situation's flexibility. Attitudes toward clerical unions emerged from the overall context of the priest's behavior. Discreet relations of responsible adults prospered, while scandalous behavior like that of Mendoza—by any calculus only one facet in the totality of relations between priest and parishioner—brought complaints.[62]

A third type of complaint involved behavior that was indecorous though not necessarily sexual. The rural clergy's tendency to blend into rural bourgeois culture enabled it to survive socioeconomic changes, but it also left the priests open to attacks by rivals. This was particularly true in regard to the priests who enjoyed the free and easygoing customs of the countryside, the same kind of worldly joy seen in religiously based fiestas of the larger cities. For example, when a faction of Sabán, a town in the deep southeast, launched a campaign against Francisco María Carrillo, they made a great deal of his fondness for nightlife. Vecinos accused the priest of meddling in local elections, probably the true heart of the conflict, but for good measure they also reported that Carrillo was raising "tumultuous gatherings" of nearly one hundred people, in which he paraded through the streets strumming a *guitarrilla* and singing verses "denigrative to the honor of certain married women." Sent to investigate, the cura of Ichmul had little difficulty finding witnesses to contradict these accounts. The "tumultuous gatherings," they explained, were merely the strolling serenades so popular in provincial towns.[63] Exactly the same thing happened when Luis Castro of Sahcabchén went after his enemy, Padre Manuel Urruña; the latter's admitted participation in serenades became public lewdness.[64] In the case of Carrillo, however, the padre's enthusiasm for public revelry does seem to have overstepped the bounds of innocent fun, since the vecinos of Hopelchén made an identical complaint against him eleven years later. The priest said mass only when paid, wore inappropriate clothing such as rings and "high shoes," fraternized with soldiers of the local national guard unit, gambled, and went through the streets at night with a guitar, singing bawdy songs.[65]

Even beyond the usual assortment of human shortcomings, these rustic towns occasionally produced misfits who were unsuited for existence in a settled and regulated society. One such man was José Ignacio Espinosa, deacon of Oxkutzcab. The Espinosa family was native to the region, and Espinosa's brother José Leocadio would eventually serve in a long and influential career in the parish, overseeing many of the ceremonies of the regional cofradía, San Antonio Xocneceh. José Ignacio was an intelligent man who preached in both Spanish and Maya. But by the age of thirty he had become a restless drunk. When intoxicated the deacon would barge into private homes in search of aguardiente, and if disappointed he would carry off anything he could lay his hands on. Espinosa engaged in brawls and public shouting matches. These actions often landed him in the public jail, "among the Indians, thieves, drunks and other criminals who are kept there." In 1835 the exasperated cura suspended Espinosa and placed him in shackles, locked within the quarters of the local convent. But the deacon contrived to pick the lock, scaled the walls of the convent, and set out for the tavern to make up for lost time. The cura eventually shipped Espinosa off to the custody of his brother, José Leocadio, who was then serving in Tecoh, but the brother's influence also failed, and the wayward deacon soon returned home. Of his later life we know nothing.[66]

The larger point here is that in the early to mid-1800s, rural priests, an accepted part of a hegemonic Catholic society, lived on social and cultural terms quite close to those of their parishioners. Doubtless much of this had to do with the isolation of Yucatán in general and of rural villages in particular. In the long run, its effect was ambiguous. It strengthened the ties between rural creoles and their pastors but also lent ammunition to those who wanted to deprive the priesthood of whatever privileges that had survived the Bourbon reforms. Complaints of bizarre or scandalous behavior thus pointed in two directions; some originated with incompetence, immorality, or a belligerent personality, while others reflected little more than the casual eccentricities of popular culture in the rural towns.

Finally, some of rural Mexico's quarrels originated not between priest and parishioner but, rather, among the priests themselves. The peninsular church was neither monolithic nor homogenous, but incorporated a diverse range of opinions and interests, all of which led to incidents that contributed to the image of an institution in crisis. Moreover, at bottom it was an institution of human beings, and it suffered all the factionalisms and personality conflicts that plague other organizations.

For the most part, intraclerical controversies fall into two categories. The first involved cases of horizontal division, or "turf wars," within the institution itself. At the highest level this meant rivalry for the office of bishop, as already seen in the struggle between José María Guerra and José María Meneses. The same high-level factional rivalries persisted well into the Porfiriato, as has been documented by Hernán Menéndez (1995).[67] At a much lower level, horizontal division meant priests quarreling over the scant resources of the parish. In a previous publication I have already explored what was probably the biggest bone of contention: rights to outlying peasant settlements. Such conflicts erupted in Hoctún, Pencuyut, and Tekax.[68] But certainly there were other sources of friction. Incoming administrators, for example, occasionally found themselves confronted by the chaotic bookkeeping of their predecessors. The missing doors of Kopomá were only one such example. Priests also had to guard their imágenes with great care, since the temptation for outgoing curas to take them to their new parishes was strong. Precisely this sort of argument erupted in Teabo in 1836, when the cura came to suspect that a predecessor had made off with the church's reliquary.[69] The problem resulted not necessarily from moral laxity but from the ambiguity of church-related property rights, particularly in cases when a cura had paid for parish refurbishing and iconography from his own pocket.

In some cases the accusations were a bit more serious. Among those dogged with suspicions of mismanagement and malfeasance was Antonio Mais, the longtime cura of Tihosuco and the man who had personally known the great Maya leaders of the Caste War. The rector of the seminary college prior to his resignation during the anti-Spanish movement of 1812, Mais was plagued for years by suspicions that he had grafted some four thousand pesos from the seminary funds. Mais himself changed his story on the matter as circumstances demanded; after a brief return to his native Málaga in the late 1820s, he reinvented himself as a wealthy sugar grower in the deep south, first in Ichmul, then in Tihosuco. The matter of the missing funds was never resolved.[70]

Other cases, if less sensational, confirmed the tendency. Quarrels over budgetary shortfalls, lost *cuentas de fábrica* (financial accounts), and rights to peasant taxes could smolder for years. In large part they stemmed from the limitations of this social and economic backwater. Records keeping was haphazard, travel was slow, jurisdictions often remained ill-defined, and despite the church's image of centralization, the bishop's office had little real idea of what was going on in individual parishes, particularly in remote areas like Tihosuco or Ichmul. These problems, together with the inevitable human tendency to treat office as personal property, contributed to disputes.

A second and much more interesting type of intraclerical conflict had certain class dimensions. Almost without exception these involved lower-ranking members of the clergy who were discontented with the supervision and privileges of their superiors. In Tixmeuac, Padre José Bruno Romero joined with the alcalde and other anticlerical vecinos in making fun of the cura as he passed by during a procession for the santo of Christ the Nazarene. There was no choice but to send Romero out of the parish altogether.[71]

William B. Taylor's study of the eighteenth-century church in Mexico and Guadalajara suggests that the growing state assault radicalized priests such as José María Morelos in defense of what they saw as a virtuous, if hierarchical, society under siege.[72] Why then was there no Padre Morelos in Yucatán? There has been a tendency to see the peninsular church as parasitic and socially disengaged. This view has been somewhat overstated, for, as nearly as can be determined, priests *did* perform all of the social functions described for other parts of Mexico: charity, health care, confessions, legal advice, public employment, personal loans, community investment, travel to the backlands, and many others. The tendency to overlook this has in turn been part of a larger tendency to overestimate the autonomy and disengagement of the Maya peasantry. The fact is that small radical elements did emerge from within the church. What made the difference was the clergy's dual role as spiritual institution and bourgeois partner and the peninsula's overall poverty.

From Words to Deeds: Legal Harassment and Violence against Priests

Accusations were one thing. But anticlericalism became a very different matter when the anticlerics translated their thoughts into actions. Doubtless this, too, had precedents in colonial times, although there has been little attempt to explore this aspect of peninsular history. Whatever the precedent, anticlerical actions emerge on a grand scale in the nineteenth century.

The first full-blown instance was the sanjuanista movement, something I have already analyzed in a previous study.[73] Largely a struggle for greater creole political power, the sanjuanista movement included players with a wide spectrum of goals, from stark anticlerics like Pablo Moreno to dissident clergy who saw the movement as a way of reforming both church and society. As happened with both the Caste War and the brief presidency of Francisco Madero (1911–1913), the profound injustices of the society caused attempts at limited popular mobilization to escape elite control.[74] Independence only took place after the restoration of control over the lower classes, although a strong popular memory of the episode lingered, informing later demands for tax relief.

Certainly the most interesting of the anticlerical troublemakers was Joaquín Lestón, interesting in part because he left fragments of his own ideas in the historical record. This man's origins, background, age, and ultimate fate are unknown, but his rootless wanderings argue that he was no patriarch. He appeared in Yaxcabá in late April of 1824. Whatever his origins and whatever his purpose in coming to Yaxcabá, Lestón represented that latent but powerful anticlericalism that has always been a feature of Hispanic society. Lestón soon took to lounging about the plaza with the town's collection of underemployed creoles and advancing his views on religion and society. When the loungers invited Lestón to accompany them to mass, he replied that the others might go if they wished, but in so doing they were mere fools. Heaven and hell did not exist, he told them, but rather were mere inventions used to frighten Christians into behaving. He even denied the divinity of Christ.[75]

Certainly the most distinctive feature of Lestón's heresy was his hostility to priests. He had a favorite joke, to the effect that when the priest held up the sanctified chalice he would say, "The smell for thee and the broth for me!"

("*El olor para ti y el caldo para mi*"). Lestón loved this quip so much that he always used it when drinking a cup of aguardiente. "The blood of Christ, the smell for thee and the broth for me: that's what the priests do to deceive people," he would remark. On other occasions Lestón added that the priests would drink the consecrated wine, then "they would go to take a shit."

In at least one instance, however, Lestón's comments suggested that a more thoughtful attitude lay behind these blasphemies. When the discussion turned to the origins and nature of humankind, his commentary became less derisive. Lestón argued that the soul died with the body, "as happens with the beasts and the plants." Nor had the human race sprung from Adam, the great father; on the contrary, Lestón held that "men are born as plants are born." On one hand, his stray remarks may have been cavalier denials of dogma, but, on the other, Lestón's insistence on an analogy of plant and animal life echoed an Enlightenment view of a world in which universal laws govern both nature and humanity. His was a popularized version of the same radical French writings with which late colonials such as Miguel Hidalgo had flirted prior to independence and that had become the particular target of the Mexican inquisition during that institution's final years.[76]

Whatever their intellectual pedigree, these blasphemies raised eyebrows when spoken under the pious porticos of Yaxcabá, where saintly José Bartolome del Granado Baeza had served since 1782.[77] Lestón himself skipped town one step ahead of the alcalde whom Baeza sent to arrest him. One month later, Baeza received word that Lestón had surfaced in the more cosmopolitan but no less religious community of Izamal. Thereafter, the wandering heretic vanished for several years. His only recorded words are stray opinions and his joke, a turn of events that probably would have been to his satisfaction. However, the distasteful incident put the elderly Father Baeza in his grave. After his death on February 13, 1830, Baeza was buried within the north wall of his church at Yaxcabá. A plaque placed there by his successor, Eusebio Villamil, commemorates the spot, an unusual touch in this land of the forgotten past.

Lestón may have fled, but there were other instances in which the anti-clerics took their cases to the legal arena. Like so many other symptoms of social entropy, legal attacks increased sharply after 1840. The full dimensions of these cases remain unknown: to some extent they were frame-ups, but others had at least some basis in reality. We find at least three such cases. First, in October 1843 Matías Ek of Cenotillo accused Padre Andrés María Avila of murder.[78] Second, a certain Padre Guerrero of Tihosuco was arrested and taken to Peto for having taken part in a federalist revolt linked to the Imán movement in Tizimín.[79] Both cases were dismissed after the priests in question had spent a few days in confinement. When Mexican troops invaded the rebellious peninsula in 1842–1843, a rumor erupted in Xcan that three curas had opened a road to allow those troops to enter from the northeast; this story, which turned out to be false, apparently began among local peasants who had picked up on the post-Imán mood. Passing from the república to local military officials to the state powers in Mérida, it sparked an investigation, which yielded nothing.[80]

Few priests spent as much time in the law courts—or the jails—as Juan de Dios Helguera, longtime cura of Chichimilá. On three different occasions, Helguera was dragged into legal battles that amounted to little more than harassment. The first of these took place in 1830, a few months after Centralists briefly seized national and regional power; Helguera, along with Juan Nepomuceno Pérez, the ex-Franciscan and then minister in Sisal de Valladolid, were arrested as part of a supposed plot of rebellion. In reality, their crime had consisted of little more than open grumbling against the centralist system. One of the Valladolid politicians advancing the accusations was none other than Joaquín Lestón, who had come to occupy a low-ranking role on the city's ayuntamiento: a village folk liberal, Lestón had gravitated toward politics. After several months and endlessly repetitive testimony, the two men were acquitted. But the effect of these harassments comes through in Helguera's angry statements to the court.[81] The entire matter came up again in 1835, when Centralism once more took power. Again the local juez de paz had Helguera, along with his minister, Juan Pablo Escalante, thrown in jail for purported sedition against the new order. This time the scene of the crime was the celebration of *fiestas patrias* in the Valladolid plaza, although the sedition in question amounted to little more than Helguera venting his "outspoken federalist views." Bishop Guerra and the juez spent some time arguing over clerical immunity from imprisonment before the two priests were eventually acquitted and released.[82]

Helguera entered the law courts one final time in 1843 when the peasants of Chichimilá and Xoccen turned against the cura and Escalante. The complaints included "concubinage," poor and infrequent service, forced personal service, and what probably lay at the bottom of all this, pressuring the villages for money to continue land-related lawsuits that they were willing to settle out of court. The plaintiffs included Manuel Antonio Ay, one of the batabs involved in the plot that became the Caste War; Secundino Loría, the alcalde of Chichimilá (also a plotter) who turned state's evidence against Ay;

and Manuel Nahuat of Xoccen, later the voice of the Speaking Cross. Escalante, at least, was convinced that the suit was a plot by one of his enemies, Vicente Rivero. More likely it was another instance of the temporary, cross-ethnic coalitions that characterized rural society immediately prior to the war, but Escalante, who was forced to resign and leave the parish, was correct when he identified the law courts as the tool ambitious vecinos used to harass their economic and political rivals.[83] Helguera, exhausted by these conflicts, also chose to relocate; he served as cura of Xcan until the outbreak of the war, then fled to Isla del Carmen, where he died peacefully in 1850.[84]

Perhaps the most sensational instance of anticlerical violence in peacetime was the murder of Friar Laureano Loría, guardian of the Franciscan convent of Mejorada in Mérida. More than anything, this gory history demonstrates the lack of respect that some of Mérida's lower element held for priests. The murder in question was the brainchild of Ramón Avila, a former servant who had already tried to rob the monastery once before and who was then incarcerated in Mérida's slipshod prison. On the evening of June 16, 1840, three rogues secretly liberated Avila and another accomplice. They broke into the Mejorada in search of the strongbox that Avila knew to be in Loría's keeping. After a brief but intense struggle, the bandits slashed the friar's throat all the way to the spinal column, making off with some fourteen ounces of gold, which represented the once-mighty Franciscans' savings. Inexplicably, however, Avila chose to return to his prison cell; suspicions focused on him, leading authorities to unravel the plot. Forensic and material evidence, down to the claw marks that Loría had inflicted in his death throes, indicted the perpetrators. After a florid trial (the prosecutor was none other than Gregorio Cantón, a versatile meridano who later negotiated one of the most important peace treaties of the Caste War), the five were convicted and sent to a firing squad on the outskirts of town. An extensive account of the case appeared nine years later in the journal entitled *Miscelánea instructiva*.[85]

The murder of Friar Laureano Loría captured a variety of different cultural attitudes toward religious sanctity. Obviously, not everyone here respected the church and its servants. This disrespect surfaced among elements of the urban lower classes throughout the peninsula, for although in some ways the murder was an inside job, the Avila gang also drew from diverse places: Mérida, Campeche, Maxcanú, and even the profoundly religious Izamal. The murder also mirrored some of the popular anticlerical harassment that was then erupting in rural areas; Loría had died at the very moment that Santiago Imán's revolt was drawing strength by promising to break the economic power of the church.[86] However, the devout upper classes who recorded the story tried to emphasize its silver linings. The first of these concerned the undercurrent of pious outrage that the crime aroused. There was still enormous public sentiment regarding the inviolability of the priest's sacred person, a fact that the socially conservative journalists of the *Miscelánea* were careful to report. Between the murder and the arrests, one of the assassins had worked as a *picador* in the bullfights of Santiago; after he wounded one of the bulls, a spectator cried out, "Barbarian! I can swear that you murdered the friar!" There is no reason to doubt that most of the urban lower classes *were* incensed by the crime. In fact, the writers of the story used its blasphemous overtones to sell it. Readers were astounded to learn that the gang had been seen prowling about Mejorada several evenings before disguised in bed sheets: "It had been observed," the reports ominously noted, "that they extinguished a light that burns in the gateway before the image of San Salvador." [87] Pious meridanos could still see the hand of God in such symbolism, and they understood the captures and executions as the triumph of moral order.

The timing of the story was also significant. The story itself did not appear in newspapers until the *Miscelánea* covered it in 1849, year two of the Caste War, by which time this sort of violence had become daily fare. Mérida's urbanites would soon forget about the war, but at this point it remained prominent in their consciousness, and they were still searching around for explanations for the tragedy. The authors did not directly make the connection for the simple reason that they did not have to: the murder of Loría provided a self-evident symbol for what happened when the lower classes of a society lost respect for traditional elites.

In 1834 Federick de Waldeck, after visiting the great Cathedral of Mérida, wrote the following indictment of the peninsular priests: "In a large chapel you can still see the openings which lead to the extensive vaults in which, at no advantage to the earth, have decomposed the bodies of the friars whose death has thus been as useless as their life." [88] It was a sentiment that a small but aggressive minority of Yucatecans shared. In reviewing these cases of anticlericalism, lawsuits with priests, and often ungodly behavior, it is impossible not to be struck by certain profound ambiguities and inconsistencies in the society. People loved the church but sometimes hated it. They honored the priests—collectively and as individual persons—but made them the target of demagogy and political persecution. It was one of the fundamental ambiguities that permeated Mexico's nineteenth century, and it was felt keenly in the small towns and hamlets where the majority of the nation still resided.

To be sure, the conflicts with priests contributed to the Caste War. They did so, however, in complex ways. Many of the dynamics described, particularly the secular-clerical rivalry, had been implicit in the colonial situation from the beginning, as the story of Diego de Landa's ill-fated inquisition reveals.[89] What had changed, however, was the state's gradual constriction of church power, something that had begun under the Bourbon reforms and continued, if fitfully, through the nineteenth and twentieth centuries. Doubtless the institution was suffering from a growing laxity that came from its ancient privileges of monopoly and internal review. But as some of its old economic advantages slipped away, priests were forced into difficult choices or callous attitudes that did not endear them to their parishioners. The parishioners, in turn, became ever more resentful of the economic leverage that did exist and tried to eliminate it. The church was thus caught in a vicious circle. Most people probably did accept the Catholic Church and the padres as basic units of the society, but at key moments the latent hostilities toward them could gather and explode, as they did in the attack on Valladolid in February 1847, in which Maya peasants killed a priest for the first time in recorded history.[90]

Nevertheless, even in wartime the old ambiguities persisted. Anticlerical violence during the Caste War itself was fairly limited. A peasant mob killed Padre Alejandro Villamil, cura and *vicario* (ecclesiastical judge) of Uayma, during the January 1847 attack on Valladolid that presaged the rebellion; hostilities apparently related to some of his rulings in the Helguera lawsuits (other priests of Valladolid went unharmed).[91] Similarly, the death of Eusebio García Rejón of Tixcacalcupul seems to have been a convergence of two events: his unpopularity among peasants and his failure to escape from towns where the Caste War initially erupted. These, however, were war-related, and wars necessarily generate extraordinary violence. Anticlerical Caste War violence therefore in some ways resembled the destruction of churches. It did not necessarily follow conscious plan but rather suggests inadvertency; it was counterbalanced by examples of continued warm relationships between priests and Mayas, including rebel Mayas; and, above all, it has been exaggerated, a case of simplification in a rural social world where nothing was black-and-white.

Later Evolution of Non-Catholic Ideas: The Law of Love

The anticlerical mood remained a part of Yucatecan life for the next half-century. When the dust had finally settled from the Caste War and the Liberal reform, the church no longer controlled peninsular loans and savings, and the last remaining convent was closed. New religious doctrines gradually began to enter Yucatán. It was at this moment that a few people, at least, began to experiment with ways of thinking church authority out of the picture altogether.

Any serious discussion of dissident nineteenth-century religious ideologies begins with spiritualism, an esoteric amalgam of doctrines centered around the belief in communication with the spirit world. Like many of the intellectual currents that have swept Latin America, Mexico's spiritualist movement was in part a delayed, modified version of beliefs that had gestated elsewhere.[92] The roots of a belief in spirit worlds lay deep in Western civilization and, indeed, within the human psyche itself. But heterogeneous doctrines of a spirit world and a spiritual pseudoscience began to flourish in the eighteenth century as a reaction to the mechanistic views of the Enlightenment; as a result of industrialization, scientific advances, deepening rural capitalism, demographic expansion, and the consequent collapse of older social norms; and as a result of increasing personal freedom from monolithic established religions. Throughout Europe and the Americas, religions across the board lost much of their influence as arbiters of human behavior and beliefs. Mexico was no exception.

The guru of Mexico's own particular branch of spiritualism was a French pedagogue and mystic who adopted the pseudonym Allan Kardec (1804–1869). The dissonance between his Catholic background and the Protestant ambience of his Swiss education eventually compelled him to seek some form of mediation. His studies of German exposed him to the then-dominant Hegelian doctrines of *geist,* the spirit or consciousness whose growth Hegel taught to be part of an unstoppable world evolution. From 1850 onward, Kardec unveiled his doctrines of the spirit world in a series of books and a newspaper known as *Revue spirite.*[93] Spiritualist doctrines entered Mexico during the French occupation of 1860 to 1867, when Kardec's teachings were at the height of their influence. At the same time, however, Mexican spiritualism drew from a wealth of folk beliefs, Catholic and otherwise. Among simple people of the countryside, the existence of ghosts was an article of faith. Even today, spirits will return to pester the living if the survivors fail to perform a periodic ritual meal known as the *mesada,* in which the departed's photograph is placed at a table setting. There is simply too little evidence to gauge the prevalence of ghost beliefs among city folk, but the force of such beliefs usually diminishes with increasing urbanization. Beyond the matter of ghosts, it is undeniable that divination, hexes, potions, and talismans all figure prominently in the folkloric landscape of both Spanish and indigenous cultures.

Meanwhile, Mérida itself was undergoing the same social, political, and material transformations that affected the other large cities of Mexico. It had recently passed through a long phase of ideological wars between conservatism and liberalism, and while a synthesis of the two prevailed, the church emerged badly weakened. Freedom of religion was now a national right; the church lost a great deal of its material wealth; and social privileges such as control of the peasantry and dominance in education were all but ended. New paths of thought were gradually opening for those who chose to follow them. Beyond this, however, new scientific technologies were redefining urban life. During the French Empire (1863–1867) Mérida had seen its first telegraph and artesian wells, while plans for railroad development existed at least on paper. Photography was becoming more common. In no small part, then, spiritualism emerged as a paradigm for a society that had deep experience with Catholicism, where freedom of thought and association were easier than ever and where science and material progress were introducing new concepts that in some way had to be reconciled with the old.

Members themselves had trouble sorting out the spiritualist genealogy, but it appears that Mexican spiritualism first began in the city of Guadalajara, then spread to Guanajuato, then branched out into other cities and provinces.[94] By 1876 Mexico had the fifth-largest number of spiritualist newspapers in the world, exceeded only by the United States (with 7), France (6), Spain (5), and England (5).[95] A brief insert in Mérida's spiritualist newspaper, drawing upon a Mexico City counterpart, asserted that there were sixty thousand believers in all the republic; the figure was undoubtedly inflated, but it is nonetheless clear that the spiritualist movement was more widespread than previously imagined.[96] The origins of Mérida's spiritualist community remain appropriately shrouded. The group's own version is that it began to meet in 1873 in the salon of a *licenciado* named Rodulfo Cantón. Their séances were guided by the oracles of a tutelary spirit known simply as Peralta (the maiden name of the late governor Miguel Barbachano's mother).[97] In November 1874 they officially constituted themselves as the Círculo Peralta. Among other activities, the Círculo translated and published several French pamphlets debating the validity of Kardec's revelations.[98] However, spiritualism reached beyond the avenues of Mérida. By 1878 there were spiritualist circles in Campeche, Valladolid, Progreso, Izamal, Temax, Acanceh, and Carmen; as with cofradías, these smaller cities and towns followed the lead of the provincial metropole.

Who were the spiritualists? The groups left few records of their meetings and activities, but most evidence points to an urban petit-bourgeois intelligentsia. The mainspring was Cantón himself, member of a large and, in some branches, wealthy family that had led armies, built haciendas, and occupied the governorship. Cantón was the son of Gregorio Cantón, the Mérida lawyer who had negotiated peace treaties during the Caste War and prosecuted the assassins of Friar Loría.[99] Another founding member was Jacinto Cuevas, director of a local music conservatory. Cuevas had grown up a devout Catholic but, on discovering the writings of Kardec, threw himself into spiritualist activity with such fervor that even fellow members feared for his sanity.[100] Justo Sierra O'Reilly's son Santiago (brother of high-Porfirian elite Justo Sierra Méndez) became a devout spiritualist and engaged in polemical debates with the movement's detractors. The group also attracted dissident members of the Catholic clergy, never a monolithic body in thought or action. For example, the spiritualist movement included Manuel Antonio Sierra O'Reilly, cura of Halachó and uncle to Santiago Sierra, who kept a reading salon that included tidbits such as *Spiritualism in the Modern World*.[101] Also present was José María González, a former Catholic priest who for reasons unknown left his vocation and took up the spiritualist banner. West of Campeche the driving force of the movement was Manuel Foucher, a Tabascan poet and journalist whose political passions led to his murder in 1882; Foucher founded circles not only in Villahermosa but in Isla del Carmen as well.[102] The most prominent of Mérida spiritualists was Ambrosio Cervera, *regidor* (councilman) of the ayuntamiento. Another well-known member, Felipe de la Cámara Zavala, had served as colonel during the Caste War and is best known for his memoir on the military occupation of Chan Santa Cruz in 1850. Most seem to have come from similar backgrounds: urban, professional, well-educated, and, with certain poorly documented exceptions, male.

Over time, however, the movement found a wider audience. In barrio San Francisco of Campeche, for example, adherents formed a circle "composed in large part of artisans and people of the town; an honorable shoemaker is the medium."[103] More difficult to explain is the limited female participation. Spiritualism in North America and Europe had attracted large numbers of women. This included not only humble enthusiasts but also international celebrities, such as the Fox sisters and Katie King. In these cases, the sudden and unrestrained growth of the movement provided greater access to women. In southeast Mexico, however, the situation evolved in a different fashion. The Catholic Church's long-standing influence over women appears to have helped limit female participation in the spiritualist movement, at least in its early stages.[104] Nevertheless, by 1876 there were signs of growing gender inclusion. For example, the San Francisco Campeche circle listed an elderly woman as medium.[105] Outside of Yucatán women found a place for themselves in spiritualism. Ciudad Victoria's circle was female.[106] Similarly, the Tabascan capital of San Juan Bautista (now Villahermosa) had a women-only spiritualist circle headed by a local writer named Catalina Zapata.[107] Foucher's Carmen circle, "*La Hermandad*," also included female membership.[108]

The result of these efforts was a journal that for three years was one of the most unusual and intriguing publications of nineteenth-century Mexico. *La ley de amor*, or *The Law of Love*, appeared every two weeks during the years 1876–1878; all seventy-two issues still survive in mint condition in Mérida's Hemeroteca Pino Suárez and provide unparalleled access to the minds of Mexico's small but energetic spiritualist community. Certainly the most unusual feature of this magazine was its list of contributors. The largest number of articles came from Peralta him- (or her-?) self. Readers could find brief articles by the spirits of such deceased luminaries as Ignacio Comonfort and the empress Josephine, usually items of two or three paragraphs that offered homilies on any number of difficult moral topics. Spirit submissions did not always bear direct connection with the histories of the spirit personality in question, but there were exceptions. In an article entitled "The Messengers," Miguel Hidalgo y Costilla returned, not one bit rueful of his disastrous rebellion in the Bajío. History, he explained, advanced through the action of certain prophets, or messengers, who come to improve the human race. "The French Revolution was a hurricane of all the unleashed passions, but it was also the door to a less intransigent era." As an afterthought, however, Hidalgo remarked that perhaps bloodshed would not be necessary for future advances.[109]

In a nutshell, the spiritualist doctrine ran something as follows: The universe was composed of immortal spirits that, over a series of innumerable reincarnations, struggled toward self-knowledge and moral enlightenment. After a time in the otherworld, where there were no punishments other than the terrible knowledge of one's past failures and imperfections, each spirit voluntarily returned to Earth to give life another try. Knowledge from past lives persisted; much like the Buddhist concept of *karma* it determined present fortunes and personality, and furnished a stock of innate ideas that conditioned our ability to comprehend. Learning, in fact, was merely a form of remembering. (Spiritualists repudiated the notion of original sin, although never explained how spirits began, or in what condition, or why; the implication was that they emerged from a primordial passion that John Calvin would have recognized instantly.) God existed; all spirits moved ineluctably toward his presence, so that seen in its long arch, history would indeed arrive at a final moral perfection. Spiritualism's key innovation was the reciprocal aid between the living and the dead. Through séances the members learned the wisdom of spirits but also helped those tortured souls who, even in the afterlife, struggled with such primal urges as pride, self-centeredness, and willful ignorance. Messengers — ectoplasmic or otherwise — figured prominently in this schema, and though the spiritualists rejected messianic doctrines, they greatly emphasized the personality of Christ and his message of universal love against the hellfire of the Old Testament. Finally, the believer, being a good nineteenth-century bourgeois, seized on the benefits of technology, particularly photography, in his quest for spirit truth.[110]

What to make of these exotic doctrines? Mexican spiritualism is best seen as a maverick cousin to several other important national movements of the nineteenth century, particularly liberalism and Protestantism. None of these were monolithic in and of themselves; rather, they drew from a smorgasbord of related ideas and attitudes that adherents of the day and age combined, disassembled, and recombined in various forms. Most immediately, spiritualism was an intellectual cousin to the far more prominent liberal movement. Both drew from a broad faith in improvement, progress, and uplift that permeated much of urban nineteenth-century culture, not only in Mexico but throughout the world. Insistence on public education served as one of the common denominators of the two groups. *The Law of Love* ran a series of redundant and repetitious articles on the need for education — seen here as helping spirits work out their problems but in practice contributing toward the growth of a secular education system — and published regular updates on clubs founded to promote schooling at the local level.

Mexican spiritualism was also a form of Protestantism in a society not ready or willing to be Protestant. It performed many of the same historical functions that Protestant sects did in the United States and Europe, and in its overall concept and orientation shared many tenets with Protestantism. First and most importantly, spiritualism rejected hierarchy and substituted direct revelation. It did, however, connect with an older, explicitly Catholic tradition of intercession: the spiritualists did not speak directly with God but rather with a series of incorporeal beings that stood closer to the spiritual source than themselves. A second and equally critical tenet was spiritualism's stress on deep personal reform, a hallmark of Protestant conversion. Believers normally arrived at the new belief only after a period of long and difficult soul searching. Third, spiritualists wrestled mightily with the problem of freedom and predestination, the obsession of seventeenth-century Protestant theology. Fourth, the spiritualists shared Protestant emphasis on the New Testament and the personality of Christ as the most important of biblical doctrines. Fifth, though positively enamored of science and technology (Cantón was the representative for a Yucatecan railroad company), believers of the doctrine rejected a purely materialist point of view.[111] The spiritualists criticized positivism far more often than they did Catholicism, even though an indirect attack of the latter was implicit throughout.

The Law of Love might have gotten a reading from heterodoxes like Joaquín Lestón, but it infuriated orthodox Catholics who saw it as heresy. Despite gentlemanly disclaimers, there can be little doubt that much of the writings were intended as broadsides against traditional church doctrine. Not surprisingly, spiritualists dedicated much of their energies and copy space to polemics against their Catholic critics. Chief among these was Crecencio Carrillo y Ancona, the priest and later bishop who functioned as the principal ideologist and leader of the Catholic Church in southeast Mexico during the post–Caste War years and whose journal, El mensajero (The Messenger), repeatedly attacked the spiritualist heresy. It was not that the church denied the intervention of spirit forces in daily life; in 1887, for example, priests of Campeche attributed the case of a mentally disturbed girl to possession by demons.[112] Rather, the point of difference was one of surrounding intellectual frameworks and how spiritualists used their beliefs as a justification for breaking with Mexico's traditional authorities on moral and religious affairs.

After the 1870s peninsular spiritualism entered a decline. It is difficult to attribute this decline to official repression, since criticism of the Catholic Church was more permissible than ever after 1867, while anticlerics continued to play leading roles in state politics; Carlos Peón, for example, went on to become governor in 1894. The abeyance of spiritualism owed in part to the death and illnesses of key members. The movement also suffered from its own internal contradictions. Sustained, meaningful communication with spirits was more difficult to achieve than the fleeting, highly subjective apparitions and wonder cures that, to the popular mind, nourished and substantiated Catholic belief. In addition to this, the spiritualists, proponents of science and learning, could not integrate their own highly esoteric doctrines with the emerging forces of modernity.

But spiritualism and other alternative beliefs did not die, a point well illustrated by Francisco Madero's earnest probings of the Ouija Board. Spiritualists became ardent supporters of the saint of Cabora, Teresa Urrea, and some eventually used her popular appeal as way of drawing support for an abortive revolt against Porfirio Díaz.[113] Peninsular spiritualism laid low for several decades but in the 1920s made a sensational comeback in the form of Theosophy. This esoteric doctrine had its origins in the teachings of Madame Helena Blavatsky. Theosophy and spiritualism shared several important features. Most importantly, both emerged after periods of profound social crisis. Spiritualism followed the Caste War, the Liberal reform, and the French Empire; peasant church taxes were largely abolished, the institution lost considerable amounts of property and rights to mortgage repayments, priests lost their privileged status as cultural arbiters and economic actors, and the Catholic Church in general had to find new ways to relate to its parishioners. Similarly, Theosophy emerged during the revolutionary "antifanaticization" campaign that destroyed or confiscated church icons and drove Yucatán's conservative archbishop, Martin Trischler, into exile. In both cases, larger social and political developments allowed members of the urban middle classes to find a home in esoteric doctrines that, like Protestantism, allowed the faithful to speak directly with spiritual forces. As nearly as can be determined, both movements drew from the same socioeconomic strata. Theosophy also shared virtually all of the spiritualist doctrines but was far more packaged and prefabricated than its forerunner. Its regional mouthpiece, *Teosofía en Yucatán,* drew combined Chichén Itzá motifs with the neo-Egyptian styles and fascinations of the Blavatsky group. Production values were higher, but it lacked the creativity and raw homegrown energy of *The Law of Love.*[114] Mérida's later Rosecrucian journal, *Revista rosacruz,* was merely a translated import with no local contributions.[115]

For a long time Protestantism itself made only glacial inroads. Here there were only the faintest glimmers of a European-style reformation led by dissident members of the clergy; differences between priests could fall into extremes (see Chapter 7 for a case study), but clergy members still kept their differences within the institution and the faith. The closest thing to a peninsular Martin Luther involved the case of Padre Lorenzo Gutiérrez, interim cura of Tixcacalcupul, who was charged in 1859 with being a partisan of the longtime Valladolid caudillo and revolutionary Agustín Acereto. The church sectors allied with the governor, and rival Liborio Irigoyen summoned Gutiérrez to answer charges of sedition. At first Gutiérrez refused to appear; the Liberal reform laws, he correctly noted, had abolished religious courts. He then announced that he was leaving the Catholic Church altogether and becoming a

Protestant, "because it is the only true religion." In the end, however, Gutié-rrez decided to submit and went through eight days of spiritual exercises to cleanse his heretic tendencies. The past persisted in spite of what he himself pointed out, the new and legally guaranteed freedom of religion.[116]

Protestant conversion, like the later Revolution, would ultimately come from without. When the first authentic evangelical, the Reverend Maxwell Phillips, arrived in 1877, he came bearing a gift to ingratiate himself with authorities, a hand-carved chair that had once belonged to the liberal caudillo Juan Alvarez of Guerrero, which Phillips sold to the recently formed Museo Yucateco for a token fee.[117] But Protestantism proved a tougher sell, and five long years would pass before he had drawn enough converts to celebrate a public service. Phillips abandoned the Yucatán mission after his two sons died of yellow fever, but others took his place, and by 1893 Mérida had some 121 Protestants, with additional small branches in Ticul, Muna, Maxcanú, and Kanasín.[118] Their early struggles, their role in the Mexican Revolution, their subsequent fortunes—all remain little studied and poorly understood.

The real boom in Protestant conversion came when missionary groups began to target rural areas. It would take the arrival of modern evangelicals, with their promise of sobriety and individual wealth, to attract the Yucate-can masses.[119] Yucatán is now approximately 85 percent Catholic, 9 percent Protestant/Evangelical, with the remainder divided between Judaism, Islam, and no religion at all. Evangelization has been stronger in the country (16.6 percent) than in Mérida itself (10.7 percent), although overall rates of conversion appear to be declining from the evangelical explosion of the 1970s.[120] Studies of Yucatecan rural conversion lag behind the more dramatic histories of Guatemala, but most link Protestant religions' appeal to the economic decline of rural life as well as to the political exclusivity practiced by traditional Catholic factions associated with the ruling PRI.[121]

Meanwhile, Yucatán's fabled *casta divina* included factions of both pro- and antichurch extremes. The latter enjoyed their strongest power under the governorship of liberal hacendado Carlos Peón (1894–1898), when it became clear that their old-time liberalism clashed with Porfirio Díaz's policy of rapprochement. Fearing that their tendencies might cause excessive social discontent, Don Porfirio retired the priest haters and after a decent interval appointed moderate Olegario Molina, who, in addition to already being the richest and most powerful man on the peninsula, was also favorably disposed to the church and its conservative doyen, Archbishop Martin Trischler. The prerevolutionary era ended with proclerics back in command.[122] However, hostility to religion, popular or otherwise, merely retreated during these years, and in fact would reassert itself soon enough. Organized middle-class opposition to Porfirio Díaz first expressed itself in 1900 through Camilo Arriaga's liberal clubs, an attempt to bring progressive Mexicans (mostly of Hidalgo and San Luis Potosí) back to their anticlerical roots.[123] When General Salvador Alvarado brought revolutionary policy to Yucatán, he unleashed anticlerical forces that had been brewing in the peninsula for decades: anarchosyndicalists, church-hating liberals, and anti-Catholic and anti-iconic Protestants. These gave the church a drubbing that conservative quarters have neither forgotten nor forgiven.[124] As in other parts of Mexico in the period of 1917 to 1929, attempts to suppress Catholicism found little popular resonance and in fact provoked a backlash against the new revolutionary governments. In the case of Yucatán, the faithful hid their saints and, in isolated cases, lynched would-be iconoclasts.

Since the heyday of Alvarado's self-styled "antifanaticism campaign," the situation has calmed; the church once more occupies a prominent role in this quite conservative province. But like Catholicism itself, the religion of anti-religion has never gone away. This is not a subject that enjoys a long paper trail or, given its sensitive nature, a great deal of scholarly attention. But prolonged exposure to Yucatecan society, or to Mexico in general, is bound to reveal the anticlerical streak sooner or later. What I hope to have shown in this chapter is that the conflicts that erupted in the 1910s in fact had deep roots in the society, and the folk cultures (always plural) included not merely reverence toward Catholicism but also an opposition to the faith, its customs, and the men who administered it. Probably a minority in any circumstances, anticlerical or even antireligious subculture was nonetheless potent in the minds of its adherents. It is only the recognition of this opposition that makes nineteenth-century and later revolutionary developments comprehensible.

CHAPTER
7

"Burning the Torch
of Revolution"

*Religion, Nationalism,
and the Loss of the Petén*

IN HIS PRISON CELL in Mérida, Padre Amado Belizario Barreiro would remember the Petén. Now, in 1860, he was broken and impoverished, relieved of his religious duties. His thoughts wandered beyond the stone walls to a vast expanse of tropical forest—bananas, mangos, cahoon palms, towering mahoganies—and more particularly to the people of the picturesque villages nestled throughout that exotic land. They had destroyed him.

But Barreiro had not suffered alone. Along with his health and reputation had perished a huge portion of the Yucatecan church. Owing to the scandals and controversies in which he had played a central role, Rome had transferred the Guatemalan Petén from the bishopric of Mérida to that of Guatemala itself. Within a few years' time, the geographic scope of Yucatán's ecclesiastical space was contracted by some thirty-six thousand square kilometers, roughly the size of South Carolina. If anything, the disaster showed that sects and ecclesiastical jurisdictions not only molded the workplace and the inner person; they also helped define national territories. The Roman Catholic Church had come to life long before the nation-state made its appearance. Over time, specific European religions came to parallel national identities: imperial Spain building itself on Roman Catholicism, northern German principalities taking Lutheranism as their creed, England with its Anglican church, France at times dealing in antipopes and, later, Bourbon and revolutionary deism. Following the policies of the mother country, the Spanish American colonies made the church a parallel world to the state, coterminous at all points and with no space outside save for that the heretic-rebel. The Bourbon assault of the eighteenth century had weakened ecclesiastical authority, but only to make room for a heightened state power that either failed to materialize or was lost in the decade of independence wars. Given the pervasiveness of the church at both the elite and folk levels, many of the early national leaders still clung to the church-state monolith and hoped that religious and cultural unity might hold their new nations together in the face of poverty and provincialism. For this reason the new states continued to identify themselves with their own ecclesiastical divisions. Mexico, for example, retained its own archbishopric. After the dictatorship of Juan Manuel de Rosas, Argentina at last gained its own archbishopric during the presidency of Bartolomé Mitre (1862–1868), separating itself from the ecclesiastical rule of the far more chaotic Bolivia.[1] In short, the colonies did manage to expel the Spanish political presence, but the Catholic Church was too deeply rooted in the social order to be removed. The coexistence was not always peaceful, but it has proved workable to the present day.

Nor did the people want it gone. In spite of the vocal anticlerical minority, most Mexicans, including Maya peasants, saw themselves as good Catholics. At the core of the matter was the church's multifaceted quality. While still the official cult of men like Raymundo Pérez and José María Guerra, the church was also much more. The doctrines and annual cycles of Catholicism were part of the imagined structure that governed life on earth. Religion offered hope: San Antonio of Xocneceh, the cult of the ciruela, and the mysterious kindling crosses all promised redemption, relief, even power and wealth in lives that were otherwise abysmal. Of equal importance, the claim of being a devout Catholic, however subjective the standard, entitled one to what today might be called civil or human rights, the former grounded in individual state laws, the latter implying a moral standard that transcends political boundaries. As twentieth-century Mexican revolutionaries learned, they could not violate these folk standards without incurring popular hostility.[2]

Perhaps the greatest peculiarity of the Yucatecan church was that even to the mid–nineteenth century it clung to an old ecclesiastical arrangement that violated national boundaries. Though based in Mérida and focused on the people of the ex-colony, the Yucatecan bishop also governed places that had little to do with Yucatecan polity or economy. One of these was Campeche, which broke from Yucatán politically in 1858 and received its own bishopric in

1894.[3] The list also included Tabasco, whose people regarded the Yucatecans as exploiters, and which separated in 1880.[4] A far greater anomaly, however, was the Petén, a tangle of rivers and tropical forest that formed the northern third of Guatemala. Mérida controlled religious administration of this remote backland for some 150 years; its last Yucatecan vicario was Amado Belizario Barreiro. And it would be here that power, piety, personality, and a new nationalist politics collided in 1858.

The Times and Travails of the Petén

The forest world that was the Petén had certainly seen its ups and downs. As late as 400 B.C. the area held little more than small family settlements, with real regional power in the hands of the Olmecs, further to the west. But within five hundred years the Petén had become one of the most dynamic regions of the entire world. Technical innovations and a strategic position along Mesoamerican trade lines had spurred the growth of city-states, dense populations, and an intelligentsia whose cultural production continues to intrigue scholars and public alike. After 600 A.D., however, increasing population pressures, changing trade routes, and a profoundly top-heavy class structure began to take their toll; within three centuries the collapse of classic lowland Maya civilization reconverted much of the core area to monte. By the time the Spanish arrived, the Petén was once more a tropical forest.[5]

The Yucatecan presence here had its origins in colonial patterns of conquest. The Itzá Maya, formerly of Chichén Itzá and Mayapán, had relocated to the western shore of Lake Petén between 1200 and 1450, eventually basing their capital on the lake's island, Noj Petén. Here they held out against half-hearted Spanish-settlement and missionary efforts for over a century; the Maya words *noj petén* in fact mean "large island," and from this comes the region's name.[6] In the end, fears that British influence might spread into the Petén region via Belize prompted action; the Spanish launched simultaneous campaigns of conquest from Guatemala and Yucatán in 1695, the latter eventually driving out the Itzáes two years later.[7] Although the Crown awarded the Petén to the captaincy of Guatemala, the Yucatecan secular clergy, fending off attempts by Franciscans of the same province, quickly consolidated their presence there, and the area remained a Yucatecan mission thereafter.[8]

For fifteen decades it hardly mattered. The Petén was poor, thinly populated, and inaccessible from any point. The main settlement was the lake's island city of Remedios. One often-cited history by a local antiquarian recounts that it originally served as an island prison, although it is doubtful that the physical prison structure was anything more than a wooden building.[9] Over the years a handful of towns sprang up: Dolores, San Andrés, San José, Guadalupe Sacluk, and San Benito, a lakeside pueblo founded by escaped Belizean slaves and dedicated to the veneration of their patron saint, an appropriately black-skinned San Benito de Palmero.[10] In 1831 Guatemalans changed the name of Remedios to Flores after a Liberal bureaucrat who had perished at the hands of an un-liberal lynch mob five years earlier in the highlands.[11]

There had been no encomienda, or forced Indian labor, in this region, owing to the late settlement and thin native population.[12] The residents devoted themselves either to subsistence farming or, toward the end of the eighteenth century, to trading livestock products to Belizean woodcutters. Their methods of cattle production were crude. Ranchers had small herds that they neither fed nor watered nor tended, instead relying on local ponds and salt licks to keep the animals in place. Even into the late 1800s officials complained about the lack of animal husbandry among peteneros.[13] Prior to the Caste War, ranchers drove the bulk of these animals northward to Yucatán for sale during the dry season of October through May.[14]

In culture the Petén was strongly Yucatecan. The indigenous peasantry lived in a material culture virtually identical to that of their northern neighbors; even the Lacandons, an elusive people who prowled the district's northwestern riverine forests, spoke a form of Yucatec Maya.[15] Milpa farming, pigs, chickens, and indigenous fruits provided the mainstays of survival. Throughout the eighteenth and early nineteenth centuries, the population hovered at around three thousand.[16] After 1847 new waves of Maya peasants fled here to escape the violence of the Caste War, further deepening the continuities between the two regions. The refugees had also managed to liberate themselves from the hated obventions of Yucatán; the limited church funding that existed here came from a tax on herds of cattle greater than ten, and on the production of corn and chickens.[17] Civil taxes amounted to an annual three pesos. It is clear that even into the 1860s Mayas considered the Petén a low-tax region and, presuming that one could stand the isolation, a good place to live. There, too, they had the indigenous *cabildos,* or local municipal governments, much like the repúblicas de indígenas to the north; instead of a batab or cacique, the chief continued to use the title *gobernador,* a term that despite earlier usage had largely disappeared in Yucatán itself by the dawn of the nineteenth century. These existed in the Petén before the Caste War and

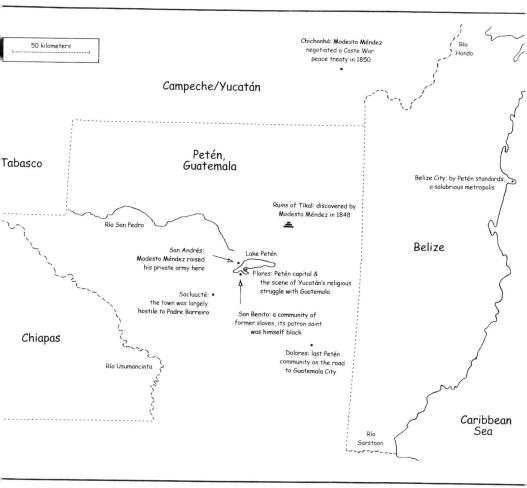

Map 4. *The Petén district of Guatemala.*

simply continued their operations as new Mayas arrived.[18] However, no vast quantities of papers survive to open a window to their daily lives.[19]

One index of the Petén's material poverty was its housing—or lack thereof. Except for a church of *mampostería* (rubble masonry), which the elderly vicario Tomás Salazar had constructed in Flores, the entire region had not a single permanent construction. They built everything—houses, barns, churches—out of the ubiquitous pole and palm thatch. People of Spanish ancestry lived in circumstances only slightly elevated from those of village Indians.

The region's creoles were a complex bunch. They, too, enjoyed strong ties to Yucatecan culture, right down to the serenades and aguardiente that were the standards of evening life. Many of the founding families had in fact come from Campeche.[20] Although poor, the peteneros had their own forms of entertainment and sociability. As in Yucatán, dances known as *jaranas* were common affairs; in certain versions, the women asked the men to dance. Cultural and familial links to the peninsula exerted such an influence that when independence came in 1821 one faction of the local ayuntamiento wanted to join formally with Yucatán, then the second largest state in Mexico and in some ways an autonomous nation. The rival, pro-Guatemalan faction prevailed, but in Flores the elites—such as they were—maintained cultural and social ties with the north, while the Petén itself remained a kind of halfway house for refugees, discontents, or mere travelers from either world. Despite their Yucatecan genesis, however, the creoles of the Petén added their own distinct touches. The men, for example, were partial to sessions of drinking and card playing that could stretch over days.[21] People traveled in canoes festooned with ribbons and made their clothes from the brightly colored fabrics of the Guatemalan highlands. They punctuated all arrivals, departures, and official ceremonies with marimba music, a regional signature. In general, peteneros were more ebullient, less repressed, and less repressive than their Yucatecan cousins.

In practice, neither the Guatemalan nor Yucatecan state had much say over what went on in the region. Given the problems of transportation, as well as a lack of interest, real control devolved to the peteneros themselves. In nineteenth-century Guatemala, even during the conservative and centralist rule of Rafael Carrera (1838–1865), the *corregidores* exercised great political authority in their respective domains; this was especially true of the Petén, where local government was virtually a one-man show. Between 1846 and 1859 the prince of this petty principality was Modesto Méndez, the corregidor, juez de paz, and all-around wise man. Born in 1801 to a humble family, the young

Modesto had shown a gift for learning and had gone to Mérida for an education; in later years he continued to read at home by firelight. In 1844 he showed his mettle by negotiating a treaty with a rebellious northern cacique named Juan Ke (of which episode no documents have survived).[22] Despite these Lincolnesque touches, however, Méndez remained every inch the Spanish autocrat. He carefully cultivated his image as a military man, complete with sword, epauletted uniform, and dashing sideburns. In 1848, following a tip by local milpa farmers, Méndez discovered Tikal, one of the world's greatest archaeological marvels.[23] The fact is still commemorated there. He corresponded with some of the great leaders of the Caste War insurgency and in 1850 negotiated the first of the critical treaties establishing communities of *pacíficos,* or ex-rebels who agreed to lay down their arms and live peacefully in the southern forests.[24] In gratitude, the Yucatecans heaped honors on both Méndez and his partner, local priest Juan de la Cruz Hoil; Méndez's son Mariano Delfín received free admission into the seminary of San Ildefonso in Mérida. There was a touch of imposter to this Guatemalan functionary, but he was also a bedrock of real talent, a man capable of maintaining rural order and of negotiating in good faith with indigenous peasants.

Méndez alone ran the Petén, but it was with less of the regality of Philip II than the whimsical fiat of Judge Roy Bean. Locals continued to go about their free-and-easy ways; the portly and gregarious corregidor understood that visions of progress meant little here and in fact were probably detrimental to public tranquility.[25] His principal administrative techniques were two: first, he operated an arbitrary system of fines and licensing fees for small matters; this money went directly to his own discretionary funds. Second, in cases of serious disorder he relied on hastily mobilized militias, usually drawing on Maya peasants from the hamlets around Flores and San Andrés. These had all the flavor of a private army, but without the diabolical dimensions of Guatemala's later paramilitary forces. In turn, Méndez distributed the rewards of his system among a slew of relatives—less capable but at least loyal. More professional bureaucrats from Guatemala City rolled their eyes at his "at times patriarchal use of authority" but ultimately chose not to interfere. As a later and relatively hostile critic conceded, "He knows a great deal about his countrymen; he knows how to handle them, and it is he more than anyone who brings together the qualities needed to discharge the office of corregidor."[26]

Outside of creole politics and family structures, the church served as virtually the only coherent institution. Yet even it operated on a shoestring. The Petén seldom enjoyed more than two or three priests; these resided in Flores or one of the other more sizable pueblos but shared the unhappy burden of traveling through the monte in order to provide services for far-flung Maya communities. On Sundays and fiesta days the black settlers of San Benito had to fetch their padre via canoe from Flores.[27] Caciques of the Petén Maya transported back to Guatemala for religious education proved haughty and difficult for their would-be instructors.[28] Indians had killed priests in the early eighteenth century and burned the first church erected in Dolores, but though they continued to resist chores like gathering firewood, the Petén's newly colonialized peasants eventually came to an understanding with the new spiritual order, and by the early nineteenth century they petitioned Mérida for priests when services were lacking.[29] Still, new obstacles arose. The padres set up cofradías for the Mayas, but as with cofradías elsewhere, these often lacked sound management and, by the time of independence, had fallen into decay.[30] Yucatecan priests who worked in the area remembered the region's epidemics above all else, and in later applications for professional advancement wore their service in northern Guatemala like purple hearts.[31] Finally, and despite the Catholic Church's centrality to Spanish colonialism, the Petén suffered from church-state antagonisms dating back to the colonies' beginnings, as missionaries quarreled with the Spanish settlers over the rights to tithe money, Indian labor, and the various fees the church attached to its services.[32] It did not escape the settlers' attention that they themselves were Guatemalans while the priests were Yucatecans, and that, at least when looked at in a certain way, they were handing over their money to foreigners.

Some of the problems that later troubled Barreiro were already evident decades earlier. A royal inspector noted in 1817 that "the dependence of Petén province on the bishopric in Mérida in its ecclesiastical jurisdiction makes establishing curacies difficult."[33] Five years later the church sent Padre Domingo Fajardo of Hecelchakán to investigate affairs in the Petén, a routine visita that had previously required no more than a few weeks. Instead, Fajardo disappeared for three years as he became embroiled in problems of funding, bureaucracy, poor roads, and the general indifference that permeated the Guatemalan state. The liberal government, which ruled after independence, had little interest in the rural priests, and even though it theoretically assumed responsibility for their salaries, it seldom had the money or inclination to pay. Nor did the Indian cofradías function as planned; without careful supervision, their cattle herds dwindled to a few scrawny cows. Only Fajardo's cajolings kept his priests from leaving. The visitador spent months lobbying for better treatment but secured only promises; eventually he was recalled.[34]

The Carrera revolt of 1838 restored many of the curas' old prerogatives—even though it failed to alter northern Guatemala's economic stagnation—and though the Petén had entered the national period with five priests (one a *vicario incápite,* or regional administrator and ecclesiastical judge), the number had shrunk to three by 1858.[35]

Clerical behavior remained lax by European standards. Consider, for example, the French traveler Arthur Morelet's account of a ball he and Corregidor Méndez attended in 1847:

> Every eye was fixed on a young man singing to his own accompaniment on a guitar. He was not wanting in taste, and certainly not in assurance. The relatively elegant cut of his garments, his easy air of gallantry with the women, all pronounced him to be a stranger. A burst of applause succeeded his song, after which, making a sign to the musicians, he offered his hand to one of the ladies, and led off a fandango with such ease, grace, and agility as to excite the utmost enthusiasm of the spectators. Frantic bravos echoed from every corner of the apartment. The gentleman smiled his thanks, wiped his face carelessly with an embroidered handkerchief, and then seated himself among the señoras, who seemed enraptured with his grace of person and elegance of manner. "Who is this extraordinary personage?" I inquired, turning to my neighbor. "He is a *cura* from Honduras," was the reply.
>
> To me the accomplishments of the *padrecito* (as he was affectionately called) were scarcely less anomalous and extraordinary than his manners and general bearing; but I concealed my surprise. I cannot better illustrate the state of society and morals in these countries than by saying, that no one saw the least impropriety in having as their minister and confessor in religion, a man who was the gayest dancer and the most gallant in manner of the entire community. "Ah!" exclaimed the corregidor as we sauntered home, "isn't the *padrecito* an elegant fellow? He has taught our young folks many a lesson in good breeding, by which they cannot fail to profit. But I presume, señor, that your padres are by far his superiors?" I was tempted to tell him how his *padrecito* would be treated in Europe, but thought better of it, and left the corregidor to his delusions.[36]

As the anecdote suggests, the Petén priesthood was in the world but also of the world. The charm, the vitality, and the casual frontier simplicity of their region all helped blur the line between pious and popular behavior.

There was one final note to the Petén's cultural formation, something that would affect priest and parishioner alike. In the popular imagination, Yucatán had once served as the point of mythic origins, an Aztlán from which the best creole families had migrated. But time tarnished the Source's image.

After 1847 the Caste War sent thousands of Maya refugees into the Petén. Méndez's shrewd diplomacy merely heightened the area's reputation as a safe haven.[37] Nevertheless, political instability continued to rage in the north, and despite the best efforts of rebels and peteneros alike, the old north-south trade lines never resumed their original vigor. The Petén increasingly traded with Tabasco and Belize and came to regard Yucatán as a kind of seismic center from which one could expect nothing but new shock waves. Next came the Mexican reform, which demoted church power in the interests of modernization and state building. Guatemala, meanwhile, moved in the opposite direction. Under Rafael Carrera, the church resumed its old colonial powers and retained its property, while the paternalistic vision articulated by parish priests formed part of the ideological basis for Guatemala's national political structure.[38] Yucatán's church, like Mexico's politics, began to look terribly unstable next to the conservative kingdom of Rafael Carrera.

The Crisis of 1858

The event that inadvertently set the Petén controversy in motion was the death of vicario Tomás Salazar on September 3, 1856. Salazar was quite old and had been sick for a long time.[39] Unable to sleep, he also refused to leave his house and remained caught in a kind of paralysis that both foretold and postponed the end. At last his doctor slipped a sedative into the vicario's lemonade. Méndez, who was present, maintained that Salazar was so startled by his own sleepiness that he assumed death had come, and simply gave up the ghost.[40] Whatever the truth, Salazar never woke up after that fatal glass of lemonade. His house, his possessions, the cofradías he administered, and the curacy that he occupied all fell vacant.

There was thus an ecclesiastical vacuum in the region, and to fill the void of services the church appointed a now forgotten rogue priest named Fernando González. Born into a large Petén family, González had studied in the seminary in Mérida. He worked briefly in Tabasco's curacy of Rios del Usumacinta, where he learned about the needs and mentality of the backwoods river folk.[41] But within two years of Salazar's death, while serving in Flores, González became discontented with the poverty and subservience of the local parishes and so decided to take control of his own career. Without bothering to obtain the licenses that were an indispensable part of the church's system of regulating its priests, González left the province and headed north. His exact movements are unclear, but we know that he traveled to Campeche, where he learned of the state's successful campaign to break away from Yucatán. Schism was in the air, and the priest's actions in certain ways epitomized the new readiness to defiance. Basing himself in Flores, González launched his own unauthorized ministry along the Mexico-Guatemala borderland, where refugee Mayas had carved innumerable tiny settlements out of the wilderness. For Bishop Guerra it was an unorthodox and embarrassing situation; even the most intrepid of church travelers, priests such as José Ascención Tzuc and Manuel Antonio Sierra O'Reilly, had always kept in close contact with the cathedral.[42] González's audacity revealed publicly that Mérida was no longer in control.

How to rein in the situation? Méndez's friend Padre Hoil was too old, too fond of aguardiente, and too familiar to the peteneros to command much respect. Bishop Guerra's first choice, Juan Manuel Pasos, flatly refused to go. Guerra then dispatched a temporary minister named Juan Irenea Milán, convenient because he was stationed in nearby Tenabo.[43] But Milán's obesity, poor health, and dubious character disqualified him as a new permanent vicario; in fact, he died soon after reaching Flores. The bishop still needed someone to discipline González and restore a measure of integrity to Yucatán's churches in the Petén. As Guerra himself later confessed, "the Yucatecan priests in general do not lend themselves to go to the Petén," which they regarded as a cultural exile and, given the high incidence of mosquito-borne diseases, a possible death sentence. This left only the least qualified and least desirable element in an age where the missionary spirit was becoming a vestigial memory.[44]

But at the last moment a volunteer came forward. Amado Belizario Barreiro was an obscure Mérida priest who was then serving as a functionary in the cathedral.[45] Up to that point his life had suffered from hard luck and frustrated dreams. His father, a merchant, was murdered in Havana in 1851 under circumstances unknown.[46] Barreiro's career as a priest proved disappointing. Coming of age at the precise time when comfortable parish rents were disappearing, he had been unable to establish himself as a cura. A friend offered him temporary work in Carmen, but Barreiro found it too remote and uncertain.[47] Appointed cura and military chaplain of Bacalar in 1854, he fell sick and had to surrender the position before it began—a stroke of fortune, it turned out, since it spared him from being on hand when Maya rebels overran the town in early 1858.[48] But whatever his later shortcomings as a pastor, it is clear that in accepting the *vicariato* of the Petén he was sacrificing a great deal. Young Amado had the benefit of his own capellanía, whose revenues he managed to convert into real-estate investment. The padre failed to procure a second capellanía in 1854, but this did not stop him from becoming a significant money lender throughout the peninsula.[49] By 1856, for example, he held four thousand pesos in mortgages over rural properties belonging to Felipe Peón, the prominent oligarch who had haciendas in the Ticul and Maxcanú regions.[50] Barreiro also owned a store in Mérida and held the rights to a dozen other mortgages throughout Yucatán.[51] In short, he could easily have stayed in the capital living in comfort off his revenues. Instead, Barreiro saw the Petén as a chance to do something significant with his life, so much so that he offered to go without benefit of the *viático,* the grant used to cover travel expenses.[52] As soon as he had official permission, Barreiro appointed an attorney to look after his mother, then set out for Flores.[53]

Tracking González into the Petén was no mean feat. The poor quality of roads made travel by horse impossible. (The Yucatecans' inability to deploy cavalry here had helped save the Caste War rebels seven years earlier.) Barreiro and his small retinue of servants had to proceed through endless hills and gullies, down paths covered in "branches, sticks, reeds, and all sort of nuisances." Worse still were the rivers that tore through the region during the rainy season of late summer. Many of these were neck-deep; Barreiro could only cross by carrying his clothes in a bundle on his head, wearing nothing but his shoes to protect against the rocks of the river bottom. In some places travel stopped for days on end as they waited for the swollen waters to subside. Jaguars prowled the jungle but kept a respectful distance from humans; the real killers of this area, the mosquitoes, had no such fear, and tortured whatever traveler dared to sleep without a campfire. The relentless humidity made it hard to keep candles lit, while diarrhea and fever put in their inevitable appearance. Barreiro's only consolation was a cask of aguardiente that he brought along from Bolonchén.[54]

Once in the northern Petén, Barreiro found reminders of the Caste War at every turn. The monte was dotted with innumerable small hamlets of Maya refugees. Even in these squalid camps, however, the Mayas had constructed huts to serve as chapels. González, it turned out, had made a lively business out of servicing the hamlets at high rates.[55] The refugees had doubts as to whether González was even really a priest at all, but they had complied in order to be on the safe side. The rogue minister also carried a collection of religious trinkets known to appeal to rustics.[56] The other recent appointment, Juan Milán, had come through here as well. The corpulent priest cut an unusual figure, waddling through the tropical forest with his Indian porters and his common-law wife. Here he had performed marriages for the locals, including a cacique in Xtanché, where the bride's daughter had already given birth to this same man's child. Such actions infuriated Barreiro but were no doubt concessions to the realities of life in the remoter parts of the Petén.[57]

The fact was that warfare and calamity had in no way diminished the Mayas' zeal for old-time religion, particularly for the sacrament of confession. The concept of drawing in spiritual grace through acts of absolution bore resemblances to pre-Conquest practices of bloodletting and penitence; moreover, unlike baptism, marriage, and burial, confession was a free church service upon which peasants could repeatedly draw to build up spiritual strength.[58] Despite recent visits by González and Milán, which had garnered nearly four hundred pesos out of these hardscrabble rancherías, the refugee Mayas were once more brimming with fresh transgressions. In San Antonio, Barreiro, now delirious under the early stages of malaria, lay in his hammock as a procession of penitents recounted sin after sin, utterly indifferent to his illness. For two days Barreiro listened to their tireless accounts, then collapsed.[59]

Eventually the new vicario picked himself up and resumed his journey, reaching San Andrés exactly two months and two days after leaving Mérida. The locals gave Barreiro a royal welcome in the best Petén style: fireworks, marimbas, and a throng of well-wishers. A mile out from the city, a horde of beggars attached themselves to his company. "This day," he later reminisced, "I drank only my own tears." Meanwhile, however, all was not well, for an omen—the worst lightning storm in living memory—terrorized Flores for the entire night following Barreiro's arrival. One bolt sent the church's altar decorations crashing to the feet of El Señor de Esquipulas, even though the santo himself escaped unharmed. Another bolt struck the home of Modesto Méndez, while in the fields two cattle were killed.[60] To a people raised on the creencias, these events told that the heavens had something terrible in store for their frontier community—and that it would involve the corregidor, the vicario, and the church.

In San Andrés the long struggle between the Yucatecan and the Guatemalan began. The vicario opened by issuing his decree of suspension for the rogue priest of Flores. González, dressed in scandalous multicolored pants and "high shoes," arrived to dispute the charges. The matter of his clothing, which would recur again and again throughout the two men's quarrel, to some degree touched on issues of local, even national, identity: Guatemalans were known for their flashy, decorative textiles, while Yucatecans dressed conservatively in simple dark or white. But for the moment Barreiro said little; he was well aware of González's influence in the town and his considerable popularity among some quarters.

The looming power struggle split Flores into factions. Barreiro wasted no time in allying himself with Méndez and Hoil, men he later came to despise but whose help he desperately needed. Many of the peteneros also supported the suspension and pressured Barreiro to maintain the hard line. But González had his own network of allies, for the most part his family and friends and the not inconsiderable group that loathed Modesto Méndez. Moreover, practical considerations intruded. The chronic shortage of priests meant that Barreiro had to give occasional permission for González to travel into local hamlets. This humiliating indecision did the vicario's cause little good.

The situation deteriorated rapidly after this first interview. González hoped to settle the matter with an initial show of force, so he rallied his supporters and began a campaign of intimidation against the vicario. This began as drunken public threats but soon bordered on real violence. Matters came to a head on the evening of September 14, when an angry mob of *gonzalecistas* forced Barreiro, Méndez, and the town's ayuntamiento (*mendecista,* naturally) to take refuge in the Flores church. For four days they could not leave for fear of assault. During that time González and Barreiro held several parlays; these resulted in nothing, but when it became clear that González could dislodge them only by force (an option he was apparently unwilling to take), he agreed to a compromise. The rogue priest offered to leave Flores, providing that Barreiro grant him a license to continue his work in outlying parts of the Petén. But Méndez, González insisted, would have to die; the mob was apparently more interested in getting rid of their autocratic corregidor than in tampering with ecclesiastical structure. Barreiro, of course, could not agree to a lynching. At last he promised to surrender the vicariato to González and that together he and Modesto Méndez would leave the Petén within a week. The mob withdrew and crisis ended, at least for the moment.[61]

Once free, Modesto Méndez did indeed leave Flores; but stealing a page from Rafael Carrera he immediately proceeded to raise a peasant army from the outlying villages, principally San Andrés, where his word was law. Arming these followers with weapons from the public armory, the corregidor divided them into patrols of fifteen, leading a vanguard of some thirty-five himself. This organized repression quickly dissolved the mob; the rebel leaders, now imprisoned, wasted no time in laying all blame at the feet of González. But Méndez apparently thought it prudent to leave the priest at large, since the latter continued to enjoy the support of a sizable faction. For his part, Barreiro quickly reneged on his agreement to leave the Petén. Instead, he took the only remaining step, which was to publicly excommunicate his rival.[62]

In the days after the September siege the people of Flores continued to live with clinched teeth. González purposefully antagonized Barreiro by parading through town in the hated pants of many colors. He sent repeated letters demanding that Barreiro and Méndez leave the Petén—something that neither man had any intention of doing. Flores still had a strong gonzalecista faction, but hope of an uprising had ended, since armed mendecistas now patrolled the streets. It is probable that the majority wanted peace in both church and state but were not prepared to take up arms for either side. That left Méndez with his immediate circle of followers and his ascendancy over the rural hamlets and Barreiro with the considerable moral authority of his position as vicario.

The following Sunday Barreiro and González fell into a public quarrel once more when González demanded to be allowed to go to San José to say mass. Denied, González shoved the vicario; he told onlookers that they were fools for paying the tithe, which had been abolished in Yucatán years ago—true enough, although other forms of revenue had made up for it. Barreiro retorted that hell awaited blasphemers. At last a pious woman stepped forward and urged the two to stop; she fainted and had to be carried away. Barreiro himself went off to dine with Méndez, at which point he succumbed to another attack of malaria, which laid him up for the next three days.[63]

A month later Barreiro seemed more in control. The threat of an armed uprising was gone, and repeated confessions to Hoil had momentarily helped tranquilize his tortured soul. But a change was coming over the vicario. Always excitable and defensive, he began to deteriorate—perhaps a result of malaria, perhaps the stress of his situation. Odd fantasies now intruded into his waking thoughts. He continued to live in fear of armed men, partisans of González whom he believed were plotting his overthrow: "burning the torch of revolution," as he put it. Barreiro became convinced that González was planning to steal the church's decorations and abscond to Africa disguised as a layman. Worst of all, González continued to wear the high shoes and multicolored pants that had brought such shame upon the church.[64]

Frustrated, Barreiro now dramatically announced his own intention to leave for Belize to recover his health. Perhaps it was merely a ruse, for this news had the immediate effect of rallying sympathy and support. A group of citizens came forward urging him to stay, reminding him, somewhat against the facts, that he had quelled the González revolution single-handedly. This was all that Barreiro's ego needed to hear. Barreiro partisans now promised a militia of mendecistas to arrest González and carry him to Mérida in chains. Such an offer, at least to the mind of Barreiro, threatened to undermine the authority of the church. Instead, he drew up a notarized decree ordering González out of the province within two days. And indeed, González did leave, escorted by his supporters "with marimbas, shouting, and laughter." But he headed straight for Guatemala City, where he hoped for an audience with President Rafael Carrera and the bishop. Meanwhile, his supporters broke out of their cell and fled to join him. Their escape was hardly surprising, since the jail, like virtually all other buildings in the Petén, was made of nothing more than wood poles and a thatch roof. They left behind a thoughtfully composed letter of farewell: the *cuates* (cronies), as Barreiro called them, threatened to return with a new corregidor and an ecclesiastical transfer; if not, they promised armed raids.[65]

Much of the confrontation had been smoke and ego, but beneath it all lay the critical issue of frontier attitude toward legality, in this case the legality of the church. The strength of ecclesiastical authority resembled the way physicists describe gravity: a relatively weak force but without spatial limits. González could flout the commands of the bishop, but even in this tropical backwater the threat of excommunication and the prohibitions of the vicario still carried weight. A pious Catholic might rebel against the specifics of the church as long as he could reconcile himself with church policy in the long run. Doubtless this understanding derived from old colonial experience, whereby the colonists' right of initiative in matters such as the impromptu and unauthorized granting of land titles always waited on the Crown's right of approval.[66] Royal rulings came at a glacial pace, but come they did, and they had to be factored into all reckonings. Local factions thus required the girder of a larger authority to support their decisions and activities, and therein lay the connection between the Petén's ecclesiastical feuds and the emergence of allegiance to national structures.

A Residue of Hard Feelings

It was at this point—and perhaps because such clear-cut authority was now in doubt—that hostilities and mutual suspicions began to proliferate. First and most surprisingly, latent differences between Barreiro and the corregidor began to emerge. Barreiro, who desperately needed allies, instead began to create new enemies. He now focused his powers of suspicion on Modesto

Méndez. Although the corregidor had saved his authority and perhaps his life, the one-man nature of his rule did not escape the vicario. Méndez's ascendancy over Hoil, his autocratic bearing, his tendency to meddle in the business of others, his love affairs: these were matters better left undisturbed, but Barreiro's unsettled state of mind now elevated them to primary importance.

For those willing to listen, there was no shortage of rumors concerning the famous Modesto Méndez. Many believed that he had gained his position by betraying the previous corregidor. Others maintained that he shot prisoners without trial (actually the crime of his predecessor, not of Méndez himself, but time tended to jumble responsibility). His brother and brother-in-law had murdered with impunity, they said. And was it true that one of his many lovers had exposed her new-born infant on a beehive, where it was stung to death? These were dark stories indeed, and probably reflected no more than a resentment over the corregidor's autocratic rule. But in the shadow of conspiracy and factional warfare, all stories seemed true.

To Barreiro the most disturbing of all was a persistent rumor that Méndez had in fact murdered the late Salazar with a glass of poisoned milk (no longer barbiturated lemonade). The night that Salazar had died, Méndez and a black manservant from San Benito had purportedly searched his house and made off with a strongbox that was hidden under the bed. As in surviving peninsular folklore, blacks and mulattos served as stock figures in rumors of the time, more than anything else a comment on the ethnic stereotypes spun out of old colonial relationships. To the popular mind, their sadism was born in cruel Africa and nursed in the slave's vengeful heart; as with the black whipmaster that Raymundo Pérez purportedly kept in Macuspana, their mere mention suggested malevolent deeds. (Even old Padre Hoil had his own stories about Africans. Barreiro, he claimed, had brought with him a pair of black manservants whom he insisted on using as sacristans. Bumbling and irreverent but loyal to the vicario, they ran roughshod over church decorum.[67]) As it turned out, however, there was a basis of truth to at least some of the Méndez stories: the corregidor *had* impounded Salazar's estate, together with the cofradía funds the old prelate had administered. As later documents show, he did it legally and with only modest levels of corruption.[68] But Barreiro accepted all the rumors at face value. It was only a matter of time, it seemed to him, before someone poisoned his own milk.[69]

Judging from their private correspondence, it sometimes seems that everyone in the Petén hated and distrusted everyone else. The case of Padre Hoil was representative. Universally considered a crony of the corregidor, Hoil had no qualms about attacking Méndez in private and affirmed that "it doesn't suit him for anyone here to oppose his depraved system of justice, and particularly when he sees that Sr. Barreiro is highly popular with the people." Indeed, Barreiro, his personal demons notwithstanding, could be strangely charismatic. He entered into the pueblos a bundle of energy, preaching in both Spanish and Maya. His youth allowed him into places that Hoil and Méndez could go only with great effort. Most importantly, his energy and facility with the Maya language were allowing him to cut into the corregidor's traditional base of support, the surrounding Maya communities.[70] It is also a fact that paranoiacs are sometimes compelling individuals; their intense struggles with imagined enemies can dominate the mundane lives of the people around them.

But not all villages enjoyed the same political climate. Hostility in Sacluucté was so intense that Barreiro tried to avoid the place altogether. Still, his occasional visits did take some strange turns. The locals tried to draw Barreiro into *jaranas,* card games, and drinking bouts, things to which the sociable vicario was not averse (all-night games of *manille* were popular here). Given the filter of Barreiro's paranoid personality, it is difficult to penetrate to the real dynamics of the situation. Were locals trying to entrap the priest in compromising situations? Or were they simply fun-loving country people who wanted to bury the hatchet and have a good time? Nothing in the Petén was as simple as it appeared.[71]

In the end, this brief period of calm exposed an odd cross-hatching of commonality and mutual distrust. On one hand, Flores and the surrounding villages looked tranquil; differences of wealth were smaller here than in many parts of Mexico or Guatemala, and institutions such as fiestas, card games, and shared religious culture mediated between peoples and classes. But, on the other hand, the villages were also hives of envy, suspicion, and mutual jealousy, the unhappy features that so many ethnographers point to as subcurrents of the rural community.[72] Petty elites such as Hoil and Méndez feared the success of their fellows and were constantly on the lookout for signs of potential rivals. They fought against such concentrations of power with a variety of weapons, but the front line of defense was always the rumor. Religion was not exempted from this dissonance. People shared the Catholic culture, but within that cultural field lay quarrels of rank, authority, and personal and regional loyalties; it was through such anguishing quarrels that the people of a given place would pass while working out larger matters such as faith, political goals, and national identity.

The First Visita

While people in Flores jealously compared status, Barreiro's enemy Fernando González continued his work. Much to his fortune, González found an entrée to President Carrera. Among the priest's closest friends was Juan José Baldizón, a comrade from his days in Rios de Usumacinta and someone who had been decorated for military service. This friend of a friend arranged to bring González to court, along with a letter of presentation from "a certain General Zapata."[73] In Guatemala he found a ready audience, since both the secular and religious hierarchies of the nation were eager to consolidate their territorial control.

The man sent to investigate the mess in Flores was Colonel Joaquín Saenz, a military officer whom Carrera had decorated for his services in the Central American wars. Although married and in his sixties, Saenz proved to be quite the ladies' man, and once in the Petén he immediately struck up a flirtation with one of the local damsels. Married men kept their wives away from the gallant colonel at dances. On a professional level, however, Saenz dedicated himself to advancing the interests and sovereignty of his master, Rafael Carrera, and he now saw in González's petty complaint the key to eliminating the Mexican ecclesiastical presence.[74]

Saenz's arrival was no surprise. Barreiro and others had known for some time that a *juez pesquizador,* the modern equivalent of the old Spanish *visitador,* was coming. In some quarters public respect for the vicario declined as Saenz's entourage neared. For example, Barreiro happened to be in the village of Chachacluum, not far from Sacluucté, when the juez pesquizador first reached the Petén. The locals had learned of his arrival, which they correctly interpreted as a victory for their man González, and they began to bait the vicario publicly. Their choice of accusations is interesting. Now, twenty-four years after the fact, the peteneros still accused Guerra of having stolen the bishopric from José María Meneses! Old animosities died hard in this land. Other insults were cruder, if not necessarily more cutting: "We shit on your crown and miter, and may the Devil take you!"[75] The vicario could do nothing more than swear out an impotent complaint.

Saenz's first interview with Barreiro immediately staked out the political divisions. The juez pesquizador was blatantly pro-Guatemala. Cutting to the point, he began by laying the Caste War at the feet of the Mérida-based church, charging that the cause of the Indian revolt had been nothing more than the despotism, mistreatment, lack of charity, poor example, and egotism, of the Bishop and the curas, since these took the grinding stones, the huipiles, and even the most basic necessities from the poor Indians to pay for burial, baptism, marriage, or whatever other administrative function . . .

Nor did Saenz overlook the hated obvention system. The accusations stung because they were at least partly correct: obventions and religious fees had been the main grievance of the peasant masses in 1847. However, the church had been only one part of a more complex social breakdown, one that involved many elements of the Yucatecan world.[76] Saenz also confronted Barreiro with the decrepit state of the Petén's churches. But the vicario had an answer for this. Yucatán's churches had been desolated by the war, whereas Guatemala's were just as bad despite prolonged peace; what hope, then, that an ecclesiastical transfer would actually favor the Petén? The situation would only go, as Barreiro's inevitable joke put it, *de Guatemala a Guatepeor* ("from Guatebad to Guate-worse").[77]

This opening interview produced no practical results. To make matters worse, González now reappeared. A childish exchange between the two priests followed; González taunted Barreiro with the fact that while traveling with the juez pesquizador he had said mass "because he felt like it." Predictably, Barreiro continued to uphold the ban and the excommunication.[78] What followed was a long period of negotiation between Barreiro and Saenz. The former remained intransigent, but the latter, while openly partisan, still needed to observe the appearance of respect for Mérida's religious authority. The colonel's first proposal was that the two men compose a joint letter to Guerra asking for González's reinstatement, a suggestion that Barreiro rejected point-blank. Saenz then tried a more conciliatory approach: he would make González the chaplain of his military regiment, where he could keep him under strict watch. Barreiro again refused, but counteroffered to buy off González by placing him on a retainer (fifteen pesos per month, no mean salary for the Petén) while upholding his suspension from active service. Saenz in turn refused this, since, as he accurately perceived, González's proud and truculent personality would make further conflict inevitable. The juez's final offer, also rejected, was that they simply reinstate the priest without bothering to inform the bishop.[79]

The situation was hopeless. Saenz could not remove Barreiro or reinstate González, but before departing he did what to his eye was the next best thing. By handing the corregidorship to a certain José Eduviges Vidaurre, he left secular power in the hands of one of Barreiro's worst critics, thus ensuring that further conflict and harassment would follow. He thus set forces in motion that were certain to work against Barreiro's interests. Thus ended the first of Saenz's two visitas.

Corregidor Vidaurre

One of the more baffling features of nineteenth-century Mexico's political culture is its instability. Particularly at the local level, political factions often organized around the personality of powerful officials or land-owning caudillos; but these factions could join forces, fragment, and realign themselves with a facility that puzzles the modern observer accustomed to thinking in terms of ideological orientation and relatively stable blocs of support. Some of the main instigators of the Caste War, for example, switched political allegiances two or three times in the decade prior to the 1847 uprising. The instability owed in large part to the forces that had generated caudillo politics in the first place: weak and underfunded central governments gave birth to regional strongmen who could not reward, and therefore could not retain, the loyalty of followers once in power. The picture is somewhat clearer for high-profile national caudillos—Juan Alvarez supporting and then pronouncing against Santa Anna, Santiago Vidaurre of Monterrey doing the same to Juárez.[80] But the picture normally remains elusive at local levels because of the lack of detailed information concerning conditions and personalities. Barreiro's adventures in the Petén are unique in the degree to which they reveal the pressures that led people to form alliances with men who had been their worst enemies only weeks before—and how those same political tendencies could trace fault lines generated by differences of religious culture.

Rapid factional realignment was particularly evident with the entrance of a new personality, José Eduviges Vidaurre. Far from calming the atmosphere, the appointment of a new corregidor simply generated new patterns of discontent. To begin with, Vidaurre's sudden rise brought new quarrels with Yucatecan churchmen, long accustomed to preferential treatment under Modesto Méndez. After a long day with the aguardiente bottle, Padre Hoil had a tendency to make rambling public complaints against the new order. The changing political situation had also taken its toll on Barreiro, whose own writings grew more disoriented. The vicario dreamed of punishing his enemies, of renovating the Petén with a staff of associates hand-picked from his days at the Cathedral. These ends, however, prompted Barreiro to an unfortunate decision. Rather than abide by traditional tithe practices, he now extended tithe obligations to all owners of cattle and to a wide variety of fruits, vegetables, and domestic animals.[81] A watermelon tax looks trivial from the distance of 150 years, but at the time these minor manipulations of long-standing custom were capable of generating enormous discontent and, as the Caste War itself has shown, contributing to a larger destabilization.

Vidaurre, who detested Barreiro, seized on these irregularities as the opening shots in his own anti-Yucatecan campaign. The accusations served as useful and necessary distractions, because Vidaurre had his own set of reforms that in and of themselves would prove unpalatable to the average petenero. This was especially true in regard to the livestock industry. Though an exporter of pigs and cattle, the region had difficulty maintaining sufficient herds. Since locals consistently refused to adopt better ranching methods, the corregidors had little choice but to impose periodic prohibitions on slaughter and export in order to maintain herd sizes. This is precisely what Vidaurre himself ordered.[82] The prohibition on exports and slaughter inconvenienced the large cattle owners such as Modesto Méndez but also hurt many less illustrious peteneros who eked by on the returns of their five or six cows. (Maya immigrants themselves came to own small herds, picking up on an industry they knew from the old country; their brands appear in the massive registry of 1873.[83]) At the same time, Vidaurre began construction of a highway leading to Yucatán. The aim was twofold: to revive the region's former trade and to better control the dispersed refugee settlements that were multiplying north of Flores in the wake of renewed Caste War violence. Both projects were sound enough but could be accomplished only through economic hardship and forced peasant labor (*fagina*) and therefore had the potential of generating popular discontent. An attack on Barreiro and the Yucatecan church could help siphon off public anger.

The anticipated resistance to these plans crystallized around Vidaurre's own former partisans. New power has a way of destroying friendships, and local jealousy and resentment flared when peteneros learned that their old manille partner was now the law north of the sixteenth parallel. Creoles like Domingo Segura and Juan José Baldizón felt that they and not Vidaurre should have been the next corregidor. These former cronies of Vidaurre now turned against him and began a tide of complaint, something that brought them, ironically, into the company of the vicario that so many of them had disliked. Indeed, Barreiro had one facility that served him well: a hypersensitivity for the potential ally, something that allowed him to survive in this hostile environment for as long as he did. Within the space of a few months, then, Barreiro found that he shared certain common interests with some of the very men who had once barricaded him in the church. Charged with resentments, Domingo Segura began a campaign of backbiting and defamation against the new corregidor. His principal ally was Belizario Barreiro, still bitter over how the visita had embarrassed him; church money was now scarcer than ever, and the vicario's dreams of renovating the Petén looked increasingly improbable. Barreiro was particularly useful, since through his office as vicario he still carried a considerable influence among the common people.

It was this last point that was crucial: the discontents enraged Vidaurre by appealing to the masses for help. The corregidor came to the belief, or at least cynically insisted, that Barreiro had told local Mayas that they had no obligation to do real work, that the entire Yucatecan tax system was coming to the Petén, and that the best thing they could do was sell their belongings and leave for the monte. It was this popular appeal, so redolent of Santiago Imán and other recent rabble-rousers, that drove Vidaurre to action. In June 1859, accusing the entire collection of malcontents of treason, the corregidor hastily convened an inquiry. Vidaurre stacked the witness box with allies, thus making the results a foregone conclusion. His investigation "discovered" that the political dissidents were drunks and malingerers, and their arrest was ordered. For political purposes the vindictive corregidor converted what was little more than low-level resistance into a sinister and sweeping conspiracy against the Guatemalan state.[84] The vecinos who participated in the "conspiracy" feared political persecution—justifiably so—and fled to Usumacinta. But this was the rainy season. By December they were exhausted, starving, and sick with malaria and so returned to surrender themselves to the authorities.[85]

Barreiro, however, refused to accept his fate. "The inhabitants of Flores," wrote Morelet in 1847, "have a lurking notion that no one can leave their island without tears in his eyes and regret in his heart."[86] Something like this applied to the deeply aggrieved ex-vicario. But one last hope remained. Nursing his wounded pride beside a river outside of town, Barreiro managed to intercept a letter from Guerra to the corregidor; in this, he inserted incongruously belligerent warnings between Guerra's otherwise innocuous paragraphs. For example, to the bishop's perfunctory closing Barreiro added, "but watch your step" (*pero mira como camina*). In a second forgery Barreiro threw caution to the wind. This, a minutely written diatribe purportedly from Guerra, blasted virtually everyone in the Petén for conspiring against the saintly Padre

Barreiro. Composed in the same breathless, unpunctuated style that characterized Barreiro's other correspondence, the latter bore no similarity whatsoever to the bland prose of Guerra. A sample: "There have reached my hands the calumnious accusations which by seditious attempts Dn. Joaquín Saenz and other impious vecinos of that district make, which, together with the accursed Padre González have planted discord and schism in the Petén . . ." and on and on, for four bombastic pages. Indeed, it was unlikely that the mild-mannered Guerra would have referred to the locals as "rogues and worms" (*pícaros y polillos*).[87] Seizing upon these cumulative misdoings, Vidaurre had deported Barreiro to Yucatán. Upon his arrival, the church placed him under arrest, where he remained during the year of investigation that surrounded the episode.

Ecclesiastical frauds were serious business. Bishop Guerra himself had already been the victim of one such incident when his rival, José Manuel Pardío, the cura who had once quarreled with the peasants of Tabi, somehow contrived to have the Pope grant him the outlandish title "Bishop of Germanicópolis," in theory a sort of alternate chief of Yucatán's ecclesiastical hierarchy; the matter ended only when the archbishops of Mexico and Puebla refused to ratify the papers. The Imán revolt drove the pretender from the peninsula, and Santiago Imán himself bought up some of Pardío's properties at ecclesiastical auction. Incredibly, Pardío managed to repeat the same trick in Caracas, Venezuela, until the Vatican caught on and suspended this religious bounder. Many years later stray documents still referred to him as "the bishop Pardío." He clung to his unusual title for years, living in obscurity in both Veracruz and, later, Mexico City, where he died in 1861 in a carriage accident while en route to hear the confession of a nun.[88]

Interrogations of Barreiro were therefore repeated and intense, far beyond the inquiries that followed more quotidian parish complaints. After initially denying the accusations, Barreiro broke down before mounting evidence of his forgeries.[89] This admission ended the priest's career. For several months he lingered in Mérida's prison. His defense attorney tried to move him to house arrest in the rectory of San Cristóbal; old Silvestre Antonio Dondé, the priest who had spearheaded economic development in Tekax before the Caste War, offered to serve as a sort of parole officer. But the request fell on deaf ears, and Barreiro lingered on in his joyless cell.[90] At last the provisor, acknowledging that Barreiro had acted under unusual pressures and harassments, cleared him of charges of sedition, drunkenness, and ministerial abuses, but convicted him of tithe irregularities and falsification of documents. He was sentenced to time served, court costs, a six months' suspension of clerical duties, and a week of "spiritual exercises." [91] At first glance a petty reprimand, this was probably the harshest sentence the Yucatecan church had ever handed to one of its members—their way of telling Barreiro that his days as a priest were over.

This strange tale of intrigue in the Petén opens into a number of interpretive issues regarding the early national period. On the one hand, it shows the kind of secret wars that took place beneath the level of national and even state and provincial history. The Barreiro-González crisis, hitherto unknown, traumatized the Petén far more profoundly than any of the more high-profile struggles, including the Caste War, Mexico's Liberal reforms, the filibustering of William Walker, or the federalist-centralist jihads that scourged early Central America. On the other hand, this story shades into the emergence of national identities at an extremely local level. Studies of nationalism often choose more recognizable entities—the Mexican revolutionary state, for example—as their subject. There is a strong directedness to such work for the simple reason that its endpoint is well known and preordained. The script calls for Mexico's inhabitants to become Mexican, China's to become Chinese, and so forth. The Petén, however, was an unusual case for its indeterminacy: perhaps Yucatecan, perhaps Mexican, perhaps Guatemalan, perhaps all of the above, or perhaps merely the private fiefdom of Modesto Méndez. In 1858 many peteneros didn't seem to know the answer, nor did they always appear terribly concerned.

But the answer did matter to a small and divided nucleus of the community. Goaded by career problems and the quest for personal power, their incipient nationalism coalesced around administrative problems, family connections, trade, roads, cultural quirks, and changing political vicissitudes outside the province. The language that it chose was what was still a universal medium for postcolonial Hispanic Americans: their religion. Indeed, Catholicism was both the language and the issue itself. Peteneros and Yucatecans alike struggled to dominate Petén religious space, while their ammunition in this struggle was the values their church articulated: peace, decorum, social harmony, and religious services for all. Both Barreiro and González advanced themselves (and their patron nations) as the best guarantor of those values.

Religion still reigned as a popular culture as well. Humble citizens made little impact on surviving documentation, but reading between the polemical lines, it appears that most peteneros were not strong partisans of either camp and certainly were not disbelievers or heretics. They found themselves instead in the crosscurrents of shared belief and bitter rivalries. That church services should continue was never in question. Rather, their insistence on mass, confessions, cofradías, and public veneration of the santos was the demand that framed the competition between Barreiro and González. Their occasional appearances principally underscore their desire to reassert the mediating role of religious culture over its darker undercurrent of domination and distrust. In practical terms, the people of Flores wanted the protagonists to make up and be friendly. That, after all, was what Christians were supposed to do; it was what the santos wanted. The search for moderation, middle ground, and postponed decisions is in fact a common reaction of ordinary people confronted by revolution or momentous change.[92] Faced with ecclesiastical quarrels that were beyond the ken—or at least the concern—of the average citizen, sometimes the wisest thing to do was to faint.

The Guatemalans Arrive

Before closing this odd and scandalous tale, there are still some dangling threads that need attention, including the matter of the ecclesiastical transfer itself. To begin with, the principal characters in the Petén story did not survive for long. Troublemaker Fernando González simply vanished. For Amado Belizario Barreiro, the spiritual exercises came too late to save his worldly career. He died in his home in Mérida on the night of April 13, 1861, without having resumed a position of responsibility in the church. In death as in life, the padre sparked controversy. Barreiro owned few material possessions beyond a scattering of furniture, but he did hold some capellanías, and since the Liberal reform was now in effect, the fate of these looked uncertain. Former debtors, like Felipe Peón, sued for the rights to this money, while a woman came forward claiming to be Barreiro's daughter and heir (indeed, his will makes reference to certain secret arrangements whose contents will never be known).[93] In the end, however, surviving family members managed to win out. The inquest into Barreiro's property in the Petén dragged on for years, with Rodulfo Cantón, leader of the Mérida spiritualists' Peralta Circle, serving as court-appointed executor.[94]

The dissipated Hoil died in 1861. Fortune had thrown a difficult lot to the padre. A mestizo in a Spaniard's world, Hoil had managed to carve out and defend his own nook only in the remoteness of Flores. In the afternoon of his old age he was inclined to sit on the porch of his home and, between tugs at the aguardiente bottle, reflect on his life and times. News of the fighting in Italy and the papal states troubled him deeply; it was a nationalist conflict too much like his own struggles with González and Saenz. But in the end the details of mundane affairs offered an escape, and his final letter shows him still fretting about the sacristy's thatch roof.[95]

Modesto Méndez died two years later, in 1863. According to one account, Méndez was offered his old job of corregidor but, with his pride mortally offended, declined.[96] Always to be found in his dashing military uniform, the colonel continued to dabble in minor intrigues until the very end. More than any other individual, he *was* the Petén, an exotic mixture of virtue and cynicism, folksiness, outlandish pretension, and real jungle heroics. This finder of lost cities and negotiator of Indian peace treaties has no peer in the history of Guatemala's northernmost province. Born in the colonial era, he was saddened by the return of European imperialism as French legionnaires occupied Mexico. A lifelong defender of the established church, he saw the changes of the time reflected in his own family: while his beloved son Mariano Delfín labored on as a priest in the Petén for many years, his second son, Félix, abandoned the seminary to study law, the language of the new secular age.[97]

As though from a screenplay by Robert Bolt, the decisions of the national powers took their course in spite of these men. The Petén was to become purely Guatemalan. At the last possible moment, however, the Yucatecan faction won a reprieve. In the spring of 1863 Guatemala fell into new conflicts with its rival, El Salvador, and Carrera decided to postpone the transfer. The news was of small comfort to the last temporary minister from Yucatán, Ignacio Berzunza, then laid up with malaria in a remote village.[98] But it meant that José María Guerra would not live to see this truncation of his spiritual kingdom. After surviving the Santiago Imán revolt, the Caste War, the Liberal reform, and a dozen other minor rebellions and palace coups, the old conservative prelate died in 1863. He was buried in a chapel on the family hacienda.[99] The onus of transition fell to his successor, Leandro de Gala.[100]

The final ironies of this story belonged to the Guatemalans themselves. The long-threatened transfer at last arrived in 1865 with the coming of the first Guatemalan vicario, Teodoro Mazeriegas. However, it was not to be the religious revitalization that Saenz, González, and others had promised. Accustomed to the colonial solidity of Carrera's Guatemala, Mazeriegas found the vicariate in its usual state of abandon. The effects of seventeen years of Caste War were evident in the countless dispersed settlements that made parish organization so difficult.[101] Among other things, Mazeriegas singled out a large number of refugees from Bécal, Yucatán, living in the northern Petén.[102] Many of the so-called towns had no more than two or three families; their churches were mere *palapas,* open pole constructions with thatch roofs. Furthermore, the people here had no custom of paying the priests for their services, "so that I do not know how the padres that lived here were able to maintain themselves," the new vicario tellingly confessed. The climate was also distressing: sultry heat alternated with periods of deluge, a curse to priests accustomed to the more temperate highlands.[103] The limitations of frontier life were beginning to sink in.

Moreover, political strife soon undermined the clerical project. Five years after Rafael Carrera's death on Good Friday in 1865, a new revolution brought to power a group of Guatemalan liberals even more savagely anticlerical than those in Mexico. Strongman-president Justo Rufino Barrios slashed the powers of the church, abolished the regular orders, and confiscated their monasteries and properties. To be certain, the church and popular religiosity survived, but no longer was Guatemala to serve as a haven for conservative prelates fleeing Mexico.

Momentary economic conditions also hurt the new Guatemalan initiative. By all evidence, 1865 was a bad year. Droughts had depressed agricultural production in many places throughout the south. Both the Petén and the adjacent pacífico communities were now suffering from several successive years of bad harvests.[104] Lacking proper temperatures and soils, the region failed to prosper from Rufino Barrios's state-sponsored coffee boom, while the Petén's remoteness and thin workforce kept it out of the pocket of banana magnate United Fruit, later infamous for its cloak-and-dagger intrigues on Guatemala's Atlantic coast.[105] Real commercial penetration came only with the development of tropical forest products, specifically chicle, from the 1890s onward, long after the church here had fallen on the liberal chopping block.[106] However, even then the rural communities continued to retain a strong Yucatecan cultural presence, particularly in their use of Yucatec Maya as the language of daily life.[107]

Finally, there was the matter of popular justice. Barreiro's excesses notwithstanding, the peteneros still retained their traditional Catholicism, something that invested the person of the priest with a certain inviolability. Hence, for several years thereafter, a mythical hue, potent if *post facto,* came to surround the events of 1858 to 1859. That hue only deepened as one calamity after another scourged the province. Flores, tropical namesake of the fallen bureaucrat, burned to the ground on May 14, 1872, for what was not the first or even second time.[108] Droughts continued throughout the decade. The people knew only too well the real cause of fires, murders, and natural disasters; confronted by such terrifying signs, they responded by shaking their heads and issuing a verdict based on their understanding of the world and its moral and spiritual order: "Make no mistake, the Petén is paying for having imprisoned Señor Barreiro!"[109]

CONCLUSION

The Motives for Miracle

The morning of January 3, 1996, began much like any other in the city of Izamal. Truckers roared in and out of town, bringing goods from Mérida. A few tourists made their way to this ancient town with its picturesque convent and courtyard. It had been an unseasonably cool winter, and old men warmed themselves with coffee in the restaurants. Little did the citizens of this tranquil scene suspect that a miracle was about to visit them.

That morning a local woman named Lourdes Alcocer was washing clothes in the patio of her home when a silhouette appeared on the patio's stucco wall. The mysterious red stain, some eighty centimeters tall, was none other than Baltazar, the dark-skinned king and wise man who along with Melchor and Gaspar brought gold for the newborn Jesus. The discovery sparked a sensation; at that very time, thousands of faithful were making their way to Tizimín to brush leaves of rosemary against the statues of those very same santos, the ancient patrons of the town. Few could doubt that a supernatural sign had arrived. Padre Román Gómez urged caution: Who knew, he asked from the pulpit, whether this was in fact a true apparition? Predictably, many local people ignored these warnings. Yucatecans began making pilgrimages from as far away as Xanabá and Temax, and the Alcocer residence soon became a blaze of votive candles.[1]

Newspaper photographs told a somewhat different tale. They showed a formless blob that, with a little imagination, might be taken for a crude sketch of a human being wearing a cloak. Clearly, however, this particular blob was less an unambiguous message than a spiritual Rorschach test. While sophisticated urbanites rolled their eyes, the poor rural folk of the area chose to read other signals. Their vulnerable position at the heart of Yucatán's henequen industry meant hardship when the industry entered its final collapse in the 1980s and 1990s, while the catastrophic peso devaluation of 1994 hurt them far more than it did professionals in the big cities. In the red blob they found yet another message that their lives mattered, that something grand was about to happen, that some imponderably powerful and benevolent spiritual force had them in mind. In the final analysis, what *izamaleños* were asserting was their right to read the blob for themselves, a right that Padre Gómez tolerantly respected.

As I have hoped to show, episodes like the Lone Wise Man apparition emerged from a complex religious popular culture whose features we can document not only in the present but also in Mexico's early national period. Religion at that time had many roles in both urban and rural society. It was a mode of identification, something that allowed people to map out what was important in their lives and world. It set out a history of time and a cultural geography in which everything and everyone had a place.

Several points stand out in these stories. The first is that religious culture encompassed an enormously complex gamut of activities, functions, and social needs. Rather than a unified set of doctrines, it was more like Wittgenstein's language games: diverse threads that bore family resemblances but held no single common denominator. Religion meant High Church, with theological doctrines and elaborate hierarchy. But it also included public activities with features that had little to do with otherworldliness but a great deal to do with social prestige, business connections, sexual flirtation, and all-around good times. It allowed for pious literature, whether imported or homegrown, that provided its writers and readers with a sense of depth and antiquity. Much of that literature focused on social conservatism in the face of recent world revolution, the devout provincial's answer to Mexican liberalism in the age of Mora, while genres such as the novenario still appealed to popular religiosity through their emphasis on wonder cures, mystical praises, and verbal self-flagellations.

Popular religious culture served as explanatory knowledge. Printed almanacs told people where they stood in biblical time, something that the Book of Mormon did for a whole generation of dispossessed farmers and craftsmen in upstate New York.[2] Through creencias people learned what was wrong with the world and how to rectify it. The liturgical year gave structure and meaning to lives often characterized by dull suffering and the unrelieved passage of days. Above all, the oral tradition of the countryside preserved an unprinted almanac of values, beliefs, stories, and nonscientific histories that were the contours of the peasant's intellectual universe, born in large part from nineteenth-century experiences. Thanks to the creencias, every man could be a wise man.

The fibers of popular religious culture also fed, however, into regional and even national identities. The process of hearing mass together explained to a people who they were: "liturgy capital," to play with Benedict Anderson's term for a print-created nationalism. So did the countless retellings of the creencias. Guatemalan nationalism in the Petén coalesced not around invasions or newspapers or industrialization but rather from the peteneros' awareness of faraway ecclesiastical offices that sent strangers into their midst, aggressive men who shunned manille and did not understand the magic of the marimba. The rise and fall of cofradías may have been microcycles, but in many cases they synchronized with larger national contours, such as the end of Spanish rule, the early national period's instability, or the Porfirian era's standards of order and economic growth.

Popular religious culture gave a place to people who had no place, or had less of one than they wanted. This was particularly true for Hispanic women. Never to be found in the ayuntamiento, women nevertheless carved an identity for themselves in the churches, in the company of priests, in the public piety of the beata. Wealthy doñas, like Margarita Guerra in Chapter 3, used their fortunes to found entirely new cults of imagen that became symbols of urban identity. Above all, women sought out and colonized the nineteenth-century cofradías as places where they could exercise leadership and creativity.

Religious culture, particularly its popular strains, also offered a medium of negotiation between the highs and lows of society. Activities like the peasant cofradías were partially intended to direct indigenous behavior into submissive and politically nonthreatening channels. And doubtless in many cases they did so. But hegemony always breeds counterhegemony: peasant cults, rebel religion, and spiritualism remained important features of the religious life of the peninsula in the 1800s. Though enormously important, pastors ultimately had to negotiate with the interests of peasants. Peasants could put up effective resistance to manipulations and abuses. They could also fabricate their own religious cults and worldviews out of the very stuff of Hispanic Catholicism, always retaining large amounts of pre-Hispanic culture.

In all of this the priest played an intriguing role: spiritual guide, community leader, lawyer, politician, banker, psychologist, records keeper, tax man, benefactor, and many other things besides. His role had begun to fray during the Bourbon reforms of the 1700s, but the larger structure of his office remained intact. Only with the dissolution of larger bands of power did the latent anticlericalism of Hispanic society come to full force. Several ambiguities run through the pages of this book, but one of the greatest is the relationship between peasant and priest. The matter cannot be summarized in a catchphrase, because for both these parties, as for most human beings, it was possible to have contradictory impulses simultaneously. Peasants loved and warred with their curas. Their own particular forms of religious piety at times demanded his presence, at times tolerated it, at times excluded him altogether. Perhaps the fairest thing to say is that popular Catholicism accepted most of the doctrines, the symbolism, and the hierarchy of the church but reserved the people's rights to make innovations of their own and to keep what they wanted of their old ways. How far they would go in demanding those rights depended in large part on the flexibility of the church itself, or better said, of the individual priests, for final decisions usually lay within their own discretionary power.

Perhaps most importantly to historians, popular religious culture was dynamic and could only survive through periodic evolution. On one hand, cultural evolution took place at relatively elite levels, since the role of cura required certain modifications, as Raymundo Pérez learned in both Macuspana and Hoctún. Moreover, the mode of life that he represented—the organization of life into religiously based parishes that aspired to encompass the totality of the parishioners' social, moral, and intellectual world—entered into serious crisis by the mid–nineteenth century. Mexico's world of rural parishes proved the perfect system that could not continue. As originally designed, it was unable to meet the challenges posed by state formation, growing population, economic change, increasing communication and travel, and the gradual absorption of many of the padres themselves into secular economic activities. The pomp and corporate wealth of the institution deteriorated markedly during the nineteenth century. Along with the rest of Mexico, Yucatecans downgraded many of their religious trappings; ecclesiastical control of loan capital disappeared under pressure from the political center, while Campeche, the Petén, and finally Tabasco broke from the control of the archbishopric in

Mérida. The church had to find new ways of maintaining a role in the society, something it achieved by reinventing itself as a voluntary organization in a world that became increasingly pluralistic over time.

On the other hand, however, cultural evolution continued at more popular levels as well. Folktales and beliefs had to be modified or retold to retain their immediacy. Cofradías started and went under like small businesses, while the objects of their veneration, the saints and imágenes, experienced dramatic appearances, gradual declines, and even stunning revitalizations. Maya peasants also learned to change their ways when ancient customs were prohibited or when economic developments rendered those customs difficult to maintain. Many of these examples amounted to little more than microscopic fibers of the society, but they loomed large in a consciousness that was intensely local and personal. Like the salient features in supernatural geographies, they stood forth out of the chaos—or monotony—of daily life's totality.

But permanence has accompanied change. In the Yucatecan case, folkways at times offer a study more of continuity than of change, and the peninsula's popular religiosity has proved to have enormous staying power. In part this owes to the culture's internal cohesion, to its prevalence within a base large enough to keep reproducing it; Yucatecan folk beliefs are well connected to the people's material life, and five centuries of experience have permanently etched the right to apparitions and processions into the popular mind. People knew what they wanted and kept with it. At the same time, real material factors have helped conserve many of the old ways. Historically, southeast Mexico has been rural, economically dependent, ethnically colonial, and intensely local in consciousness. The current exodus to urban centers like Cancún or the slums of south Mérida is a relatively new phenomenon, something that has only begun within the past generation. The marginality and isolation of today's rural peasantry have helped conserve features that the urban intelligentsia retail and romanticize. These features tended to retard change, and they continue to do so in the present day.

Taking all this into consideration, I am skeptical of seeing the Caste War as the angry protest of cultural beliefs—or at least cultural beliefs narrowly defined—under attack. The cultural values of rural southeast Mexico, or at least huge portions of them, weathered the post-1821 changes intact, and have continued to the present day. Peninsular peasants did not rise up as a defense against antisuperstition campaigns, or to resist forced castellanization, or, as in the Cristero revolt, to defend an established Catholic faith against revolutionary state builders. The real conflicts that came to a head in 1847 were explicitly material and political. Particularly critical were the tax systems, the survival of formal systems of indigenous self-government, and the postindependence attempts to incorporate peasant elites and masses alike into the fracas of militias and municipal and state politics. In all of this, popular religious culture played an important but strictly supporting role. From 1800 onward the church made only sporadic and fitful attempts to rectify the peasants' composite version of doctrinal orthodoxy. Indeed, most of the features of Maya folk-Catholicism were perfectly compatible with later hacienda society; these included santo cults, witchcraft, a folklore of wonders, heavy drinking, and strong paternalism. They became part of the hacienda system because the people demanded them. Indeed, that system's successful tolerance—even cultivation—of these tendencies helps to explain the relatively lessened revolutionary ferment in what is generally recognized as a world of harsh labor conditions. What this in turn means is that the Maya story, like the Yucatecan story in general, is not necessarily or entirely declensional. One may choose to see the long arch of the nineteenth century as a time of growing peasant population, dwindling land base, and crumbling community; but one can also see it as a time of increasing peasant cultural innovation and adaptation, in the sense that the church's social hegemony declined relative to popular belief while new elements entered the almanac of folk knowledge to form an expanded repertoire of stories and histories. That the hacienda in some ways replaced the parish system does not invalidate the persistence of popular culture in at least that aspect.

Finally, while I have tried to point toward shared filaments and common beliefs as an antidote for what I think has been an excessively dichotomized history, in the end it is still necessary to admit a general (not total) difference in orientation. Wonders and wise men did not always coexist easily. Elite religiosity emphasizes the social and the ethical; at its darkest, it can function as a class or state ideology—a justification for questionable deeds—but in a better spirit can be a spur to self-realization for both the individual and the society, a beneficial means of organizing life and perpetuating positive values. Popular religiosity tends toward deliverance, wondrous cures, subjective apparitions, and literal intercessions; it can amount to little more than misguided escapes, even disasters, but can also provide a tool for coping, a way of keeping families and communities together, or even a means of sustaining some alternate vision of how the world could be. These various tensions and ambiguities permeate the history of religion in southeast Mexico and, I hope, have provided the reader with a fruitful approach for reexamining a time and place already visited so often and by so many talented historians.

But the story is far from exhausted. Mexico's nineteenth-century elite culture remains insufficiently understood; conversely, if it is ever written, a complete compilation of the nation's popular miracles, apparitions, and walking and talking crosses will run into whole volumes. A contemporary belief in the town of Xoccén holds that somewhere in the village there was once a prophetic ancient book that told how to make submarines, atomic bombs, airplanes, and other technological cargo. But the book disappeared, or was stolen. Representatives of the town somehow persuaded then-president Carlos Salinas de Gortari to help them find it. He set up a special office of investigation in Xoccén itself, but after a few months its out-of-state directress ran afoul of local sentiment; men of the village did not like being told to stop beating their wives. The town rebelled, the initiative bogged down, and the Lost Book remained as elusive as ever.[3] What stories like those of the Kindling Crosses, the Lost Book, and the Lone Wise Man tell us is that cultural tendencies can have an enormous permanence and that people, particularly the poor and marginalized, will continue to build their houses of refuge and resistance in the land of the wondrous.

Reform and revolution have come and gone. The motives for miracle remain.

Notes

Notes to Introduction

1. Archivo Histórico de la Arquidiócesis de Yucatán (AHAY), Decretos y Oficios (DO), microfilm roll 94, January 19, 1815. The investigator uses the Latin word *quidam,* literally meaning "a certain person." In this case, the somewhat looser translation as "nobody" I think more accurately captures the true meaning of the comment.

2. I refer to the constitutional crisis and its fomenters, the liberal political club known as the *sanjuanistas.* See Terry Rugeley, *Yucatán's Maya Peasantry and the Origins of the Caste War, 1800–1847* (Austin: University of Texas Press, 1996), 33–60.

3. Literature on the Speaking Cross is now voluminous. See Nelson Reed, *The Caste War of Yucatan* (Stanford: Stanford University Press, 1964), particularly Chapters 7, 8, and 11. Post-Reed ethnohistorical treatments include Victoria Bricker, *The Indian Christ, The Indian King: The Historic Substrate of Maya Myth and Ritual* (Austin: University of Texas Press, 1981), 87–118; and Nancy M. Farriss, *Maya Society under Colonial Rule: The Collective Enterprise of Survival* (Princeton: Princeton University Press, 1984). Don E. Dumond offers a new narrative history of the Caste War and its Speaking Cross in *The Machete and the Cross: Campesino Rebellion in Yucatán* (Lincoln: University of Nebraska Press, 1997), especially pp. 177–185, 240–261. A new analysis of the cross cult and its history appears in Lorena Careaga Viliesid, *Hierofanía combatiente: Lucha, simbolismo y religiosidad en la Guerra de Castas* (Chetumal: Universidad de Quintana Roo, 1998). For some recent ethnographic observations on *cruz* religion in Quintana Roo, see Miguel Alberto Bartolomé, *La dinámica social de los*

mayas de Yucatán: Pasado y presente de la situación colonial (México: Instituto Nacional Indigenista, 1988); Jorge Franco Cáceres, "Religiosidad y convivencia mayas," *Unicornio* (weekly literary supplement to *Por Esto!*) 249, January 7, 1996, 3–7; Cáceres, "Eclesialidad católica maya," *Unicornio* 278, July 28, 1996, 3–9.

4. Farriss, *The Maya Under Colonial Rule.*

5. Eric Hobsbawm, "Introduction: Inventing Tradition," in Eric Hobsbawm and Terence Ranger, eds., *The Invention of Tradition* (Cambridge: Cambridge University Press, 1983), 1–14.

6. William B. Taylor, *Magistrates of the Sacred: Priests and Parishioners in Eighteenth-Century Mexico* (Stanford: Stanford University Press, 1996), 20–26.

7. The importance of Cancún in the lives of modern-day Yucatecans is hard to overestimate, despite the fact that the city as we know it did not come into existence until 1971. For a discussion of Cancún's influence on rural society, see Alicia Re Cruz, *The Two Milpas of Chan Kom: A Study of Socioeconomic and Political Transformations in a Maya Community* (Albany: State University of New York Press, 1996).

8. Hemeroteca Pino Suárez (HPS), *Diario de Yucatán,* June 24, 1993.

9. Redfield wrote widely on this point, but his most developed statement appears in *The Folk Culture of Yucatan* (Chicago: University of Chicago Press, 1941). Chapters 9 and 10 in particular deal with the religious transformation of rural communities.

10. Luis González, *San José de Gracia: Mexican Village in Transition,* trans. John Upton (Austin: University of Texas Press, 1974); Paul Vanderwood, *The Power of God Against the Guns of Government: Religious Upheaval in Mexico at the Turn of the Nineteenth Century* (Stanford: Stanford University Press, 1998).

11. Murdo J. MacLeod, "Some Thoughts on the Pax Colonial, Colonial Violence, and Perceptions of Both," in Susan Schroeder, ed., *Native Resistance and the Pax Colonial in New Spain* (Lincoln: University of Nebraska Press, 1998), p. 142.

12. For a beginning on English-language writings on nineteenth-century peninsular history, see Reed, *The Caste War of Yucatan;* Gilbert M. Joseph, *Revolution From Without: Yucatán, Mexico, and the United States, 1880–1924* (Cambridge: Cambridge University Press, 1982): Allan Wells, *Yucatan's Gilded Age: Haciendas, Henequen, and International Harvester, 1860–1915* (Albuquerque: University of New Mexico Press, 1985); Robert W. Patch, *Maya and Spaniard in Colonial Yucatán, 1648–1812* (Stanford: Stanford University Press, 1993); Rugeley, *Yucatán's Maya Peasantry* (1996); Allan Wells and Gilbert M. Joseph, *Summer of Discontent, Seasons of Upheaval: Elite Politics and Rural Insurgency in Yucatán, 1876–1915* (Stanford: Stanford University Press, 1996); and Dumond, *The Machete and the Cross* (1997).

13. The best ethnographic descriptions of Maya peasant religion are still, and will probably always be, Robert Redfield and Alfonso Villa Rojas, *Chan Kom: A Maya Village* (Chicago: University of Chicago Press, 1934); and Alfonso Villa Rojas, *The Maya of East Central Quintana Roo* (Washington, D.C.: Carnegie Institute, 1943).

14. For a review of some of the difficulties associated with interpreting popular cul-

ture, see David Hall, "Introduction," in *Understanding Popular Culture: Europe from the Middle Ages to the Nineteenth Century,* ed. Stuart Kaplan (New York: Mouton Publishers, 1984), 5–18; Peter Burke, *Popular Culture in Early Modern Europe* (Cambridge: Scholar Press, 1996), xi–xxvii.

15. Burke, xi.

16. As much as I admire the work of James C. Scott, I do think that the impression that comes from books such as *Domination and the Arts of Resistance: Hidden Transcripts* (New Haven: Yale University Press, 1990) is one of extreme polarization and relentlessly adversarial relations.

17. For a review of this point, see Bob Scribner, "Is a History of Popular Culture Possible?" *History of European Ideas* 10, 2 (1989), pp. 175–191.

18. In addition to Farriss, see Matthew Restall, *The Maya World: Yucatec Culture and Society, 1550–1850* (Stanford: Stanford University Press, 1997).

19. The three principal works on the pre-Porfirian nineteenth-century church, while extremely useful, are also institutional and economistic and deal almost entirely with events of central Mexico. See Michael P. Costeloe, *Church Wealth in Mexico: A Study of the "Juzgado de Capellanias" in the Archbishopric of Mexico, 1800–1856* (Cambridge: At the University Press, 1967); Jan Bazant, *Alienation of Church Wealth in Mexico: Social and Economic Aspects of the Liberal Revolution, 1856–1875,* trans. and ed. Michael P. Costeloe (Cambridge: At the University Press, 1971); and Robert Knowlton, *Church Property and the Mexican Reform, 1856–1910* (Dekalb: Northern Illinois University Press, 1976).

20. Howard F. Cline, "Regionalism and Society in Yucatan, 1825–1847: A Study of 'Progressivism' and the Origins of the Caste War" (diss., Harvard, 1947), pp. 599–601.

21. Ludwig Wittgenstein, *Philosophical Investigations* (New York: MacMillan, 1953), pp. 11–12, 32.

22. For this observation I am indebted to Aletta Biersack, "Local Knowledge, Local History: Geertz and Beyond," in Lynn Hunt, ed., *The New Cultural History* (Berkeley: University of California Press, 1989), pp. 72–96.

23. This view is particularly associated with James C. Scott. As only one of many applied examples in recent scholarship, see William H. Sewell Jr., *Work & Revolution in France: The Language of Labor from the Old Regime to 1848* (Cambridge: Cambridge University Press, 1980).

24. These issues and methods came late to Latin American studies. In some ways the study that was fifty years ahead of its time was Irving A. Leonard's *Baroque Times in Old Mexico: Seventeenth-Century Persons, Places, and Practices* (Ann Arbor: University of Michigan Press, 1959), which attempted to trace "the baroque," a culture of ostentatious form but politically repressed substance, through its many manifestations in the seventeenth century. Subsequent seminal works include William Beezley's study of Porfirian culture, *Judas at the Jockey Club and Other Episodes of Porfirian Mexico* (Lincoln: University of Nebraska Press, 1987); and William H. Beezley, Cheryl En-

glish Martin, and William E. French, eds., *Rituals of Rule, Rituals of Resistance: Public Celebrations and Popular Culture in Mexico* (Wilmington, Del.: Scholarly Resources, 1994).

25. For a discussion of this point, see Gerald Strauss, "Viewpoint: The Dilemma of Popular History," *Past and Present* 132 (1991), pp. 130–149; see also Burke, xv–xvi.

Notes to Chapter 1

1. Southeast Mexican folk knowledge conforms to Walter Ong's analysis of "oral literature" with all of that literature's inconsistencies and unassimilated variation; see Ong, *Orality and Literacy: The Technologizing of the Word* (London: Routlage, 1982), especially Chapters 1–3.

2. T. A. Willard, *The City of the Sacred Well* (New York: Century Company, 1926), p. 199. Consider also the remark of Oliver LaFarge II and Douglas Byers regarding the Jacalteca Mayas of Guatemala: "The Indians are very fond of telling stories, particularly around the fire at night. Certain ones enjoy a reputation as storytellers, either from their knowledge of old myths, or lively styles in narrating recent events"; see LaFarge and Byers, *The Year Bearer's People,* Middle America Research Series No. 3 (New Orleans: Department of Middle American Research, Tulane University, 1931), p. 112.

3. Allan F. Burns, *An Epoch of Miracles: Oral Literature of the Yucatec Maya* (Austin: University of Texas Press, 1983), p. 93. As a collection of Maya folk literature, this book is in a class by itself.

4. Alan Dundes argues against the relevance of literal belief as the measure of folktales; see his essay "Texture, Text, and Content" in *Interpreting Folklore* (Bloomington: Indiana University Press, 1980), pp. 20–32. I am inclined to agree.

5. Peter Burke identifies the European "discovery of the folk" as an event of the late eighteenth and early nineteenth centuries; see Burke, 3.

6. Two colonial-era Franciscan chronicles include some mention of folk beliefs and popular religion. The first is Diego de Landa, *Relación de las cosas de Yucatán,* ed. Miguel Rivera Dorado (Madrid: Hermanos García Noblejas, 1985); the second is Diego López de Cogolludo, *Historia de Yucatán,* 3 vols. (Campeche: Comisión de Historia, 1954). The earliest nineteenth-century recording of folklore is Padre José Bartolomé del Granado Baeza's 1813 ethnography of the Maya peasants of his parish, Yaxcabá; his account includes certain peasant beliefs regarding rain gods and spirits of the field and forest, as well as material on witchcraft. The complete text of Baeza's report was published by Rodolfo Ruz Menéndez in "Los indios de Yucatán de Bartolomé del Granado Baeza," *Revista de la Universidad Autónoma de Yucatán* 4, 168 (1989), pp. 52–63. In 1861 ex-governor Santiago Méndez reprinted the Baeza report with a few additional tidbits, one being an intriguing belief that sugar mills were inhabited by spirits resembling small boys, who turned the mills at night. See F. W.

Hodge, ed., "Reports on the Maya Indians of Yucatan by Santiago Méndez, Antonio García y Cubas, Pedro Sánchez de Aguilar, y Francisco Hernández," *Indian Notes and Monographs* IX, 3, 1921.

7. Daniel G. Brinton, "The Folklore of Yucatan," *Folklore Journal* 1, 8 (1883). Reprinted as *El folk-lore de Yucatán,* trans. Enrique Leal (Mérida: Museo Arqueológico Histórico de Yucatán, 1937). Among other sources, the author drew from a manuscript by a certain "Licenciado Zetina from Tabasco, originally from Tihosuco." I have been unable to locate this work.

8. Manuel Rejón García, *Supersticiones y leyendas mayas* (Mérida: 1905). Rejón García liked to couch his stories in the form of fictional conversations, such as that between a priest and his bumpkin *mayordomo,* Remigio Chávez.

9. The classic products of this endeavor were the studies by Robert Redfield and Alfonso Villa Rojas cited above in note 13 of the Introduction; to these must be added Redfield, *The Folk Culture of Yucatan* (Chicago: University of Chicago Press, 1940); and Redfield, *A Village that Chose Progress: Chan Kom Revisited* (Chicago: University of Chicago Press, 1950). Attacking, revising, or deconstructing the Carnegie Project and its resulting work has become an anthropological right of passage; this far-ranging follow-up literature is beyond the scope of the current work. For an overview of criticisms of Redfield, see Irwin Press, *Tradition and Adaptation: Life in a Modern Yucatecan Village* (Westport, Conn.: Greenwood Press, 1975), pp. 4–11. On the overall contours of Carnegie Institute studies in Yucatán, see Herman W. Konrad, "Anthropological Studies in Yucatan and the Historical Dimension," *Mexican Studies* 3, 1 (1987), pp. 163–180. For the history behind the history of the Carnegie Project in Yucatán, see Paul Sullivan, *Unfinished Conversations: Mayas and Foreigners Between Two Wars* (New York: Alfred A. Knopf, 1989); and Quetzil E. Castañeda, *In the Museum of Maya Culture: Touring Chichén Itzá* (Minneapolis: University of Minnesota Press, 1996).

10. Margaret Park Redfield, *The Folk Literature of a Yucatecan Town,* Contributions to American Archaeology, No. 13 (Washington, D.C.: Carnegie Institution, 1935). Somewhat earlier, Willard (1926, pp. 150–165) had reproduced two folktales that he learned from longtime U.S. resident Edward Thompson.

11. These have been edited and published by Manuel Andrade and Hilaria Máas Collí, in *Cuentos mayas yucatecos,* 2 vols. (Mérida: Universidad Autónoma de Yucatán, 1991).

12. A collection of the original three volumes of this journal are housed in the "Impresos" section of the CAIHY. Hilaria Máas Collí has collected and republished these in *Leyendas yucatecas* (Mérida: Universidad Autónoma de Yucatán, 1993).

13. The "Colección letras" series consists of forty-nine brief but highly interesting volumes, each in Maya and Spanish and published jointly by the National Indigenous Institute (INI) and the Secretaría de Desarrollo Social. It includes not only stories but also songs, prayers, herbal remedies, and local oral histories. We also possess two important collections by Ana Patricia Martínez Huchim: *K-maaya tsikbal: jaahil t'aan*

("Maya Conversation: True Words"). *Estudio de género cuento de la tradición en maya-yukateko (El caso de Xocén, municipio de Valladolid, Yucatán, México* (thesis, Universidad Autónoma de Yucatán, Facultad de Antropología, 1996), and *Cuentos enraizados* (Mérida: Compañía Editorial de la Península, 1999). Finally, there are also relatively recent collections by Domingo Dzul Poot, María Luisa Góngora Pacheco, Roldán Peniche Barrera, and Eduardo Medina Loría; I have provided complete bibliographical information on these when first noted.

14. The issue of the origins of Mesoamerican folklore was the first major debate in the field; it accompanied the initial collection process and involved some of the giants of early anthropology. Franz Boas himself was the first to note the overwhelming European presence in early twentieth-century Mexican lore; see Boas, "Notes on Mexican Folklore," *Journal of American Folklore* 25 (1912), pp. 204–260. A similar reading formed the basis of Aurelio Espinosa's monumental studies of Spanish folklore in the U.S. Southwest, summarized in *The Folklore of Spain in the American Southwest: Traditional Spanish Folk Literature in Northern New Mexico and Southern Colorado,* ed. J. Manuel Espinosa (Norman: University of Oklahoma Press, 1985). Ralph L. Beals offered a more systematic statement on European origins in "Problems of Mexican Indian Folklore," *Journal of American Folklore* 56 (1943), pp. 8–16. Paul Radin attacked both Boaz and Beals, arguing that indigenous plots and motifs were in fact prevalent among the Zapotecs of Oaxaca but required more extensive fieldwork than did their European counterparts; see Radin, "The Nature and Problems of Mexican Indian Folklore," *Journal of American Folklore* 57 (1944), pp. 26–36. Finally, George M. Foster's "Some Characteristics of Mexican Indian Folklore" and "The Current State of Mexican Indian Folklore Studies" reviewed the first fifty years of Mexican folklore research and concluded that we are dealing with a syncretic lore; see *Journal of American Folklore* 58 (1945), pp. 225–235, and 61 (1948), pp. 368–382, respectively. The two Foster articles called for moving beyond a sterile Spanish/Indian duality and for greater attention to the ways that various motifs combine.

15. For the European version, see Peter Burke, 162. The Maya version appears in María Luisa Góngora Pacheco, *Cuentos de Oxkutzcab y Maní* (Mérida: Editores Maldonado, 1990), pp. 7–10.

16. "Aladino," in Andrade and Máas Collí, vol. 2, pp. 169–199.

17. I recount a number of the "impossible task" stories in the course of this chapter. Pedro de Urdemalas, an archetypal idiot trickster, is described briefly in "Pedro de Urdemalas and the Gringo," in Américo Paredes, *Folktales of Mexico* (Chicago: University of Chicago Press, 1970), pp. 155–156; and in J. Manuel Espinosa, "Aurelio M. Espinosa: New Mexico's Pioneer Folklorist," in *Folklore of Spain,* 48. The old Urdemalas motif of the filling of the donkey's rectum with gold coins in order to fool a prospective buyer appears in "El yerno mentiroso," Andrade and Máas Collí, vol. 2, pp. 323–361.

18. Albert S. Gatschet recorded riddles virtually identical to the Maya versions in

Matamoros in 1889; see "Popular Rimes from Mexico," *Journal of American Folklore* 2 (1889), pp. 48–53. For New Mexico versions, see Aurelio M. Espinosa, "Traditional Spanish Proverbs in New Mexico," in Espinosa, 165–167.

19. Long-lived Yucatecan folk motifs include the *x-tabay*, the *alux*, the garbled versions of biblical doctrine, and encounters with the *balams*. I borrow the term "fakelore" from Richard M. Dorson, *Folklore and Fakelore: Essays Toward a Discipline of Folk Studies* (Cambridge: Harvard University Press, 1976). Dorson provides no strict rules, but for the most part he upholds folklore as information transmitted by oral performance, not by technological mediums. He also appears to have special disdain for stories such as those of Paul Bunyan, which originate more from modern authors and less from a body of preliterate traditions. Alan Dundas takes a more inclusive view in "The Fabrication of Fakelore," in *Folklore Matters* (Knoxville: University of Tennessee Press, 1989), pp. 40–56. For further discussion on the problem of authentication, see Regina Bendix, "Diverging Paths in the Scientific Search for Authenticity," *Journal of Folklore Research* 29, 2 (1992), pp. 103–132.

20. I suspect that there is insufficient pre-1900 collection to permit an analysis of Mexican motif evolution for the period in question. Moreover, I share Robert A. Georges's skepticism of the quest for *ur*-versions; see Georges, "The Pervasiveness in Contemporary Folklore Studies of Assumptions, Concepts, and Constructs Usually Associated with the Historic-Geographic Method," *Journal of Folklore Research* 23 (1986), pp. 87–103. My own inspiration for a linking of narrative motifs and historical dynamics has been Peter Taylor and Hermann Rebel, "Hessian Peasant Women, Their Families, and the Draft: A Social-Historical Interpretation of Four Tales from the Grimm Collection," *Journal of Family History* 6, 4 (1981), pp. 347–478; Eugen Weber, "Fairies and Hard Facts: The Reality of Folk Tales," *Journal of the History of Ideas* 52 (1981), pp. 93–113; and Robert Darnton, "Peasants Tell Tales: The Meaning of Mother Goose," in *The Great Cat Massacre and Other Episodes in French Cultural History* (New York: Vintage Books, 1984), pp. 9–72. These writings stress the historical basis for such folktale motifs as poverty, famine, vagrancy, injustice, debt, delousing, high infant mortality, family conflicts, and military conscription. Weston La Barre attempted a little-noticed earlier version of the same in "The Aymara: History and Worldview," *Journal of American Folklore* 79 (1966), pp. 130–144, by tracing historical themes of hunger and external exploitation in the lore of these Andean peoples.

21. Michel Antochiw, *Historia cartográfica de la península de Yucatán* (México: Comunicación y Ediciones Tiacuilo, S.A. de C.V., 1994), pp. 283. The best of the pre–Caste War maps was "Mapa corográfico de la provincia de Yucatán que comprende desde la Laguna de Términos en el ceno mexicano hasta de los Zapatillos en el Golfo de Honduras, 1798."

22. Jorge Victoria Ojeda analyzes military defense as an impetus for coastal mapping. See Victoria Ojeda, *Mérida de Yucatán de las Indias: Piratería y estrategia defensiva* (Mérida: Ayuntamiento de Mérida, 1995).

23. Redfield and Villa Rojas, 110–211; Villa Rojas, 97–131.

24. Catherine J. Allen, *The Hold Life Has: Coca and Cultural Identity in an Andean Community* (Washington, D.C.: Smithsonian Institution Press, 1988), pp. 51–52. Aliaja Iwanska makes a similar point in her study of peasants in Mexico state; see *Purgatory and Utopia: A Mazahua Village of Mexico* (Cambridge, Mass.: Schenkman Publishing Company, 1971), p. 76.

25. "El hombre de la tierra," in Andrade and Máas Collí, vol. 1, pp. 26–55.

26. Brinton, 20–21; the source of the story is the missing Zetina manuscript. Compare this to other stories of balam encounters, such as "The Owners of Rain," in Burns, 110–121.

27. For the Zacatecas version, see "The Priest Who Had One Small Glimpse of Glory," in Paredes, 122–123. In this version, a priest gets his wish for a glimpse of heaven but returns to find that years have passed and that his church has fallen into ruins. The Oaxacan version appears in Elsie Clews Parsons, "Zapoteca and Spanish Tales of Mitla, Oaxaca," *Journal of American Folklore* 45 (1932), pp. 292–296.

28. Redfield, *The Folk Culture of Yucatán,* 114–121.

29. Restall, 13–40.

30. Variations of the story of the monster in the monte are particularly common in the excellent Roldán Peniche Barrera collection, which apparently reflects late-nineteenth-century folklore from the Hunucmá region. See "Extraña experiencia" (7–8), "La culebra aldana" (9–10), "La Xtabay" (11–12), "El huay-chivo" (17–19), "Dámaso y el demonio" (20–22), "Lo que ocurrió al Sr. Juan de la Cruz al ir a cazar al pavo del monte" (25–27), and "El hombre sin cabeza" (28–29), in *Relatos mayas* (Mérida: Maldonado Editores, n.d.). Penich Barrera's source was a h-men from the Hunucmá region, born around 1910 (personal communication from author). On child-abduction stories, see the report of Richard Fletcher in the Wesleyan Methodist Missionary Society Archives (WMMSA), 30 December 1967, Corozal.

31. Archivo General de la Nación de México (AGNM), Bienes Nacionales (BN), IX, 18, November 11, 1839.

32. Serapio Baqueiro, *Ensayo histórico sobre las revoluciones de Yucatán desde el año de 1840 hasta 1864,* vol. 2 (Mérida: Manuel Heredia Argüelles, 1878), pp. 103–104; on the subsequent disenterral of his remains, see CAIHY, Manuscritos, XLIV, 25, March 8, 1851, Tepich, José Eulogio Rosado to José Canuto Vela.

33. Rejón García, 69–77.

34. Victoria Ojeda, 96–99, provides an intriguing discussion of the possibility of tunnels in the center of Mérida. Although excavation of some older house foundations suggests underground construction (perhaps cellars), the installation of water lines in the inner city failed to turn up evidence of tunnels. We also find tunnel belief among the Mazahuas; see Iwanska, 117. Finally, Silvia Limón Olvera identifies caves as places of mythic origin in both Inca and Aztec culture; see *Las cuevas y el mito de origen: Los casos inca y mexica* (Mexico: Consejo Nacional para la Cultura y las Artes, 1990).

35. Ludovic Chambon, *Un gascón en México,* trans. Rocío Alonzo (México: Consejo Nacional para la Cultura y las Artes, 1994), p. 40.

36. Redfield, *The Folk Culture of Yucatan,* 118–119. Iván Vallardo Fajardo records some interesting cenote lore collected in Sudzal in 1987–1988; see Vallardo Fajado, "Cambios en la religiosidad popular en Sudzal, Yucatán," in *Religión y sociedad en el sureste de México,* vol. 4 (México: Centro de Investigaciones y Estudios Superiores en Antropología Social, 1989), especially pp. 149–153.

37. Vallardo Fajado, 149–151. Special thanks to Teófilo Cocom and Don Inocencio for taking me to see the burro tuunich.

38. For a review of various mythical creatures of Yucatán, see Padre Estanislao Carrillo (1798–1846), "Papeles sueltos del P. Carrillo: Fantasmas," in *Registro yucateco,* vol. 4 (1845), pp. 103–106. A far more recent and highly readable bilingual collection on the same topic is Roldán Peniche Barrera's *Mitología maya: 15 seres fabulosos* (Mérida: Comercializadora Editorial, 1999); my account of the *ek chapat* comes from pp. 52–53 of this latter work.

39. "El novio de la xtabay," in Eduardo Medina Loría, *Leyendas de los mayas de Quintana Roo: Colección del taller de la lengua maya* (Mérida: Estudios Bassó, 1982), pp. 45–61. A version of this same story was recently told to me by a thirty-year-old woman from Espita; sadly, the wáay-chivo in question was none other than her grandfather, who spent the rest of his life in a hammock, an invalid. Wizard transformation stories are fairly common throughout Mexico; see, for example, Ralph L. Beals, "Two Mountain Zapotec Tales from Oaxaca, Mexico," *Journal of American Folklore* 48 (1935), pp. 189–190. In this case, however, the wizard takes the form not of an animal but of lightning.

40. This story appears in Evelio Tax Góngora's memoir of his childhood, "El huay chivo o (chivo brujo)." See HPS, *Por Esto!,* January 11, 1996. The barber spent three years in prison as a result of his masquerade.

41. "El silbido misterioso," in Medina Loría, 25–37.

42. Burns, 36.

43. "The Story of the Flood," in Park Redfield, 24–25; Redfield and Villa Rojas, 330–331; and "The Story of the Hunchbacks," in Burns, 50–61.

44. Roberto López Méndez, "Se devela el misterio de los pu'ses: Raza de pigmeos sobrevive en Yucatán, afirman," *Por Esto!* August 17, 1998, pp. 18–19. López Méndez's informants were from Motul and pointed to the existence of tiny masonry wells as evidence of the little people.

45. The Park Redfield collection contains a number of these; see "The Story of Creation" (8–11), "Jesu Cristo and the *Pozole*" (11–14), "The Birth of Jesu Cristo" (16–17), and "The *Ejemplo* of the Mocking Bird" (17). A Oaxacan variant appears in "María and San José," in Parsons, 1932, pp. 288–290. For the Veracruzan version, see Stanley L. Robe, *Mexican Tales and Legends from Veracruz,* Folklore Studies #23 (Berkeley: University of California Press, 1971), pp. 48–53; Robe collected this story in 1965, in Tecolutla, Veracruz.

46. For Campeche, see Enrique Pino Castilla, *Las esquinas de Campeche* (Campeche: Universidad Autónoma de Campeche, 1997). Curiously, there seems to be no comprehensive history of Mérida's own street corners.

47. See "La esquina del 'venado,'" in Ramiro Briceño López, *Leyendas izamaleños* (Mérida: Universidad Autónoma de Yucatán, 1990), pp. 47–50.

48. Frank P. Saul, "Disease in the Maya Area: The Pre-Columbian Evidence," in T. Patrick Culbert, *The Classic Maya Collapse* (Albuquerque: University of New Mexico Press, 1973), pp. 301–324.

49. CAIHYTTL, Correspondencia del Ayuntamiento de Mérida, August 11, 1825, p. 172. Réjon García (52–57) also reports bloodletting with serpent's teeth or the quill of a porcupine.

50. For example, in 1876 the town of Hunucmá decided to rename itself Hunucmá de Mateo in honor of padre Lorenzo Mateo Caldera (cura from 1794 to 1799), whose legacy to the townsfolk had provided for victims of the 1827 smallpox epidemic; see Archivo General del Estado de Yucatán (AGEY), Poder Ejecutivo (PE) 205, Ayuntamientos, September 25, 1876.

51. On the Balmís expedition, see Sherburne F. Cook, "Francisco Xavier Balmís and the Introduction of Vaccination to Latin America," *Bulletin of the History of Medicine* 11, 5, 1942, pp. 543–560; and Part II, 12, 1, 1942, pp. 70–101.

52. CAIHY, Correspondencia del Ayuntamiento de Mérida, July 14, 1825, p. 168; July 26, 1825, p. 170; August 8–10, 1825, p. 171; July 22, 1825, pp. 173–174.

53. Ruz Menéndez, "Los indios de Yucatán de Bartolomé del Granado Baeza, 59.

54. There is a significant body of literature on Maya herbal and folk healings. For a nineteenth-century description, see CAIHY, Manuscritos, XLVIII, 2, 1865, "Superstición de los indios yucatecos, por el padre Juan Pablo Ancona." A more recent and less hostile account appears in Miguel Antonio Güémez Pineda, "Estado actual de las prácticas médicas tradicionales en Pustunich, Yucatán" (thesis, Universidad Autónoma de Yucatán, 1984); and Lucilia Caballero Salas, et al., *Prácticas médicas mayas,* Collección Letras Mayas Contemporáneas #12 (México: INI/SEDESOL, 1993).

55. Redfield, *The Folk Culture of Yucatan,* 308.

56. "Curado por nueve sacerdotes," in Andrés Tec Chi, ed., *Cuentos sobre las apariciones en el mayab,* Colección Letras Mayas Contemporáneas #6 (México: Premiá Editores, 1993), pp. 21–22.

57. "El espanto de las albarradas que se caen," in Tec Chi, 35–37.

58. A complete listing of the recorded x-tabay stories would be enormous; for a representative case, see José González, "Los amores de Toribio con la *x-tabay,*" in Tec Chi, 53–54. X-tabay legends can also be found among the Lacandons of Chiapas; see R. Jon McGee, "The Influence of Pre-Hispanic Yucatecan Maya Religion in Contemporary Lacandon Maya Ritual," *Journal of Latin American Lore* 10, 2 (1984), pp. 175–187.

59. "El cazador," in Andrade and Máas Collí, vol. 1, pp. 64–105.

60. "Two Short *Ejemplos* Told by Doña Pilar's Mother," in Park Redfield, 29.

61. "La muchacha que se convirtió en rey," in Andrade and Máas Collí, vol. 1, pp. 184–209.

62. "El viejo enamorado," in Andrade and Máas Collí, vol. 1, pp. 452–471.

63. "An *ejemplo* of the *balams* and a woman," in Park Redfield, 21.

64. "Dámaso y el demonio," in Peniche Barrera, 20–22.

65. In compiling the superstitious beliefs mentioned in this chapter, I have drawn from a variety of sources. They include Santiago Pacheco Cruz, *Usos, costumbres, religión y supersticiones de los mayas: Apuntes históricos con un estudio psicobiológico de la raza* (Mérida: 1947); Oswaldo Baqueiro López, *Magia, mitos y supersticiones entre los mayas* (Mérida: Maldonado Editoriales, 1983); Sylvanus Morley, *Maya Civilization* (Stanford: Stanford University Press, 1946); and Jesús Amaro Gamboa, "Miscelánea de hábitos y creencias," serialized in *Diario del Sureste*. To this I have added many that I have heard in Yucatán between 1990 and 1997.

66. Baqueiro López, 37–45; Brinton, 14; Pacheco Cruz, 114–115. Ralph Steele Boggs found the identical proverb in 1938 in the state of Tlaxcala ("Cuando el tecolote canta, el indio muere"); see Boggs, "A Folklore Expedition to Mexico," *Southern Folklore Quarterly* 3, 2 (1939), pp. 65–73. Special thanks to Patricia Martínez Huchim for her explanation of the phrase *tamax chi'*.

67. The dream interpretations cited in this paragraph appear in Baqueiro López, 37–45.

68. Burns, 87–88.

69. "Creencias sobre insectos," in Santiago Domínguez Aké, *Creencias, profecías y consejas mayas,* Colección Letras Mayas Contemporáneos, #20 (Mérida: INI/SEDESOL, 1993), pp. 18–19.

70. Morely, 49–52.

71. Baqueiro López, 37–45.

72. Morely, 49–52.

73. "Creencias sobre mujeres," in Domínguez Aké, 25.

74. Ibid.

75. Baqueiro López, 37–45. John G. Bourke, the commander of U.S. troops at Fort Ringgold, Texas, reported the same belief among Rio Grande valley Hispanics in his early and important collection, "Popular Medicine, Customs, and the Superstitions of the Rio Grande," *Journal of American Folklore* 7, 24 (1894), pp. 199–146. Here, millstone water was commonly used to relieve swollen breasts (see p. 122). The fear of lunar-inflicted birthmarks was also widespread, turning up in collections from the Teotihuacán area as early as 1918; see E. M. Gómez Maillifert, "Supersticiones de la región de San Juan Teotihuacán est. de México," *Journal of American Folklore,* 31 (1918), pp. 488–495.

76. The three preceding creencias appear in Domínguez Aké, 27, 32.

77. Examples of these childbirth punishments appear in two stories recorded by

Park Redfield: "You Should Not Make Fun of or Say Evil Things About Other People," and "You Should Not Speak Recklessly." See Park Redfield, 26.

78. Mary Elmendorf, *Nine Maya Women* (New York: Schenkman Publishing Co., 1976), pp. 65–66, 71.

79. Redfield and Villa Rojas, 95; Elmendorf, 91.

80. Baqueiro López, 37–45; Domínguez Aké, 28.

81. Pacheco Cruz, 114–115.

82. For examples of this see "Tigre y Napoleón," in Andrade and Máas Collí, vol. 1, pp. 244–277; and "El cazador," in Andrade and Máas Collí, vol. 1, pp. 64–105.

83. Park Redfield, "Dogs and Jesu Cristo" and "Jesu Cristo and the Dog," 23–24.

84. Martínez Huchim, *Cuentos enraizados,* 26–29.

85. Domínguez Aké, 17.

86. Rejón García, 2–3; Pacheco Cruz, 114–115.

87. Domínguez Aké, 18.

88. Pacheco Cruz, 114–115; Domínguez Aké, 19. We find prophetic powers attributed to birdsongs in central Mexico as well; see Gómez Maillifert, 488–495.

89. Morely, 49–52.

90. These two folktales about the inoffensive and ubiquitous Yucatecan iguana come from Frederick A. Ober, *Travels in Mexico and Life Among the Mexicans* (Boston: Estes and Lauriat, 1884), p. 93.

91. Baqueiro López, 37–45.

92. Belief in the tulix is so common even today that it hardly requires a source.

93. Morely, 49–52.

94. Baqueiro López, 37–45.

95. Claude Lévi-Strauss, *The Savage Mind* (Chicago: University of Chicago Press, 1966) offers Lévi-Strauss's best formulation of the antinaturalist (i.e., structuralist) reading of myth.

96. "*Tzutzuy* and *zacpakal,*" Park Redfield, 25. Another version of the same appears in "Jesucristo y las palomas sakpakal y la tzutzuy," in Góngora Pacheco, 21–22.

97. Pacheco Cruz, 60–61.

98. Henry C. Schmidt identifies animal life as a common theme of rural Mexican verse, animals often serving as a way to engender a sense of locality and immediacy. See Schmidt, "History, Society, and the Popular Lyric in Mexico: A Study in Cultural Continuity," *Mexican Studies/Estudios Mexicanos* 4, 2 (1988), pp. 295–318.

99. "El cuento del murciélago," in Domingo Dzul Poot, *Cuentos mayas,* vol. 1 (Mérida: Maldonado Editores, 1985), p. 59.

100. "El pajarito de siete colores," in Góngora Pacheco, 31–32.

101. Park Redfield noticed this inconsistent respect toward dogs in her work in Dzitás: "Dogs in Dzitás, as in most Mexican small towns, swarm everywhere, mangy, starved, snarling, barking curs. Dog bites are 'the shame of the country,' to quote from the newspapers. Now and then agitation starts to reduce the number of these dogs, most of which appear to be unwanted and uncared for. Is it merely apathy or

is it something stronger which preserves them from destruction? Somehow the dog, which was domesticated in pre-Hispanic times, has a very deeply rooted place in folk society. To the older people, it is a sin to abuse a dog" (p. 24).

102. The *conejo/coyote* stories occur in folktale collections of many parts of Mexico, particularly the south. For Oaxaca, see William H. Mechling, "Stories from Tuxtepec, Oaxaca," *Journal of American Folklore* 25 (1912), pp. 199–203; and Mechling, "Stories from the Southern Atlantic Coastal Region of Mexico," *Journal of American Folklore* 29 (16), pp. 547–552. See also, Boas, 1912, and Radin, 1944. For Jalisco, see J. Alden Mason, "Four Mexican-Spanish Fairy-Tales from Azquetlán, Jalisco," *Journal of American Folklore* 25 (1914), pp. 191–198. For Mexico state, see Franz Boas and Herman K. Haeberlin, "Ten Folktales in Modern Nahuatl," *Journal of American Folklore* 37 (1924), pp. 345–370. On Puebla, see Elsie Clews Parsons, "Folklore from Santa Ana Xalmimilulco, Puebla, Mexico," *Journal of American Folklore* 45 (1932), pp. 342–344. On Veracruz, Robbe, 1971 (collected in 1965).

103. "A Cuento of Juan Conejo," Park Redfield, 35.

104. Versions of Juan Tul differ radically. In the earliest known version, that of Rejón García, Juan began as an inept cowboy whom a supernatural being tutors in the ways of the cattle; see Rejón García, 14–30. In this version, Juan eventually becomes *juez de paz* of an eastern town, where his abilities and wisdom became legendary. The version in Andrade and Máas Collí portrays him as a foundling left in a corral, who is raised by cows and who somehow transforms into a spiritual entity. See "El origen de H Wáan Tuul" in Andrade and Máas Collí, vol. 2, pp. 128–141.

105. "Milpero al que le liberan su esposa por un conejito," in Dzul Poot, vol. 1, pp. 75–84.

106. "La muchacha que se convirtió en rey," in Andrade and Máas Collí, vol. 1, pp. 184–209.

107. See, for example, "The Story of Creation" (8–10), "Jesu Cristo and the Pozole" (2 versions, 11–13), "The Virgin Veronica" (14), and "Jesu Cristo and San Diego" (22).

108. "El zorro, el diablo y el niño," in Dzul Poot, vol. 2, pp. 25–29.

109. "El pobre carbonero," in Andrade and Máas Collí, vol. 1, pp. 426–433.

110. "El sacerdote y el pecado de una mujer," in Góngora Pacheco, 15–18.

111. Iwanska, for instance, notes the dichotomy of good/bad devils in her study of the Mazahuas. As she put it: "The devil himself, far more than any saint, acts as a social controller, and a guardian of El Nopal morality. He does what no one of the legitimate saints has been able to do: he punishes deviations from cherished communal norms" (116–117).

112. "El batab Cazuela," in Andrade and Máas Collí, vol. 1, pp. 274–289.

113. "El flojo," in Andrade and Máas Collí, vol. 1, pp. 106–137.

114. "Joselito y Petrona," in Andrade and Máas Collí, vol. 2, pp. 292–301. The Tabascan version appears in "The Little Guava," Paredes, 89–91. See also the more recent Veracruzan version in "Los niños perdidos," in Robe, 29.

115. "El rey y las tres hermanas," in Andrade and Máas Collí, vol. 2, pp. 144–167.

116. "A Story about an Unusual Marriage," in Burns, 163–170.

117. The 1840–1841 censuses, found in AGEY, PE 39–41, frequently break down villages into family units, providing a firm basis for the analysis of family structure. Rather than regale the reader with innumerable case studies, I offer the case of a single town, Cantamayec. This contained 269 families of two or more; four single-person households; and two priests. The figures are fairly representative for the peninsula; see AGEY, PE 39, Censos y Padrones, 1, 4, April 28, 1841.

118. "X-waay chivo," in Tec Chi, 40–44. For the Veracruzan version, see "El que se casó con una bruja," in Robe, 99–104.

119. "La x-wáay y el campesino," in Martínez Huchim, 37–38.

120. A Chiapan variation appears in "The Witch Wife," in Paredes, 27; in this version, the woman takes off her skin so that her skeleton can go out cavorting. Some outstanding examples from Mexico state appear in María del Socorro Caballero, *Supersticiones populares* (Toluca: Imagen Editores, 1995), pp. 115–124; the oldest of Caballero's informants on this particular motif, Candelaria Quiroz, was born in 1890, a point underscoring the story's antiquity.

121. Morely, 49–52.

122. This is particularly true among the stories collected by Andrade in 1930.

123. "El hijo de la yegua" in Andrade and Máas Collí, vol. 1, pp. 414–425.

124. Modern-day witchcraft struggles do not have the anthropological literature they deserve, but there is some information in Redfield, *The Folk Culture of Yucatan*, Chapter 11; and Press, 188–198.

125. The imperial subprefect managed to persuade the villagers to send the *hechiceras* in question, two women, to Mérida for imprisonment; we know nothing more of the case. See AGEY, PE 162, Gobernación, July 17, 1866, Mérida.

126. Villa Rojas, 74–75.

127. See Thomas W. F. Gann, *The Maya Indians of Southern Yucatan and Northern British Honduras*, Smithsonian Institution Bureau of Indian Ethnology Bulletin 64 (Washington, D.C.: Government Printing Office, 1918), pp. 35–36. The term *pul yah* or *pul yaaj* simply means "witch."

128. Dorson, "Folklore, Academe, and the Marketplace," in *Folklore and Fakelore*, 6–7.

129. The opportunity for a large-scale oral history of the *Porfiriato* and the revolution in Yucatán has probably slipped away, although fragments of individual recollections can be found in various publications. A person who was twenty years old in the pivotal year of 1910 would now be over ninety. Some historical folklore relating to the nineteenth century appears in Burns, "The First Thing I Said to Dr. Morley" (79–81), "The Patrón, I" (81–82), "The Story of Venancio Puc" (82–85), and "The Patrón, II" (85–87). The most thorough and systematic attempt to relate current Maya lore to documented history is still Paul Sullivan's *Unfinished Conversations*.

130. Watanabe, 77–78, makes a similar point regarding the similarity between the Chimaltecan spirit known as a *witz*, whose ambiguous behavior closely resembles that

of real-life patrons. Franco Savarino Roggero makes a strong case for the reinforcement of patronage ties in *Pueblos y nacionalismo, del régimen oligárquico a la sociedad de masas de Yucatán, 1894–1925* (México: Instituto Nacional de Estudios Históricos de la Revolución Mexicana, 1997), p. 127.

131. "El dios del fuego y el dios de la lluvia," in Góngora Pacheco, 45–46.

132. Following a line of peasant analysis that begins with A. V. Chayanov, James C. Scott identifies risk avoidance as a key factor in peasant decision making; see Scott, *The Moral Economy of the Peasant: Rebellion and Subsistence in Southeast Asia* (New Haven: Yale University Press, 1976), pp. 15–26.

133. Regarding the beginnings of these key technologies, I have drawn on Allen Wells, "From Hacienda to Plantation: The Transformation of Santo Domingo Xcuyum," in Jeffery T. Brannon and Gilbert M. Joseph, eds., *Land, Labor, & Capital in Modern Yucatán: Essays in Regional History & Political Economy* (Tuscaloosa: University of Alabama Press, 1991), pp. 124–125; and Herman W. Konrad, "Capitalism on the Tropical-Forest Frontier: Quintana Roo, 1880s to 1930," in the same volume, 150–152.

134. The Living Rope is one of the most widespread and, apparently, indigenous of Yucatecan folktales. The earliest version that I have found is that of a Chihuahuan traveler in *Viaje a Yucatán del Lic. José Fernando Ramírez, 1865,* ed. Carlos R. Menéndez (Mérida: Compañía Tipográfica Yucateca, 1926), p. 66. More recent versions of this story appear in "La soga de sangre," in Góngora Pacheco, 1–12; Burns, "The History of Don Francisco Xiu," 74–78; and Irene Dzul Chablé, et al, *Cuentos mayas tradicionales* (Mérida: SGEYINI/SEDESOL, 1993), "Sastunat," 55–57.

135. Linda Schele and Peter Mathews, *The Code of Kings: The Language of Seven Sacred Maya Temples and Tombs* (New York: Scribners, 1998), p. 206.

136. This story appears in both Park Redfield and Góngora Pacheco. However, the Park Redfield rendering ("About Dogs," 24) omits the laguna story altogether. In this more ribald version (Góngora Pacheco, 45–46), the dog sings "kok xix peel a mamá," or "Your mother's a dried-up vagina." The dog becomes an alligator, which explains that animal's ability to emit barking sounds.

137. I have encountered at least two versions of this. First, "El hombre que vio a los difuntos," in Medina Loría, 9–19; and "El aullido de los perros a medianoche," in Tec Chi, 10–12.

138. For an introduction to some of the legends associated with Day of the Dead in the peninsula—not necessarily the same as those found in other parts of Mexico—see Miguel Angel Orilla, *Los días de muertos en Yucatán (hanal pixan)* (Mérida: Maldonado Editores, 1996), especially pp. 41–49. Among others, these include the widespread story of the Vanishing Hitchhiker; unfortunately, dates and provenances are unstated. I have heard three versions of stories relating to the procession of the dead in Seyé, near Mérida, in 1997–1998.

139. This story comes from my wife's grandmother, Aurora Alcocer Espinosa viuda de Sauri, who for many years operated a small store in Cansahcab. Another version of the same folktale appears in Tec Chi; see *"Ixtab, Ixtabay e Ixtabentún,"* 47–49.

140. Redfield, *A Village that Chose Progress,* 157.

141. "María la sapita," in Dzul Poot, vol. 2, pp. 35–43; the girl-in-animal-skin motif also appears in "Siete rayos del sol," in Andrade and Máas Collí, vol. 1, pp. 278–311, although in this case she disguises herself as a bird.

142. See "The Frog-Woman," in Mason, 191–198. This extremely early Jalisco collection is strongly informed by the Grimm stories, including Cinderella and the Seven-League Boots. Another version appears in Boas and Haeberlin, "The Tomato Peeler," 354–356.

143. Material presented by Burns in his section on "Counsels" (pp. 79–87) carries a similar message: things are bad and no one can do anything about it.

144. "Un hombre de poca fe," in Peniche Roldán, 23–24.

145. Joseph Campbell, *The Hero With a Thousand Faces* (New York: Pantheon Books, 1949), p. 51.

146. Pacheco Cruz, 114–115.

147. Juan José Hernández briefly describes the snake cure in HPS, *Museo yucateco,* 1841, pp. 238–239.

148. Pacheco Cruz, 114–115.

149. Amaro Gamboa, "Miscelánea de hábitos y creencias."

150. Baqueiro López, 37–45.

151. This last creencia features in the folktale "A Cura who Lived with his Comrade," in Park Redfield, 19–21. The priest's common-law wife protected him from the devil by means of paper soles.

152. J. Eric S. Thompson, *Maya History & Religion* (Norman: University of Oklahoma Press, 1970), p. 210; Linda Schele and Mary Ellen Miller, *The Blood of Kings: Dynasty and Ritual in Maya Art* (New York: George Braziller, Inc., 1986), p. 49.

153. Baqueiro López, 37–45.

154. Elmendorf, 98.

155. Baqueiro López, 37–45.

156. Morely, 49–52.

157. AGNM, BN, V, 22, July 24, 1841. The term *república* referred to *república de indígenas,* a form of peasant town council that governed certain internal affairs in the village. For an examination of *repúblicas* in the early national period, see Rugeley, *Yucatán's Maya Peasantry,* 91–97.

158. Both soldiers and officers complained when the morning ration of aguardiente was missing; see Archivo Histórico de la Defensa Nacional (AHDN), xi/481/2914, Col. Juan María Rosado to Micheltoreno, Tihosuco.

159. William Wroth, *Images of Penance, Images of Mercy: Southwestern Santos in the Late Nineteenth Century* (Norman: University of Oklahoma Press, 1991), p. 41.

160. B. A. Norman, *Rambles in Yucatan; or, Notes of Travel Through the Peninsula, Including a Visit to the Remarkable Ruins of Chi-Chen, Kabah, Zayi, and Uxmal* (New York: J. & H. G. Langley, 1843), pp. 60–61.

161. Ruz Menéndez, "Los indios de Yucatán de Bartolomé del Granado Baeza," 57.

162. Baqueiro López, 37–45.

163. I came across this item of information from several people in Mérida, here to remain anonymous. Bourke reports the same belief in South Texas, 1894; see Bourke, 130.

164. These were identical to the "vows" that William Christian describes for six-teenth-century Spain. See Christian, *Local Religion in Sixteenth-Century Spain* (Princeton: Princeton University Press, 1981), pp. 22–69.

165. Archivo Notarial del Estado de Yucatán (ANEY), July 7, 1819, pp. 72–74.

166. ANEY, 30 December 1835, pp. 151–155.

167. See "Curado por nueve sacerdotes" ("The man who was cured by nine priests"), in Tec Chi, 21–22.

168. Campbell also notes the frequency of supernatural aid; see *Hero With a Thousand Faces,* 69–77.

169. "El bueno y el malo," in Andrade and Máas Collí, vol. 1, pp. 210–243. Impossible tasks, a stock item in world folklore, is common in the Hispanic world. For example, we have the Zapotec version in "The Suitor Tested," in Parsons, "Zapotec and Spanish Tales," 312–313. See also, "Blancaflor," Paredes, 78–88; and, in the same collection, "The Poor Woodcutter," 112–115.

170. See "Buried Treasure," in Parsons, "Zapotec and Spanish Tales," 339–341. The classic reading of buried-treasure stories comes from George Foster and his vision of the "limited good"; see George M. Foster, *Tzintzuntan: Mexican Peasants in a Changing World* (Boston: Little, Brown and Company, 1967), particularly Chapters 6 and 7.

171. WMMSA, 30 December 1867, report of Richard Fletcher, Corozal; report of John Carmichael in Archives of Belize (AB), Record #96, November 15, 1867, p. 396. See also the 1918 account of the lost fortune of an Icaiché chieftan in Gann, 18. This latter account, possibly little more than folklore, describes how the chieftan died without revealing where he had buried his crock of gold coins, accumulated from chicle cuttings and from a stipend paid to him by the Mexican government.

172. "Chipitín el cazador," in Andrade and Máas Collí, vol. 1., pp. 138–181.

173. "Las tres muchachas," in Andrade and Máas Collí, vol. 1, pp. 348–379.

174. "Los siete rayos del sol," in Andrade and Máas Collí, vol. 1, pp. 278–311; "El rey y los tres bandidos," in Andrade and Máas Collí, vol. 2, pp. 302–319; "El yerno mentiroso," in Andrade and Máas Collí, vol. 2, pp. 322–361.

175. Redfield and Villa Rojas, 190–192.

176. Villa Rojas, 81–82, 89; Redfield and Villa Rojas, 91.

177. Villa Rojas, 71: "The offices which carry prestige are almost always occupied by men of ripe age who, by their exemplary conduct and specified aptitudes have become worthy of such posts." On age and public office in the pre–Caste War peninsula, see Rugeley, *Yucatán's Maya Peasantry,* 99–100.

178. This, at least, is the picture left by numerous anthropological studies of the

twentieth century. On the western highlands of Guatemala, see Ruth Bunzel, *Chichicastenango: A Guatemalan Village* (Seattle: University of Washington Press, 1952); and Charles Wagley, *Economics of a Guatemalan Village,* American Anthropological Association Memoir #58 (Menasha: American Anthropological Association, 1941). On the Mazahua of Mexico state, see Iwanska, 43–44. George A. Collier and Elizabeth Lowery Quaratiello make a similar argument regarding modern-day Chiapas in *Basta! Land and the Zapatista Rebellion in Chiapas* (Munroe: Institute for Food and Development, 1994), pp. 114–116.

179. "Chipitín el cazador," in Andrade and Máas Collí, vol. 1, pp. 138–181. Regarding the motif of animal body parts as gifts, see "Juan Oso," in Paredes, 63–78. Oaxacan counterparts appear in "La serpiente de las siete colores" (112–113) and "Juan Pescador" (114–115), in John Turner Reid, "Seven Folktales from Mexico," *Journal of American Folklore* 48 (1935), pp. 109–124. The motif of an eloping couple who escape the angry father by means of magical transformations appears in Pablo González Casanova's brief "Cuento en Mexicana de Milpa Alta D.F.," in *Journal of American Folklore* 33 (1920), pp. 25–27.

180. Rejón García (31–51) includes what is probably the oldest recorded reference to the tuunich keej. See also, "El cazador," in Andrade and Máas Collí, vol. 1, pp. 64–105, for the revenge of the deer. Paul Eiss (personal communication) informs me that stories of the use and abuse of the deer-stone are well known among the deer hunters of modern-day Tetiz.

181. "El siete colores," in Andrade and Máas Collí, vol. 1, pp. 312–345. In "The Horse of Seven Colors" (102–112) Paredes reports an extremely similar siete-colores story from La Encantada, Texas; he links the motif itself to such remote places as Hungary and Israel.

182. Keith Thomas, *Religion and the Decline of Magic* (New York: Scribners, 1971).

183. For an intriguing discussion of *ekmuleños* and their many ghosts, see Roberto López Méndez, "Los espantos se pasean libremente en Ekmul," *Por Esto!,* September 11, 1998, 22.

184. Irwin Press, borrowing from George Foster, referred to this process of anthropological change in Yucatán as "simmering." See Press, 9–10.

185. Robert Redfield, *The Folk Culture of Yucatan,* 229–230.

Notes to Chapter 2

1. The faded photographic reproduction of this portrait is found in *Retratos y biografía de yucatecos ilustres,* an unpublished album located in the CAIHY book collection.

2. For a sketch of the representative Mexican conservative, see Michael Costeloe in *The Central Republic in Mexico, 1835–1846: Hombres de Bien in the Age of Santa Anna* (Cambridge: Cambridge University Press, 1993), pp. 19–26; on Conservatism, and particularly the church's attitude toward the state, see Richard N. Sinkin, *The Mexi-*

can Reform, 1855–1876: A Study in Liberal Nation-Building (Austin: Institute of Latin American Studies, 1979), pp. 27–29, 115–116.

3. The principal national-level studies of church wealth are Costeloe, 1967; Bazant, 1971; and Knowlton, 1976. Yucatecan church studies include Michael J. Fallon, "The Secular Clergy in the Diocese of Yucatan: 1750–1800" (diss., The Catholic University of America, 1979); Raymond P. Harrington, "The Secular Clergy in the Diocese of Mérida de Yucatán, 1780–1850: Their Origins, Careers, Wealth and Activities" (diss., The Catholic University of America, 1982); Edgar Augusto Santiago Pacheco, "La política eclesiástica borbónica y la secularización de parroquias franciscanas en Yucatán: 1750–1825" (thesis, Universidad Autónoma de Yucatán, 1992); Beatriz Eugenia Carrillo y Herrera, "Iglesia y sociedad yucateca en el siglo XIX (1800–1840)" (thesis, Universidad Autónoma de Yucatán, 1993); Lynda Sanderford Morrison, "The Life and Times of José Canuto Vela: Yucatecan Priest and Patriot (1802–1859)" (diss., University of Alabama, 1993); and Hernán Menéndez Rodríguez, *Iglesia y poder: Proyectos sociales, alianzas políticas y económicas en Yucatán (1857–1917)* (México: Consejo Nacional para la Cultura y las Artes, 1995).

4. ANEY, May 14, 1864, pp. 98–100. See also, CAIHY, Fabian Carrillo, "Elogio fúnebre del señor doctor D. Raimundo Pérez y González, cura proprio de la parroquia de Hoctún" (Mérida: Rafael Pedera, 1857).

5. Grant D. Jones, *Maya Resistance to Spanish Rule: Time and History on a Colonial Frontier* (Albuquerque: University of New Mexico Press, 1989), pp. 213–230.

6. See Rugeley, *Yucatán's Maya Peasantry,* 7, 150–151.

7. Sosa, 1884, pp. 813–815. On the socioeconomic origins of San Ildefonso students, see Fallon, 68. A fuller analysis appears in Harrington, 77–177.

8. AHAY, Concursos a Curatos (CC), exp. 30, January 15, 1807.

9. Fallon, 129.

10. AHAY, Visitas Pastorales (VP), exp. 18, 1804.

11. AHAY, Asuntos Terminados (AT) 13, exp. 33, April 26, 1845.

12. For a biographical sketch of Eusebio Villamil, see Rugeley, *Yucatán's Maya Peasantry,* 110–111.

13. A census of 1868 reports both communities as Chontal; see Manuel Gil y Saenz, *Compendio histórico, geográfico y estadístico del Estado de Tabasco* (México: Consejo Editorial del Gobierno de Tabasco, 1979, facsimile of 1872 edition), 238.

14. AHAY, VP, Box 5, exp. 81, 1804.

15. Chambon, 59; Desiré Charnay, *Mis descubrimientos en México y en la América Central,* in *América pintoresca: Descripción de viajes al nuevo continente por los más modernos exploradores Carlos Wiener, Doctor Crevaux, D. Charnay, etc., etc.* (Barcelona: Montaner y Simón, Editores, 1884), pp. 320–321.

16. AHAY, CC, 1800.

17. In 1811, a year before Spain's constitutional crisis, he had bonded the cura of Tacotalpa, Tabasco, José María de Rivas Rocaful y Cámara, as collector of the *real*

mesada; see ANEY, January 1, 1811, pp. 10–11. For further information on Quintana's career, see Morrison, 40–56.

18. AHAY, CC, exp. 130, January 15, 1807.

19. Carol Steichen Dumond, and Don E. Dumond, eds. *Demography and Parish Affairs in Yucatan, 1797–1879: Documents from the Archivo de la Mitra Emeritense, Selected by Joaquín de Arrigunaga Peón* (University of Oregon Anthropological Papers #27, 1982), p. 373.

20. The best population statistics come from the year 1828, by which time the number of haciendas had grown to thirty-five (Dumond and Dumond, *Demography,* 91).

21. Pérez's removal from Macuspana followed the sort of delayed response identified in William B. Taylor's study of colonial rebellions. See Taylor, *Drinking, Homicide, and Rebellion in Colonial Mexican Villages* (Stanford: Stanford University Press, 1984), p. 120.

22. Regarding tax rebellions in Homún, see Rugeley, *Yucatán's Maya Peasantry,* Chapter 2.

23. AHAY, Cofradías (CF), r. 216, "Cuenta y razón de un ornamento entero que trabaje para encargo del Sr. cura D. Raymundo Pérez para su iglesia," March 27, 1811. It appears that Pérez spent somewhere around five hundred dollars for his project. Regarding the refurbishing of churches in the late eighteenth century, see Taylor, *Magistrates of the Sacred,* 103–104, 167.

24. HPS, *Razón del pueblo,* July 29, 1881, travel narrative of Serapio Baqueiro.

25. See Rugeley, *Yucatán's Maya Peasantry,* 40–44.

26. Conservative forces within Yucatán fabricated a legislative body called the *diputación,* so called because it purportedly planned to report as a deputation to the recently convened Spanish *cortes.* In reality it had no legal basis for issuing laws or decrees. See Justo Sierra O'Reilly, *Los indios de Yucatán: Consideraciones históricos sobre la influencia del elemento indígena en la organización social del país,* vol. 2 (Mérida: Compañía Tipográfica Yucateca, 1954), Chapters 13–17.

27. CAIHY, exp. 1, #7, 1813, misc. dates.

28. *El aristarco,* #18, 1813.

29. CAIHY, Expedientes, box VI, 66, December 16, 1841, P.C.A., "Al público."

30. On Spain's mystical illuminist movement, see John Lynch, *Spain Under the Hapsburgs,* vol. 1 (Oxford: Basil Blackwell, 1964), pp. 62– 64.

31. AGEY, Fondo Colonial (FC), Tierras, 1, 16, June 17, 1816; June 19, 1816.

32. ANEY, March 20, 1813, pp. 65–70. The junta de electores for the Spanish Cortes was in fact heavily weighted toward the church: thirteen of its twenty members were priests.

33. CAIHY, Expedientes, box VI, #66, P.C.A. (author), "Al público," printed by the *Boletín Comercial,* December 16, 1841: ". . . no soy de los que por una extraña y peregrina transformación se convierten por pocos días en liberales, como sucedió a nuestro teólogo [Pérez] el año de 1820".

34. Studies of the peninsular clergy unanimously point to key stratifications of wealth among priests. At the top lay a wealthy strata of curas and prominently placed cathedral bureaucrats; at the bottom, a large group of "floating clergy" who traveled from town to town, working as temporary help. Between these extremes lay a middle strata of assistant curas, ministers, and minor cathedral functionaries who enjoyed permanent or semipermanent conditions but who lacked access to obvention money. The most detailed analysis of this matter appears in Harrington, 282–345; see also Carrillo y Herrera, 47–50.

35. AHAY, AT 12, exp. 16, January 14, 1832; November 21, 1835; February 8, 1836; and January 16, 1838. See also, Rugeley, *Yucatán's Maya Peasantry,* Chapter 3, for a discussion of this issue in the context of peasant mobility.

36. The price of Canicab is cited in the postmortem investigation into Pérez's property. See AGEY, Fondo Justicia (FJ), box 64, "Juicio sobre ocultación de bienes en la testamentaría del finado Sr. Cura Dr. Raymundo Pérez," April 16, 1860.

37. AGEY, FJ, "Investigación."

38. AGEY, PE 51, G, Secretaría General de Gobernación, Jefe Político de Mérida, June 1, 1843; June 16, 1843.

39. Carrillo, 10.

40. Other plans of the time included forced labor for prisoners; see "Proyecto de presidio correcional para dar ocupación a los presos" (Mérida: 1823), CAIHY, Impresos. The final resolution to the matter was the labor law of the 1840s; see "Ley de trabajo agrícola," in CAIHY, October 30, 1843.

41. For information on the loans mentioned, see AGNM, BN, XXXXIII, 41, June 27, 1822; ANEY, July 30, 1821, 122; June 30, 1827, pp. 113–115; May 25, 1829, pp. 298–299; and August 2, 1832, pp. 170–171. This list could be extended to some length.

42. ANEY, August 19, 1846, pp. 227.

43. AGNM, BN, X, 20, April 14, 1820.

44. On the lives of Villamil and Dondé, see Rugeley, *Yucatán's Maya Peasantry,* 110–112, 82–83, 135. Following the Caste War, the powerful Dondé left Tekax to assume the high office of Chantry in the cathedral. There is no worthwhile study of the life of Meneses, despite his historical importance and the ample documentation in the Mérida archives; the only available work is still the hagiography by Justo Sierra O'Reilly entitled *Noticia biográfica del Sr. Dr. D. José Ma. Meneses"* (Mérida: Mariano Guzmán, 1856), found in CAIHY, Impresos, XI, 19, 1856.

45. Carrillo y Herrera, 129–145.

46. Copies of these sermons can be found in the CAIHY, Impresos mayas, *Colección de sermones para los domingos de todo el año, y cuaresma, tomados de various autores, y traducidos libremente al idioma yucateco, por el padre Fray Joaquín Ruz* (Mérida: José D. Espinosa, 1846), 2 vols. Volumes 3 and 4 appeared in 1850.

47. AHAY, AT 12, exp. 15, January 24, 1835.

48. Bricker, *The Indian Christ,* 160–161.

49. Interim appointments were common during times of liberal government because they did not require state approval.

50. Justo Sierra O'Reilly; Crescencio Carrillo y Ancona. See below, Chapter 7, regarding later accusations against and rivals of José María Guerra.

51. Morrison explores the political activities of the Yucatecan church as seen through the life of Padre José Canuto Vela; in particular, see pp. 82–83, 86, 125, 220.

52. Carrillo, 12–13. Congressional records of 1834 list Pérez as a deputy for Valladolid, a fact reinforcing the idea that politics of the centralist period tended to manipulate or override local desires. See AGEY, Poder Legislativo (PL), Acuerdos, November 24, 1834, p. 82.

53. AHAY, DO r. 99, December 11, 1834. This was ratified by conservative governor Francisco Toro; evidently Pérez had friends in that political quarter.

54. Carrillo, 12.

55. AGEY, FJ, "Juicio sobre ocultación de bienes," April 15, 1862.

56. A brief account of the procession, written eight years after Pérez's death by his successor, Luis Francisco Ricalde, appears in AHAY, DO r. 113, August 25, 1862, Hoctún.

57. AHAY, DO r. 110, December 17, 1856, Hoctún.

58. HPS, *Razón del pueblo,* July 29, 1881, travel narrative of Serapio Baqueiro.

59. ANEY, August 29, 1858, pp. 158–159. In a later document, her name appears as Francisca; see AGEY, FJ-Civil, 33, November 29, 1860, "Demanda puesta por la Sra. Francisca Medina contra Manuel Medina, exigiendo el inventario de los bienes del cura Raymundo Perez."

60. The registry of students at St. Louis University lists Manuel Medina as a student of classics in those years. Special thanks to Luis Millet for alerting me to Medina's years in the United States.

61. AHAY, DO r. 110, September 20, 1856, Motul.

62. CAIHY, Actos de Cabildo/Ayuntamientos Municipales (AC/AM), Libro de Manuscrito (LM) #32, January 1, 1854.

63. Manuel Medina, "Discurso leído por su autor, D. Manuel Medina, socio nato de la Academia de ciencias y literatura, en sesión pública del 23 de septiembre de 1849," in HPS, *Mosaico: Periódico de a Academia de Ciencias y Literatura,* 1849, pp. 121–131. Two years later, Medina was named associate to Mérida's tribunal of justice; see AGNM, Justicia (J) 396, January 11, 1851, p. 299.

64. Raymundo Pérez does not appear in the records of denuncias de terrenos baldíos found either in the ANEY or the CAIHY.

65. AGEY, PE, Ayuntamientos, IV, 30, May 4, 1840.

66. AHAY, AT 13, July 14, 1843.

67. Even though above the legal age limit of forty, Domingo Barret served for one year (1841–1842) as captain in the second company of the Sixteenth Battalion, based in Campeche; see AGEY, PE 47, M, I, 22, March 8, 1842.

68. José María Meneses tied for first with ex-governor José Tiburcio López and capitalist Lorenzo Peón. See AGEY, PE 26, Gobernación, April 12, 1847.

69. See Rugeley, "Rural Political Violence and the Origins of the Caste War," *The Americas* 53, 4 (April 1997), pp. 469–496.

70. For the most recent examination of the rebel offensive's decline and reversal, see Dumond, *The Machete and the Cross,* especially Chapters 6 and 8.

71. HPS, *El constitucional,* 120, June 8, 1859.

72. CAIHY, Carrillo, "Elogio fúnebre," 11.

73. A roster of property evaluations listing Pérez at two thousand dollars was a massive underevaluation, since his urban properties in Mérida alone far exceeded that figure. The list apparently demonstrates property taxable according to a now-lost formula; it nonetheless places Pérez among the wealthiest of the Hoctún-Izamal region. See AGEY, PE 39, G, "Padrón," misc. dates, 1850. Morrison's study of the life of José Canuto Vela reaches much the same conclusion: the more successful members of the church retained their wealth into the 1850s (Morrison, 228).

74. CAIHY, Carrillo, "Elogio fúnebre," 18.

75. AHAY, DO r.114, 24 October 150, Hoctún.

76. AGEY, PE 36, "Disposiciones y decretos en respuesta a exposiciones y solicitudes," April 12, 1849, p. 25.

77. In 1853, for example, he loaned two thousand pesos to Ildefonso Gómez. See ANEY, August 17, 1853, pp. 135–136.

78. ANEY, May 16, 1855, pp. 111–116. The document identifies the house as standing on the corner opposite "Toro." If this is the same corner as that currently identified as Toro, then Pérez's house is now an auto lubrication center.

79. Peón liquidated the debt three years later; this money allowed him to weather the most critical years of the Caste War catastrophe. See ANEY, November 19, 1851, pp. 227–278.

80. A roster of curas for the year lists him as eighty-one, six years older than his closest rival. See AHAY, DO r. 114, July 1849.

81. CAIHY, Carrillo, "Elogio fúnebre," 17.

82. AHAY, DO r. 118, July 12, 1854.

83. AHAY, DO r. 106, November 17, 1856. The times and dates given in the eulogy of Fabian Carrillo—10:00 P.M. on November 19, 1856—were mistaken.

84. Within a week of his passing, a force of some one thousand rebels attacked Tihosuco; people could no longer count the number of raids on this old epicenter of the war. See AHAY, DO r. 110, November 23, 1856.

85. Knowlton, 19–55.

86. For more on the career of Hurtado, see Carrillo y Herrera, 19–20.

87. CAIHY, Carrillo, "Elogio fúnebre," 18.

88. The author has spent considerable time searching for Pérez's will, to no avail.

89. Three examples suffice. First, there is the gift of 200 pesos to José Inocencia Miguel, son of Pérez's old friend Olaya Miguel (ANEY, Protocolos de Izamal #12, December 17, 1857, pp. 199–200). Second, there was the 1,168 pesos left to Felipe Cámara González, son of Caste War hero Felipe Cámara Zavala (AGEY, Registro Pú-

blico de Propiedad (RPP) #704, May 16, 1857, pp. 65). Third, Pérez left 3,000 pesos as a wedding gift for Luis María Gamboa, a posthumous act of kindness that Gamboa remembered in his will many years later (ANEY, Protocolos de Izamal #19, June 2, 1871, pp. 93–96).

90. AGEY, FJ, box 64, "Juicio," April 16, 1860.

91. "Documentos justificativos de la memoria que el C. Antonio G. Rejón presentó a la legislatura de Yucatán como secretario general del gobierno del estado, en 8 de septiembre de 1862" (Mérida: José Dolores Espinosa, 1862), p. 3. This particular item is to be found in CAIHY, Libros, Crescencio Carrillo y Ancona, ed., *Documentos interesantes de Yucatán, 1857–1902* (unpublished volume).

92. AGEY, FJ, "Ocultacion de bienes," misc. dates. The other haciendas were Tixcancal, Xcehus, Chetdzan, and Tzimché.

93. HPS, *Razón del pueblo*, July 29, 1881, travel narrative of Serapio Baquiero.

94. ANEY, August 29, 1858, pp. 158–159. The two granddaughters were Pérez's designated heirs in the case that Manuel Medina predeceased him.

95. AGEY, PE 119, G, February 12, 1859. This petition to reinstate the Caste War–related slave traffic is explicit: ". . . many times we have seen that in a lifeboat filled with castaways on the high seas, some are thrown into the water in order to save the lives of the others . . ."

96. HPS, Fabian S. Carrillo, "Estudios morales: El avaro," *Registro yucateco*, III, April 30, 1846, pp. 301–310.

97. AGEY, Registro Público de la Propiedad (RPP), #704, May 16, 1857, p. 65. This was certainly questionable by modern standards, but Ek's mother and father appear to have accepted the arrangement.

98. AGEY, FJ, "Ocultación de bienes," December 9, 1865.

99. AGEY, DO 47, March 10, 1887, Hoctún.

100. Many of these folk-art gravestones are the work of sexton Anacleto Cobá, who has worked at the Hoctún cemetery since 1960.

101. I base these observations on a visit made on June 8, 1997. Special thanks to the locals of Canicab for taking the time to speak with me. A few days after my visit, incidentally, Canicab experienced the apparition of a cross.

102. As with the last will and testament, the author has spent considerable time trying to locate Pérez's grave in Hoctún, with no success. There appears to be no living memory of the man. In fact, it is rare to find any commemoration of the dead in Yucatán before the 1890s.

Notes to Chapter 3

1. Key works on public festivals and parades include Natalie Z. Davis, *Society and Culture in Early Modern France* (Stanford: Stanford University Press, 1975), pp. 109–121; Darnton, *The Great Cat Massacre*, 116–124; Susan G. Davis, *Parades and Power:*

Street Theatre in Nineteenth-Century Philadelphia (Philadelphia: Temple University Press, 1986); Mary Ryan, "The American Parade: Representations of the Nineteenth-Century Social Order," in Lynn Hunt, ed., *The New Cultural History* (Berkeley: University of California Press, 1989), pp. 131–153; Linda A Curcio-Nagy, "Giants and Gypsies: Corpus Cristi in Colonial Mexico," in Beezley, et al., *Rituals of Rule,* 1–26; and Barbara A. Tenenbaum, "Streetwise History: The Paseo de la Reforma and the Porfirian State, 1876–1910," also in Beezley, 127–150.

2. J. Derek Holms and Bernard W. Bickers, *A Short History of the Catholic Church* (New York: Paulist Press, 1984), pp. 223–256.

3. CAIHY, Impresos, X, 28, 1855, "Carta pastoral del exmo. e ilmo. Sr. Obispo de Yucatán, Tabasco, etc., a sus diocesanos, con motivo de la definición dogmática de la inmaculada concepción de la Santísima Virgen María" (Mérida: Rafael Pedrara, 1855).

4. HPS, anonymous, *Registro yucateco,* 1, 1845, p. 233.

5. On the "Generation of 1840," see John F. Chuchiak IV, "Intellectuals, Indians and the Press, Polemical Journalism of Justo Sierra O'Reilly," *Saastun: Revista de la cultura maya* 2 (1997), pp. 6–16.

6. Chuchiak, 5.

7. Perry Miller, *Errand into the Wilderness* (Cambridge: Belknap Press of Harvard University Press, 1956), pp. 1–15.

8. Leonardo Boff and Clodovis Boff, *Liberation Theology: From Dialogue to Confrontation,* trans. Robert R. Barr (San Francisco: Harper and Row, 1986); for an examination of liberation theology's trajectory and its relationship with less intellectual and more "populist" elements of the Catholic Church, see Jeffrey L. Klaiber, "Prophets and Populists: Liberation Theology, 1968–1988," *The Americas* 46, 1 (1989), pp. 1–15.

9. The quote itself is from H. Richard Niebuhr; cited in Syndey E. Ahlstrom, *A Religious History of the American People* (New Haven: Yale University Press, 1972), p. 940.

10. Rodríguez Cantón, *Seis meses primeros del calendario para el año de 1827, tercero después de bisiesto,* found in Archivo Parroquial del Obispado de Campeche (APOC), among materials under reclassification at time of research.

11. Ralph Gibson notes the decline of hellfire Catholic preaching in France at this time, the combined effect of revolutionary skepticism and a changing family structure; see "Hellfire and Damnation in Nineteenth-Century France," *The Catholic Historical Review* 74, 3 (1988), pp. 383–402.

12. The literature on U.S. evangelism is enormous. I have drawn on Nathan O. Hatch, *The Democratization of American Christianity* (New Haven: Yale University Press, 1989). Hatch stresses nineteenth-century evangelicalism as part of a broader revolt of popular culture against the authority of traditional social elites. Doubtless other factors played a hand as well in the proliferation of this movement; the fire-and-brimstone quality of that evangelism, however, is beyond dispute.

13. CAIHY, Impresos, III, 2, 1838, *Sumario de las gracias e indulgencias que hay concedidas a los Archicofradías del Santísimo que visitaren la iglesia en donde estuviera instituida dicha Cofradía, para orar o velar a su Divina Magestad, acompañarle en las procesiones y viáticos y por asistir a las juntas, entierros y demás de sus respectivas obligaciones.*

14. HPS, "El pueblo y el clero," *Museo yucateco,* vol. I, 1841, p. 80: "Todo en la sociedad está arreglado/ Cada estado subsiste en su estado;/ Por eso el pueble se mantiene *arando*/ Y los ministros del altar *orando.*"

15. *Devocional a la Escala Santa, su origen, traslaciones y culto* (Mérida: Manual Isac Rodríguez, 1816), in CAIHY, Impresos, I, 6, 1816.

16. HPS, "Canto histórico-religioso en alabanza de la virgen María," advertised by A. Gonzalez in *La nueva época* #60, March 18, 1864.

17. HPS, J. A. Cisneros, "A la religión," *Registro yucateco,* II, November 4, 1845, pp. 380–382.

18. HPS, José Turrisa (Justo Sierra O'Reilly), "D. José María Loría. Necrología," *Registro yucateco,* II, March 22, 1846, pp. 232–236.

19. HPS, V. Calero, "La cuaresma," *Registro yucateco,* III, 1846, pp. 150–153; "La biblia y la literatura contemporánea," *Registro yucateco,* III, 1846, pp. 161–165; "El gran elemento de la conquista: La religión," *Registro yucateco,* IV, 1846, pp. 21–27. It is difficult to tell where Calero derived his ideas on the direction of contemporary poetry, although it is clear that the Romantic period did witness a decline in classical themes such as Greco-Roman mythology.

20. HPS, José Turrisa (Justo Sierra O'Reilly), "La catedral de Mérida," *Registro yucateco,* I, August 28, 1845, pp. 131–142.

21. HPS, Sandalio de Noda (pseudonym), "Interior de la Catedral de la Habana," *Registro yucateco,* III, February 1846, pp. 177–186; HPS, Gerónimo Castillo, "El camposanto," *Registro yucateco,* I, January 2, 1845, pp. 485–491.

22. HPS, L.G., "Una visita: Las ruinas de Uxmal," *Registro yucateco* I, 1845, pp. 275–279. In volume 3 of the same (1846), see Vicente Calero, "Ruinas de Chichén Itzá," 298–300.

23. HPS, "Dr. Fr. Francisco Toral," *Registro yucateco* I, 1845, pp. 31–36; "El convento de la Mejorada," in same volume, 38–40. I cite only two of numerous examples. Church historical writing reached its apogee late in the century with bishop Crescencio Carrillo y Ancona's *El obispado de Yucatán: Historia de su fundación y de sus obispos desde el siglo XVI hasta el XIX.* (Mérida: R. Caballero, 1895).

24. HPS, Juan José Hernández, "El indio yucateco," *Registro yucateco,* III, 1846, p. 429.

25. See Redfield and Villa Rojas, 148–153.

26. The thirty-one novenarios I consulted for this study originally formed part of the collection of Crescencio Carrillo y Ancona, the conservative bishop (1884–1897) and man of letters. Today they are part of the "Impresos" collection of the CAIHY.

27. See, for example, *Voto o donación que en manos de María Santísima nuestra*

Señora podrá hacer el que guste en favor de las afligidas almas del purgatorio, con los actos de fe, esperanza y caridad (Mérida: José Dolores Espinosa, 1842), in CAIHY, Impresos, III, 30, 1842. The voto measured seven by eleven centimeters and ran eleven pages. See also *Devocionario para el día siete de cada mes, en memoria y honra de los dolores de la Sacratísima Virgen María, nuestra señora al pie de la cruz* (Mérida: José Dolores Espinosa, 1839), in CAIHY, Impresos, III, 4, 1839.

28. "Novena de la Sacratísima Virgen de Itzmal," CAIHY, Impresos, I, 14, 1824. In a personal communication, William B. Taylor pointed out that the novenarios of eighteenth-century Mexico typically carried an introductory history concerning the icon or saint in question; this does not seem to have been the case with the nineteenth-century works I have examined.

29. "Novena a Santa Apolonia, virgen y mártir," CAIHY, Impresos, VI, 5, 1847; "Novena a la gloriosa virgen y mártir Santa Lucía, abogada de los ojos," in CAIHY, Impresos, X, 8, 1853.

30. "Novena del Imaculado Corazón de María Santísima, Señora Nuestra," CAIHY, Impresos, X, 36, 1855. The same construction appears in "Novena de la Sacratísima Sangre de Ntro. Sr. Jesucristo," CAIHY, Impresos, X, 9, 1853.

31. *Manual de la virtud, o sea explicación y razonada de la oración del Padre Nuestro, escrita por el Presbítero D. Mucio Valdovinos, domiciliario de este arzobispado* (México: J. M. Lara, 1851), in CAIHY, Impresos, VIII, 10, 1851.

32. Ong, 57.

33. "Novena y día ocho al Abraham de la Ley de Gracica y Padre de los Pobres San Juan de Dios, para implorar su patrocinio en todas las necesidades y enfermedades," CAIHY, Impresos, X, 21, 1854.

34. *Devocionario*, op cit.

35. *Oraciones para antes y después de las sagradas confesión y comunión, con otras alabazas al Señor y a su santísima madre* (Mérida: R. Pedrera, 1849), in CAIHY, Impresos, VI, 21, 1849. Like certain novenarios, this work provided a long series of attributes and actions that helped the reader to better comprehend the divine nature.

36. Benedict Anderson, *Imagined Communities: Reflections on the Origin and Spread of Nationalism* (London: Verso Editions, 1993).

37. Nicholas Terpstra, "Confraternities and Mendicant Orders: The Dynamics of Lay and Clerical Brotherhood in Renaissance Bologna," *Catholic Historical Review* 82, I (1996), pp. 1–22.

38. Cofradía literature is extensive. For a beginning on Mexico, see D. A. Brading, "Tridentine Catholicism and Enlightened Despotism in Bourbon Mexico," *Journal of Latin American Studies* 15 (1983), pp. 1–22. On Colombia, see Gary Wendell Graff, "Cofradías in the New Kingdom of Granada: Lay Fraternities in a Spanish American Frontier Society, 1600–1755" (diss., University of Wisconsin, 1973). On Brazil, see Manuel Cardozo, "The Lay Brotherhoods of Colonial Bahia," *Catholic Historical Review* 33, I (1947), pp. 12–30; A. J. R. Russell-Wood, "Prestige, Power, and Piety in

Colonial Brazil: The Third Orders of Salvador," *Hispanic American Historical Review* 69, 1 (1989), pp. 61–89; Patricia A. Mulvey, "Slave Confraternities in Brazil: Their Role in Colonial Society," *The Americas* 39, 1 (1982), pp. 39–68; and Taylor, *Magistrates of the Sacred,* 301–323.

39. Literature on Yucatecan cofradías has dealt overwhelmingly with rural peasant organizations. See Chapter 5, note 6, for a review.

40. See Rugeley, *Yucatán's Maya Peasantry,* 25–31.

41. Prior to the Imán revolt, the annual obvention payment for each peasant, male or female, was approximately twelve reales. The revolt eliminated obventions for women, while the government subsequently slashed obventions in 1850 in an effort to quiet the peasantry. Governor Miguel Barbachano's orders to this effect appear in APOC, Mandatos, box 142, "Libro de mandatos, 1805–1857," January 12, 1850.

42. AGNM, Justicia Eclesiástica (JE) 22, misc. dates, 1822.

43. AGNM, JE 183, January 21, 1856, pp. 253–255.

44. Ibid.; see also "Constituciones para las cofradías de Nuestro Amo, en las parroquias de la sagrada mitre de Sonora" (México: Imprenta de Aguila, 1845), in AGNM, JE 183, pp. 229–250.

45. AGNM, JE 188, June 2, 1856, pp. 196–198.

46. AGNM, JE 183, May 26 1856, p. 309.

47. AHAY, Cofradías Generales, r. 217, May 15, 1809, "Libro de la Cofradía de Nuestra Santísima Madre y Señora la Purísima Virgen de la Merced . . ." The current classification system of the AHAY no longer uses Cofradías Generales; most of that section's papers are to now in Oficios de Cofradías.

48. APOC, Cofradías 2/3, November 13, 1851, padre Gregorio Ximénez to Bishop Guerra.

49. CAIHY, Impresos, XX, 18, 1868, "Reglamento de la venerable cofradía del santísimo sacramento en la parroquia de Santiago."

50. AHAY, DO r. 108, February 2, 1846.

51. AHAY, DO r. 111, June 28, 1859.

52. APOC, Cofradías box 2/3, March 12, 1886.

53. For this point and all subsequent information on Santísimo Sacramento, I have drawn from José María Oliver de Casares's unpublished memoir, *Noticia histórica de la fundación de la antigua cofradía y de otros hechos relativos a ella.* This document of nineteenth-century social history can be found in APOC, Cofradías, 2/3, 1878–1880. The author wrote it in installments, hence the range of dates. Concerning Santísimo Sacramento's twentieth-century return, see APOC, "Libro de caja de la archicofradía de la adoración perpetua del Santísimo Sacramento, establecida en la santa iglesia catedral el 25 de julio de 1932," unclassified document, 1932–1940.

54. AHAY, Cofradías Generales, r. 216, July 24, 1828, "Cuenta de cargo y data de la cofradía de Nuestra Señora del Rosario."

55. AHAY, DO r. 146, Cenotillo, September 14, 1910. The group was busily rounding up scapulars and a portrait of the Virgin as part of its rebirth.

56. AGEY, PE 4, Beneficiencia, 1, 2, February 25, 1831.

57. No biography or study of Ximénez exists, although quite a bit of information appears in APOC, *Noticia histórica.*

58. On Vario Canto y Sosa, see APOC, "Patente de admisión a la cofradía del Piadosa Corazón inmaculado de María Santísima," unclassified document, 1888.

59. APOC, Cofradías 4, "Cristo de San Román," July 8, 1878.

60. "Restablecimiento de la cofradía del Santísimo Sacramento," APOC, Cofradías 2/3, March 17, 1877, Campeche.

61. On the archicofradía in eighteenth-century Chihuahua, see Cheryl English Martin, *Governance and Society in Colonial Mexico: Chihuahua in the Eighteenth Century* (Stanford: Stanford University Press, 1996), pp. 110–113.

62. AHAY, DO 31, June 18, 1852, Mérida; DO 34, May 19, 1855, Mérida. Regarding the election of officers, see AHAY, DO 21, June 25, 1838, Izamal.

63. CAIHY, Impresos, XV, 1, August 26, 1862.

64. CAIHY, Impresos, X, 3, May 15, 1853, "Constitución de la venerable archicofradía del santísimo sacramento, establecida en la santa iglecia catedral de Mérida."

65. Membership statistics on the archicofradía are based on CAIHY, Impresos, X, 29, October 5, 1855; XII, 18, August 1, 1858; XVII, 20, January 12, 1865; and XXVI, 6, March 18, 1874.

66. CAIHY, Impresos, "Constitución."

67. CAIHY, Impresos, "Constitución."

68. CAIHY, Impresos, XX, 18, 1868, "Reglamento de la venerable cofradía del santísimo sacramento en la parroquia de Santiago."

69. CAIHY, Impresos, XIV, 1, 1861, "Asociación católica del centro de Mérida, suburbio de S. Sebastián y su partido."

70. AHAY, DO r. 99, December 5, 1834.

71. AHAY, DO r. 116, October 27, 1853, "Reglamento de la Cofradía del Santísimo Sacramento de Hunucmá."

72. Ibid.

73. APOC, Oliver de Casares, *Noticia histórica,* 472–475.

74. CAIHY, Manuscritos, XXXIII, 12, May 1, 1840, "Nóminas de los empleados, comerciantes y demás."

75. CAIHY, Impresos, XXIV, 24, 1872, "Reglamento de la sociedad católica del gremio de barberos de Mérida."

76. CAIHY, AC/AM, LM #33, October 5, 1857.

77. Cheryl English Martin noted that owing to the different structure of eighteenth-century Chihuahua's workforce and workplace, the workers made relatively little use of gremios and cofradías for burial assistance, relying instead on loans from employers; see Martin, 117–118.

78. Membership statistics on the archicofradía are based on CAIHY, Impresos, X, 29, October 5, 1855; XII, 18, August 1, 1858; XVII, 20, January 12, 1865; and XXVI, 6, March 18, 1874.

79. Archivo Histórico del Arzobispado (AHA), Temax, V5–C-1, "Cofradías," "Libro de la Cofradía de la Sma. Virgen del Monte Carmelo fundada en esta parroquia de San Miguel de Temax el año de 1817," various dates.

80. For respective gender breakdowns on these three organizations, see APOC, Cofradias, 1, "Libro de asientos de los hermanos de la real cofradía de nuestra Señora del Carmen, Pbro. Mamerto Ojeda, Campeche, julio 16 de 1864"; "Libro de asientos de los Hermanos de la Real Archicofradía de Nuestra Señora de la Merced, Redención de Cautivos," 1809–1881; and "Libro de asientos y cuentas de la cofradía del Sagrado Corazón de María," 1851–1914. As a rule, Campeche's cofradías are much better documented than their peninsular counterparts. In this case the list of enrollments extends from 1864 to 1909. Men were somewhat better represented in the cofradía's early years, although still a distinct minority; by the last decade they had virtually disappeared.

81. Norman, 78.

82. Regarding this argument of piety as an underlying theme of *machismo,* see John M. Ingram, *Mary, Michael, and Lucifer: Folk Catholicism in Central Mexico* (Austin: University of Texas Press, 1986), particularly Chapter 8.

83. Luis Martín, *Daughters of the Conquistadors: Women of the Viceroyalty of Peru* (Albuquerque: University of New Mexico Press, 1983), pp. 280–309. By my own calculation, carried out in a number of different churches on different Sundays, female church attendants outnumber male counterparts by about two to one.

84. "Las beatas," HPS, *El mus, periódico satírico de política y costumbres,* 1, 1861, pp. 56–59.

85. During a recent (1998) forum on social change in Yucatán, an anthropologist working in rural Campeche remarked that "Pentacostalism is the peasant's version of Alcoholics Anonymous." That is to say, it carries a strong antialcohol message and a ready-made support group. On some of the larger dynamics of Protestant conversion in rural Yucatán, see Ivan Vallado Fajardo, "En busca de la esperanza y la salvación: Resocialización religiosa en Sudzal, Yucatán," in Esteban Krotz, coord., *Cambio cultural y resocialización en Yucatán* (Mérida: Universidad Autónoma de Yucatán, 1997), pp. 165–185.

86. APOC, Oliver de Casares, *Noticia histórica.*

87. I refer to Natalie Davis's essay "Women on Top," in *Society and Culture in Early Modern France,* 124–151.

88. AGEY, JF-Penal, 30, February 16, 1858, Ixil. *Mestiza* came to be a euphemism for a rural Maya woman.

89. I say "significantly" in order to be on the safe side; the fact is, I have never seen a single example.

90. Ana Patricia Uribe Euán and Felipe de Jesús Castro Medina, "El convento de Nuestra Señora de la Consolación de Mérida" (thesis, Universidad Autónoma de Yucatán, 1992), pp. 35, 40, 109–139.

91. Uribe and Castro, 54–57, 63–76, 89, 94; Federico de Waldeck, *Viaje pintoresco y arqueológico a la provincia de Yucatán (América central) durante los años 1834 y 1836,* trans. Dr. Manuel Mestre Ghigliazza (Mérida: Compañía Tipográfica Yucateca, S. A., 1930, orig. 1837), p. 94.

92. Uribe and Castro, 160–170; CAIHY, Impresos, XIX, 29, 1867, "Documentos para la historia de la exclaustración de las RR.MM. Concepcionistas de Mérida de Yucatán" (Mérida: M. Guzman, 1867).

93. The vision of carnival as a time of tolerated anarchy and social inversion is a running theme throughout histories of popular culture. To take only the most prominent examples, see Burke, 178–204, and Beezley, 97–108.

94. As, for example, in Frank Cancian, *Economics and Prestige in a Maya Community: The Cargo System in Zinacantan* (Stanford: Stanford University Press, 1965); see also, Waldemar Smith, *The Fiesta System and Economic Change* (New York: Columbia University Press, 1977); and Ingram, *Mary, Michael, and Lucifer.*

95. John Lloyd Stephens, for example, describes limited integration in the fiesta of Halachó; see John Lloyd Stephens, *Incidents of Travel in Yucatan* (New York: Dover Publications, Inc., 1963) I, 206–207.

96. Martin, 102–103.

97. CAIHY, LM, AC/AM, #22, February 11, 1831, 153.

98. Waldeck, 88.

99. "El carnaval," in Manuel Barbachano y Tarrazo, *Vida, usos y hábitos de Yucatán al mediar el siglo XIX* (Mérida: Maldonado Editores, 1986, orig. 1951), pp. 37–40.

100. HPS, Gerónimo Castillo, "Una escena de carnaval," *Registro yucateco,* III, 1846, pp. 375–380.

101. Eighteenth-century birth records of the Campeche cathedral identify San Román as a barrio of Mayas, Spaniards, Blacks, and "chinos." See APOC, "Baptisms, San Román." Unfortunately, the archive contains virtually no information on urban cofradías between the colonial period and the postreform years.

102. This description of Campeche's *haute couture* comes from HPS, *El grano de arena,* #80, September 3, 1852.

103. For a brief but illuminating review of the fiesta and its origins, see Gaspar A. Cauich and Mayra Aguayo Mena, *La feria de San Román: Historia de una mentalidad, 1565–1997* (Campeche: Campeche XXI, 1998), particularly pp. 57–74.

104. HPS, *El grano de arena,* #74, August 13, 1852.

105. HPS, *El grano de arena,* #6, December 19 1851.

106. HPS, *Repertorio pintoresco,* March 29, 1861, reproducing the comments of Justo Sierra O'Reilly in *El fénix* I, #32, April 5, 1849.

107. HPS, *Diario de Yucatán,* April 2, 1994.

108. AHAY, DO r. 114, April 12, 1852, Tenabo.

109. Norman, 8–10.

110. APOC, Oliver de Casares, *Noticia histórica,* passim. No such corresponding

documents exist for the larger Mérida archicofradía, since, as the mayordomo himself reported in 1853, they had mostly been destroyed during the preceding seven years of revolution and civil war; see AHAY, DO 32, May 25, 1852, Mérida.

111. This, at least, was the interpretation that a local priest passed on to Oliver de Casares; it was not necessarily correct or definitive.

112. Cauich and Aguayo Mena (pp. 88–89) refer to this as the transition from fiesta, or religious celebration, to the more explicitly secular feria.

113. On the suppression of carnival-associated popular customs, see Curcio-Nagy, 17–22.

114. APOC, Oliver de Casares, *Noticia histórica,* 445.

115. AGEY, PC, Acuerdos, r. 20, February 28, 1824, pp. 73–74.

116. CAIHY, AC/AM, LM #31, August 8, 1853.

117. AHAY, DO r. 115, September 20, 1852. José Clemente Romero sent printed circulars announcing the fiesta of Tixkokob to Mérida, Campeche, "and all the towns."

118. HPS, *Las garantías sociales,* #176, November 12, 1856.

119. HPS, *Museo yucateco,* II, 1841, pp. 15–19, José Turrisa, "Las diligencias y la feria de Izamal."

120. HPS, *La nueva época,* #116, September 30 1864. In 1821 Cacalchén had a mere 2,017 inhabitants, as opposed to the 7,428 of Izamal; see Salvador Rodríguez Losa, *Geografía política de Yucatán. Tomo I: Censo inédito de 1821* (Mérida: Universidad Autónoma de Yucatán, 1985), p. 98.

121. HPS, *Las garantías sociales,* #176, November 12, 1856.

122. HPS, *Museo yucateco,* II, 1841, pp. 15–19, José Turrisa (Justo Sierra O'Reilly), "Las diligencias y la feria de Izamal."

123. "To Epifanía Rodríguez," in Clements Library (CLE), Yucatecan Collection, "Revista de salón en el primero y segundo baile de Carnaval de 1877, Izamal," February 12, 1877. The anonymous author had a poem for each of his eleven favorite sweethearts.

124. Turrisa, "Las diligencias."

125. See, for example, the itinerary for the fiesta of Dzidzantún, in HPS, *La nueva época,* #61, 3–21–1864. The majority of the ads promise dances.

126. Barbachano, 27. Barbachano's colorful vignettes of *costumbrismo* first appeared in 1845, when his brother Miguel was governor. As his humorous sketch explains, the stands suffered a tendency to collapse. See also John Lloyd Stephens's description of a Mérida bullfight in Stephens, vol. I, pp. 26–38.

127. HPS, *Periódico oficial,* #1, October 3, 1864.

128. HPS, *El regenerador,* #24, April 8, 1853.

129. HPS, *Las garantías sociales,* #174, November 7, 1856.

130. HPS, *La nueva época,* #60, March 18, 1864.

131. For records of bullfight money accruing to the Ayuntamiento of Mérida, see CAIHY, LM, AC/AM, #22, June 4, 1830, 52.

132. University of Texas Nettie Lee Benson Collection (TEX), G559, June 1878,

"Apuntes y datos sobre el estado actual de la guerra de los indios sublevados y los remedios posibles de abrir una campaña decisiva para darle término."

133. HPS, *La nueva época,* #116, September 30, 1864.

134. HPS, *La sombra de Morelos,* no number, January 8, 1862.

135. HPS, *Las garantías sociales,* #174, November 7, 1856.

136. HPS, *La nueva época,* #95, July 18, 1864; *Periódico oficial,* #1, October 3, 1864.

137. AHAY, DO r. 124, May 25, 1856.

138. AGEY, PC, Acuerdos, February 28, 1824, pp. 73–74. This particular reference deals with the license the state congress granted to Oxkutzcab's ayuntamiento for organizing fiestas; the license came with a list of prohibitions.

139. See, for example, AGEY, FJ-Penal, 7, January 22, 1855, Campeche; and 10, July 5, 1855, Mérida.

140. AGNM, BN, XXXVIII, 13, February 5, 1844.

141. Stephens, II, 205.

142. CAIHY, LM, AC/AM, #18, October 14, 1823, pp. 118–119.

143. Regarding both the economics and aesthetics of the national lottery, see Juan José Reyes, *Cuestión de suerte* (México: Editorial Clío, 1997), pp. 42–55.

144. Barbachano, 25–28.

145. ANEY, July 1, 1853, pp. 82–83. Miguel Barbachano acted as guarantor of his in-law Ignacio Quijano y Cosgaya for a state contract to manage the lottery for four years at an annual profit of 2 percent of the total revenues.

146. AGEY, PE 189, Milicias, March 27, 1874, Mérida. This document, a report from the state council, reviews the history of the Mérida lottery.

147. Turrisa (Justo Sierra O'Reilly), "Las diligencias."

148. AGEY, PE 99, G, November 18, 1854, Mérida; WMMSA, 30 December 1867, report of Richard Fletcher, Corozal.

149. Burke, 270–281; Beezley, 6.

150. HPS, *Registro yucateco,* I, 1845, pp. 155–156.

151. On urban change in the late nineteenth and early twentieth centuries, see Allen Wells and Gilbert M. Joseph, *Summer of Discontent,* 120–141.

152. For a rundown on the sodalities and their mayordomos, see AHAY, DO 45, 1879, Mérida.

153. The statutes of the four above-mentioned cofradías are to be found in CAIHY, Impresos. See XXXV, 14, September 9, 1880, "Estatutos de la cofradía de las benditas almas del purgatorio"; XXXV, 21, June 16, 1882, "Patente y sumario de todas las indulgencias que de una manera auténtica consta han sido concedidas a todas las hermandades o congregaciones de Nuestra Señora de las Mercedes"; XXXVII, 12, 1883, "Patente de la cofradía de Nuestra Señora del Carmen"; and XXXVI, 14, 1883, "Guía práctica de los hermanos de la archicofradía del cordón de S. Francisco de Asís."

154. The papers of the underutilized Archivo de la Parroquia de la Arquidiócesis de Campeche contain a significant body of materials dealing with the these organizations in both Porfirian and revolutionary times. In addition to the cases of San Román and

Santísimo Sacramento described in the text, see "Expediente de erección de cofradía de Animas en Campeche," in APOC, Cofradías 2/3, May 8, 1880; and "Patente de admisión a la cofradía del Piadosa Corazón Inmaculado de María Santísima," (1888), in APOC, unclassified document.

155. See "Cuentas de cargo y data . . . correspondiente a la cofradía del Señor de San Román extramuros de la ciudad de Campeche," in APOC, Cofradías 4, August 12, 1883.

156. APOC, Cofradías 1, "Cofradía de Nuestra Señora del Rosario," October 1870–October 1879; "Nuestra Señora de Carmen," 1860-1894.

157. APOC, Asociaciones 2, "Legajo sobre asociaciones de caridad, 1807 a 1882, varios lugares."

158. AHAY, DO 47, March 11, 1887, Conkal; DO 47, November 8, 1887, Temax.

159. AHAY, DO 47, January 8, 1887, Peto.

160. There is little study of the Porfirian cultural life in the Yucatecan pueblos. Some information on fiestas appears in Savarino, 104-108, although his argument for a mapping of "symbolic territories" seems dubious.

161. Victor M. Suárez Molina, *Historia del obispado y arzobispado de Yucatán, siglos XIX y XX,* (Mérida: Fondo Editorial de Yucatán, 1981), pp. 1124-1128. This book was intended as a continuation of Carrillo y Ancona's two earlier volumes on the history of the peninsular church.

162. On the history of Acción Católica in the national context, see Peter Lester Reich, *Mexico's Hidden Revolution: The Catholic Church in Law and Politics Since 1929* (Notre Dame: University of Notre Dame Press, 1995), pp. 93-103.

163. Savarino, 204-207.

164. CAIHY, Impresos, VII, 17, March 21, 1850. This was the Sociedad de Jesús María.

165. The library of the CAIHY contains two useful Carnival albums: *Recuerdo del Carnaval, Mérida 1919* and *Album-Recuerdo, Carnaval de 1920, Mérida.* Significantly, both are packed with commercial advertising.

166. As happened in 1994, for example, when Pope John Paul II said mass at Izamal.

Notes to Chapter 4

1. Reed, 159-269; Dumond, 179-198.

2. For a traditional analysis of Yucatec Maya iconography, see Thompson, 10-25, 169, 176-177, 277-278. For a revisionist interpretation, see Schele and Miller, 41-55, and Schele and Mathews, 197-289.

3. Patrick J. Geary, "The Ninth-Century Relic Trade: A Response to Popular Piety?" in James Obelkevich, *Religion and the People, 800-1700* (Chapel Hill: University of North Carolina Press, 1979), pp. 8-19.

4. Wroth, 8–9.

5. AGEY, PE 226, G, March 22, 1884.

6. AHAY, DO 20, February 1, 1836, Izamal. The local soldiers there kept a statue of Our Lady of Carmen.

7. See Taylor, *Magistrates of the Sacred,* 53–59, for a review of interpretations of syncretism.

8. Marshall Sahlins, *Tribesmen* (Englewood Cliff: Prentice-Hall, 1968), pp. 96–113, analyzes the roles of sky gods and intermediaries.

9. Transportation of holy oils is a common motif in Cathedral-parish correspondence. See, for example, AHAY, DO, August 28, 1859, Flores.

10. AHAY, DO 28, September 7, 1846, Izamal.

11. Relatively little is known concerning Maya craftsmen of the colonial and even the national period. Some preliminary information appears in Miguel A. Bretos's enchanting *Iglesias de Yucatán* (Mérida: Producción Editorial Dante, 1992), a study of various Yucatecan churches, with photographs by Christian Rasmussen. See, for example, pp. 20, 27–28 on the development of indigenous sculptors and artisans.

12. AHAY, DO 19, August 1, 1836.

13. This information appears at the museum of the Church of Izamal.

14. AHAY, DO r. 115, June 5, 1851, Nolo.

15. AHAY, DO r. 128, July 17, 1872, Hunucmá.

16. AHAY, DO r. 115, August 26, 1851, Telchac.

17. Christian, 21.

18. HPS, *Por Esto!,* January 7, 1996. Although little survives describing its activities, we know that the cult of the *tres reyes* was alive and well in the pre–Caste War period, since the town's ayuntamiento worked feverishly to restore it in the 1850s; see AGEY, PE III, Gobernación, Ayuntamiento de Tizimín, March 27, 1857.

19. See Cogolludo (III, 354–362) for wonders attributed to San Diego.

20. See "Dios y San Isidro," in Robe, 25–26.

21. Taylor argues that the Virgin of Guadalupe was primarily a creole Spanish cult from the beginning and only began to be promoted outside of the Mexico City area in the mid–eighteenth century. See *Magistrates of the Sacred,* 277–300; see also Taylor, "The Virgin of Guadalupe in New Spain: An Inquiry into the Social History of Marian Devotion," *American Ethnologist* 14 (1987), pp. 9–33. For the colonial career of Mexico's second most important Marian cult, see Linda A. Curcio-Nagy, "Native Icon to City Protectress to Royal Patroness: Ritual, Political Symbolism and the Virgin of the Remedies," *The Americas* 52, 3 (1996), pp. 367–391.

22. Bernardo de Lizama, *Historia de Yucatán. Devocionario de Ntra. Sra. de Izamal y conquista espiritual* (México: 1893).

23. For the only source I have been able to locate for the history and legends surrounding the Virgin of Izamal, see Diego López de Cogolludo, *Historia de Yucatán,* II, 112–122. Cogolludo's tendency to see wonders at every turn makes him an exceptional

source for tracing popular miracles of the seventeenth century. A detailed history of the Virgin of Izamal from colonial times to the present day would make an intriguing monograph, but thus far there has been little research on the subject of this, one of Mexico's most important Marian cults.

24. Cogolludo, III, 368–377.

25. AHAY, DO, November 10, 1842.

26. Morrison (43–44) briefly reviews the literature on the Virgin of Tekax. Cogolludo (III, 397–406) provides a lengthy history of this statue, supposedly found in a tree by Maya fishermen of the village of Hampolol. Gerardo Can Pat's brief but interesting monograph, *La virgen de la Candelaria: Entohistoria de la Patrona de Tibolón* (Mérida: INI/SEDESOL, 1993), basically explores the cult's contemporary activities, with a bit of twentieth-century history by way of introduction.

27. AGEY, FJ-Penal, 7, January 5, 1855.

28. Ruz Menéndez, 57; Villa Rojas, 159.

29. Méndez et al., "Report on the Maya Indians of Yucatan." in F. W. Hodges, ed., *Indian Notes and Monographs* IX, 3 (1921), p. 170 (orig. October 24, 1861). Charged with preparing a report on Maya customs and culture, Méndez took the easy way out by simply reproducing Padre Baeza's well-known 1813 ethnography. However, he did make a few minor additions, including a reference to this particular myth of supernatural forces in the sugar *engenios*. My comments on forced acculturation and the folk meanings of the devil are indebted to Michael Taussig, *The Devil and Commodity Fetishism in South America* (Chapel Hill: University of North Carolina Press, 1980), although, I hope, without the absoluteness of his construction. See also Irene Silverblatt, *Moon, Sun and Witches: Gender Ideologies and Class in Inca and Colonial Peru* (Princeton: Princeton University Press, 1987), pp. 161–163.

30. To take only one example, in the story "D-Juso y San Antonio," the santo repeatedly ignores God's warning and showers his attention on an unworthy peasant. The peasant's harvest is so great that he throws out San Antonio's statue to make room. See Dzul Poot, vol. 2, pp. 9–11.

31. Park Redfield, 28.

32. For a critique of the theory of peasant socialism, see Grant Evans, *Lao Peasants Under Socialism* (New Haven: Yale University Press, 1990). Evans stresses the often invisible peasant role as petty commodity producers in local and regional capitalist markets.

33. On the retention (and loss) of Maya family wealth, see Restall, *The Maya World*, 110–120, 124–130.

34. On the bequeathing of icons in central Mexico, see Stephanie Wood, "Adopted Saints: Christian Images in Nahua Testaments of Late Colonial Toluca," *The Americas* 47, 3 (January 1991), pp. 259–293.

35. ANEY, July 1, 1819, pp. 232–234, will of Nasario Encalada. Encalada was apparently active in the south or east, since he possessed two sugar ranchos.

36. ANEY, April 28, 1847, pp. 371–374, will of Jacobo Machado.

37. ANEY, September 18, 1847, pp. 107–111.

38. ANEY, September 16, 1845, pp. 31–35, will of Rita Mugártegui.

39. ANEY, November 26, 1817, pp. 298–301, will of Gregorio Domínguez.

40. AGNM, BN, 11, 31, March 29, 1845.

41. ANEY, September 17, 1847, p. 84.

42. ANEY, May 27, 1837, pp. 127–129, will of Marcela Cen.

43. My argument regarding the introduction of Spanish property rights and their subsequent effect on indigenous culture borrows from William B. Taylor's analysis of sixteenth-century changes in alcohol production and consumption in the vicinity of Mexico City; see Taylor, 1979, pp. 34–45.

44. AHAY, DO r. 108, August 1, 1845.

45. Without mentioning specific cases, suffice it to say that people in *pueblos* throughout the peninsula have told me variants of this same story.

46. Parsons, 1932, p. 278. In this case the santo refused to stay put until locals constructed a chapel for him.

47. HPS, *Diario de Yucatán,* July 30, 1997.

48. The oldest of these apparitions, the visions at Lourdes, came in 1858, apparently the combination of seer Bernadette Soubirous's personal anguish and the rural anxieties concerning the Crimean War, attempts against the life of Louis Napoleon, and the proclamation of the Second Empire; see Robert Tombs, *France, 1814–1914* (London: Longman, 1996), p. 244. Portugal's Virgin of Fátima appeared in 1917, a year of convergence for the First World War, the Russian Revolution, and the anticlerical strife of the Portuguese Republic (1910–1926). The Virgin's strongly anticommunist message helped set the stage for the corporatist state of António de Oliveira Salazar in 1932. See Tom Gallagher, *Portugal: A Twentieth-Century Interpretation* (Manchester: Manchester University Press, 1983), pp. 31, 94–95. Finally, the background of the 1981 Medjugorje apparition included the crisis of late communism, since the miracle of this Herzegovinian town appealed to Catholic Croats rather than Orthodox Serbs. Moreover, it involved a last-ditch effort by Yugoslavia's Franciscan order to prevent their parishes' takeover by the diocesan church; the Virgin there has spoken in favor of the Franciscans, and the bishop of Mostar, appointed by Rome to investigate the miracle's authenticity, "stacked the commission with known skeptics." Regarding the historical context of the Medjugorje miracle, see Sabrina Petra Ramet, *Balkan Babel: The Disintegration of Yugoslavia from the Death of Tito to Ethnic War* (Boulder: Westview Press, 1996), pp. 156–157.

49. Regarding the Tzeltal uprising, see Bricker, 55–69; Robert Wasserstrom, *Class and Society in Central Chiapas* (Berkeley: University of California Press, 1983), pp. 71–87; and Kevin Gosner, *Soldiers of the Virgin: The Moral Economy of a Colonial Maya Rebellion* (Tucson: University of Arizona Press, 1992), pp. 106–121. In similar cases outside of Latin America, the teachings of inspired prophets often laid the groundwork

for rebellion; see Michael Adas, *Prophets of Rebellion: Millenarian Protest Movements Against the European Colonial Order* (Chapel Hill: University of North Carolina Press, 1979), pp. 92–121.

50. For the most recent studies of the religious-based community uprising of Tomóchic, see Vanderwood, 1998. See also Jesús Vargas Valdez, ed., *Tomóchic: La revolución adelantada* (Ciudad Juárez: Universidad Autónoma de Chihuahua, 1994), 2 vols.

51. Ralph della Cava, *Miracle at Joaseiro* (New York: Columbia University Press, 1970).

52. On the career of Antonio the Counselor, see Euclides da Cunha, *Rebellion in the Backlands,* trans. Samuel Putnam (Chicago: University of Chicago Press, 1957); and Robert M. Levine, *Vale of Tears: Revisiting the Canudos Massacre in Northeastern Brazil, 1893–1897* (Berkeley: University of California Press, 1992). Regarding José Maria, see Todd A. Diacon, *Millenarian Vision, Capitalist Reality: Brazil's Contestado Rebellion, 1910–1916* (Durham, N.C.: Duke University Press, 1991).

53. AHAY, DO r. 105, February 17, 1838.

54. Dumond and Dumond, *Demography,* 389–390.

55. AHAY, DO r. 107, November 10, 1842.

56. AHAY, DO r. 101, October 14, 1836.

57. AHAY, DO 19, December 19, 1836.

58. AHAY, DO 108, December 17, 1844.

59. Anthony F. C. Wallace, *Religion: An Anthropological View* (New York: Random House, 1966), pp. 86–96.

60. On the h-men, see Redfield and Villa Rojas, 74–77; Farriss, 317; Bartolomé, 219–238.

61. John A. Grim, *The Shaman: Patterns of Siberian and Ojibway Healing* (Norman: University of Oklahoma Press, 1983), pp. 3–32.

62. Redfield, *The Folk Culture of Yucatan,* 68–71.

63. AHAY, DO r. 94, July 11, 1815.

64. Silverblatt, *Moon, Sun, and Witches;* for a similar reading on the Yucatec Maya case, see Inga Clendinnen, "Yucatec Maya Women and the Spanish Conquest: Role and Ritual in Historical Reconstruction," *Journal of Social History* (Spring 1982), pp. 427–442.

65. See Ruth Behar, "Sexual Witchcraft, Colonialism, and Women's Powers: Views from the Mexican Inquisition," *Sexuality and Marriage in Colonial Latin America,* ed. Asunción Lavrin (Lincoln: University of Nebraska Press, 1989), pp. 178–206.

66. Bruce Love and Eduardo Castillo, "Wahil Kol: A Yucatec Maya Agricultural Ceremony," *Estudios de la cultura maya* XV (1984), pp. 251–301; Redfield and Villa Rojas, 127–147. I have had various opportunities to attend the wahil kol in the region of Tecoh and have used my own observations in addition to the ethnographic literature.

67. See Carlos Montemayor, *Rezos sacerdotales mayas,* 2 vols., Colección Letras

Mayas Contemporáneas (Tlahuapan: Instituto Nacional Indigenista/SEDESOL, 1994).
See also Love and Castillo, "Wahil Kol."

68. AHAY, DO r. 94, September 2, 1816.

69. Gerónimo Castillo, "Costumbres de los indios de Yucatán," *Registro Yucateco*
III (1845), p. 291; AHAY, DO r. 94, January 21, 1815; Villa Rojas, 122–125; Farriss, 343–351.

70. Ruz Menéndez, 57–58.

71. CAIHY, LM, AC/AM #16, May 18, 1821, pp. 41–42.

72. AHAY, DO r. 119, August 25, 1845.

73. The remainder trailed off into a highly garbled transcription offering bloodletting (*kikil*) and corn gruel (*kum*) for the benefit of the village (*cacab*). See AHAY, DO
r. 119, August 25, 1845. Compare this with more recent samples of Maya ceremonial
prayers in Montemayor, *Rezos sacerdotales*.

74. "Cultos gentilicios de nuestros indios," in Barbachano, 75–80.

75. Taylor reports a similar decline of anti-idolatry and an increase in theological
optimism in his study of Guadalajara and the archdiocese of Mexico; see *Magistrates
of the Sacred*, 18–19.

76. AGEY, PC, Acuerdos, r. 20, May 18, 1823; May 27, 1823.

77. On Hurtado's ongoing problems with his parishioners/laborers, see AHAY, DO
11, March 7, 1822, and AGNM, BN, XXVIII, 14, May 28, 1832. For additional information
of Hurtado's career, see Chapter 6.

78. AHAY, DO box 11, April 19, 1822; April 23, 1822.

79. On the tax-debt-labor system, see Rugeley, *Yucatán's Maya Peasantry*, 74–78.

80. AHAY, DO box 10, May 5, 1824; May 7, 1824. Presumably they used the Maya
term *San Antonio Abal*.

81. The Jacinto Canek episode is now clearer than ever thanks to a recent publication by Robert W. Patch; see "Culture, Community, and 'Rebellion' in the Yucatec
Maya Uprising of 1761," in Susan Schroeder, ed., *Native Resistance and the Pax Colonial in New Spain* (Lincoln: University of Nebraska Press, 1998), pp. 67–83. See also
Rugeley, "Jacinto Canek revisitado," *Unicornio* 294, November 17, 1966, pp. 3–7.

82. AHAY, DO box 10, May 5, 1824; May 7, 1824.

83. The issue of symbolic reversal as a counterhegemonic act enjoys several noteworthy discussions. Again, see Taussig, *The Devil and Commodity*. Another interesting
study is Paul Diener, "The Tears of St. Anthony: Ritual and Revolution in Eastern
Guatemala," *Latin American Perspectives* 5 (1978), pp. 92–116.

84. Batabs did indeed own santos, but, I would argue, it was the individual santo
that determined prestige and not necessarily the social position of its owner. Here,
too, icon wealth mirrored the larger patterns of wealth.

85. The tendency for drinking to become more egalitarian paralleled changes in
the central Mexico region; see Taylor, 40–41. For an instructive review of theories of
the cultural interpretation of drinking, see Mac Marshall, *Weekend Warriors: Alcohol
in a Micronesian Culture* (Palo Alto: Mayfield Publishing Company, 1979), pp. 99–

III. Unfortunately, little documentation exists for native drinking patterns in villages except for a handful of the usual pejorative comments by creoles. But there is no reason to assume that all or even most drinking among Mayan peasants was communal, as found in the case of the Pan-Tun cult. As I have pointed out, Yucatecan towns and rural villages were fairly awash in aguardiente long before independence.

86. The source on a Sotuta-Yaxcabá rivalry is Baqueiro, vol. 1, pp. 338–339.

87. AGEY, FJ, Civil, XIII, 28, 1842.

88. AGEY, PC, Correspondencia, r. 23, October 31, 1829, p. 49.

89. AHAY, DO box 13, July 18, 1827.

90. It's still there. Locals will be happy to point it out, and will proudly recount the story, whose details vary according to the teller.

91. Norman, 136–137.

92. AHAY, DO r. 107, January 23, 1845.

93. AHAY, DO box 13, July 13, 1827, multiple testimonies.

94. AHAY, DO box 13, August 4, 1827. Nohitzá continued to grow over the next decade, now at the expense of terreno baldío land, which the peasants of Yaxcabá had considered to be rightfully theirs (CAIHY, Decretos, October 17, 1845, pp. 242–245).

95. AHAY, DO box 13, August 7, 1827.

96. AHAY, DO box 13, August 11, 1827; August 12, 1827. In this case, I was fortunate enough to have the Sotutans' own description of their fiesta, from a petition they sent to the bishop. On the semiotics of parades and other public processions, see Beezley, *Judas at the Jockey Club*, 89–124; Leonard, 117–129; and Ryan, 131–153.

97. AHAY, DO box 13, August 11, 1827.

98. AHAY, DO box 17A, November 17, 1835.

99. ANEY, February 26, 1840, pp. 67–70. The hacienda, apparently of modest proportions, cost Pardío a mere fifty pesos. He acquired it from Joaquín Esquivel of Sotuta.

100. See Rugeley, *Yucatán's Maya Peasantry*, 169–171.

101. AHAY, DO r. 110, December 22, 1858, Sotuta.

102. AHAY, DO r. 112, December 17, 1859, Tixkokob.

103. AHAY, DO r. 111, February 22, 1858, Sotuta; r. 128, October 22, 1872, Sotuta; AHAY, DO 46, August 11, 1879, Mérida.

104. Gann, *The Maya Indians of Southern Yucatan*, 40.

105. See Dumond for a chronicle of the Speaking Cross's post-1870 history.

106. CAIHY, XIIV, 57, January 5, 1854, José Eulogio Rosado to José Canuto Vela.

107. AHDN, xi/481.3/3257, February 24, 1851, Bonifacio Novelo to the Santa Cruz.

108. AHAY, DO, March 1, 1866. The statue became a controversial item after his death, as various factions sought to control it.

109. Archivo General de Centroamérica (AGCA), B, 28624, 232, November 28, 1869.

110. AHDN, xi/481.3/3257, March 17, 1851, Pedro Regalado Ek to Manuel Nauat.

III. See "Las memorias inéditas de D. Felipe de la Cámara Zavala," *Diario de Yuca-*

tán, September 9, 1923, p. 6. Zavala's memoir describes a military campaign against Chan Santa Cruz that began in December 1851; on reaching the rebel stronghold, the soldiers discovered that its miraculous crosses were believed to inhabit a large tree, which Zavala immediately ordered to be cut down.

112. AHDN, xi/481.3/3256, April 24, 1851, summary of a report on the testimony of rebels surrendering to the military canton in Tixcacal.

113. As described in Christopher Hill, *The World Turned Upside Down: Radical Ideas During the English Revolution* (New York: Viking Press, 1972).

114. Gann, *The Maya Indians of Southern Yucatan,* 40.

115. Fallon, 101–102; Levine, 124–131.

116. Secretaría de Hacienda y Crédito Público, *Catálogo de construcciones religiosas del estado de Yucatán* (Mexico: Talleres Gráficos de la Nación, 1945), misc. pages; see also Bretos, 16.

117. AHAY, DO r. 98, August 22, 1828.

118. AHAY, DO r. 98, February 11, 1828.

119. AHAY, DO 17A, September 26, 1835.

120. AHAY, DO r. 117, March 10, 1841.

121. AHAY, DO r. 109, May 12, 1846.

122. AHAY, DO r. 111, July 25, 1859, Conkal.

123. APOC, unclassified imprint, *Cuenta de recaudación e inversión de los fondos reunidos para la composición de la parroquia principal de Campeche con motivo de la descarga eléctrica que recibió una de sus torres en septiembre del año próximo pasado* (Campeche: Sociedad Tipográfico, 1887). To rebuild, the cathedral raised some nine hundred dollars from Mexico, Veracruz, Mérida, and primarily from within Campeche itself.

124. AHAY, DO 46, September 3, 1880, Campeche.

125. AGEY, PE 44, Gobernación, 4, 101, May 30, 1841.

126. AHAY, DO r. 110, December 16, 1848.

127. AGEY, PE 168, Jefe Político de Sotuta, November 16, 1867. Information regarding the destruction of the Tihosuco church comes from the testimony of six Mayas who had fled Tihosuco during the Imperial conflict of 1865–1866 and had briefly returned to see what had become of their town.

128. Rugeley, *Yucatán's Maya Peasantry,* 148–149.

129. On the Tepeuano revolt, see Susan M. Deeds, "First-Generation Rebellions in Seventeenth-Century Nueva Vizcaya," in Susan Schroeder, ed., *Native Resistance and the Pax Colonial in New Spain* (Lincoln: University of Nebraska Press, 1998), particularly pp. 8–12. On the Pueblo revolt, see Ramón A. Gutiérrez, *When Jesus Came, the Corn Gods Went Away: Marriage, Sexuality, and Power in New Mexico, 1500–1846* (Stanford: Stanford University Press, 1991), pp. 135–136.

130. Savarino, 138–139.

131. For an introduction to the ideological and stylistic differences between these

two newspapers, see Mark I. Pinsky, "Under Repair, Under Fire," *Quill* (May 1997), pp. 13–17.

132. Observations based on a visit to the fiesta of the Tres Reyes in Tizimín, January 6, 1996.

Notes to Chapter 5

1. Pedro Carrasco, "The Civil-Religious Hierarchy in Mesoamerican Communities: Pre-Spanish Background and Colonial Development," *American Anthropologist* 63 (1961), pp. 483–497; Cancian, *Economics and Prestige* (1965); Evon Z. Vogt, *Zinacantan: A Maya Community in the Highlands of Chiapas* (Cambridge: Harvard University Press, 1969).

2. The most explicit attack on the functionalist reading has been Smith, *The Fiesta System and Economic Change* (New York: Columbia University Press, 1977), pp. 21–33.

3. Billie R. DeWalt, "Changes in the Cargo Systems of Mesoamerica," *Anthropological Quarterly* 48, 2 (1975), pp. 87–105; Jan Rus and Robert Wasserstrom, "Civil-Religious Hierarchies in Central Chiapas: A Critical Perspective," *American Anthropologist* 7, 3 (1980), pp. 466–478; John D. Early, "Some Ethnographic Implications of an Ethnohistorical Perspective on the Civil-Religious Hierarchy Among the Highland Maya," *Ethnohistory* 30, 4 (1983), pp. 185–202; John K. Chance and William B. Taylor, "Cofradías and Cargos: An Historical Perspective on the Mesoamerican Civil-Religious Hierarchy," *American Anthropologist* 12, 1 (1985), pp. 1–26; Brad R. Huber, "The Reinterpretation and Elaboration of Fiestas in the Sierra Norte de Puebla, Mexico," *Ethnology* 62, 4 (1987), pp. 281–296; John M. Watanabe, *Maya Saints & Souls in a Changing World* (Austin: University of Texas Press, 1992), especially Chapter 5; and Dagmar Bachtloff, "La formación de una sociedad intercultural: Las cofradías en el Michoacán colonial," *Historia mexicana* 43, 2 (1993), pp. 251–263.

4. For this perspective I am indebted to William Roseberry, whose *Anthropologies and Histories: Essays in Culture, History, and Political Economy* (New Brunswick, NJ: Rutgers University Press, 1989) repeatedly challenges the notion of "pure" peasantries, communities, institutions, and modes of production.

5. Genny Mercedes Negroe Sierra, "La cofradía de Yucatán en el siglo XVIII" (thesis, Universidad Autónoma de Yucatán, 1984), p. 20.

6. Literature on Yucatecan cofradías offers several intriguing examples. First, Robert Patch's "Una cofradía y su estancia en el siglo XVIII, notas de investigación" (*Boletín E.C.A.U.D.Y.*, 8, 1981, pp. 56–66) examines the accounts of the cofradía Purísima Concepción de Nuestra Señora la Virgen María, a brotherhood located in Euán, eighteen miles east of Mérida. Second, Negroe Sierra (1984) studies these institutions in Hecelchakán and Lerma, both near Campeche. Third, Farriss's *Maya Society* studies cofradía properties in the broad sweep of Yucatecan history, culminating in the expropriation of cofradía properties in the late colonial period. Finally, Grant D. Jones

analyzes modified cofradía activity among Yucatecan refugees in Belize in the 1860s; see "Symbolic Dramas of Ethnic Stratification: The Yucatecan Fiesta System on a Colonial Frontier," *University of Oklahoma Papers in Anthropology* 22 (1981), pp. 131–155.

7. Negroe Sierra, 23–24.

8. Negroe Sierra, 27, 40–54, 55–58.

9. Patch, "Una cofradía," 64; Negroe Sierra, 22.

10. Negroe Sierra, 36–40.

11. Patch, "Una cofradía," 58–59; Negroe Sierra, 36–40.

12. The fondo de cofradías still held numerous mortgages at this time. See AGEY, Fondo Municipios (FM), Ticul, box 7 (252), Legajo 9, exp. 6, "Capitales impuestos manifestados por sus propietarios administradores." This document apparently dates from the period 1856–1859.

13. Farriss, 362–366.

14. AGEY, PE, Correspondencia, I, August 18, 1823. Telá's liquid capital at that moment stood at 542 pesos, 7 reales.

15. On Baca and Tekantó, see ANEY, January 20, 1814, pp. 25–26; on Teya, see ANEY, November 3, 1846, pp. 544–545.

16. Farriss, 360–377; Molina Solís, C, I, 60–61; and Robert Patch, *Maya and Spaniard in Colonial Yucatán, 1648–1812* (Stanford: Stanford University Press, 1993), pp. 187–188. Patch argues that the elimination of the cofradías was less a land grab than an attempt to eliminate an institution long associated with abuses and manipulations.

17. ANEY, March 4, 1846, 180–182.

18. AHAY, DO r. 96, October 1, 1821. Manzanilla oversaw the liquidation of the cofradías Kuchel, Cumpich, Canchakan, and Oxholom between 1816 and 1819.

19. AGEY, PC, Acuerdos, r. 20, March 15, 1824, p. 78.

20. AGEY, PC, Acuerdos, r. 20, December 18, 1823, p. 53.

21. Bartolomé, 101.

22. Taylor, *Magistrates of the Sacred,* 322.

23. AHAY, DO r. 110, December 17, 1856, Hoctún.

24. ANEY, February 19, 1816, pp. 54–57. Sacalaca itself was not a cabecera. Brito was probably the cura of Ichmul, although it is not clear when this would have been.

25. Baeza's ongoing concern for financing the village fiesta, a project entirely in keeping with his character and predilection for the old colonial ways, can be found in ANEY, February 23, 1829, p. 226. In *Yucatán's Maya Peasantry* (p. 37) I examine the sale of Yaxleulá to a certain Yaxcabá vecino named José Francisco del Castillo. This same Castillo also purchased liquidated cofradía property of Xiat. In the case of Yaxleulá, however, Baeza provided the mortgage on the stipulation that the 5-percent interest be used "with the object of perpetuating with its returns the memory of the Septenario of the Most Precious Blood of Our Lord Jesus Christ which up till now he has celebrated in that parish, and will celebrate during his life, and afterward his succes-

sors will continue to celebrate . . .," using, among other funds, a twenty-peso annual return on a pious work, and performing seven masses annually for the souls of his parishioners. Baeza had also loaned two hundred pesos to a Francisco Yrigoyen of Mérida on the condition that the repayments be applied to celebrate the same fiesta in the convent of Mérida (ANEY, January 31, 1828, 1).

26. AHAY, DO r. 96, July 16, 1819.

27. Stephens, I, 228–229.

28. AHAY, DO r. 110, September 6, 1848, Abalá.

29. Redfield and Villa Rojas, 153–158; Villa Rojas, 100.

30. Francisco Javier Fernández Repetto, "Resistencia cultural y religiosidad popular: Los gremios en Chuburná de Hidalgo, Mérida, Yucatán" (thesis, Universidad Autónoma "Benito Juárez" de Oaxaca, 1988), p. 30. Chan Kom's gremio of San Diego dates back to at least 1954, when its founder discovered a statue of the santo in a nearby cave (see Elmendorf, 74). A recent newspaper article on the Tixkokob gremio of Cristo de la Misericordia dates it to 1905 (*Diario de Yucatán,* September 16, 1997).

31. Thus far there is little literature on these modern grandchildren of the cofradía. Some descriptive information appears in Richard A. Thompson, *The Winds of Tomorrow: Social Change in a Maya Town* (Chicago: University of Chicago Press, 1974), pp. 45–49; Fernández, 65–157; Ella F. Quintal Avilés, *Fiestas y gremios en el oriente de Yucatán* (Mérida: Consejo Nacional Para la Cultura y las Artes, 1993); and ReCruz, 133–134.

32. See Rugeley, *Yucatán's Maya Peasantry,* 156. The APOC contains numerous such requests; see Correspondencia, box 119, various dates. The Campeche papers allude to at least thirty of these requests, of which about fifteen possess extant paperwork.

33. Savarino, 131–132. My own reading is that Savarino, in his attempt to revise our vision of the Porfirian era, overestimates the benevolence of the later Yucatecan hacienda system. Nevertheless, I am willing to go at least part of the way with him on one point: the change to hacienda culture was more gradual and more voluntary than portrayed in revolutionary writings.

34. Jones, "Symbolic Dramas," 132–139.

35. These cases are all drawn from AHAY, DO. See r. 114, October 14, 1849, Calkiní; r. 114, November 22, 1849, Maní; r. 113, April 21 and 22, 1850, Telchac; r. 115, June 5, 1851, Nolo; r. 115, August 9, 1852, Sotuta; r. 112, November 25, 1859, Mochá; and r. 125, September 11, 1866, Campeche.

36. The argument here against historical essentialism is, I think, identical to the case Cynthia Radding makes for an ongoing evolution, or "ethnogenesis," of the native peoples of Sonora; see Radding, *Wandering Peoples: Colonialism, Ethnic Spaces, and Ecological Frontiers in Northwestern Mexico, 1700–1850* (Durham, N.C.: Duke University Press, 1997), p. 300.

37. Ralph L. Roys, *The Book of Chilam Balam of Chumayel* (Norman: University of Oklahoma Press, 1933), p. 72.

38. Margarita Rosales González, *Oxkutzcab, Yucatán, 1900–1960: Campesinos, cambio agrícola y mercado* (México: Instituto Nacional de Antropología e Historia, 1988), p. 62.

39. Farriss, 333.

40. AHAY, Oficios de Cofradías (OC), June 15, 1861; *Católogo de construcciones religiosas,* 698.

41. AGEY, FJ, January 27, 1854.

42. S. Baring-Gould, *The Lives of the Saints* (Edinburgh: John Grant, 1914, 13 vols.), vol. 6, pp. 188–189.

43. ANEY, November 6, 1760, pp. 596–600.

44. ANEY, March 22, 1831, pp. 102–107. Thanks to Chris Nicholls for calling this reference to my attention.

45. HPS, *El noticioso,* January 12, 1847, 1; ANEY, September 6, 1855, pp. 44–47.

46. The physical description comes from my own observations of the chapel's remains, as well as the description provided in the *Catálogo de construcciones religiosas,* 698–699.

47. On *gallinas ciegas,* "the delight of generations of Yucatecan doves and bats," see Bretos, 22. This author informs us that such upper passageways usually denote eighteenth-century construction.

48. AHAY, OC, January 27, 1852.

49. Fabio (pseudonym), "Fragmentos de un viaje hecho a la Sierra Alta, en enero de 1845, y escrito en el mismo año por Fabio," *Mosaico, Periódico de la Academia de Ciencas y Literatura de Mérida de Yucatán* (Mérida: 1849), p. 102. As with other Maya words, we find varied spellings in the historical documents: *Xocnequej, Xocnequeh, Xocnaceh,* and so forth. *Xocneceh* is the most common.

50. The first known transaction of San Antonio Xocneceh, María del Castillo's sale to her daughter Petrona de Solís, includes an itemized inventory of the hacienda's wealth (see ANEY, November 6, 1760, pp. 596–600). These included: 1,313 branded cattle (5,252 pesos), land and plantings (2,000 pesos), 173 branded horses (865 pesos), 40 mules (600 pesos), vaquero debts (515 pesos), 190 becerros (380 pesos), 6 burros (180 pesos), 247 colmenas (123 pesos), 20 foals (50 pesos), 30 sheep (16 pesos), and 1 newborn mule (7 pesos). Rounding off the stray reales, its assets totaled 9,989 pesos.

51. Description of the house comes from the detailed inventory of 1898; see ANEY, Protocolos de Ticul, January 15, 1898, pp. 1–10.

52. Several pieces of evidence suggests this. Irwin Press, while gathering information on the region in 1964 when the property was totally abandoned, was informed that it had been a sugar ingenio. In addition, the Sierra Alta was a major sugar producer in the early national period. Finally, the extant ruins include what appears to have been a furnace with a Jamaica train for cooking sugar. See AHAY, Capellanías, box 5, exp. 27, June 16, 1843; AHAY, CC box 35, June 8, 1845; and Press, 28.

53. On the paucity of early regional markets, see Farriss, 152–158.

54. The other cofradía in question was Hool, in southern Campeche; see AHAY, CC box 35, May 16, 1842. Information on early national markets of the Sierra Alta comes from AGEY, PC, Acuerdos, r. 20, February 28, 1824, pp. 73–74.

55. Honey did not factor into the equation, since wax production meant more frequent harvesting of the hive, which in turn reduced honey yield.

56. Negroe Sierra, "La cofradía de Yucatán," 102; AHAY, CF box 5, November 16, 1846.

57. AHAY, CF box 5, November 16, 1846.

58. AHAY, "Libro en que se toma razón de los autos de aprobación de cuentas de fábrica, cuentas decimales y obras pías de las parroquias del obispado, 1827–1855."

59. AHAY, OC, January 18, 1835; January 14, 1842; "Libro en que se toma razón," passim.

60. ANEY, September 9, 1828, p. 107 (found among 1841 documents); December 14, 1836, pp. 101–102 (in 1842 documents); May 22, 1841, pp. 97–98; November 10, 1837, pp. 454–456.

61. A forthcoming study by Chris Nicholls of Tulane University promises to shed much light on the Pu'uk, or Sierra Alta region, during the late eighteenth and early nineteenth centuries.

62. Woodrow Borah and S. F. Cook, *The Population of Central Mexico in 1548: An Analysis of the Suma de Visitas de Pueblos* (Berkeley: University of California Press, 1960), p. 122.

63. Robert Patch, "Agrarian Changes in Eighteenth-Century Yucatán," *Hispanic American Historical Review* 65, 1 (1985), pp. 21– 49.

64. Dumond and Dumond, eds., *Demography and Parish Affairs in Yucatán* (1982), p. 192; AHAY, VP box 5, exp. 3, 1803.

65. Salvador Rodríguez Losa, ed., *Geografía política de Yucatán. Tomo 1. Censo inédito de 1821, año de la independencia* (Mérida: Universidad Autónoma de Yucatán, 1985), p. 100; José María Regil and Alonso Manuel Peón, *Estadística de Yucatán* (1851), in CAIHY. Of the three censuses—1806, 1821, and 1845—the first is probably the most accurate. It was conducted during the Bourbon colonial days, prior to the time of constitutional upheaval. Moreover, it offers the most detailed breakdown of racial distribution. The 1821 and 1845 censuses are presumably the work of government officials. Although both probably reflect overall contours, the 1845 information probably suffers from underrepresentation, possibly due to the internal migrations and political instabilities of the time.

66. AGEY, PE 40, Censos y Padrones, Pustunich, May 26, 1841.

67. See Rugeley, "Rural Political Violence," 469–496.

68. AHAY, CC box 35, May 26, 1845. These same documents are the basis for the following account.

69. AHAY, OC, October 22, 1844.

70. As nearly as can be determined, these individuals were not peons of the ha-

cienda. There is no correlation between the hacienda census of 1841 and the petition of 1845. See AGEY, PE 40, Censos y Padrones, Pustunich, May 26, 1841.

71. This particular complaint was added by Méndez in his separate letter. See AHAY, CC box 35, June 26, 1845.

72. AHAY, CC box 35, May 26, 1845.

73. AHAY, CC box 35, June 26, 1845.

74. Information on the founding of the Hool cult comes from a visita to Campeche state by Padre Juan Manuel Pasos Gala; see AHAY, DO 45, January 2, 1878, Campeche.

75. On Hool, see APOC, Correspondencia, box 118, April 26, 1855; box 119, December 13, 1860; box 118, October 22, 1865; box 119, November 9, 1893; and box 118, December 12, 1893.

76. AHAY, DO 45, March 24, 1879, Champoton.

77. AHAY, CC, May 16, 1842.

78. AHAY, DO 47, February 3, 1882, Hool. The fiesta's obligatory skyrockets went astray, hitting a keg of gunpowder.

79. We find references to Talavera as *jefe político* in those towns in HPS, *La unión,* April 13, 1837, 1; and *El constitucional,* May 11, 1839, 4, respectively.

80. For an interesting case study in violent peasant reaction to changes in the 1840s, see Arturo Güémez Pineda, "La rebelión de Nohcacab, prefacio inédito de la guerra de castas," *Saastun: Revista de cultura maya* 2 (1997), pp. 51–79.

81. See Rugeley, *Yucatán's Maya Peasantry,* Chapter 6.

82. AHAY, DO r. 115, November 18, 1852, Oxkutzcab.

83. Espinosa originally arranged for himself to act as *"patrón* of the funds" for the cult; see AGEY, RPP #704, July 1857, pp. 69–70. On Espinosa's loan to himself, see AGEY, RPP #780, October 16, 1855, p. 8. Espinosa arranged for a 383 peso loan, mortgaging the hacienda Santa Rita Komak, which he had purchased at auction from the estate of the late Bernardo Cetina.

84. AGEY, FJ (material under reclassification at time of writing), "Lista nominal de los varones, desde la edad de diez y seis hasta la de sesenta años, que viven en las haciendas, sitios y ranchos de la comprensión de los pueblos de este partido." The census lists only seventeen men, apparently heads of families. My figures on the percentage of decline in resident laborers derive from projections of estimated family size: an average family of four would therefore mean sixty-eight residents, a family of five increases the hypothetical total to eighty-five.

85. ANEY, September 6, 1855, pp. 44–46,

86. See, for example, AHAY, OC, May 8, 1861. However, some of the haciendas that had obtained loans from the cult were completely destroyed.

87. ANEY, August 26, 1853, pp. 67–68.

88. AGEY, FM, Ticul, box 7, v. 8, exp. 17, March 22, 1862; box 9, vol. 12, exp. 13, April 25, 1862. Census figures tend to vary widely, however, even in the same year. The 1862 "Documentos justificativos" reports a mere twenty-nine residents, a figure that

perhaps fails to account for children; see CAIHY, *Documentos interesantes de Yucatán, 1857–1902*, 16.

89. AGEY, FM, Ticul, box 22, v. 34, exp. 29, June 15, 1877.

90. See, for example, AGEY, PE 81, Gobernación, Jefe Político-Ticul, June 23, 1859.

91. AHAY, OC, May 8, 1861, June 15, 1861, July 27, 1861; AGEY, PE 97, Jefe Político-Ticul, April 12, 1863; AGEY, PE 105, Gobernación, April 29, 1865. Thanks to Barbara Angel for calling this last reference to my attention.

92. AHAY, DO r. 113, December 28, 1861.

93. From *El constitucional* 409 (May 22, 1861), found in AGEY, FJ, box 61.

94. On this score I plead to be as guilty as anyone.

95. ANEY, Protocolos de Ticul #5, January 15, 1898, pp. 1–10. Only two of the estate's six servants actually lived at Xocneceh; the others now made their home in Pustunich.

96. AGEY, RPP #684, January 8, 1910, 18.

97. Park Redfield, 31. Cantón supposedly promised the *santa* elaborate new church decorations in exchange for victory in battle.

98. AGEY, FM, Ticul, 14, 18, 4, June 21, 1865. The political prefect of Ticul continued to receive complaints that the cult was suffering from "*entorpecimientos.*"

99. Information on property titles appears in HPS, *Diario oficial,* May 16, 1910, p. 26. Xocneceh was now valued at 15,000 pesos; Santa Rita, property of Banco Peninsular Mexicano, S.A., ran at 30,000 pesos. But the great plantations were valued at 100–600,000 pesos. These figures appeared in *Diario* as a reprint from the *oficina de catastro,* or property register. There are two useful secondary sources on the life of Francisco Cantón. The first is Hernán Menéndez Rodríguez, *Iglesia y poder,* 60, 209–210; the second is Wells and Joseph, 24–27, 33–43.

100. Lourdes Rejón Patrón, *Hacienda Tabi: Un capítulo en la historia de Yucatán* (Mérida: Gobierno del Estado de Yucatán, 1993), p. 53. This comes from the testimony of Nicolás Villareal, who was peon on the estate from 1894 to 1915 (see pp. 94–102).

101. AGEY, RPP #684, January 8, 1910, p. 18. Cantón had contracted a loan of forty thousand pesos from the Vales company.

102. *Diario de Yucatán,* May 12, 1997; interview with Saúl J. Pompeyo Vales, current owner of San Antonio Xocneceh, June 14, 1997.

103. I base these comments on my observations of the festival of San Antonio in 1995 and 1998. The latter was better attended, perhaps because it fell on a Saturday.

104. *Catálogo de construcciones religiosas,* 698: "Su estado de conservación es bastante malo."

Notes to Chapter 6

1. Charles A. Hale, *Mexican Liberalism in the Age of Mora, 1821–1853* (New Haven: Yale University Press, 1968). Even Hale's principal protagonist, the urbane intellectual José María Luis Mora, had his own gut hostility to the Catholic Church; see Hale, 297–298.

2. The quest for folk liberalism began with Alan Knight, "El liberalismo mexicano desde la Reforma hasta la Revolución (una interpretación)," *Historia mexicana* 35, 1 (1985), pp. 59–91. A more recent and more fully developed exploration appears in Guy P. Thomson and David G. LaFrance, *Patriotism, Politics, and Popular Liberalism in Nineteenth-Century Mexico: Juan Francisco Lucas and the Puebla Sierra* (Wilmington, Del.: Scholarly Resources, 1998).

3. Landy Elizabeth Santana Rivas, "Protestantismo y sus implicaciones sociales en el campo yucateco" (thesis, Universidad Autónoma de Yucatán, 1987), pp. 43–46.

4. Although isolated cases existed, non-Catholic religions made little headway in the peninsula until after the 1910 Revolution and, more particularly, not until the recent arrival of evangelical sects. No history on this phase of peninsular revolution exists; the principal study of early Protestantism in Mexico, Deborah J. Baldwin's *Protestants and the Mexican Revolution: Missionaries, Ministers, and Social Change* (Urbana: University of Illinois Press, 1990), deals primarily with the north of the country.

5. Timothy Mitchell, *Violence and Piety in Spanish Folklore* (Philadelphia: University of Pennsylvania Press, 1988), pp. 72–73.

6. William J. Callahan, "The Spanish Parish Clergy, 1874–1930," *Catholic Historical Review* 75 (1989), pp. 405–422.

7. On the persecution of priests, see José M. Sánchez, *The Spanish Civil War as a Religious Tragedy* (Notre Dame: University of Notre Dame Press, 1987).

8. See Robert Haskett, " 'Not a Pastor, But a Wolf': Indigenous-Clergy Relations in Early Cuernavaca and Taxco," *The Américas* 50, 3 (1994), pp. 313–314.

9. AGNM, JE 164, May 15, 1855, p. 562. This remark, by General Pedro Ampudia, appears in a request to Mexico City to send whatever available friars to help pacify rural Mayas during the Caste War.

10. Harrington, 261–271; Morrison, 60, 63.

11. See Taylor, *Magistrates of the Sacred,* particularly Chapter 1, on the effect of Bourbon reforms on the parish priest.

12. Waldeck, 48–50.

13. Harrington, 32–35.

14. See, for example, the complaint of Captain Robert Hunston in ANEY, October 23, 1872, pp. 241–244; or of Captain Joel Bonney, in ANEY, June 14, 1832, p. 83.

15. This interpretation appears to have begun with Howard Cline, 599–601, but it has survived in virtually all subsequent publications.

16. The reading of a top-down anticlericalism with but tenuous rural connections recurs in Jean Meyer, *La cristiada. 2: El conflicto entre la iglesia y el estado, 1926–1929* (México: Siglo XXI, 1973); see, for example, the analysis on pp. 206–211.

17. On the history of Imán, see Rugeley, "En busca de Santiago Imán, el caudillo de Tizimín," parts 1 and 2, *Unicornio* 408 (February 21, 1999), pp. 3–9; and 409 (February 28, 1999), pp. 3–9.

18. AGNM, BN, 19, 2, February 2–6, 1851.

19. Not too many priests were rags-to-riches cases like Raymundo Pérez, although some did begin at the middle to lower-middle strata of urban society. See Fallon, 80–85.

20. Sinkin, 45–46, cites exclusion from and conflicts with the church as a key ingredient in the formation of Juárez-era liberalism.

21. AB, Records 29, February 4, 1849, pp. 227–229.

22. AGEY, PE 4, Beneficiencia, 1, 2, February 25, 1831.

23. See APOC, "Consiertos y casamientos de la montaña del Sur en el año de 1863," as well as accompanying volumes for 1865, 1867, and 1884 (the latter found in Defunciones, box 103).

24. Haskett, 313–314.

25. AHAY, DO r. 96, September 11, 1818, Chikindzonot Escalante to Estévez y Ugarte.

26. See Rugeley, *Yucatán's Maya Peasantry,* 164–171.

27. "El hijo de la yegua," in Andrade and Máas Collí, vol. 1, pp. 414–425.

28. "Dámaso y el demonio," in Peniche Barrera, 20–22.

29. "X-waay chiva," in Tec Chi, 40–44.

30. "The Boy who Killed the Priest," in Parson (1932), pp. 356–357.

31. "El hombre de pene pequeño," in Andrade and Máas Collí, vol. 1, pp. 472–481.

32. Again, see Tombs, 243–244.

33. Concerning popular resentments against priests, I am indebted to Vanderwood, 187–189.

34. A tip of the historical hat to the incomparable Sones Jarochos for their rendition of "La paloma."

35. Postimperial Brazil's two great popular religious phenomena—Antonio the Counselor and Father Cicero—both emerged in the poor northeast. See Chapter 4, note 49.

36. AGNM, BN, XXXV, 5, misc. dates, 1824.

37. AGEY, PE 44, Gobernación, IV, 101, March 30, 1841.

38. HPS, *El mus, periódico satírico de política y costumbres,* 1, 1861. García authored the journal single-handedly.

39. Inga Clendinnen, *Ambivalent Conquests: Maya and Spaniard in Yucatan, 1517–1570* (Cambridge: Cambridge University Press, 1987), pp. 72–92.

40. T. G. Powell makes much the same point in "Priests and Peasants in Central Mexico: Social Conflict During 'La Reforma,'" *Hispanic American Historical Review* 57, 2 (1977), pp. 296–313. Powell's treatment is, I think, a bit overdrawn, as the papers of the National Archives' Bienes Nacionales tend to overemphasize the negative.

41. AGNM, BN, VII, 285, September 22, 1851.

42. AGNM, BN, V, 22, July 21, 1841.

43. AHAY, DO r. 107, August 8, 1843.

44. AGNM, BN, XV, 30, July 16, 1855; July 28,1855; and August 14, 1855.

45. See Rugeley, "Rural Political Violence," 469–496.

46. The only other priest proscribed on the broadside—Bishop Estévez y Ugarte—was also a peninsular Spaniard; see University of Texas Nettie Lee Benson Collection (TEX), "María de Arrigunaga Coello Archive," #54, 1822.

47. Hurtado's inabilities with Maya were revealed during the investigation of misconduct of a fellow priest in Nunkiní; see AGNM, BN, XXVIII, 14, May 28, 1832.

48. Rejón Patrón, 113.

49. See ANEY, May 9, 1845, pp. 125–126; October 1, 1845, pp. 57–60.

50. AHAY, DO box 11, March 27, 1822; April 20, 1822.

51. Stephens, vol. 2, p. 114.

52. AGNM, BN, XXXV, 8, July 28, 1824; September 7, 1824; September 23, 1824; and November 14,1824.

53. AGEY, FJ-Penal, box 30, February 4, 1858.

54. AHAY, DO r. 96, April 27, 1815.

55. AHAY, DO r. 96, February 17, 1816. For further information on the career of Miguel Cabañas, see Rugeley, *Yucatán's Maya Peasantry,* 28–29.

56. AGNM, BN, VIII, 31, April 2, 1842; April 26, 1842.

57. AHAY, DO r. 96, December 17, 1815.

58. AHAY, CC, January 18, 1814.

59. AHAY, DO box 12, November 19, 1825.

60. I first heard this story when traveling with Nelson Reed through Quintana Roo in July 1995. It seems to be a well-entrenched part of local lore.

61. Reed, 24.

62. For more on the problem of priest-related sexual indiscretions, see Taylor, *Magistrates of the Sacred,* 185–189; and Haskett, 318–322.

63. AGEY, PE 19, Gobernación, April 9, 1845.

64. AGNM, BN, IX, 8, May 1839.

65. AGNM, BN, XV, 28, December 8, 1856.

66. AHAY, DO 17A, September 15, 1835.

67. See Menéndez Rodríguez, 66–72, 214–227. Menéndez points in particular to the repeated defeated campaigns of Norberto Domínguez and to the eventual designation of an "outsider" bishop, Martin Trischler, during the late Porfiriato, as critical cases of intrainstitutional fissures.

68. Rugeley, *Yucatán's Maya Peasantry,* 78–84.

69. AHAY, DO r. 101, September 13, 1836; and September 20, 1836.

70. AGNM, BN, XIII, 15, misc. dates, 1827.

71. AHAY, DO r. 106, April 12, 1842.

72. Taylor, *Magistrates of the Sacred,* 461–473.

73. Rugeley, *Yucatán's Maya Peasantry,* 33–60.

74. Regarding the mobilizations of 1907–1915, see Wells and Joseph, particularly Chapters 8 and 9.

75. AHAY, DO box 10, May 17, 1824; May 18, 1824; May 21, 1824; May 22, 1824.

76. Richard E. Greenleaf, "The Mexican Inquisition and the Enlightenment, 1763–1805," *New Mexico Historical Review* 11, 3 (1966), pp. 181–196.

77. Fallon, 1979.

78. AHAY, DO r. 118, October 17, 1843; October 24, 1843; October 31, 1843; and January 16, 1844.

79. AHAY, DO r. 105, July 4, 1839.

80. AGEY, PE 51, Gobernación, Jefe Político Accidental, Tizimín, April 16, 1843.

81. The source on this case is the massive trial transcript found in AGNM, BN, XX, 10, misc. dates, 1830.

82. Stephanie Jo Smith, "A Reconstruction of Early Nineteenth-Century Valladolid, Mexico" (thesis, University of Oklahoma, 1997), pp. 26–28.

83. AGNM, BN, IX, 24, January 18, 1839 and September 2, 1839; IX, 22, April 16, 1839, May 22, 1839, May 27, 1839, and July 3, 1839.

84. AHAY, DO r. 114, December 26, 1849.

85. The papers of this interesting case are reprinted under the title "Causa célebre: Los asesinos del R. P. Loría," in HPS, *Miscelánea instructiva y amena* 1 (January 10, 1849), pp. 87–104.

86. Regarding problems of the rural church in the 1840s, see Rugeley, *Yucatán's Maya Peasantry,* 134–141.

87. Ibid.

88. Waldeck, 46.

89. Clendinnen, *Ambivalent Conquests,* 82–83.

90. Rugeley, *Yucatán's Maya Peasantry,* 167–169.

91. See Rugeley, *Yucatán's Maya Peasantry,* 168–169, for a discussion of these events.

92. As Jorge Castañeda notes, the major political ideologies that have defined Latin America since independence—liberal constitutionalism, communism, neoliberalism—have all been superimpositions taken from other societies and cultures. See Castañeda, *Utopia Unarmed: The Latin American Left After the Cold War* (New York: Alfred A. Knopf, 1993), pp. 179–180.

93. HPS, *Ley de amor,* 1, 9, May 1, 1876, pp. 67–69, "Allan Kardec"; see also, Allan Kardec, *Caracteres de la revelación espírita* (Mérida: Librería Meridana de Cantón, 1874), in CAIHY, Impresos, XXVII, 4, 1874.

94. HPS, *Ley de amor,* 1, 12, June 15, 1876, pp. 94–95, "Miscelánea." This particular bit of information came from a Guanajuato reader who felt that he had to acknowledge Guadalajara's primacy.

95. HPS, *Ley de amor,* 1, 1, January 1, 1876, p. 8.

96. HPS, *Ley de amor,* 1, 8, April 15, 1876, pp. 63–64.

97. HPS, *Ley de amor,* 1, 1, January 1, 1876, "Introduction," 5–6.

98. Attacking Kardec was Abate Guame, *El espiritismo condenado y reprobado según la doctrina católica* (Mérida: J. D. Espinosa e Hijos, 1874). A defense of the beliefs

came from Enrique Manera, *La verdad ante todo: Carta dirigida al presbítero D. Felix Sardá y Salvany por un neofito del espiritismo* (Mérida: Edición del Círculo Espirita Meridano, 1874).

99. Special thanks to Michel Antochiw for clarifying this bit of genealogy.

100. HPS, *Ley de amor,* III, 10, May 19, 1878, pp. 77–80, "Necrología: J. Jacinto Cuevas."

101. HPS, *Ley de amor,* III, 9, May 4, 1878, p. 72; HPS, *Razón del pueblo* 28, January 18, 1875.

102. "Foucher, Manuel," in Francisco J. Santamaría, *Semblanzas tabasqueñas* (Villahermosa, Tabasco: Universidad Juárez Autónoma de Tabasco, 1995, orig. 1946), pp. 69–71; HPS, *Ley de amor,* I, 8, April 15, 1876, pp. 63–64, "Miscelánea."

103. HPS, *Ley de amor,* I, 12, June 15, 1876, pp. 94–95, "Miscelánea."

104. There is another possible interpretation: that the early writers and pamphleteers were a clique of men who downplayed or overlooked female contributions.

105. HPS, *Ley de amor,* I, 12, June 15, 1876, pp. 94–95, "Miscelánea."

106. HPS, *Ley de amor,* I, 7, April 1, 1876, p. 56, "Miscelánea."

107. HPS, *Ley de amor,* I, 11, June 1, 1876, pp. 86–88, "Miscelánea."

108. HPS, *Ley de amor,* I, 8, April 15, 1876, pp. 63–64, "Miscelánea."

109. HPS, *Ley de amor,* I, 9, May 1, 1876, pp. 70–71, "Los enviados."

110. Key doctrinal essays from *Ley de amor* include "Las expiaciones terrestres" (I, 1, January 1, 1876, pp. 5–6); "Pluralidad de las existencias del alma" (I, 5, March 1, 1876, pp. 31–32); "Pluralidad de las existencias del alma. II" (I, 6, March 15, 1876, pp. 41–43); "El pecado original" (I, 7, April 1, 1876, pp. 49–51); and "Olvido del pasado" (I, 8, April 15, 1876, pp. 57–58).

111. On Rodulfo Cantón's work with the railroads, see AGEY, PE 212, July 16, 1880. He worked for the "Empresa del ferrocarril de Mérida a Peto" and also played a major hand in the construction of the Mérida-Progreso track.

112. AHAY, DO 47, January 1887, Campeche. Padre José Bacilio López's theory was that an incorrectly performed baptismal ceremony had allowed the devil to enter the girl.

113. Vanderwood, 178–184, 299–302.

114. See HPS, *Teosofía en Yucatán;* numbers from the years 1925–1930 survive.

115. See HPS, *Revista Rosacruz;* surviving numbers cover the years 1940–1945. Though homegrown Rosecrucian literature has yet to turn up, we know that there was a Centro Fraternidad Rosacruz in downtown Mérida.

116. AGNM, BN, 4, 14, September 26, 1859, other dates.

117. AGEY, PE 208, G, April 8, 1879, Mérida. "El sillón es una notable obra de artista, muy hábil, hecho de la preciosa madera de bálsamo, hermosamente grabado en flores, frutas, etc., y está muy bien conservado." Museo directo Juan Peón Contreras bought it for twenty-five pesos, a steal.

118. Santana Rivas, 43–46.

119. Research into evangelical conversion in the Yucatán peninsula is still limited. Among others, see Antonio Higuera Bonfil, "Los testigos de Jehová en la frontera México-Belice," paper presented at the twentieth international congress of the Latin American Studies Association, Guadalajara, Mexico, April 18, 1997. The Guatemalan case has thus far received a far more thorough examination. Perhaps the two most critical works are Sheldon Annis, *God and Production in a Guatemalan Town* (Austin: University of Texas Press, 1987), and David Stoll, *Between Two Armies in the Ixil Towns of Guatemala* (New York: Columbia University Press, 1993), especially Chapter 6. Both stress economic polarization within communities, an increasingly well-developed infrastructure of foreign missionary service, and the peasants' need to distance themselves from the Catholic activists believed to be in league with revolutionaries. Stoll, however, lays greater stress on community expectations raised by, though not necessarily satisfied through, the Catholic Action movement.

120. HPS, *Diario de Yucatán,* March 6, 1994.

121. The work of two scholars stand out here. First, Ivan Vallardo Fajardo has published a number of studies on conversion in Sudzal, a small community near Izamal. See Vallardo, "Cambios en la religiosidad popular"; and "En busca de la esperanza," 165–185. Second, José Juan Cervera Fernández's study of Uayma, while primarily an analysis of the community's political factionalism, contains useful information linking political alliances to different religions; see Cervera Fernández, "Iglesias no católicas y estructura política: Los campesinos de Uayma, Yucatán" (thesis, Universidad Autónoma de Yucatán, 1991).

122. Menéndez Rodríguez, 307–311, briefly reviews some of the social and economic ideas of the deeply conservative Martin Trischler; Chapter 3 of Savarino also examines the reconstruction of the Yucatecan church under Crescencio Carrillo y Ancona and Martin Trischler y Córdova.

123. On the genesis of these anticlerical clubs, see James D. Cockcroft, *Intellectual Precursors of the Mexican Revolution, 1900–1913* (Austin: University of Texas Press, 1968), pp. 91–110. Arriaga's revived liberalism, the direct forerunner of the Madero movement, came about largely in reaction to open clerical violations of the 1857 constitution, particularly in regard to the prohibitions on Catholic schools and the wearing of sacerdotal vestments in public.

124. On the antifanaticism campaigns of Alvarado, see Ramón D. Chacón, "Salvador Alvarado and the Roman Catholic Church: Church-State Relations in Revolutionary Yucatán, 1914–1918," *Journal of Church and State* 27, 2 (1985), pp. 245–266; a more detailed if distinctly anti-Alvarado history appears in Savarino, 358–367.

Notes to Chapter 7

1. David Rock, *Authoritarian Argentina: The Nationalist Movement, Its History and Its Impact* (Berkeley: University of California Press, 1993), pp. 29–30.

2. Western Mexico seems to have been particularly prone to postrevolutionary conflicts between the emerging national state and local religious customs. See González, Chapter 5; and Marjorie Becker, *Setting the Virgin on Fire: Lázaro Cárdenas, Michoacán Peasants, and the Redemption of the Mexican Revolution* (Berkeley: University of California Press, 1995).

3. CAIHY, Impresos, LV, 3, 1896, "Primera carta pastoral que dirige el primer obispo de Campeche al clero y pueblo de su diócesis."

4. Gil y Saenz, xiii. Bishop Gala had supported the separation of Tabasco as early as 1864, but the process was delayed by the Reform War and subsequent French invasion.

5. William T. Sanders, "The Cultural Ecology of the Lowland Maya: A Reevaluation," in T. Patrick Culbert, ed., *The Classic Maya Collapse* (Albuquerque: University of New Mexico Press, 1973), pp. 325–365.

6. See Jones, *Maya Resistance* (1989), particularly Chapters 5 and 6. A more complete analysis of the Petén conquest appears in Jones's recent *The Conquest of the Last Maya Kingdom* (Stanford: Stanford University Press, 1998).

7. Jones, *Maya Resistance* (1989), pp. 269–270; and Linda C. Marcus, "English Influence on Belize and the Petén Region of Northern Guatemala, 1630 to 1763" (diss., Southern Methodist University, 1990), pp. 107–112.

8. Norman B. Schwartz, *Forest Society: A Social History of Petén, Guatemala* (Philadelphia: University of Pennsylvania Press, 1990), pp. 46–50; Jones, *Conquest*, 387–397.

9. José María Soza, *Pequeña monografía del departamento del Petén* (Guatemala: Ministerio de Educación Pública, 1957), pp. 115–117. There are no material remnants of a fortress here, and it would have been easy to swim to shore.

10. Schwartz, 65–66.

11. Schwartz, 37.

12. Schwartz, 39.

13. The 2,500–3,500 head of the state-owned hacienda San Felipe was probably exceptional; see Schwartz, 57–58. Observers from the 1870s reported much smaller herds.

14. Schwartz, 58.

15. Lacandón itself is extremely close to Yucatec Maya. Jan de Vos maintains that the people now known as Lacandón—the tunic-clad forest people famous for being among the most elusive in Mesoamerica—do not represent the historical Lacandones, who were wiped out in the seventeenth century through relocations, epidemic disease, and political reorganizations. Rather, de Vos argues, the current Lacandones are an amalgam of Caribs and Yucatec Mayas. See de Vos, *La paz de Dios y del Rey: La conquista de la Selva Lacandona (1524–1821)* (México: Fondo de Cultura Económica, 1980), pp. 212–231.

16. Schwartz, 43.

17. AGNM, BN, 48, 3, February 19, 1859, Vidaurre to Guerra; this letter reviews past tithe-collection policy.

18. AHAY, CC 34 1820, petition of the república of San Andrés.

19. The principal work on Maya refugees in the Petén is Grant D. Jones, "Levels of Settlement Alliance Among the San Pedro Maya of Western Belize and Eastern Petén, 1857–1936," in Grant D. Jones, ed., *Anthropology and History in Yucatán* (Austin: University of Texas Press, 1977), pp. 139–190; and Rugeley, "The Caste War in Guatemala," *Saastun: Revista de la cultura Maya,* 3 (1998), pp. 67–96. On the *repúblicas* in Yucatán, see Rugeley, "Maya Elites of the Nineteenth Century," 42, 1 (1995), pp. 477–493; and Restall, *The Maya World.* A handful of scattered papers regarding the Petén repúblicas are to be found in the Archivo General de Centroamérica, but the quantity in no way approaches that of the Yucatecan collections.

20. Schwartz, 51.

21. AHAY, DO 35, January 1859, Flores, Barreiro to Guerra.

22. On the life of Méndez, see Soza, 125–128; and Julián A. Pinelo, "Hombres notables del Petén: El Coronel Modesto Méndez," *Petén Itzá,* January 1943, p. 15; found in the Hemeroteca of AGCA.

23. Franz Blom, "Coronel Modesto Méndez," *Antropología e historia de Guatemala* 7, 2 (1955), pp. 3–16. This article includes a partial reproduction of Méndez's original report on Tikal. See also Ernesto Schaeffer, "El corregidor del Petén: Coronel Modesto Méndez y el encargado de negocios de Prusia von Hesse," *Antropología e historia de Guatemala* 3, 7 (1951), pp. 55–60.

24. See Michel Antochiw, "Los tratados de paz de Chichanhá," *Saastun: Revista de la cultura maya* 2 (1997), pp. 83–112.

25. The description of Méndez's personality and physical stature come from Arthur Morelet, *Travels in Central America, Including Accounts of Some Regions Unexplored Since the Conquest,* trans. M. F. Squier (New York: Leypoldt, Holt & Williams, 1871), p. 201.

26. AGCA, B, 28577, 77, February 10, 1859, report of Colonel Joaquín Saenz.

27. HPS, *Museo yucateco,* "Documentos inéditos," II, 1841, pp. 19–22, a reproduction of the letter of the Guatemalan bishop José de Bustamente to Agustín Estévez y Ugarte, dated March 27, 1817.

28. See "El documento Canec: Documentos relativos a los caciques José Pablo Canec y Francisco Exquin-Canec, señores que fueron del Petén, encontrados en el Archivo General del Gobierno de Guatemala, por J. J. Joaquín Pardo, Director de dicho Archivo," *Maya Studies* 3 (1936), pp. 294–295. I encountered this journal in the book collection of the CAIHY; the date of the original document is February 20, 1705.

29. AHAY, CC 34, 1820, petition of the república of San Andrés.

30. See the report of *visitador* Domingo Fajardo in AHAY, AT 157, "Disposición del cura de Hecelchakán sobre lo que ha gestionado y sobre indemnización por suspensión en la visita," October 15, 1824. But as David McCreery has argued, cofradía decline may in reality have been a reorientation toward Indian-controlled associations, with most of the financial burdens assumed by a voluntary *patrón* or *mayordomo;* see McCreery, 135–138.

31. AHAY, CC exp. 128, March 13, 1806, application of Juan Xavier Mendoza; see also Rugeley, *Yucatán's Maya Peasantry,* 110–111.

32. Schwartz, 42, 46–50.

33. HPS, *Museo yucateco,* "Documentos inéditos," Bustamente to Estévez y Ugarte, 1817.

34. AHAY, AT r. 157, "Disposición," September 15, 1824.

35. AGNM, JE 23, June 7, 1822, p. 80.

36. Morelet, 211–212.

37. For analyses of how the Caste War affected the Petén, see Grant D. Jones, "Levels of Settlement Alliance," pp. 139–189; and Rugeley, "The Caste War in Guatemala," 67–96.

38. On the important relationship between the parish-level church and the Carrera state, see Douglas Creed Sullivan-González, "Piety, Power, and Politics: The Role of Religion in the Formation of the Guatemalan Nation-State, 1839–1871," (diss., University of Texas at Austin, 1994).

39. Residents of Flores had put up with Salazar's poor health for at least a decade before his eventual death; see AHAY, DO 29, March 28, 1846, Flores.

40. AHAY, DO r. 110, September 9, 1856, Flores, Méndez to Guerra.

41. AHAY, DO 34, 29 January 1855, Usumacinta.

42. As testified by their surviving correspondence in AHAY, Decretos y Oficios.

43. AHAY, DO r. 110, March 28, 1858, Tenabo, Juan Irenea Milán to Guerra.

44. AGCA, B, 28594, 1, April 5, 1859.

45. Barreiro was assistant to the *sacristán mayor* of the cathedral; see AGNM, JE 183, April 30, 1856, p. 174.

46. ANEY, August 8, 1851, pp. 107–109. This interesting document, a *poder general,* or power of attorney, outlines Barreiro's immediate family tree.

47. AHAY, DO r. 114, October 23, 1850, Mérida, Amado Belizario Barreiro to Vicario Simón Escolástico Ocorrio.

48. On the Bacalar appointment, see AHAY, DO r. 116, April 14, 1853; r. 117, May 11, 1853; r. 116, July 20, 1853. At about this same time, Barreiro also turns up momentarily as a witness to a public row in Mérida; see AGEY, FJ-Penal, box 7, January 12, 1855, Mérida.

49. On the capellanía, see CAIHY, LM, AC/AM #32, April 3, 1854.

50. AGEY, FM, Ticul, 3, 11, 3, 1856. Barreiro owned a debt of 1,000 pesos on Peón's hacienda Yokut, near Ticul. He also held slightly over 50 percent of a 2,075 pesos mortgage on the hacienda Yaxhá, a property near Muna owned by Paulino González.

51. AHAY, DO r. 114, October 23, 1850, Mérida, Amado Belizario Barreiro to Simón Escolástico Ocorrio; AGEY, Fondos Municipio, Ticul, caja 7 (252), Legajo 9, exp. 6, "Capitales impuesos."

52. AGNM, BN, 48, 3, February 19, 1859.

53. Barreiro's mother and the eventual heir to his property was María Gertrudis Fernández Remedios. To care for her in his absence he appointed none other than Pilar

Canto Sosaya, the prominent attorney who received pilgrims to Izamal in his palatial hom (see Chapter 3). Canto Sosaya was Barreiro's brother-in-law, having married the latter's younger sister Josefina.

54. AHAY, DO box 38, September 15, 1858.

55. Barreiro reported that González had charged two pesos for mass, six reales for baptism.

56. AHAY, DO box 38, September 15, 1858.

57. Ibid.

58. Robert Ricard noted the Indian affinity for confession decades ago in his study of the early colonial church; see Ricard, *The Spiritual Conquest of Mexico: An Essay on the Apostalate and the Evangelizing Methods of the Mendicant Orders in New Spain, 1523–1572* (Berkeley: University of California Press, 1966), pp. 116–122.

59. AHAY, DO box 38, September 15, 1858.

60. Ibid.

61. Ibid.

62. Ibid.

63. AHAY, DO box 38, October 15, 1858, Flores, Barreiro to Guerra.

64. Ibid.

65. Ibid.; January 1859, Flores, Barreiro to Guerra.

66. This particular example comes from Francois Chevalier, *Land and Society in Colonial Mexico: The Great Hacienda,* trans. Alvin Eustis (Berkeley: University of California Press, 1963), pp. 222–226.

67. AHAY, DO r. III, February 22, 1859, Flores, Hoil to Guerra. Regarding the Yucatecan folklore motif of the evil Negro, see "Las tres muchachas," in Andrade and Máas Collí, vol. I, pp. 349–379; the story draws upon the motif of a wicked black woman who wrongfully assumes the place of a princess, only to be burned in the end. "The Bad Negress" also appears in Paredes (p. 95), collected from Jalisco in 1947; Paredes traces the motif to Germany.

68. AHAY, DO box 38, October 15, 1858, Flores, Barreiro to Guerra.

69. Ibid.

70. AHAY, DO III, October 15, 1858, Flores, Hoil to Guerra.

71. AHAY, DO box 35, January 1859, Flores, Barriero to Guerra.

72. One thinks first and foremost of George M. Foster's "image of the limited good"; see Foster, *Tzintzuntzan,* 123-124. But Oscar Lewis has perhaps been more vivid in his capturing the real acrimony of intravillage conflicts; see *Pedro Martínez: A Mexican Peasant and His Family* (New York: Vintage Books, 1964). See also Cynthia Nelson's depiction of rival elites in Erongarícuaro, Michoacán, in *The Waiting Village: Social Change in Rural Mexico* (Boston: Little, Brown and Company, 1971), pp. 33–53.

73. This was not the General Dionicio Zapata of Chan Santa Cruz, but rather a former member of the army of Rafael Carrera. See AHAY, DO 35, January 1859, Flores, Barreiro to Guerra.

74. Ibid.

75. As reported by the vicario, "que se cagaban en nuestra corona y en su mitra y que el Diablo había de cargar de nosotros." AHAY, DO box 35, January 1859, Flores, Barreiro to Guerra.

76. AHAY, DO box 35, January 1859, Flores, Barreiro to Guerra.

77. Ibid.

78. Ibid.

79. Ibid.

80. I am thinking of some of its key creole instigators, men such as Augustín Acereto and Antonio Trujeque. See Rugeley, "Rural Political Violence." On the instability associated with caudillo-based politics, see Sinkin, 96; as well as Wells's and Joseph's discussion of Porfirian politics in *Summer of Discontent,* 27–33.

81. Barreiro's lengthy and critical letter of January provides a basic source of events between August and December 1858. The accusations of tithe irregularities first appear in AGNM, BN, 48, 3, February 19, 1859, Vidaurre to Guerra; however, they are substantiated in an item from the same folio, Barreiro's own tithe roster for products such as ducks, turkeys, coffee, chicle, chiles, yucca, watermelons, and melons (August 31, 1858).

82. AGCA, B, 28584, 75, January 24, 1861; in this document, Vidaurre reflects back on policies that he adopted, in concert with the recommendations of Saenz, upon taking office.

83. AGCA, Jefatura Política, Petén, 1873, misc. dates.

84. AGCA, B, 28578, 92, May 29, 1859.

85. AGCA, B, 28579, 240, December 20, 1859.

86. Morelet, 248.

87. AGCA, B, 28579, 171, August 23, 1859.

88. The strange history of José Manuel Pardío is unwritten and poorly documented. Some of the few available facts come from Edmundo Bolio, *Diccionario histórico, geográfico y biográfico de Yucatán* (México, D.F.: I.C.D., 1944); Bolio's sources are unknown. I have been unable to find reference to the event in the Yucatecan archives. On the sale of his properties, see the auction inventories of AGEY, FJ, Civil, 13, 28, 1842, "Valores de las haciendas del cura Dr. Manuel Pardío, llamadas Hahil, Chacanchel, Xmah, y San Francisco Tsitsilché." Despite the missing pieces in regional collections, there is important information in the AGNM's Justicia Eclesiástica papers, where the bishop of Germonicópolis offers his own view of things in a series of complaints and petitions; see AGNM, JE 132, October 8, 1836, pp. 250–264; and JE 179, September 28, 1856, pp. 364–369. Pardío saw himself as the victim of conservative political persecutions, and there may be limited truth in this, even though it was the liberal faction that initially drove him from the peninsula. A search in Caracas or Rome might help clarify the story.

89. AGNM, BN, 48, 3, April 21, 1860.

90. AGNM, BN, 48, 3, June 8, 1860.

91. AGNM, BN, 48, 3, August 1, 1860.

92. Among other cases, one thinks in particular of David Stoll's recent description of the Ixil Maya as attempting to live "between two armies."

93. AGEY, FJ-Penal, box of January–August 1861, April 23, 1861; this packet of documents includes Barreiro's will, dated March 30, 1861. See also, ANEY, Protocolos de Izamal #15, October 29, 1864, pp. 143–144.

94. AHAY, DO 125, January 28, 1867, Flores, Berzunza to Guerra; AGEY, RPP #846, August 26, 1864, pp. 243–244.

95. AHAY, DO 113, April 29, 1861, Flores, Hoil to Guerra. His last letter is AHAY, DO 13, April 30, 1861, Flores.

96. Pinelo, "Hombres notables."

97. AHAY, DO 113, April 24, 1861, Flores, Méndez to Guerra; biography by Sosa.

98. AHAY, DO 119, May 30, 1863, Flores, Berzunza to Gala. Berzunza labored in the Petén until the late 1880s; see AHAY, DO 47, July 14, 1882, Champotón.

99. Carrillo y Ancona, El obispado de Yucatán, vol. 2, pp. 1050–1060. In the angry aftermath of Mexico's Reform War (1857–1859), Guerra's survivors refused to bury him in the "secularized and profaned" city cemetery, and therefore opted for the family estate of San Antonio Cucul, which lay outside barrio Santa Ana. One year later, with the French Empire in power, his remains were reburied in the cathedral.

100. There is as yet little research on the peninsular church from Porfirian times onward. For basic political contours, see Hernández Rodríguez, Iglesia y poder. On the career of Bishop Gala, see Carrillo y Ancona, vol. 2, pp. 1063–1082.

101. Archivo Histórico de la Arquidiócesis de Guatemala (AHAG), "Cartas," April 4, 1865; April 7, 1865; April 25, 1865.

102. AHAG, "Cartas," May 31, 1865, Flores, Teodoro Mazariegas to the bishop of Guatemala.

103. AHAG, "Cartas," April 4, 1865; 4-7-1865; April 25, 1865.

104. AHAG, "Cartas," May 31, 1865, Flores, Teodoro Mazariegas to the bishop of Guatemala.

105. On the emergence of an extractive tropical economy, see Schwartz, 81; Jan de Vos, Oro verde: La conquista de la Selva Lacandona por los madereros tabasqueños, 1822–1949 (México: Fondo de Cultura Económica, Instituto de Cultura de Tabasco, 1988); and Stephen Schlesinger and Stephen Kinzer, Bitter Fruit: The Untold Story of the American Coup in Guatemala (Garden City, N.Y.: Doubleday, 1982). Schlesinger's and Kinzer's version of the role of United Fruit in Guatemala's political intrigues has recently been revised by Piero Gleijeses, Shattered Hope: The Guatemalan Revolution and the United States, 1944–1954 (Princeton: Princeton University Press, 1991).

106. Schwartz, 137–139. See Chapters 4 and 5 of the same volume for an analysis of the inner workings of the chicle industry.

107. Yuri H. Balam Ramos, "Presencia de población maya peninsular en comuni-

dades de el Petén, Guatemala, en la actualidad," *Investigadores de la cultura maya 3*, vol. 2 (Mexico: Universidad Autónoma de Campeche, 1996), pp. 278–280.

108. AGCA, B, 28633, 98, September 20, 1872, Flores, report from the visita of José E. Matu.

109. AHAG, "Cartas," May 31, 1865, Flores, Teodoro Mazariegas to the bishop of Guatemala.

Notes to Conclusion

1. My account of the apparition at Izamal is drawn from newspaper accounts in HPS, *Por Esto!*, January 9, 1996.

2. Ahlstrom, 501–509. Lane interprets Smith as yet another evangelical populist, appealing to the socioeconomic losers of upper New York state: "The single most striking theme in the *Book of Mormon* is that it is the rich, the proud, and the learned who find themselves in the hands of an angry God" (117).

3. Special thanks to Nelson Reed for first alerting me to the story of the Lost Book.

GLOSSARY

Note: All terms are Spanish unless otherwise indicated.

adivino: riddle

aguardiente: crude sugarcane rum popular in many parts of rural Mexico

aj bolon pixan: (Maya) patron saint of a village

aj k'iin: (Maya) pre-Columbian term for a priest

alhaja: jewelry; often used to refer to church decorations as well

alux: (Maya) a mischievous elf believed to inhabit the woods of Yucatán

anís: a sweetened, anis-flavored liquor

archicofradía: principal cofradía of a city or town, based on the cathedral or the principal church of the parish

asiento: initial inscription fee for a cofradía

asociación de caridad: charitable association

atributos: symbols of the crucifixion normally painted on Yucatecan crosses

baile de mestizo: dance in traditional rural costume

baile serio: a formal ball reserved for Hispanics

bajada: the taking down of a saint from its niche in the church for purposes of veneration

balam: (Maya) a field god; also, *yumtsil*

balche': (Maya) beerlike alcoholic beverage popular in rural villages

batab: (Maya) a cacique or headman of a village

beata: a lay holy woman

burro tuunich: (Spanish-Maya) literally, "donkey of stone"; a rock formation near present-day Sudzal, fabled to have once been a malevolent enchanted donkey

cabecera: administrative head town

cabildo: a town council; also, *ayuntamiento* or, in the case of Mayas, *república de indígenas*

cacique: the headman of a village

campechano: resident of Campeche

campesino: a peasant

canto: a chant, prayer, or song

cantón: a military guard unit; became common throughout Yucatán with the onset of the Caste War in 1847; later renamed *colonias militares*

capellán: a chaplain

capellanía: a church-administered investment fund, often used to support members of the clergy

capitalino: resident of Mexico City

carbonero: charcoal maker

casta divina: "the divine caste"; a nickname for rich Yucatecans, popular during the Porfiriato

caudillo: a regional strongman

celador: a cofradía official responsible for guarding the organization's santo or altar

cenote: (from the Maya *ts'ono'ot*) a limestone sinkhole found throughout the Yucatán peninsula; a source of fresh water, but also associated with powerful and mysterious forces

centro comercial: a shopping mall

cháak: (Maya) one of the four rain gods

ch'a-cháak: (Maya) a rain ceremony

chicha: (Maya) beerlike alcoholic beverage common in rural villages

Chilam Balam: (Maya) any of a series of prophetic books written in Yucatec Maya

chipitín: (Maya) a type of cicada

choch: (Maya) a type of cicada

ciruela: fig

coadjutor: an assistant pastor or copastor

cofrade: member of a cofradía

cofradía: a lay religious organization

colmenero: tender of beehives; a position found in some rural cofradías

colonial militar: post-1867 term for a guard unit in rural Yucatán

concepcionistas: order of nuns based in Mérida; secularized in 1867

concubinato: cohabitation without marriage

contribución religiosa: church tax on the Maya peasantry, also known as *obvención*

corregidor: district political chief in nineteenth-century Guatemala

costumbrismo: a literary genre prevalent in early-nineteenth-century Hispanic countries; emphasized genial renditions of local custom

coyote/conejo: trickster stories featuring the characters of Rabbit and Coyote, common throughout Mexico

creencia: a popular belief or wisdom, often brief and isolated (to put it crudely, a superstition)

cuaresma: Lent

cuenta de fábrica: parish budgetary records

cuento: folktale

cura: pastor, the head priest of a parish

curato: parish

dedazo: rule by personal fiat (literally, "a stroke of the finger")

denuncia: claim for private title to previously untitled public land

devocionario: a prayer booklet

día de los muertos: Day of the Dead; see *janal pixan*

diablete: dancers disguised as devils; common in colonial street processions

diligencia: horse-drawn coach

don: Spanish honorific title; female, *doña*

donación: a gift or private donation (in this case, to a pious organization or activity)

ejido: communal land surrounding a village; after 1910, a land-based political and economic collective created by the Revolutionary government

elegidos de dios: "God's chosen people," a phrase Alfonso Villa Rojas found the Maya of Quintana Roo applying to themselves in the 1920s

embriaguez: drunken bender

encargado, empresario: organizer of village fiesta

encomienda: a system of mandatory peasant tribute and service; an *encomendero* is the recipient of such tribute and service.

esclava: an initiate nun

estancia: a form of rural cattle property that later developed into the Yucatecan hacienda

ex voto: small token of devotion given to a santo in exchange for the santo's favor or protection

fábrica: parish income

fagina: mandatory public labor performed by Maya peasants

feria: a rural fair; the term carries more secular overtones than does the closely related *fiesta*

fiesta: village celebration, often associated with the feast day of the patron saint

filipina: white collarless shirt common in rural Yucatán

fondo de cofradías: a cathedral-operated loan fund built on revenues from the liquidation of peasant cofradías

gallinas ciegas: a closed upper passageway found in some Yucatecan churches; literally, "blind chickens," a Spanish version of blind man's bluff

gigantón: a two-man costume representing a giant; worn in colonial street processions

gobernador: the Guatemalan equivalent of *cacique* or *batab;* once used in Yucatán, but increasingly rare in the nineteenth century

gremio: an organization based on trade, gender, neighborhood, or some other common denominator; usually lay-religious in nature

hacendado: owner of an *hacienda*

hacienda: a commercial estate with resident workers

hechicería: witchcraft

hechicero: (fem., *hechicera*) a witch

hermano mayor: a senior member of a cofradía

h-men: (Maya; the *h* is silent) Maya shaman

holpatán: (Maya) a colonial-era tax on the rural peasantry, used to finance the convent of Mérida

hombre de bien: an early nineteenth-century term for an urban gentleman

imagen: an icon or representation of Jesus, Mary, the cross, the saints, or other divine or spiritual entity; pl., *imágenes*

Imán revolt: (1839–1840) A regional uprising, led by Tizimín merchant and property owner Santiago Imán; established Yucatecan independence but also mobilized the Maya peasantry, leading to the Caste War of 1847

indio: colonial term for indigenous peasant

itza'ob: (Maya) the legendary founders of Chichén Itzá

jaankab: (Maya) customary period by which newlyweds live with the bride's parents

janal pixan: (Maya) Food of the Dead, a syncretic adaptation of the Christian Day of the Dead (November 2); begins on the night of October 31 but is also part of a larger series of religious ceremonies performed in Yucatán throughout the month of November

jarana: a popular dance performed in 3/4 or 6/8 time, often punctuated by witty four-line poems known as *bombas*

javelina: wild pig

jefe político: a district political official

Jesucristo: common rural Mexican name for Jesus Christ

jornal: one of the periodic dues that members of cofradías paid to support their organization; also, *limosna*

juez de paz: magistrate of a small town

junta directiva: organizing committee for the Mérida carnival

kaaj: (Maya) village

k'aax: (Maya) *monte* or overgrown wilderness

k'an xul: (Maya) a type of tree

koché: a hand-held carriage service operated by rural peasants

kool: (Maya) a milpa

kuuch: (Maya) Maya ceremony

k'uyub: (Maya) anatto seed (Sp., *achiote*)

laguna: a small pool of water

limón: a Yucatecan lemon tree

machismo: (adj., *macho*) exaggerated masculinity

maestro cantor: a Maya church assistant whose responsibility was to memorize and recite prayers

mampostería: a type of rubble construction common in rural Yucatán and Guatemala

mayorcol: hacienda or cofradía official responsible for overseeing corn cultivation

mayordomía: the office or act of serving as *mayordomo*

mayordomo: the executive director of a cofradía or gremio; also, the caretaker of a particular imagen; also, the caretaker of an hacienda

mayordomo de hachas: a ceremonial position in some rural cofradías; *hachas* were large candles

meridano: resident of Mérida

mesada: special dinner held in order to encourage the dead to avoid returning to earth

mestizo: a biological mixture of Spanish and Maya; by the late nineteenth century, this had come to be a euphemism for Mayas

milpa: a cornfield (in Maya, *kool*)

misa: Mass

mojonero: stone field markers used by Maya agriculturists

monte: the wilderness; same as *k'aax*

muuch: (Maya) frog

noriero: well operator; a position of responsibility in some rural cofradías

novena: a nine-day prayer ritual

novenario: a prayer booklet that accompanies a *novena*

obra pía: see *capellanía*

ocultación de bienes: the crime of hiding an inheritance from its rightful heirs

oriente: the eastern part of Yucatán, extending from Río Lagartos southward to Bacalar

pacíficos: former Caste War rebels who signed peace treaties and continued to live in relative autonomy in southern Campeche and other isolated pockets of the Yucatán peninsula; also, *pacíficos del sur*

padre: Spanish term for a priest

pajajtun: (Maya) one of the four rain gods

palapa: a construction common in southeast Mexico and northern Guatemala composed of a thatched roof sustained by poles

patrón: (fem., *patrona*) official sponsor or executive of a cofradía or imagen

patronato real: royal right to review ecclesiastical appointments to the Americas; later expropriated by the governments of the former Spanish colonies

peón: servant on an hacienda

petén: (Maya) island; origin of the name "Petén"

petenero: an inhabitant of the Petén

picador: a functionary of the bullfight whose job is to enrage the bull by pricking it with a lance

piñata: a brightly decorated paper maché sculpture filled with candy and treats; often used in parties

pitarrilla: (Maya) see *chicha*

pixan: (Maya) soul, spirit, or ghost; *aj bolon pixan,* "patron saint"

Porfiriato: the rule of Porfirio Díaz, 1876–1911

pozole: (Maya, *k'elem*) a drink made from partially boiled corn

prioste: administrator or administrative helper in a cofradía

promesa: a vow of special devotion made to a saint in exchange for the saint's help in solving some problem or curing an illness

pueblo: a rural village

pul ja'aj: (Maya) a witch; also, *x-pul ya'aj*

p'uuso'ob: (Maya) a race of dwarfs popularly believed to have once inhabited the peninsula

ranchería: a small settlement of milpa farmers

rancho: a commercial estate usually smaller and less highly capitalized than an hacienda; also, a small settlement of milpa farmers

real: colonial unit of money; eight reales were equal to one peso

relleno negro: a dish made from boiled fowl and dried black habanero chiles

república de indígenas: indigenous town council; abolished in 1867

sak pakal: (Maya) *turcaza,* or wild dove

salve: a prayer

sanjuanistas: Liberal party of Yucatán during the late colonial years

santo óleo: holy oil; chrism

santo: a saint, but loosely used to apply to any of the wondrous powerful beings accessed through religious icons, including Jesus and the cross

secreto'ob: (Spanish-Maya) narratives of amazing and wondrous content

Sierra Alta: hilly region along the southern border between modern-day Yucatán and Campeche; also known as *pu'uk* or *serranía*

sitio: a small and relatively undeveloped piece of land used for cattle, beekeeping, or agriculture

sorteo: a lottery drawing

stela: pre-Columbian stone monument celebrating the life of a Maya noble

sudario: a cloth decoration, similar to an hipil, applied to crosses

tamax chi': (Maya) literally, "deep speech"; refers to beliefs or *creencias* that carry a prophesy or warning

terno: elaborate dress worn by mestiza women in Yucatán

terreno baldío: untitled lands

tertulia: a formal ball, usually a private affair of prominent Hispanic families *tianguis:* an informal rural market

tich': (Maya) a Maya field ceremony

tienda, tendejón: a small rural store

ts'awayak': (Maya) praying mantis

tsutsuy: (Maya) wild dove

ts'uul: (Maya) non-Maya, foreigner; sir

tulix: (Maya) dragonfly, commonly believed to signal the arrival of visitors; also, *turix*

tuunich keej: (Maya) "deer stone," a stone found in the entrails of a deer, popularly believed to bestow magical hunting abilities on the possessor

tuunkul: (Maya) log drum

u janlikool: (Maya) see *wajil kool*

úuchben máako'ob: (Maya) "the ancient ones," the Mayas who built the pyramids

vaquero: a cowboy or cattle tender

vecino: non-Maya resident of a rural town or village

viático: a priest's journey to administer religious services to a remote area; also refers to a small stipend provided to make such journeys

vicariato: area administered by a *vicario*

vicario: ecclesiastical magistrate; also, *vicario incápite*

viejitas, las: "the old ladies"; a term of derision used by Yucatecan men

visita: periodic inspection of rural churches; also refers to any inspection of doings and misdoings in political affairs

voto: a religious vow to fulfill some act of piety or veneration in exchange for spiritual favors or protection; once completed, the token gift left for the santo is referred to as an *ex-voto*

wáay: (Maya) a sorcerer who has transformed himself into an animal; *wáay chivo,* or "phantom-goat" or "were-goat"

wajil kool: (Maya) ceremony used to propitiate field gods prior to planting

xanab k'eewel: (Maya, literally "shoe of leather") formal footwear worn during mestiza dances

x-majannaj: (Maya) a large black moth believed to signal the arrival of long-term visitors

x-tabay: (Maya) a mythical creature believed to transform itself into a beautiful woman in order to entrap and devour men

x-wáay: (Maya) a witch

Bibliography

Archives

AB	Archives of Belize
AGCA	Archivo General de Centroamérica
AGEY	Archivo General del Estado de Yucatán
	FC Fondo Colonial
	FJ Fondo Justicia
	FM Fondo Municipios
	PC Poder del Congreso
	PE Poder Ejecutivo
	RPP Registro Público de Propiedad
AGNM	Archivo General de la Nación de México
	BN Bienes Nacionales
	J Justicia
	JE Justicia Eclesiástica
AHA	Archivo Histórico del Arzobispado
AHAG	Archivo Histórico de la Arquidiócesis de Guatemala
AHAY	Archivo Histórico de la Arquidiócesis de Yucatán
	AT Asuntos terminados
	CC Concursos a curatos
	CF Cuentas de fábrica
	DO Decretos y órdenes
	OC Oficinas de cofradía
	VP Visitas pastorales
AHDN	Archivo Histórico de la Defensa Nacional
ANEY	Archivo Notarial del Estado de Yucatán
APOC	Archivo Parroquial del Obispado de Campeche
CAIHY	Centro de Apoyo a la Investigación Histórica de Yucatán
	Impresos
	Libros Manuscritos (Actos de Cabildo, Ayuntamientos Municipales)
	Manuscritos
CLE	Clements Library, University of Michigan
HPS	Hemeroteca José María Pino Suárez
TEX	Nettie Lee Benson Library, University of Texas
WMMSA	Wesleyan Methodist Missionary Society Archives

Theses and Dissertations

Carrillo y Herrera, Beatriz Eugenia. "Iglesia y sociedad yucateca en el siglo XIX (1800–1840)." Thesis. Universidad Autónoma de Yucatán, 1993.

Cervera Fernández, José Juan. "Iglesias no católicas y estructura política: Los campesinos de Uayma, Yucatán." Thesis. Universidad Autónoma de Yucatán, 1991.

Cline, Howard F. "Regionalism and Society in Yucatan, 1825–1847: A Study of 'Progressivism' and the Origins of the Caste War." Diss. Harvard, 1947.

Fallon, Michael J. "The Secular Clergy in the Diocese of Yucatan: 1750–1800." Diss. The Catholic University of America, 1979.

Fernández Repetto, Francisco Javier. "Resistencia cultural y religiosidad popular: Los gremios en Chuburná de Hidalgo, Mérida, Yucatán." Thesis. Universidad Autónoma "Benito Juárez" de Oaxaca, 1988.

Graff, Gary Wendell. "Cofradías in the New Kingdom of Granada: Lay Fraternities in a Spanish American Frontier Society, 1600–1755." Diss. University of Wisconsin, 1973.

Güémez Pineda, Miguel Antonio. "Estado actual de las prácticas médicas tradicionales en Pustunich, Yucatán." Thesis: Universidad Autónoma de Yucatán, 1984.

Harrington, Raymond P. "The Secular Clergy in the Diocese of Mérida de Yucatán, 1780–1850: Their Origins, Careers, Wealth and Activities." Diss. The Catholic University of America, 1982.

Marcus, Linda C. "English Influence on Belize and the Petén Region of Northern Guatemala, 1630 to 1763." Diss. Southern Methodist University, 1990.

Martínez Huchim, Patricia. "K-maaya tsikbal. Jaajil t'aan. Estudio del género cuento de la tradición oral en Maya-Yukateko (El caso de Xocén, municipio de Valladolid, Yucatán, México)." Thesis. Universidad Autónoma de Yucatán, Mérida, 1996.

Morrison, Lynda Sanderford. "The Life and Times of José Canuto Vela: Yucatecan Priest and Patriot (1802–1859)." Diss. University of Alabama, 1993.

Negroe Sierra, Genny Mercedes. "La cofradía de Yucatán en el siglo VIII." Thesis. Universidad Autónomoa de Yucatán, 1984.

Santana Rivas, Landy Elizabeth. "Protestantismo y sus implicaciones sociales en el campo yucateco." Thesis. Universidad Autónoma de Yucatán, 1987.

Santiago Pacheco, Edgar Augusto. "La política eclesiástica borbónica y la secularización de parroquias franciscanas en Yucatán: 1750–1825." Thesis. Universidad Autónoma de Yucatán, 1992.

Smith, Stephanie Jo. "A Reconstruction of Early Nineteenth-Century Valladolid, Mexico." Thesis. University of Oklahoma, 1997.

Sullivan-González, Douglas Creed. "Piety, Power, and Politics: The Role of Religion in the Formation of the Guatemalan Nation-State, 1839–1871." Diss. University of Texas at Austin, 1994.

Uribe Euán, Ana Patricia, and Castro Medina, Felipe de Jesús. "El convento de Nuestra Señora de la Consolación de Mérida." Thesis. Universidad Autónoma de Yucatán, 1992.

Secondary Literature

Adas, Michael. *Prophets of Rebellion: Millenarian Protest Movements against the European Colonial Order.* Chapel Hill: University of North Carolina Press, 1979.

Ahlstrom, Sydney E. *A Religious History of the American People.* New Haven: Yale University Press, 1972.

Allen, Catherine J. *The Hold Life Has: Coca and Cultural Identity in an Andean Community.* Washington, D.C.: Smithsonian Institution Press, 1988.

Amaro Gamboa, Jesús. "Miscelánea de hábitos y creencias." Serialized in *Diario del sureste,* misc. dates, 1988.

Anderson, Benedict. *Imagined Communities: Reflections on the Origin and Spread of Nationalism.* London: Verso Editions, 1983.

Andrade, Manuel J., and Máas Collí, Hilaria, eds. *Cuentos mayas yucatecos.* 2 vols. Mérida: Universidad Autónoma de Yucatán, 1991.

Annis, Sheldon. *God and Production in a Guatemalan Town.* Austin: University of Texas Press, 1987.

Antochiw, Michel. *Historia cartográfica de la península de Yucatán.* México: Comunicación y Ediciones Tiacuilo, 1994.

———. "Los tratados de paz de Chichanhá." *Saastun: Revisita de la cultura maya* 2 (1997), pp. 83–112.

Bachtloff, Dagmar. "La formación de una sociedad intercultural: Las cofradías en el Michoacán colonial." *Historia mexicana* 43, 2 (1993), pp. 251–263.

Balam Ramos, Yuri H. "Presencia de población maya peninsular en comunidades de el Petén, Guatemala, en la actualidad." *Investigadores de la cultura maya.* Vol. 2. Mexico: Universidad Autónoma de Campeche, 1996, pp. 270–283.

Baldwin, Deborah J. *Protestants and the Mexican Revolution: Missionaries, Ministers, and Social Change.* Urbana: University of Illinois Press, 1990.

Baqueiro, Serapio. *Ensayo histórico sobre las revoluciones de Yucatán desde el año de 1840 hasta 1864.* 2 vols. Mérida: Manuel Heredia Arguelles, 1879.

Baqueiro López, Oswaldo. *Magia, mitos y supersticiones entre los mayas.* Mérida: Maldonado Editoriales, 1983.

Barbachano y Tarrazo, Manuel. *Vida, usos y hábitos de Yucatán al mediar el siglo XIX.* Mérida: Maldonado Editores, 1986, orig. 1951.

Baring-Gould, S. *The Lives of the Saints.* 13 vols. Edinburgh: John Grant, 1914.

Bartolomé, Miguel Alberto. *La dinámica social de los mayas de Yucatán: Pasado y presente de la situación colonial.* México: Instituto Nacional Indigenista, 1988.

Bazant, Jan. *Alienation of Church Wealth in Mexico: Social and Economic Aspects of the Liberal Revolution, 1856–1875.* Trans. and ed. Michael P. Costeloe. Cambridge: At the University Press, 1971.

Beals, Ralph L. "Two Mountain Zapotec Tales from Oaxaca, Mexico." *Journal of American Folklore* 48 (1935), pp. 189–190.

——. "Problems of Mexican Indian Folklore." *Journal of American Folklore* 56 (1943), pp. 8–16.

Becker, Marjorie. *Setting the Virgin on Fire: Lázaro Cárdenas, Michoacán Peasants, and the Redemption of the Mexican Revolution.* Berkeley: University of California Press, 1995.

Beezley, William. *Judas at the Jockey Club and Other Episodes of Porfirian Mexico.* Lincoln: University of Nebraska Press, 1987.

Beezley, William H., Cheryl English Martin, and William E. French, eds. *Rituals of Rule, Rituals of Resistance: Public Celebrations and Popular Culture in Mexico.* Wilmington, Del.: Scholarly Resources, 1994.

Behar, Ruth. "Sexual Witchcraft, Colonialism, and Women's Powers: Views from the Mexican Inquisition." In *Sexuality and Marriage in Colonial Latin America.* Ed. Asuncion Lavrin. Lincoln: University of Nebraska Press, 1989, pp. 178–206.

Bendix, Regina. "Diverging Paths in the Scientific Search for Authenticity." *Journal of Folklore Research* 29, 2 (1992), pp. 103–132.

Biersack, Aletta. "Local Knowledge, Local History: Geertz and Beyond." In Lynn Hunt, ed. *The New Cultural History.* Berkeley: University of California Press, 1989, pp. 72–96.

Blom, Franz. "Coronel Modesto Méndez." *Antropología e historia de Guatemala* 7, 2 (1955), pp. 3–16.

Boas, Franz. "Notes on Mexican Folklore." *Journal of American Folklore* 25 (1912), pp. 204–260.

——, and Herman K. Haeberlin. "Ten Folktales in Modern Nahuatl." *Journal of American Folklore* 37 (1924), pp. 345–370.

Boff, Leonardo, and Clovodis Boff. *Liberation Theology: From Dialogue to Confrontation.* Trans. Robert R. Barr. San Francisco: Harper and Row, 1986.

Boggs, Ralph Steele. "A Folklore Expedition to Mexico." *Southern Folklore Quarterly* 3, 2 (1939), pp. 65–73.

Bolio, Edmundo. *Diccionario histórico, geográfico y bibliográfico de Yucatán.* Mexico: I.C.D., 1944.

Borah, Woodrow, and S. F. Cook. *The Population of Central Mexico in 1548: An Analysis of the Suma de Visitas de Pueblos.* Berkeley: University of California Press, 1960.

Bourke, John G. "Popular Medicine, Customs, and the Superstitions of the Rio Grande." *Journal of American Folklore* 7, 24 (1894), pp. 199–206.

Brading, D. A. "Tridentine Catholicism and Enlightened Despotism in Bourbon Mexico." *Journal of Latin American Studies* 15 (1983), pp. 1–22.

Bretos, Miguel A. *Iglesias de Yucatán.* Photographs by Christian Rasmussen. Mérida: Producción Editorial Dante, 1992.

Briceño López, Ramiro. *Leyendas izamaleñas.* Mérida: Universidad Autónoma de Yucatán, 1990.

Bricker, Victoria. *The Indian Christ, the Indian King: The Historic Substrate of Maya Myth and Ritual.* Austin: University of Texas Press, 1981.

Brinton, Daniel G. "The Folklore of Yucatan." *Folklore Journal* 1, 8 (1883). Reprinted as *El folk-lore de Yucatán,* trans. Enrique Leal (Mérida: Museo Arqueológico Histórico de Yucatán, 1937).

Bunzel, Ruth. *Chichicastenango: A Guatemalan Village.* Seattle: University of Washington Press, 1952.

Burke, Peter. *Popular Culture in Early Modern Europe.* Cambridge: Scholar Press, 1996.

Burns, Allan F. *An Epoch of Miracles: Oral Literature of the Yucatec Maya.* Austin: University of Texas Press, 1983.

Caballero, María del Socorro. *Supersticiones populares.* Toluca: Imagen Editores, 1995.

Caballero Salas, Lucilia, et al. *Prácticas médicas mayas.* Colección Letras Mayas Contemporáneas, No. 12. México: INI/SEDESOL, 1993.

Callahan, William J. "The Spanish Parish Clergy, 1874–1930." *Catholic Historical Review* 75 (1989), pp. 405–422.

Campbell, Joseph. *The Hero with a Thousand Faces.* New York: Pantheon Books, 1949.

Cancian, Frank. *Economics and Prestige in a Maya Community: The Cargo System of Zinacantan.* Stanford: Stanford University Press, 1965.

Can Pat, Gerardo. *La virgen de la Candelaria: Etnohistoria de la Patrona de Tibolón.* Colección Letras Mayas Contemporáneas No. 18. Mérida: INI/SEDESOL, 1993.

Cardoso, Manuel. "The Lay Brotherhoods of Colonial Bahia." *Catholic Historical Review* 33, 1 (1947), pp. 12–30.

Careaga Viliesid, Lorena. *Hierofanía combatiente: Lucha, simbolismo y religiosidad en la Guerra de Castas.* Chetumal: Universidad Autónoma de Quintana Roo, 1998.

Carrasco, Pedro. "The Civil-Religious Hierarchy in Mesoamerican Communities: Pre-Spanish Background and Colonial Development." *American Anthropologist* 63 (1961), pp. 483–497.

Carrillo, Estanislao. "Papeles sueltos del P. Carrillo: Fantasmas." *Registro yucateco* IV. Mérida: 1846, pp. 103–106.

Carrillo y Ancona, Crescencio, ed. *Documentos interesantes de Yucatán, 1857–1902.* Unpublished bound volume.

―――. *El obispado de Yucatan: Historia de su fundación y de sus obispos desde el siglo XVI hasta el XIX.* Mérida: Caballero, 1895.

Castañeda, Jorge. *Utopia Unarmed: The Latin American Left After the Cold War.* New York: Alfred A. Knopf, 1993.

Castañeda, Quetzil E. *In the Museum of Maya Culture: Touring Chichén Itzá.* Minneapolis: University of Minnesota Press, 1996.

Cauich, Gaspar A., and Mayra Aguayo Mena. *La feria de San Román: Historia de una mentalidad, 1565–1997.* Campeche: Campeche XXI, 1998.

Chacón, Ramón D. "Salvador Alvarado and the Roman Catholic Church: Church-State Relations in Revolutionary Yucatán, 1914–1918." *Journal of Church and State* 27, 2 (1985), pp. 245–266.

Chambon, Ludovic. *Un gascón en México.* Trans. Rocío Alonzo. México: Consejo Nacional para la Cultura y las Artes, 1994.

Chance, John K., and William B. Taylor. "Cofradias and Cargos: An Historical Perspective on the Mesoamerican Civil-Religious Hierarchy." *American Ethnologist* 12, 1 (1985), pp. 1–26.

Charnay, Desiré. *Mis descubrimientos en México y en la América Central.* In *América pintoresca: Descripción de viajes al nuevo continente por los más modernos exploradores Carlos Wiener, Doctor Crevaux, D. Charnay, etc., etc.* Barcelona: Montaner y Simón, Editores, 1884, pp. 265–340.

Chevalier, Francois. *Land and Society in Colonial Mexico: The Great Hacienda.* Trans. Alvin Eustis. Berkeley: University of California Press, 1963.

Christian, William. *Local Religion in Sixteenth-Century Spain.* Princeton: Princeton University Press, 1981.

Chuchiak, John F. IV. "Intellectuals, Indians and the Press, Polemical Journalism of Justo Sierra O'Reilly." *Saastun: Revista de la cultura maya* 2 (1997), pp. 6–16.

Clendinnen, Inga. *Ambivalent Conquests: Maya and Spaniard in Yucatan, 1517–1570.* Cambridge: Cambridge University Press, 1987.

Clendinnen, Inga. "Yucatec Maya Women and the Spanish Conquest: Role and Ritual in Historical Reconstruction." *Journal of Social History.* Spring 1982, pp. 427–442.

Cockcroft, James D. *Intellectual Precursors of the Mexican Revolution, 1900–1913.* Austin: University of Texas Press, 1968.

Cogolludo, Diego López de. *Historia de Yucatán.* 3 vols. Campeche: Comisión de Historia, 1954.

Collier, George, with Quaratiello, Elizabeth Lowery. *Basta! Land and the Zapatista Rebellion in Chiapas.* Munroe: Institute for Food and Development Policy, 1994.

Cook, Sherburne F. "Francisco Xavier Balmis and the Introduction of Vaccination to Latin America." *Bulletin of the History of Medicine* 11, 5 (1942), pp. 543–560.

———. "Francisco Xavier Balmis and the Introduction of Vaccination to Latin America. Part II." *Bulletin of the History of Medicine* 12, 1 (1942), pp. 70–101.

Costeloe, Michael P. *Church Wealth in Mexico: A Study of the 'Juzgado de Capellanias' in the Archbishopric of Mexico, 1800–1856.* Cambridge: At the University Press, 1967.

Costeloe, Michael. *The Central Republic in Mexico, 1835–1846: Hombres de Bien in the Age of Santa Anna.* Cambridge: Cambridge University Press, 1993.

Curcio-Nagy, Linda A. "Giants and Gypsies: Corpus Christi in Colonial Mexico City." In *Rituals of Rule, Rituals of Resistance: Public Celebrations and Popular Culture in Mexico.* Eds. William H. Beezley, Cheryl English Martin, and William E. French. Wilmington, Del.: Scholarly Resources, 1994, pp. 1–26.

————. "Native Icon to City Protectress to Royal Patroness: Ritual, Political Symbolism and the Virgin of the Remedies." *The Americas* 52, 3 (1996), pp. 367–391.

da Cunha, Euclides. *Rebellion in the Backlands.* Trans. Samuel Putnam. Chicago: University of Chicago Press, 1957.

Darnton, Robert. *The Great Cat Massacre and Other Episodes in French Cultural History.* New York: Vintage Books, 1984.

Davis, Natalie Z. *Society and Culture in Early Modern France.* Stanford: Stanford University Press, 1975.

Davis, Susan G. *Parades and Power: Street Theatre in Nineteenth-Century Philadelphia.* Philadelphia: Temple University Press, 1986.

Deeds, Susan M. "First-Generation Rebellions in Seventeenth-Century Nueva Vizcaya." In *Native Resistance and the Pax Colonial in New Spain.* Ed. Susan Schroeder. Lincoln: University of Nebraska Press, 1998.

della Cava, Ralph. *Miracle and Joaseiro.* New York: Columbia University Press, 1970.

DeWalt, Billie R. "Changes in the Cargo Systems of Mesoamerica." *Anthropological Quarterly* 48, 2 (1975), pp. 87–105.

Diacon, Todd A. *Millenarian Vision, Capitalist Reality: Brazil's Contestado Rebellion, 1900–1916.* Durham: Duke University Press, 1991.

Diener, Paul. "The Tears of St. Anthony: Ritual and Revolution in Eastern Guatemala." *Latin American Perspectives* 5, 3 (1978), pp. 92–116.

Domínguez Aké, Santiago. *Creencias, profecías y consejas mayas.* Colección Letras Mayas Contemporáneas, #20. Mexico: Premiá Editores, 1993.

Dorson, Richard M. *Folklore and Fakelore: Essays Toward a Discipline of Folk Studies.* Cambridge: Harvard University Press, 1976.

Dumond, Carol Steichen, and Don E. Dumond, eds. *Demography and Parish Affairs in Yucatan, 1797–1879: Documents from the Archivo de la Mitra Emeritense, Selected by Joaquin de Arrigunaga Peon.* University of Oregon Anthropological Papers #27, 1982.

Dumond, Don E. *The Machete and the Cross: Campesino Rebellion in Yucatán.* Lincoln: University of Nebraska Press, 1997.

Dundas, Alan. "Texture, Text, and Context." In *Interpreting Folklore.* Bloomington: Indiana University Press, 1980, pp. 20–32.

Dundas, Alan. "The Fabrication of Fakelore." In *Folklore Matters*. Knoxville: University of Tennessee Press, 1989, pp. 40–56.

Dzul Chablé, Irene, et al. *Cuentos mayas tradicionales*. Colección Letras Mayas Contemporáneas, #14. México: Premiá Editores, 1994.

Dzul Poot, Domingo. *Cuentos mayas*. 2 vols. Mérida: Maldonado Editores, 1985, 1986.

Early, John D. "Some Ethnographic Implications of an Ethnohistorical Perspective on the Civil-Religious Hierarchy Among the Highland Maya." *Ethnohistory* 30, 4 (1983), pp. 185–202.

Ek Chablé, Robert, Miguel Chac Han, and Irene Dzul. *Cuentos mayas de temas europeos*. Colección Letras Mayas Contemporáneas, #16. México: Premiá Editores, 1993.

Elmendorf, Mary. *Nine Maya Women*. New York: Schenkman Publishing Co., 1976.

Espinosa, Aurelio. "Traditional Spanish Proverbs in New Mexico." In Espinosa, J. Manuel, ed. *The Folklore of Spain in the American Southwest: Traditional Spanish Folk Literature in Northern New Mexico and Southern Colorado*. Norman: University of Oklahoma Press, 1985, pp. 165–167.

Espinosa, J. Manuel, ed. *The Folklore of Spain in the American Southwest: Traditional Spanish Folk Literature in Northern New Mexico and Southern Colorado*. Norman: University of Oklahoma Press, 1985.

Evans, Grant. *Lao Peasants Under Socialism*. New Haven: Yale University Press, 1990.

Farriss, Nancy M. *Maya Society Under Colonial Rule: The Collective Enterprise of Survival*. Princeton: Princeton University Press, 1984.

Foster, George M. "Some Characteristics of Mexican Indian Folklore." *Journal of American Folklore* 58 (1945), pp. 225–235.

————. *Tzitzuntzan: Mexican Peasants in a Changing World*. Boston: Little, Brown and Company, 1967.

————. "The Current State of Mexican Indian Folklore Studies." *Journal of American Folklore* 61 (1948), pp. 386–382.

Franco Cáceres, Jorge. "Religiosidad y convivencia mayas." *Unicornio* #249, January 7, 1966, pp. 3–7.

———— "Eclesialidad católica maya," *Unicornio* #249, July 28, 1996, pp. 3–9.

Gallagher, Tom. *Portugal: A Twentieth-Century Interpretation*. Manchester: Manchester University Press, 1983.

Gann, Thomas W. F. *The Maya Indians of Southern Yucatan and Northern British Honduras*. Smithsonian Institution Bureau of Indian Ethnology Bulletin No. 64. Washington, D.C.: Government Printing Office, 1918.

Gatschet, Albert S. "Popular Rimes from Mexico." *Journal of American Folklore* 2 (1889), pp. 48–53.

Geary, Patrick J. "The Ninth-Century Relic Trade: A Response to Popular Piety?" *Religion and the People, 800–1700*. Ed. James Obelkevich. Chapel Hill: University of North Carolina Press, 1979.

Georges, Robert A. "The Pervasiveness in Contemporary Folklore Studies of Assumptions, Concepts, and Constructs Usually Associated with the Historic-Geographic Method." *Journal of Folklore Research* 23 (1986), pp. 87–103.

Gibson, Ralph. "Hellfire and Damnation in Nineteenth-Century France." *The Catholic Historical Review* 74, 3 (1998), pp. 383–402.

Gil y Saenz, Manuel. *Compendio histórico, geográfico y estadístico del Estado de Tabasco.* Mexico: Consejo Editorial del Gobierno de Tabasco, 1979, fascimile of 1872 edition.

Gleijeses, Piero. *Shattered Hope: The Guatemalan Revolution and the United States, 1944–1954* Princeton: Princeton University Press, 1991.

Gómez Maillifert, E. M. "Supersticiones de la región de San Juan Teotihuacán est. de México." *Journal of American Folklore* 31 (1918), pp. 488–495.

Góngora Pacheco, María Luisa. *Cuentos de Oxkutzcab y Maní.* Mérida: Maldonado Editores, 1990.

González, Luis. *San José de Gracia: Mexican Village in Transition.* Trans. John Upton. Austin: University of Texas Press, 1974.

González Casanova, Pablo. "Cuento en mexicana de Milpa Alta, D.F." *Journal of American Folklore* 33 (1920), pp. 25–27.

Gosner, Kevin. *Soldiers of the Virgin: The Moral Economy of a Colonial Maya Rebellion.* Tucson: University of Arizona Press, 1992.

Greenleaf, Richard E. "The Mexican Inquisition and the Enlightenment, 1763–1805." *New Mexico Historical Review* 11, 3 (1966), pp. 181–196.

Grim, John A. *The Shaman: Patterns of Siberian and Ojibway Healing.* Norman: University of Oklahoma Press, 1983.

Güémez Pineda, Arturo. "La rebelión de Nohcacab, prefacio inédito de la guerra de castas." *Saastun: Revista de cultura maya* 2 (1997), pp. 51–79.

Gutiérrez, Ramón A. *When Jesus Came, the Corn Gods Went Away.* Stanford: Stanford University Press, 1991.

Hale, Charles A. *Mexican Liberalism in the Age of Mora, 1821–1853.* New Haven: Yale University Press, 1968.

Hall, David. "Introduction." *Understanding Popular Culture: Europe from the Middle Ages to the Nineteenth Century.* Ed. Stuart L. Kaplan. New York: Mouton Publishers, 1984, pp. 7–18.

Haskett, Robert. " 'Not a Pastor, But a Wolf': Indigenous-Clergy Relations in Early Cuernavaca and Taxco." *The Americas* 50, 3 (1994), pp. 313–314.

Hatch, Nathan O. *The Democratization of American Christianity.* New Haven: Yale University Press, 1989.

Higuera Bonfil, Antonio. "Los testigos de Jehová en la frontera México-Belice." Paper presented at the twentieth international congress of the Latin American Studies Association, Guadalajara, Mexico, April 18, 1997.

Hill, Christopher. *The World Turned Upside Down: Radical Ideas During the English Revolution.* New York: Viking, 1972.

Hobsbawm, "Introduction: Inventing Tradition," in Eric Hobsbawm and Terence Ranger, eds. *The Invention of Tradition.* Cambridge: Cambridge University Press, 1983.

Hodge, F. W., ed. "Reports on the Maya Indians of Yucatan by Santiago Méndez, Antonio García y Cubas, Pedro Sánchez de Aguilar, y Francisco Hernández." *Indian Notes and Monographs* 9, 3, 1921.

Holms, J. Derek, and Bernard W. Bickers. *A Short History of the Catholic Church.* New York: Paulist Press, 1984.

Huber, Brad R. "The Reinterpretation and Elaboration of Fiestas in the Sierra Norte de Puebla, Mexico." *Ethnology* 62, 4 (1987), pp. 281–296.

Ingram, John M. *Mary, Michael, and Lucifer: Folk Catholicism in Central Mexico.* Austin: University of Texas Press, 1986.

Iwanska, Aliaja. *Purgatory and Utopia: A Mazahua Village of Mexico.* Cambridge: Schenkman Publishing Company, 1971.

Jones, Grant D. *The Conquest of the Last Maya Kingdom.* Stanford: Stanford University Press, 1998.

———. "Levels of Settlement Alliance Among the San Pedro Maya of Western Belize and Eastern Petén, 1857–1936." *Anthropology and History in Yucatán.* Ed. Grant D. Jones. Austin: University of Texas Press, 1977, pp. 139–190.

———. *Maya Resistance to Spanish Rule: Time and History on a Colonial Frontier.* Albuquerque: University of New Mexico Press, 1989.

———. "Symbolic Dramas of Ethnic Stratification: The Yucatecan Fiesta System of a Colonial Frontier." *University of Oklahoma Papers in Anthropology,* 22, 1 (1981), pp. 131–155.

Joseph, Gilbert M. *Revolution From Without: Yucatán, Mexico, and the United States, 1880–1924.* Cambridge: Cambridge University Press, 1982.

Klaiber, Jeffrey L. "Prophets and Populists: Liberation Theology, 1968–1988." *The Americas* 46, 1 (1989), pp. 1–15.

Knight, Alan. "El liberalismo mexicano desde la Reforma hasta la Revolución (una interpretación)." *Historia mexicana* 35, 1 (1985), pp. 59–91.

Knowlton, Robert. *Church Property and the Mexican Reform, 1856–1910.* DeKalb: Northern Illinois University Press, 1976.

Konrad, Herman W. "Anthropological Studies in Yucatan and the Historical Dimensions." *Mexican Studies* 3, 1 (1987), pp. 163–180.

———. "Capitalism on the Tropical-Forest Frontier: Quintana Roo, 1880s to 1930." In *Land, Labor, and Capital in Modern Yucatan: Essays in Regional History and Political Economy.* Ed. Jeffery T. Brannon and Gilbert M. Joseph. Tuscaloosa: University of Alabama Press, 1990, pp. 143–171.

La Barre, Weston. "The Aymara: History and Worldview." *Journal of American Folklore* 79 (1966), pp. 130–144.

LaFarge, Oliver II, and Douglas Byers. *The Year Bearer's People.* Middle American Research Series No. 3. New Orleans: Department of Middle American Research, Tulane University, 1931.

Landa, Diego de. *Relación de las cosas de Yucatán.* Ed. Miguel Rivera Dorado. Madrid: Hermanos García Noblejas, 1985.

Laurentin, René. *Bernadette of Lourdes: A Life Based on Authenticated Documents.* Trans. John Drury. Minneapolis, Minn.: Winston Press, 1979.

Leonard, Irving A. *Baroque Times in Old Mexico: Seventeenth-Century Persons, Places, and Practices.* Ann Arbor: University of Michigan Press, 1971 (orig. 1959).

Levine, Robert. *Vale of Tears: Revisiting the Canudos Massacre in Northeastern Brazil, 1893–1897.* Berkeley: University of California Press, 1992.

Levi-Strauss, Claude. *The Savage Mind.* Chicago: University of Chicago Press, 1962.

Lewis, Oscar. *Pedro Martínez: A Mexican Peasant and his Family.* New York: Vintage Books, 1964.

Limón Olvera, Silvia. *Las cuevas y el mito de origen: Los casos inca y mexica.* Mexico: Consejo Nacional para la Cultura y las Artes, 1990.

Lizama, Bernardo de. *Historia de Yucatán. Devocionario de Ntra. Sra. de Izamal y conquista espiritual.* México: 1893.

López Méndez, Roberto. "Los espantos se pasean libremente en Ekmul." *Por Esto!* 11 September 1998.

——. "Se devela el misterio de los pu'ses: Raza de pigmeos sobrevive en Yucatán, afirman." *Por Esto!* August 17, 1998.

Love, Bruce, and Eduardo Peraza Castillo. "Wahil Kol: A Yucatec Agricultural Ceremony." *Estudios de la cultura maya* 15 (1984), pp. 251–300.

Lynch, John. *Spain Under the Hapsburgs.* 2 vols. Oxford: Basil Blackwell, 1964.

Máas Collí, Hilaria. *Leyendas yucatecas.* Mérida: Universidad Autónoma de Yucatán, 1993.

MacLeod, Murdo J. "Some Thoughts on the Pax Colonial, Colonial Violence, and Perceptions of Both." *Native Resistance and the Pax Colonial in New Spain.* Ed. Susan Schroeder. Lincoln: University of Nebraska Press, 1998, pp. 129–142.

Marshall, Mac. *Weekend Warriors: Alcohol in a Micronesian Culture.* Palo Alto, Ca.: Mayfield Publishing Company, 1979.

Martín, Luis. *Daughters of the Conquistadors: Women of the Viceroyalty of Peru.* Albuquerque: University of New Mexico Press, 1983.

Martin, Cheryl English. *Governance and Society in Colonial Mexico: Chihuahua in the Eighteenth Century.* Stanford: Stanford University Press, 1996.

Martínez Huchim, Ana Patricia. *Cuentos enraizados.* Mérida: Compañía Editorial de la Península, 1999.

Mason, J. Alden. "Four Mexican-Spanish Fairy-Tales from Azquetlán, Jalisco." *Journal of American Folklore* 25 (1912), pp. 191–198.

McCreery, David. *Rural Guatemala, 1760–1940.* Stanford: Stanford University Press, 1994.

McGee, R. Jon. "The Influence of Pre-Hispanic Yucatecan Maya Religion in Contemporary Lacandon Maya Ritual." *Journal of Latin American Lore* 10, 2 (1984), pp. 175–187.

Mechling, William H. "Stories from Tuxtepec, Oaxaca." *Journal of American Folklore* 25 (1912), pp. 199–203.

———. "Stories from the Southern Atlantic Coastal Region of Mexico." *Journal of American Folklore* 29 (1916), pp. 547–552.

Medina Loria, Eduardo. *Leyendas de los mayas de Quintana Roo: Colección del taller de la lengua maya.* Mérida: Estudios Bassó, S. A., 1982.

Méndez, Santiago, et al. "Report on the Maya Indians of Yucatan." *Indian Notes and Monographs* 9, 3 (1921), pp. 136–226.

Menéndez Rodríguez, Hernán. *Iglesia y poder: Proyectos sociales, alianzas políticas y económicas en Yucatán (1857–1917).* Mexico: Consejo Nacional para la Cultura y las Artes, 1995.

Meyer, Jean. *La cristiada. 2: El conflicto ente la iglesia y el estado, 1926–1929.* México: Siglo XXI, 1973.

Miller, Perry. *Errand into the Wilderness.* Cambridge: Belknap Press of Harvard University Press, 1956.

Mitchell, Timothy. *Violence and Piety in Spanish Folklore.* Philadelphia: University of Pennsylvania Press, 1988.

Molina Solís, Francisco. *Historia de Yucatán durante la dominación española.* Mérida: Imprenta de la Lotería del Estado, 1904–1913.

Montemayor, Carlos. *Rezos sacerdotales mayas.* Colección Letras Mayas Contemporáneas Nos. 38 and 40. Mérida: INI/SEDESOL, 1994.

Morelet, Arthur. *Travels in Central America, Including Accounts of Some Regions Unexplored Since the Conquest.* Trans. M. F. Squire. New York: Leypoldt, Holt & Williams, 1871.

Morley, Sylvanus Griswold. *The Ancient Maya.* Stanford: Stanford University Press, 1946.

Mulvey, Patricia A. "Slave Confraternities in Brazil: Their Role in Colonial Society." *The Americas* 39, 1 (1982), pp. 39–68.

Nelson, Cynthia. *The Waiting Village: Social Change in Rural Mexico.* Boston: Little, Brown and Co., 1971.

Norman, B. A. *Rambles in Yucatan; or, Notes of Travel Through the Peninsula, Including a Visit to the Remarkable Ruins of Chi-Chen, Kabah, Zayi, and Uxmal.* New York: J. & H. G. Langley, 1843.

Orilla, Miguel Angel. *Los días de muertos en Yucatán (janal pixan).* Mérida: Maldonado Editoriales, 1996.

Ong, Walter J. *Orality & Literacy: The Technologizing of the Word.* London: Routledge, 1982.

Pacheco Cruz, Santiago. *Usos, costumbres, religión y supersticiones de los mayas: Apuntes históricos con un estudio psicobiológico de la raza.* Mérida: 1947.

Pardo, J. J. Joaquín, ed. "El documento Canec: Documentos relativos a los caciques José Pablo Canec y Francisco Exquin-Canec, señores que fueron del Petén, encontrados en el Archivo General del Gobierno de Guatemala, por J. J. Joaquín Pardo, Director de dicho Archivo." *Maya Studies* 3 (1936), pp. 294–295.

Paredes, Américo. *Folktales of Mexico.* Chicago: University of Chicago Press, 1970.

Park Redfield, Margaret. *The Folk Literature of a Yucatecan Town.* Contributions to American Archaeology, No. 13. Washington, D.C.: Carnegie Institution, 1935.

Parsons, Elsie Clews. "Folklore from Santa Ana Xalmimilulco, Puebla, Mexico." *Journal of American Folklore* 45 (1932), pp. 342–344.

———. "Zapoteca and Spanish Tales of Mitla, Oaxaca." *Journal of American Folklore* 45 (1932), pp. 292–296.

Patch, Robert W. "Una cofradía y su estancia en el siglo XVIII, notas de investigación." *Boletín E.C.U.A.D.Y.* 8 (1981), pp. 55–66.

———. "Agrarian Changes in Eighteenth-Century Yucatán." *Hispanic American Historical Review* 65, 1 (1985), pp. 21–49.

———. *Maya and Spaniard in Colonial Yucatán, 1648–1812.* Stanford: Stanford University Press, 1993.

———. "Culture, Community, and 'Rebellion' in the Yucatec Maya Uprising of 1761." *Native Resistance and the Pax Colonial in New Spain.* Ed. Susan Schroeder. Lincoln: University of Nebraska Press, 1998, pp. 67–83.

Peniche Barrera, Roldán. *Mitología maya: 15 seres fabulosos.* Mérida: Comercializadora Editorial, 1999.

———. *Relatos mayas.* Mérida: Maldonado Editores, n.d.

Pinelo, Julián A. "Hombres notables del Petén: El Coronel Modesto Méndez." *Petén Itzá* (January 1943), p. 15.

Pino Castilla, Enrique. *Las esquinas de Campeche.* Campeche: Universidad Autónoma de Campeche, 1997.

Pinsky, Mark. "Under Repair, Under Fire." *Quill.* May 1997, pp. 13–17.

Powell, T. G. "Priests and Peasants in Central Mexico: Social Conflict During 'La Reforma.'" *Hispanic American Historical Review* 57, 2 (1977), pp. 296–313.

Press, Irwin. *Tradition and Adaptation: Life in a Modern Yucatecan Maya Village.* Westport, Conn.: Greenwood Press, 1975.

Quintal Avilés, Ella F. *Fiestas y gremios en el oriente de Yucatán.* Mérida: Consejo Nacional para la Cultura y las Artes, 1993.

Radding, Cynthia. *Wandering Peoples: Colonialism, Ethnic Spaces, and Ecological Frontiers in Northwestern Mexico, 1700–1850.* Durham: Duke University Press, 1997.

Radin, Paul. "The Nature and Problems of Mexican Indian Folklore." *Journal of American Folklore* 57 (1944), pp. 26–36.

Ramet, Sabrina Petra. *Balkan Babel: The Disintegration of Yugoslavia from the Death of Tito to Ethnic War.* Boulder. Co.: Westview Press, 1996.

Ramírez, José Fernando. *Viaje a Yucatán del Lic. José Fernando Ramírez, 1865.* Ed. Carlos R. Menéndez. Mérida: Compañía Tipográfica Yucateca, 1926.

Re Cruz, Alicia. *The Two Milpas of Chan Kom: A Study of Socioeconomic and Political Transformations in a Maya Community.* Albany: State University of New York Press, 1996.

Redfield, Robert. *The Folk Culture of Yucatan.* Chicago: University of Chicago Press, 1941.

——————. *The Village that Chose Progress.* Chicago: University of Chicago Press, 1950.

Redfield, Robert, and Alfonso Villa Rojas. *Chan Kom: A Maya Village.* Chicago: University of Chicago Press, 1934.

Reed, Nelson. *The Caste War of Yucatan.* Stanford: Stanford University Press, 1964.

Reich, Peter Lester. *Mexico's Hidden Revolution: The Catholic Church in Law and Politics since 1929.* Notre Dame: University of Notre Dame Press, 1995.

Reid, John Turner. "Seven Folktales from Mexico." *Journal of American Folklore* 48 (1935), pp. 109–124.

Rejón García, Manuel. *Supersticiones y leyendas mayas.* Mérida: 1905.

Rejón Patrón, Lourdes. *Hacienda Tabi: Un capítulo en la historia de Yucatán.* Mérida: Gobierno del Estado de Yucatán, 1993.

Restall, Matthew. *The Maya World: Yucatec Culture and Society, 1550–1850.* Stanford: Stanford University Press, 1997.

Reyes, Juan Jesús. *Cuestión de suerte.* Mexico: Editorial Clío, 1997.

Ricard, Robert. *The Spiritual Conquest of Mexico: An Essay on the Apostalate and the Evangelizing Methods of the Mendicant Orders in New Spain, 1523–1572.* Berkeley: University of California Press, 1966.

Robe, Stanley L. *Mexican Tales and Legends from Veracruz.* Folklore Studies, No. 23. Berkeley: University of California Press, 1971.

Rock, David. *Authoritarian Argentina: The Nationalist Movement, Its History and Its Impact.* Berkeley: University of California Press, 1993.

Rodríguez Losa, Salvador. *Geografía política de Yucatán. Tomo 1. Censo inédito de 1821, año de la independencia.* Mérida: Universidad Autónoma de Yucatán, 1985.

Rosales González, Margarita. *Oxkutzcab, Yucatán, 1900–1960: Campesinos, cambio agrícola y mercado.* Mexico: Instituto Nacional de Antropología e Historia, 1988.

Roseberry, William. *Anthropologies and Histories: Essays in Culture, History, and Political Economy.* New Brunswick, N.J.: Rutgers University Press, 1991.

Roys, Ralph L. *The Indian Background of Colonial Yucatan.* Norman: University of Oklahoma Press, 1972 (orig. 1943).

Rugeley, Terry. "Maya Elites of the Nineteenth Century." *Ethnohistory,* 42, 3 (1995), pp. 477–493.

——————. *Yucatán's Maya Peasantry and the Origins of the Caste War, 1800–1847.* Austin: University of Texas Press, 1996.

————. "Jacinto Canek revisitado." *Unicornio* #294, 17 November 1996, pp. 3–7.

————. "Rural Political Violence and the Origins of the Caste War." *The Americas* 53, 4 (1997), pp. 469–496.

————. "The Caste War in Guatemala." *Saastun: Revista de la cultura maya* 3 (1997), pp. 67–96.

————. "En busca de Santiago Imán, el caudillo de Tizimín, I." *Unicornio* #408, 21 February 1999, pp. 3–9.

————. "En busca de Santiago Imán, el caudillo de Tizimín, II." *Unicornio* #409, 28 February 1999, pp. 3–9.

Rus, Jan, and Robert Wasserstrom. "Civil-Religious Hierarchies in Central Chiapas: A Critical Perspective." *American Ethnologist* 7, 3 (1980), pp. 468–478.

Russell-Wood, A. J. R. "Prestige, Power, and Piety in Colonial Brazil: The Third Orders of Salvador." *Hispanic American Historical Review* 69, 1 (1989), pp. 61–89.

Ruz Menéndez, Rodolfo, ed. "Los indios de Yucatán de Bartolomé del Granado Baeza." *Revista de la Universidad de Yucatán* 4, 168 (1989), pp. 52–63.

Ryan, Mary. "The American Parade: Representations of the Nineteenth-Century Social Order." In *The New Cultural History*. Ed. Lynn Hunt. Berkeley: University of California Press, 1989, pp. 131–153.

Sahlins, Marshall D. *Tribesmen*. Englewood Cliffs: Prentice-Hall, 1968.

Sánchez, José M. *The Spanish Civil War as a Religious Tragedy*. Notre Dame: University of Notre Dame Press, 1987.

Sanders, William T. "The Cultural Ecology of the Lowland Maya: A Reevaluation." *The Classic Maya Collapse*. Ed. T. Patrick Culbert. Albuquerque: University of New Mexico Press, 1973, pp. 325–365.

Santamaría, Francisco J. *Semblanzas tabasqueñas*. Villahermosa: Universidad Juárez Autónoma de Tabasco, 1995 (orig. 1946).

Saul, Frank P. "Disease in the Maya Area: The Pre-Columbian Evidence." In T. Patrick Culbert, *The Classic Maya Collapse*. Albuquerque: University of New Mexico Press, 1973, pp. 301–324.

Savarino Roggero, Franco. *Pueblos y nacionalismo, del régimen oligárquico a la sociedad de masas de Yucatán, 1894–1925*. Mexico: Institution National de Estudios Históricos de la Revolución Mexicana, 1997.

Schaeffer, Ernesto. "El corregidor del Petén: Coronel Modesto Méndez y el encargado de negocios de Prusia von Hesse." *Antropología e historia de Guatemala* 3, 7 (1951), pp. 55–60.

Schele, Linda, and Mary Ellen Miller. *The Blood of Kings: Dynasty and Ritual in Maya Art*. New York: George Braziller, Inc., in association with the Kimbell Art Museum, Fort Worth, 1986.

Schele, Linda, and Peter Mathews. *The Code of Kings: The Language of Seven Sacred Maya Temples and Tombs*. New York: Scribners, 1998.

Schlesinger, Stephen, and Stephen Kinzer. *Bitter Fruit: The Untold Story of the American Coup in Guatemala.* Garden City, N.Y.: Doubleday, 1982.

Schmidt, Henry C. "History, Society, and the Popular Lyric in Mexico: A Study in Cultural Continuity." *Mexican Studies/Estudios Mexicanos* 4, 2 (1988), pp. 295–318.

Schwartz, Norman B. *Forest Society: A Social History of Peten, Guatemala.* Philadelphia: University of Pennsylvania Press, 1990.

Scott, James C. *The Moral Economy of the Peasant: Rebellion and Subsistence in Southeast Asia.* New Haven: Yale University Press, 1976.

————. *Domination and the Arts of Resistance: Hidden Transcripts.* New Haven: Yale University Press, 1990.

Scribner, Bob. "Is a History of Popular Culture Possible?" *History of European Ideas* 10, 2 (1989), pp. 175–191.

Secretaría de Hacienda y Crédito Público. *Catálogo de construcciones religiosas del estado de Yucatán.* Mexico: Talleres Gráficos de la Nación, 1945.

Sewell, William H. Jr. *Work & Revolution in France: The Language of Labor from the Old Regime to 1848.* Cambridge: Cambridge University Press, 1980.

Sierra O'Reilly, Justo. *Los indios de Yucatán. Consideraciones históricos sobre la influencia del elemento indígena en la organización social del país.* Ed. Carlos R. Menéndez. 2 vols. Mérida, 1954.

Silverblatt, Irene. *Moon, Sun, and Witches: Gender Ideologies and Class in Inca and Colonial Peru.* Princeton: Princeton University Press, 1987.

Sinkin, Richard N. *The Liberal Reform, 1855–1876: A Study in Liberal Nation-Building.* Austin: Institute of Latin American Studies, 1979.

Smith, Waldemar. *The Fiesta System and Economic Change.* New York: Columbia University Press, 1977.

Soza, José María. *Pequeña monografía del departamento del Petén.* Guatemala: Ministerio de Educación Pública, 1957.

Stephens, John Lloyd. *Incidents of Travel in Yucatan.* 2 vols. New York: Dover Publications, 1963.

Stoll, David. *Between Two Armies in the Ixil Towns of Guatemala.* New York: Columbia University Press, 1993.

Strauss, Gerald. "Viewpoint: The Dilemma of Popular History." *Past and Present* 132 (1991), pp. 130–149.

Suárez Molina, Victor M. *Historia del obispado y arzobispado de Yucatán, siglos xix y xx.* Mérida: Fondo Editorial de Yucatán, 1981.

Sullivan, Paul. *Unfinished Conversations: Mayas and Foreigners Between Two Wars.* New York: Alfred A. Knopf, 1989.

Taussig, Michael T. *The Devil and Commodity Fetishism in South America.* Chapel Hill: University of North Carolina Press, 1980.

Tax Góngora, Evelio. "El huay chivo o (chivo brujo)." *Por Esto!* January 11, 1996.

Taylor, Peter, and Hermann Rebel. "Hessian Peasant Women, Their Families, and the Draft: A Social-Historical Interpretation of Four Tales from the Grimm Collection." *Journal of Family History* 52 (1981), pp. 93–113.

Taylor, William B. *Drinking, Homicide, and Rebellion in Colonial Mexican Villages.* Stanford: Stanford University Press, 1979.

———. "The Virgin of Guadalupe in New Spain: An Inquiry into the Social History of Marian Devotion." *American Ethnologist* 14 (1987), pp. 9–33.

———. *Magistrates of the Sacred: Priets and Parishoners in Eighteenth-Century Mexico.* Stanford: Stanford University Press, 1996.

Tec Chi, Andrés. *Cuentos sobre las apariciones en el mayab.* Colección Letras Mayas Contemporáneas, #6. México: Premiá Editores, 1993.

Tenenbaum, Barbara A. "Streetwise History: The Paseo de la Reforma and the Porfirian State, 1876–1910." In *Rituals of Rule, Rituals of Resistance: Public Celebrations and Popular Culture in Mexico.* Eds. William H. Beezley, Cheryl English Martin, and William E. French. Wilmington, Del.: Scholarly Resources, 1994, pp. 127–150.

Tepstra, Nicholas. "Confraternities and Mendicant Orders: The Dynamics of Lay and Clerical Brotherhood in Renaissance Bologna." *Catholic Historical Review* 82, 1 (1996), pp. 1–22.

Thomas, Keith. *Religion and the Decline of Magic.* New York: Scribners, 1971.

Thompson, J. E. S. *Maya History and Religion.* Norman: University of Oklahoma Press, 1970.

Thomson, Guy P., and David G. LaFrance. *Patriotism, Politics, and Popular Liberalism in Nineteenth-Century Mexico: Juan Francisco Lucas and the Puebla Sierra.* Wilmington, Del.: Scholarly Resources, 1998.

Tombs, Robert. *France, 1814–1914.* London: Longman, 1966.

Urzaiz Rodríguez, Eduardo (Claudio Meex). Reconstrucción de hechos: Anécdotas yucatecas ilustradas. Mérida: Universidad Autónoma de Yucatán, 1992.

Vallardo Fajardo, Iván. "Cambios en la religiosidad popular en Sudzal, Yucatán." In *Religión y sociedad en el Sureste de México.* Vol. 4. Mexico: Centro de Investigaciones y Estudios Superiores en Antropología Social, 1989, pp. 109–229.

———. "En busca de !a esperanza y la salvación: Resocialización religiosa en Sudzal, Yucatán." *Cambio cultural y resocialización en Yucatán.* Ed. Esteban Krotz. Mérida: Universidad Autónoma de Yucatán, 1997, pp. 165–185.

Vanderwood, Paul. *The Power of God Against the Guns of Government: Religious Upheaval in Mexico at the Turn of the Nineteenth Century.* Stanford: Stanford University Press, 1998.

Vargas Valdez, ed. *Tomóchic: La revolución adelantada.* 2 vols. Ciudad Juárez: Universidad Autónoma de Yucatán, 1994.

Victoria Ojeda, Victoria. *Mérida de Yucatán de las Indias: Piratería y estrategia defensiva.* Mérida: Ayuntamiento de Mérida, 1995.

Villa Rojas, Alfonso. *The Maya of East Central Quintana Roo.* Washington, D.C.: Carnegie Institute, 1943.

Vogt, Evon Z. *Zinacantan: A Maya Community in the Highlands of Chiapas.* Cambridge: Harvard University Press, 1969.

Vos, Jan de. *La paz de Dios y del Rey: La conquista de la Selva Lacandona (1524–1821).* Mexico: Fondo de Cultura Económica, 1980.

———. *Oro verde: La conquista de la Selva Lacandona por los madereros tabasqueños, 1822–1949.* Mexico: Fondo de Cultura Económica, Instituto de Cultura de Tabasco, 1988.

Wagley, Charles. *Economics of a Guatemalan Village.* American Anthropological Association Memoir, No. 58. Menasha: American Anthropological Association, 1941.

Waldeck, Federico de. *Viaje pintoresco y arqueológico a la provincia de Yucatán (América central) durante los años 1834 y 1836.* Trans. Manuel Mestre Ghigliazze. Mérida: Compañía Tipográfica Yucateca, S.A., 1930 (orig. 1837).

Wallace, Anthony F. C. *Religion: An Anthropological View.* New York: Random House, 1966.

Wasserstrom, Robert. *Class and Society in Central Chiapas.* Berkeley: University of California Press, 1983.

Watanabe, John. *Maya Saints and Souls in a Changing World.* Austin: University of Texas Press, 1995.

Weber, Eugen. "Fairies and Hard Facts: The Reality of Folk Tales." *Journal of the History of Ideas* 52 (1981), pp. 93–113.

Wells, Allen. *Yucatan's Gilded Age: Haciendas, Henequen, and International Harvester, 1860–1915.* Albuquerque: University of New Mexico Press, 1985.

———. "From Hacienda to Plantation: The Transformation of Santo Domingo Xcuyum." In Jeffrey T. Brannon and Gilbert M. Joseph, eds. *Land, Labor, & Capital in Modern Yucatán: Essays in Regional History & Political Economy.* Tuscaloosa: University of Alabama Press, 1991.

Wells, Allen, and Gilbert M. Joseph. *Summer of Discontent, Seasons of Upheaval: Elite Politics and Rural Insurgency in Yucatán, 1876–1915.* Stanford: Stanford University Press, 1996.

Willard, T. A. *The City of the Sacred Well.* New York: Century Company, 1926.

Wittgenstein, Ludwig. *Philosophical Investigations.* New York: MacMillan, 1953.

Wood, Stephanie. "Adopted Saints: Christian Images in Nahua Testaments of Late Colonial Toluca." *The Americas* 47, 3 (1991), pp. 259–293.

Wroth, William. *Images of Penance, Images of Mercy: Southwestern Santos in the Late Nineteenth Century.* Norman: University of Oklahoma Press, 1991.

INDEX

Blessed Souls of Purgatory (urban
  cofradía), 97
blunders as folklore motif, 28–29
bolon (analysis of term), 29
"Bonhomme Misere" (folktale), 4
Brinton, Daniel G., 2, 7
Burns, Allan, 3, 11, 16
burro tuunich: 9–10, 101 (photograph)

Cáceres, José Concepción, 153, 163
caciques. See *batabs*
Calero, Vicente, 69–70
Campbell, Joseph, 28
"Camposanto" (essay), 70
Canek, Jacinto, 131
Canicab (hacienda), 50, 59, 62–63
Cantón, Francisco, 165
Cantón, Rodulfo, 195, 228
Cárdenas, Lázaro, 165
Carnegie Project, 2
Carnival, 87–88
cartography, 6
Carrera, Rafael: appoints *juez pesqui-*
  zador, 22; *corregidores* under, 208;
  death of, 230; and peasant militias,
  216; restores clerical privileges, 212
Carrillo, Fabián, 59, 62
Caste War: and anticlericalism, 174,
  184; and apparitions, xv–xvi; and
  cofradía liquidations, 147; and destruction of churches, 140–141;
  early careers of leaders, 190–191;
  effect on clerical zeal, 128; and
  folklore formation, 3; in Hoctún,
  55–58; and *imágenes,* 118; origins of,
  xix, 237–238; and the Petén, 206,
  207, 212, 214–215, 221–222, 229–
  230; and Raymundo Pérez, 55–58;
  reduces church funding, 74, 178;
  responsibility for, 221–222; and restrictions on popular celebrations,

95; and rural *cofradías,* 149; and San
  Antonio Xocneceh, 153, 161–162;
  and source material, xxvi; and technology, 25; topography helps saves
  rebels, 214; and violence against
  priests, 193; and the Virgin of Tabi,
  136–137
*Catalogue of Religious Constructions of
  the State of Yucatán,* 167
cenotes as folklore motif, 9
cháaks, 7–8
ch'a'-cháak (ceremony), 126–128
Chambon, Ludovic, 9
Chancenote, *cofradía* of, 148–149
Chan Santa Cruz: and anticlericalism,
  174; bullfights in, 93; and buried
  treasure, 32–33; church in, 141;
  origins, 171; and witchcraft, 23
charitable associations, 98
Chichén Itzá, 9, 26
Chilam Balam of Chumayel, 150
"Chipitín the Hunter" (folktale), 33, 34
churches: as community property, 138–
  139; construction and restoration,
  139–140; deterioration during Caste
  War, 140–141; as folklore motif,
  8–9; as icons, 138–141
Cline, Howard, xxiv
cofradías, rural: attempts to rescue,
  148; connections with church, 146;
  eighteenth-century economic activities, 144–145; and historical
  change, 143–144; liquidations,
  146–147; later fortunes, 149; organization, 145; origins, 144; recipients
  of liquidated property, 147–148
cofradías, urban: after 1867, 97–100;
  attrition and survival, 74–75; in
  barrios, 79–80; and Caste War, 75–
  76; financial constraints, 76–77;
  function, 73–74; and gender, 82–

84; and Liberal reforms, 76; origins, 73; in smaller towns, 80–81
Colección letras mayas contemporáneas, 3
Conservatism, Mexican, 40, 59–61
convents. *See* nunneries
Cord of San Francisco (*cofradía*), 97
Corpus Christi, 79, 82, 90, 94
coyote/conejo stories, 20
creencias, 2
cross: apparitions of, xiii–xiv; as *imagen,* 114–115
cuentos, 1–2
"Cured by Nine Priests" (folktale), 32

"Dámaso and the Demon" (folktale), 175
Day of the Dead, 27
devils as folklore motifs, 10, 21
Devoción a la escala santa (devotional literature), 69
Devocionario (devotional literature), 72
diabletes, 90–91
día de los muertos. See Day of the Dead
Díaz, Porfirio: culture change under, 99; restrains anticlericalism, 201–202
"Dog and the Creation of the Lagoon" (folktale), 26–27
dragonflies as folklore motif, 18, 37
dreams, 15–16
drinking, 29–30, 83

epidemics in Yucatecan history, 13

Faith, Hope and Charity (*gremio*), 149
fiestas of cities and towns: advertising, 91; in early national period, 87; and popular rowdiness, 87; as secular entertainment, 91–96; state regulation, 91
"Fire God and the Rain God" (folktale), 25

folklore, Mexican: agency in, 18–25; and Caste War, 3; collections, 2–3; European influence, 4–5; and extra-community forces, 24–25; and folklore theory, 3–4; and generational conflict, 33–34; and geography, 5–12; heroes, 20; and history, 1–37; and mythical beings, 10; persistence and change in present day, 35–37; remedies, 25–35; and sexual attainment, 33; and social mobility, 32; and technology, 25–26; villains, 21–25
Flores: omens, 215; origins, 206; photo, 110

gender inversion, 84–85
gigantones, 90–91
"Girl who Became a King" (folktale), 20
González, Fernando: disappears, 228; flees to Guatemala City, 217; origins, 212–213; struggles with Amado Belizario Barreiro, 215–216
"Good and Bad Brothers" (folktale), 32
Granado Baeza, José Bartolomé del: and *cofradía* Xiat, 148; and folk medicine, 13; investigates heresy, 188–189; investigates sexual harassment, 183
Gremio de Agricultores, 166
gremios, 81–82, 98
Grimm, brothers, 20
Guerra, José María: accusations against, 221; becomes bishop, 52; death, 229

Harris, Joel Chandler, 20
Hecelchakán (*cofradía*), 154–155
hechicería. See witchcraft
Hermandad (spiritualist club), 197

Santísimo Sacramento (urban *cofra-día*): of Campeche, 90; of Hunucmá, 80–81; of Valladolid, 75–76
santos. See *imágenes*
secreto'ob, 2
"Seven Rays of the Sun" (folktale), 33
sickness as folklore theme, 12–14
Sierra O'Reilly, Justo, 5, 67, 69–70
"Siete Colores" (folktale): first version, 19–20; second version, 35
Sotuta: photograph, 106
Speaking Cross, xvi, xix, 111, 137–138
spiritualism: adherents, 105–197; doctrines and interpretation of, 197–199; later influences, 199–200; in Mexico, 195; origins, 194–195
Spiritualism in the Modern World (pamphlet), 196
Stephens, John Lloyd: on clerical indiscretion, 180; on gambling, 94; as source for local antiquarianism, 71
stoicism as folklore theme, 26–27
"Story about an Unusual Marriage" (folktale), 22
"Story of the Two Women" (folktale), 27–28
street corners, 6, 11–12
Sumaria de gracias (devotional literature), 68
Supersticiones y leyendas mayas (book), 2

Tabi: and folklore, 134; photographs, 101, 106
Talavera, Juan Pablo, 162, 163
tamax chi', 15
"Three Girls" (folktale), 33
Three Wise Men of Tizimín, 115
tich' (ceremony), 125
tinkle dancers, 90–91
treasure, buried, 32–33
Tsahe, Bernardo (*h-men*), 125
Tsul, Francisco, 47

tulix. See dragonflies as folklore motif
tunnels as folklore motif, 9
tuunich keg, 34

Urdemalas, Pedro de, 4
urna: photograph, 105
úuchben máako'ob, 11, 26

Viduarre, José Eduviges: appointed corregidor, 223–224; quarrel with Amado Belizario Barreiro, 224–225
violence as folklore theme, 14–15
Virgin: of Guadalupe (urban *cofradía*), 76; of Izamal, 114, 115, 121–122; of Merced (urban *cofradía*), 75; popularity as santo, 115–116; of Tabi, after 1847, 136–137, 116; of Tabi, before 1847, 133–136; of Tekax, 116; of Tetiz, 114, 116; of Tibolón, 116

wáay chivo, 10, 175
winds, evil, 14, 32
witchcraft, 22–24, 124
Wittgenstein, Ludwig, xxiv, 234
Wolf, Eric, 143
women: as *beatas*, 83; and Catholic church, 82–83; folk beliefs regarding, 16–17; and pious spending, 84; and popular religious cultures, 235; and priests, 83–84; in Santísimo Sacramento, 80; and spiritualism, 196–197; in urban *cofradías*, 82–84

x-majan naj, 18
x-tabay, 10, 14

Yikal maya than (journal), 3
Yucatán: historical synopsis, xviii–xxi; map, xx; negative reputation of, xviii
Yucateco (newspaper), 176
yumtsil. See *balam*